Living Metal

Advances in Metal Music and Culture

Series editors: Keith Kahn-Harris and Rosemary Lucy Hill

Advances in Metal Music and Culture publishes monographs, edited collections, and short books on metal and its associated sub-genres.

Metal music studies is a fast-expanding interdisciplinary field that spans across subject area fields in the social sciences, performing arts, and humanities. Intellect's Advances in Metal Music and Culture book series builds on and continues the series Emerald Studies in Metal Music and Culture, with the same series editors. It continues to provide a home for the growing number of scholars—from a wide variety of backgrounds—who wish to critically reflect on metal music around the world as a cultural product.

Decolonial Metal Music in Latin America

By Nelson Varas-Díaz

Living Metal: Metal Scenes around the World

Edited by Bryan A. Bardine and Jerome Stueart

Living Metal

Metal Scenes around the World

EDITED BY

Bryan A. Bardine and Jerome Stueart

intellect

Bristol, UK / Chicago, USA

First published in the UK in 2022 by
Intellect, The Mill, Parnall Road, Fishponds, Bristol, BS16 3JG, UK

First published in the USA in 2022 by
Intellect, The University of Chicago Press, 1427 E. 60th Street,
Chicago, IL 60637, USA

A catalogue record for this book is available from the British Library.

Copy editor: Newgen KnowledgeWorks
Cover designer: Aleksandra Szumlas
Production managers: Faith Newcombe and Sophia Munyengeterwa
Typesetting: Newgen KnowledgeWorks

Hardback ISBN 978-1-78938-400-0
Paperback ISBN 978-1-78938-758-2
ePDF ISBN 978-1-78938-401-7
ePub ISBN 978-1-78938-402-4

To find out about all our publications, please visit
www.intellectbooks.com
There you can subscribe to our e-newsletter, browse or download our current catalogue, and buy any titles that are in print.

This is a peer-reviewed publication.

Contents

Figures

Acknowledgments

Bryan A. Bardine

The idea for this book came about as I spent more and more time in the Dayton metal scene. Seeing all the positive experiences that scene members had and the way they support each other made me want to learn if other scenes act in similar ways.

A huge thank you to Jerome. He has been invaluable throughout the entire process as a sounding board, outstanding editor, and patient listener when frustration set in.

I'd like to thank Tom Wilson, aka Jebeneezer Law, whose photographs appear in the book's introduction as well as in Chapter 9. He is an amazing photographer—he's shot most of Dayton's local bands as well as many national and international acts. He's the best.

As always, to my wife Molly who reads my first drafts every time. Your comments invariably point me in the right direction. Without your support over the years, much of what I do may not have been possible.

Though they don't know it—to my daughters Katie and Allie. They aren't fans of metal but they both love music, which is all I can ask for. Maybe someday I'll get them to a show!

Jerome Stueart

I'd like to thank Bryan for his unwavering support in this project, for taking me to concerts to ground me in the scene, and for offering me this chance to edit a book examining the culture of people who support the arts—because that's what fans and scenes are: valuable supporters of the arts we love. We don't examine fan communities enough—or the work they do to keep something alive. Reading these chapters lets me know how surprisingly supportive and complex metal scenes are.

I'd like to also thank Danny Chavez; Rudy Huerta; Luis, Rita, and Sandy Guerrero; and Larry Bihl, for playing metal on their boom boxes on the bus to and from the basketball away games we had in West Texas from 1985 to 1987. They were my introduction to heavy metal, and I could only turn up my earphones playing Foreigner, Air Supply, and Duran Duran so high to try and drown out the metal. I finally took my earplugs out and listened. For me, metal is tied to both getting us ready to compete and comforting us when we lost. We mostly lost. (We had only five boy basketball players from a school of fourteen high school students, the smallest high school in Texas.) Black Sabbath, Judas Priest, Iron Maiden, Metallica, AC/DC, Mötley Crüe, Ozzy—they were there for us on the bus win or lose. Tell me how metal can be both the anthem of the powerful and the powerless. My classmates' heavy metal soundtracks to our games were part of my cross-cultural bonding in rural West Texas on long flat highways between rural schools. No matter where we came from, we could all identify with the long, rough, scraping chorus in the dark on the bus, exhausted, defeated, but together.

Foreword

Speaking at the White House in May 2016, President Obama acknowledged Finland's special connection with metal bands. At the time Finland had the most metal bands per capita in the world. When the president of the United States brings this topic to the media, it is an indication that metal is taken seriously and that the book you are holding is needed in today's world. Metal is not an underground movement anymore. In many countries, especially Finland, metal albums dominate the charts and metal music is played in most of the households. Metal music and metal fans can be found everywhere in the world, in all segments of society.

This book is about an international and intercultural phenomenon called the metal scene. My band, Children of Bodom, has been fortunate to be able to play on five continents, in more than 50 countries. I feel privileged to have been able to explore countless cities and meet people from many different cultures. The connection that I get with a headbanging metalhead in a crowd is as strong every time, regardless of whether he or she is wearing a kipa, turban, hijab, or baseball cap. Now that I think of it, I have played in most of the metal scenes that are talked about in this book.

I sincerely wish I had had the chance to read this book before all of that. As a performing artist, I see the scene from a special vantage point. The bigger the venue you play in, the less you interact with the actual local scene, and vice versa. I see the venue, I see the backstage, maybe even get to chat with the local promoter. If I am lucky, I have time to have a few beers with the locals in a pub nearby. Nevertheless, for much of the time the artist is in the middle of the scene without interacting directly with it. It is like not being able to see the forest for the trees. Reading this book helps to distance oneself to be able to see all the regional and cultural differences in a scene.

I was amazed by how much I learned and how many new layers were exposed when looking at things from a different vantage point. For this book Dr. Bardine and Dr. Stueart have carefully gathered research by authors from different parts of the world. I had the privilege of meeting and becoming friends with some of these authors while in Dayton at the *Metal and Cultural Impact Conference*; others,

I now know through their work. I have found their research to be fresh and eye-opening, even for one who is as deeply immersed in the subject as I am.

I played with Children of Bodom from its beginning and until its final show in 2019. I joined Alexi and Jaska's band in 1994. Pretty soon after, I started high school. After graduating high school, I was accepted into the University of Helsinki. While constantly making and playing music, it took me eleven years to get my master's degree in political history from the Faculty of Social Sciences. The combination of an academic and an international metal musician is not a real rarity, but it's not a very common thing either. As a fan I know that metal is global, but reading these studies about metal scenes in faraway places underlines the amazing diversity within metal culture. It will make every metal fan think about his or her own path to the metal scene. The role of political, historical, and social environments in the rise and even the occasional fading away of metal scenes is not only interesting for fans, but also opens a gate to a largely untouched and fertile landscape for academia. For a metal musician, reading this book simply makes every show more meaningful.

Bringing metal to an academic environment is a fairly new thing. Many of the early studies confirmed the positive psychological effects of blasting drums and shredding guitars; a thing that we metalheads have always taken for granted. Now that the prejudices about the psychological consequences of listening to metal have been debunked, we need to dig deeper into its social, cultural, and historical features. Let's zoom into our beloved metal culture's most important ingredient, the metal scene itself.

Henkka Seppälä, Children of Bodom
March 2020
Helsinki, Finland

Introduction

Bryan A. Bardine and Jerome Stueart

The first time I went to Oddbody's Music Room, I took my Metal as Cultural Experience class to see the NWOBHM legends Saxon. I couldn't believe Saxon was playing in such a small venue—in Dayton, Ohio. I wondered if my students understood how big of a deal this really was. It was a weekday night and not surprisingly the place wasn't full, which I thought was okay because for my students it was their first metal show, and a more intimate setting might put them at ease a little sooner. As the night wore on and each of the bands played their sets, my students (the males especially) began moving closer and closer to the stage, so by the time Saxon came on they were at the barricade in front of the band. One of my primary goals in taking students to shows is so they can experience the music, of course, but also the rest of the people and the venues that are part of the scene. My students often come in with stereotypical misconceptions about "metal people" and metal music. One way to help break the stereotype is to take them to a show, have them interact with scene members, and have a great time. In all the years I have taught this course, I've never had a student who didn't appreciate the experience and who learned a great deal about Dayton's scene in the process. While Dayton is just one scene in a state which is known for its metal, it is important because regardless of what is going on in the world around us, people know that they have support from members of the scene, which is really what it is about, isn't it?

Metal music is played in virtually every country on earth, and scenes—both big and small—exist in those countries. But how are scenes created? What has to happen when scenes come to life, grow, become static, and sometimes die out? How are scenes maintained and nourished so that they last regardless of economic, cultural, political, and even demographic changes? What are the elements that scenes need in order to remain viable in a changing world—whether a local scene in a small town or a global scene which covers most of the planet? Regardless, certain characteristics must exist in order for a scene to grow and be relevant in whatever culture it is a part of.

Living Metal: Metal Scenes around the World is the first book devoted solely to metal scenes, and we hope it won't be the last. Previous books have looked at music scenes from different perspectives: a specific place or a type of music scene (Mortensen 2014; Bennett and Peterson 2004), but until now there hasn't been a book dedicated to studying metal scenes, and none that goes to as much depth as our authors have attempted to do with this book. We believe that *Living Metal: Metal Scenes around the World* takes a fresh look at metal music and global culture. By examining these thirteen metal scenes together in one place, readers won't just learn about various scenes, but they get to understand how these scenes are formed by and fit within their respective cultures and how they connect to other scenes across the globe. For example, not only do readers learn about the ABC Headbangers in São Paulo, Brazil, they also begin to grasp the industrial connections that the scene has to the automobile industry, and by extension similarities to Detroit, Michigan, the United States' automobile capital. These are the kinds of connections we hope readers will make with this book.

Authors have also utilized multiple methods of researching and understanding the metal scene—using different theories and approaches—that other scene researchers will find valuable for comparison. They have taken Bennet, Peterson, Straw, Wallach and Levine and expanded their theories and methods to metal scenes all over the world. We think the chapters in this book broaden the field of metal studies and expand the ways scenes can be studied. We also think metal studies has needed a book solely devoted to scenes as a comparison study, *to study scenes in tandem*. This volume explores the intricate nature of scenes and how they affect the music being produced by a culture, how they help metal music grow, nurture musicians, and reflect the values and issues present within specific cultures while still reflecting the broader characteristics of global metal.

When we started this process, we wanted to compare scenes around the world to find out how they function, what their histories are, how they affect their local communities, how they deal with ethnic, economic, political, and racial problems, and through it all, most importantly, how they survive. We learned that all of these scenes have their own specific problems that they address—some of them require more attention than others, but regardless, if the scenes don't have individuals who are willing to play leadership roles, it becomes extremely difficult to survive. In many scenes, their members are aging out, which, if not addressed in the near future, could endanger a scene, causing it to dwindle and weaken. Wallach and Levine (2013) talk about the need for a "generation gap" in scenes. Scenes addressed in this book have offered many insights into strengthening scenes by addressing age issues through mentoring, teaching in local schools, and finding unique ways to bring in younger members. Scenes examined in this book have had to address issues with governmental restrictions (Gaugeng, South Africa; Turkey), a weakened economy (Hull, United Kingdom), or the struggles inherent in just being a nascent scene (Estonia). Regardless of the situation these scenes face, their members' desire to keep the scene alive has encouraged innovation in addressing their specific issues. These methods can be applied to all scenes around the world, and we hope making them available in one volume gives any scenes concerned with survival some new ideas and new tools to use.

Through the examination of these scenes, we hope to show the reader the broad scope that metal has in the world. We only wish we could have added more chapters because we know that metal music is in virtually every country on earth, though they exist in very different structures and sizes. While it can certainly be argued that metal is one large community, where fans share many of the same values and beliefs when it comes to metal music and culture, what we have seen in these chapters is that while that may be true, by looking at these smaller scenes we see an intimacy and a togetherness that cannot exist when we try to compare it to the millions of metal fans around the world as one group. It is clear that while there are similarities among the members of these scenes like among metalheads around the world, each scene has its own specific qualities and connections among the members. While the musical core might be there for all metal people, the closeness and intimacy exist at a different local level. We aren't saying that this type of intimacy can't exist in larger groups—it is just much more difficult because so many people are separated by greater physical distances. Furthermore, many of the scenes in this book are heavily influenced by the cities or areas in which they live. They exist *because* of these places. Without this home base, these scenes would find it difficult to gather, to perform, and even to create music. Without it, the scene would suffer because not only would it be more difficult for local and outside bands to perform, but it would also take away a prime place for people to get together and share experiences and lives with one another.

While other books have included individual chapters that address a variety of topics that connect to metal scenes, including the extreme scene in Osaka, Japan (edited by Heesch and Scott), how a metal scene sits at the fringe of society (edited by Gardenour Walter et al.), the racism inherent in some extreme metal (edited by Varas-Diaz and Scott), how scenes are formed (edited by Hjelm, Kahn-Harris, and LeVine), and even a chapter examining the limitations inherent in metal scenes (edited by Wallach, Berger, and Greene), as yet there has not been a book that looks at metal scenes in depth, as ours does. By examining scenes around the world, we want to showcase the diversity of metal music—alongside the common struggle of scene survival—and add a worthy volume of research to metal studies as a whole.

How does this book, with its global perspective on scene research, change the way that metal scenes are studied in the future? First, the book gives scholars more tools and methods to analyze scenes. Furthermore, it can challenge them to consider more than just the scenes they are studying—to think about scenes in tandem—to consider how their research fits into the landscape of metal scene scholarship. We believe this opens the door for more scholars to begin examining other scenes and use other research methods. One of the goals of this volume is to show other scholars new ways to look at scenes and to learn more about metal culture in some places on earth that have not been considered yet. Some scholars may be introduced to new places: Hull's metal and hardcore scene, the oceanic black metal of Copenhagen, the rivalry between the Osaka and Tokyo scenes. Any new scholarship on metal scenes enriches the field and inspires growth.

Taken together, these chapters create a lattice of metal scholarship strengthening a new direction and give promise of more development in metal scene studies, due to the extraordinary depth of analysis that our authors have undertaken in their research of both scenes and cultures. It is clear that while some research has been done on metal scenes, much more is needed, and this book begins to fill that gap. Furthermore, we think future scholars will better understand the theories and methodologies prevalent in metal scene research through reading this collection, which by extension can assist them when they design their own studies.

Representing scenes from six of the seven continents, this book shares how scenes around the world survive and thrive despite a myriad of issues that affect them, from stagnation of metal in certain places around the world, to economic hardships, to political persecution, and even an aging population within the scene. How do they survive? Can they survive in a world which places more problems in front of people today than ever before? We believe they can, and this book will show how scenes from places as distant as Gauteng, South Africa, and as small as Dayton, Ohio, have many similarities and difficulties and yet survive.

What makes a scene? Common sense says that without fans, bands, and places to play, scenes can't exist. But it is certainly more than that. For a scene to exist, to us, there needs to be a *community*—where people come together to support each other and are available for one another when things in life get tough. Without that community, it is more difficult for scenes to do a number of things, including surviving in difficult times, growing, bringing in new members, appealing to younger members—which is often necessary to keep aging scenes together. Just because scenes are communities, though, does not mean that they are destined for survival—without leadership from a few and a foundation from a base who are willing to be sounding boards and the ability to organize membership when necessary a scene will have a difficult time staying together. While all these aspects are important for a scene to survive, and even thrive, without community a scene will crumble.

Some things about community we also learned from doing this project are the myriad of ways *community* might be expressed. Community is a nurturing aspect to a scene, and it can contribute to bolstering and creating new bands. Consider these four ways we see reflected in these chapters that community is a nurturing force.

Almost every scene we look at here has a "feeder line"—something that keeps injecting new life into the scene. For some it is the creation of a local recording studio that produces CDs of local bands and sells them at a local CD music store, and internationally online—this lets bands move from just playing to creating an album and distributing themselves locally and abroad. It also gives a different hub—not a venue to play in, necessarily, but a distribution, meeting, and marketing hub outside of a bar. It feeds the fans another way to hear their favorite local bands on par with the international bands they listen to, and gives fans a place to meet and share their interests. Furthermore, studios are valuable to moving local bands to the next step in their professional identities.

In some cases, that feeder line is a big festival—a created space for local bands to play alongside respected and more well-known bands. It gives local bands the chance to work with professional musicians active in the industry. It brings metal bands into a place giving fans a reason to stay at the local scene, respect the local scene, and see the local scene in a new light—playing with the big bands. A recognized local festival also pools fans, scenes, and bands from surrounding areas, thereby enriching the local scene, and allowing smaller scenes a chance to build an audience.

Other times, the feeder line is a school or mentorship program that happens. As is the case with Osaka, creating a space where students come to learn metal music from a professional in an educational setting feeds more interest and potential bands into the scene, and gives a place for older musicians to mentor younger ones. Several of these papers mention the aging of the metal fan and band population, but they also suggest mentoring might be an answer to keeping those scenes alive.

Geography can help feed or starve a scene and plays a role in the creation of scenes as well. Hull, while nearly too far for national bands to circuit, becomes a host for many international bands because of its port city status, allowing the scene to constantly inject new music into the scene. Sometimes, distance from other scenes isolates a scene creating unique sounds and styles, but it can also make bands feel outcast from the greater metal scene nationally. However, scenes that are right next door to larger scenes might develop a rivalry that challenge a scene to develop their own unique sound and compete with a larger market.

No matter how community is expressed, it takes enterprising individuals seeing a need in the scene to help create these supportive structures and fans to support them. When that support is present, a scene thrives, and scenes that lose this creative support struggle.

This book also serves as a history of several scenes. We asked researchers to tell us how these scenes were formed. What we now have are mini-histories of scene formation which can be valuable for scene restoration and could include tips for survival. Most of these chapters also have a state of the scene today—or at least before music scenes were hit with a global pandemic. What is valuable is that this is a snapshot of scenes working today worldwide—their similarities, their differences. What we expect to see in 2021 will be how scenes recover from COVID-19 induced lockdowns. Hopefully what these researchers have been able to collect here will serve to help rebuild and recharge scenes. It would be valuable to collect a picture of the global metal scene in a book in 2022 about how scenes recovered from a pandemic, or whether they recovered at all. Community, our linchpin in this collection we think, might also be the linchpin in scene survival right now.

***

The book is broken into thirteen chapters, each from a different country, analyzing a metal scene(s) within that country. The chapters examine the scenes through a variety of lenses—some take a historical approach which charts a scene's development over time (Osaka, Japan; Nantes, France; Styria, Austria; Québec, Canada; Estonia; Dayton, Ohio), others focus on the scene as it currently exists (Hull, England; Copenhagen, Denmark), still others attempt to compare scenes within the same region (Berlin, Germany; ABC region of São Paulo, Brazil), some address how scenes are affected by the politics of a region (Gauteng, South Africa; Turkey), and one tries to primarily define scenes by the genres of metal that are most prevalent (Tasmania, Otago; Southland, Australia, and Aotearoa/New Zealand). Regardless of the specific analytical approaches to the research, the ultimate goal within each chapter is to examine a scene or scenes to learn how the scene functions and in some cases how it has developed over time.

You will notice that the authors did not necessarily use the same definition for a scene. Several chapters use Wallach and Levine (2013) while others have defined it by referencing Bennett and Peterson (2004), and some have referenced Will Straw's definition of scene (1991). Some authors have created their own definitions or combined definitions in order to better understand the scene they are examining. Regardless of the approach, each of the chapters determines what a scene is and uses that determination as part of the analysis.

The first chapter, Edward Banchs's "From the ashes of the fallen empire: Heavy metal and community in postapartheid South Africa," examines a section of the Johannesburg scene, Gauteng. Banchs conducted an online survey as well as interviews of scene members in order to better understand the culture of this postapartheid scene. He describes the problems that scene members had during apartheid and explains how they have been able to rise above the political issues that hindered the scene then. He asked the following question: "[H]as the South African metal scene, whose nascence came under the control of an authoritarian, racist government, moved on from the past into including those who would not previously have been allowed to participate legally?" (23). Banchs's chapter focuses on how a scene that has been brutalized by hatred and racism addresses those issues as it grows into the modern world.

Chapter 2, Catherine Hoad's "Polar fate: Mapping metal at the southern edge of the world," analyzes the metal scenes in three of the southern most areas in Australia and Aotearoa/New Zealand—Tasmania, Otago, and Southland. She lays out a comparison between the notion of the "North" in metal—the importance of Scandinavia to the history and culture of metal to these three most southern parts of the world and their connections to place, gender, and history. Her chapter is divided into three sections, each one approaching the specific region by considering how scene members identify with their region through its physical and geographic characteristics. She continues her analysis by contrasting the types of metal which dominate each region—Southland's metal focuses on working-class masculinity, while the black metal bands of Otago emphasize individuality and abjection. Finally, she defines the Tasmanian bands' sound as a "lo-fi forest black metal," of which isolation is the primary theme.

Pierre Hecter and Douglas Mattsson, authors of Chapter 4, "The enemy within: Conceptualizing Turkish metalheads as the ideological 'other,'" believe that the best way for the black metal scene in Turkey to find its own identity is to address the new political agenda in the country. This agenda developed by President Recep Tayyip Erdogan stresses an emphasis on Islamic exceptionalism and to denigrate the once favorable support of a more secular society. The authors argue that though metal may have always been the "other" in Turkey, it now takes on a more important role because of the ideological nature of Erdogan's more conservative Islamist government. Furthermore, many scene members note how important it is for them to move away from the extreme conservatism of the current government and to use their music and culture as a way to resist the new government and its conservative elite within the larger society.

Chapter 4, Mei-Ra St. Laurent's "'*Métal noir épique patriotique*': Analysis of historical, sociological, and cultural discourses uniting *métal noir québécois* and Québec Society," uses the concept of eventialization to examine the key events in the *métal noir québécois* (MNQ) scene and in Québec society as a whole. She notes that the MNQ scene's primary focus comes from a nationalist ideology whose primary theme is the Patriots' Rebellion where French settlers attempted to gain independence from their British oppressors. The chapter will draw parallels between the MNQ and the primary political, cultural, and social events which take place in Québec society. She has collected her data from Québécois publications, interviews, booklet images, song lyrics, and from the *Metal Archives* database.

Chapter 5, Peter Pichler's "Living sonic knowledge in South-Eastern Austria: The sound history of the metal scene in Graz and Styria, *c.*1980 to the present," examines the cultural history of this scene. Pichler, a cultural historian, examines three periods of the sound history in the Styrian scene and presents an in-depth analysis of the Metal on the Hill festival in Graz. Pichler introduces the concept of sonic knowledge and uses it as the focal point of analysis for this study. The chapter seeks to show how the Styrian metalheads addressed the biggest challenge they faced—keeping their common knowledge (of the scene) alive.

Kei Saito in Chapter 6, "Heavy metal scene in Osaka: Localness now and then," contrasts the metal scene in Osaka, Japan, to that of its biggest rival, Tokyo. Osaka, Kobe, and Kyoto make up the Kei-han-shin region, which is in most ways opposite to Kansai—or Tokyo. Saito discusses the differences between the two regions of the country. For instance, Kai-han-shin is known as a scene with a strong technique-oriented style as well as its more friendly and straightforward approach, unlike the Kansai scene, which is where bands go when they want to become famous, and in some cases, not really focus on their music. A strong rivalry exists between the two cities/regions, with Osaka sometimes feeling like the little brother to the much bigger and sometimes more influential Tokyo. Regardless, both cities have a sense of pride in the music that comes from within.

Chapter 7, Tore Tvarnø Lind's "Heart of sadness: Fieldwork in the Copenhagen black metal undergrounds," analyzes the black metal scenes in and around Copenhagen through conducting interviews, attending concerts, and examining the music itself. He learned that Denmark's black metal scene lacks homogeneity and is highly fragmented. He primarily discusses two black metal scenes: the atmospheric scene which he calls oceanic black metal, which at times lies on the fringes of the larger more traditional scene, and the more raw black metal which is from the Korpsånd scene whose home is the Mayhem venue in Copenhagen. This scene considers itself "ultra-marginal underground." Lind notes that contrary to some current black metal bands, the bands in the Copenhagen scene strive to explore "aggression, belonging and sadness, and aspiring to dissolution."

In Chapter 8, "'Dit Is Berlin': Local metal scene building and transformation in Berlin, Germany," Wolf-Georg Zaddach contrasts the Berlin metal scene in the 1980s with the scene in the 2010s, looking at the political issues in the city as well as how the local scene has developed over time. Because of the separation of East and West Germany until 1989, metal music in East Berlin was seen as "a weapon of the enemy," which would undermine the government's ability to control the local youth population; however, in West Berlin the local scene members felt that they were outside of the metal scene in the country. Today, because Berlin is more international and diverse, the scene has become more diversified and is much more broad because there are several generations which exist together now.

The ninth chapter, Bryan A. Bardine and Jacob Hale's "Perspectives old and new: Cross-generational community in the Dayton metal scene," seeks to understand if the scene is a community, and if so, what is the impact on the overall scene? Does it make it more vibrant? More stable? More supportive of the local Dayton community at large? The authors compared and contrasted early founders' comments with those of newer scene members to better understand the scene over time. The research found that while the scene in many ways is strong, it suffers from a few issues, including an aging population, often seeing the scene through rose-colored glasses, and sometimes not recognizing the commonalities between the older and younger scene members. Without addressing these issues, it will be difficult for the scene to survive.

Gérôme Guibert and Sophie Turbé, authors of Chapter 10 entitled "*La belle endormie* awakened by Hellfest Open Air?: A study of the Nantes metal music scene," trace the history of the metal scene in Nantes, beginning in the 1980s when it was quite small and quite local, to today with the advent of Hellfest in 2006, which brought an international presence to the region and an increased local scene as well. In its early days, the Nantes metal scene was not known as a strong scene. There were not many local bands, and the city was not normally a stop for touring international bands. Over time, and with the arrival of Hellfest, things began to change—it brought international bands to the city, increased the local scene, more local venues opened which paved the way for more local shows, and then brought other people and professional music organizations to Nantes. With these additions, the Nantes metal scene has grown and flourished, and with the exception of Paris, it is recognized as the strongest scene in France.

Chapter 11, "Heavy metal in Estonia: Cohesions and divisions, past and present," by Toni-Matti Karjalainen examines the scene's history from its founding in the 1980s through the present day. By conducting interviews, analyzing articles about the Estonian scene, and conducting an online survey, Karjalainen was able to break the scene's history into three waves. The first wave was the beginning of the scene, growing with the end of Soviet occupation and Estonian independence. The second wave reestablished the scene after a slowdown occurred in the mid 1990s, and the third wave moved the scene into present day and a more active scene, in part due to Estonia's movement into the Euro currency.

In Chapter 12, "From the sound of the lathes to the noise of the amplifiers: Heavy metal and the music scene of the Greater ABC Region (São Paulo/Brazil, 1980–90)," Rui Luiz Ferreira Granado and Heloísa de Araújo Duarte Valente argue that the metal scene in the Greater ABC region of Brazil was influenced by the military repression of the time, the factory workers' culture, and the influence of punk culture. The authors note that two important questions are necessary to help better understand how influential the three points above are. First, how does the sound landscape (in the factories) influence how music in the scene is created? And second, conversely, how does the music scene reinforce and compose elements of the local sound landscape?

The final chapter of the book, Lewis Kennedy's "'This is the city of hate': Surveying the Hull metal/hardcore scene," looks at the negative and positive perceptions of the scene from its members. Hull's post–Second World War history has shown a steady decline in its economy because of deindustrialization and increasing automation, to name two reasons. These negative perceptions are expressed by the local metal and hardcore bands—who witness the state of their city and their scene—through songs that talk about their frustration and indignation with their lives. The scene is not all bad, however, as several survey respondents talk about the community and the friendly atmosphere they see among scene members. Kennedy's research sees the scene as both accommodating and restrictive, as, on the one hand, members feel a sense of community but, on the other, they find it difficult to break away, both because of scenic restrictions and the geographical location of Hull itself.

***

Metal Scenes around the World brings up some important questions that need to be considered in metal studies in the future.

1. Is this research showing that the diversity of metal music is not an anomaly—but the norm? That the media concentration on whiteness or the research on whiteness is skewing the face of metal music? This book works to prove the strong diversity in this musical genre.
2. Do bands form from scenes, or do scenes form from local bands playing? There is a real conversation going on here in these chapters about a dialogue of inter-creation between bands and scenes. Are they co-creational? Are they building their scene/message/look/culture together?
3. How does the history of a region influence the metal of today? We have several chapters that rely on the history of the place—the history of Québec separatism, the history of Hull's isolation, the history of Denmark's seafarers—that channel some very ancient ideas into today's music, sometimes fueling political movements.
4. How does the landscape affect the scene—the distances between places, the nearness of others? Does nearness create rivalry, or cooperation? Does isolation create uniqueness, or does it prohibit growth of bands and scene? How are scenes determined by landscape?

5. Are bands expressing thoughts of the scene in their music—or do bands teach the scene how to think about the culture? Are bands the voices of scenes? Or are they co-creational? Do bands, venues, fans, studios create a voice? Or are they created because of a strong voice?
6. How do political events both strengthen and weaken scenes? When bands take a more political stance, does that help? Or do bands shun political association and remain completely an outsider?
7. Peter Pichler's sonic knowledge applied to scenes could give scenes everywhere a way of understanding their history not as something that formed around a specific band or bands, but as a supportive community creating and launching bands and culture, and seeing the scene itself as a historic player in the creation of music.
8. How would studying scenes in tandem (Saito, Hoad, Kennedy, Granado, Zaddach) also help us understand the unique qualities of scenes? Can we find the tension and energy between scenes that cause scenes to develop in specific ways—as reactions possibly to each other?

***

For metal music to remain viable throughout the world, it needs strong metal scenes with dedicated people who are working to keep the music and culture alive. Without those people, we believe that scenes will suffer and by extension so will, ultimately, the music. Because even though at the very least a scene just needs fans, bands, and places to play, without the necessary foundation and support it is quite difficult for scenes and metal to avoid becoming stagnant and to weaken over time. A goal of these chapters is to examine scenes from diverse countries, looking at their scenes from a variety of perspectives in order to show how they are able to exist and often thrive. We don't often see at first glance how a scene creates community. Walking with my students into Oddbody's, I noticed a bit of apprehension from a few of them, clearly not knowing what to expect from the evening. The venue was dark with a lot of people with long hair, wearing black t-shirts, patched battle jackets, or leather. It can be intimidating for someone not used to such a scene. But once they spent some time at Oddbody's and talked to the locals, they felt the camaraderie that the scene members not only had for each other, but also for the students because they came to the show and wanted to take part in the show. This welcoming attitude dispelled so many stereotypes and misrepresentations that some groups like to pin on metal people and metal culture. My students were able to see the connections among the fans and the band, and as the night wore on they became part of that relationship. I will never forget the sight of my students headbanging to "Princess of the Night" at one point during the show. They got it. We want our readers to get what keeps these amazing metal scenes around the world together.

Working on this project got me thinking in new ways about a music and culture that I love. Maybe it isn't a good thing for a scholar to be too close to his "scene," but I don't think so, at least not in this case. Not only have I learned a great deal about Dayton's metal scene, I have also been able to look at it with fresh eyes because of all the other metal scenes I've learned about during this process. It would not have been possible if Jerome and I had not decided to put together a book on metal scenes. Without the excellent chapters from our contributing authors, you the reader wouldn't have the opportunity to learn as much as I have over the past two years.

I have always been a fan of metal music; but growing up in Akron, Ohio, a city with a good scene, I really didn't have any friends who liked metal, and I was too insecure to go to shows alone in my youth. I never felt like I was part of a metal scene until I started going to shows in Dayton, mostly at Oddbody's Music Room. The first show I went to at Oddbody's was Saxon and Fozzy. I had never seen a metal show in such a small venue (Oddbody's can hold maybe 600 people), and it was an amazing experience because I felt like I was part of the show since I was so close to the band. Another reason it was so great was that I was in close contact with other metalheads who were just as into the music as I was. It was a freeing night for me. I met a few people and always felt welcomed and safe—which for someone who only heard about the stereotypical negative aspects of metal music and culture growing up it greatly added to my experience that night.

FIGURE I.1: Dayton's Forces of Nature opening for Exodus at Oddbody's Music Room. Photo by Tom Wilson.

That show was my first taste of what a metal scene can be. It opened my eyes more clearly to metal culture—more than I had ever encountered before. I had been going to metal shows for many years, but always at big venues that felt much more impersonal, and I felt less connected to the audience. They were great shows, but once I began going to smaller venues there was a more immediate and intense feeling—I found myself feeling closer to the band and the other fans much more than I ever felt at any big venue. But it wasn't just the venue that brought this out of me it was that I met and talked to many people in Dayton's scene who had similar metal interests than I did, and we all came from many different walks of life. It opened my eyes to a world I'd never known before, which at times was a bit scary because it was new but also exciting for that same reason.

This book came, at least in part, from these experiences at small venues like Oddbody's because I was able to see the connections among the fans and the bands. Walking into the show and getting a hug or a hardy handshake from a few people you haven't seen in a while is a very cool occurrence. You feel welcomed and you feel part of the group. I hadn't had that at other types of concerts or events. I wanted to learn more about other scenes around the world to see how they experience the music and the culture. Obviously, if you've read the chapter coauthored by Jacob and me you would know that Dayton is not all roses, but it certainly isn't all bad either. That is the purpose of this book—to explore scenes around the world and to begin to understand what makes them what they are. It was about time we learn more about metal scenes, if for no other reason than there are millions of metal fans all over the world: with fans in almost every country from such diverse cultures listening to and creating metal music, Jerome and I felt it was time to continue the conversation in more detail.

A major goal of this book is to introduce the readers to more research on metal scenes from as broad a perspective as possible. Jerome and I wanted to put a collection together that brought in an array of scholarship about metal scenes from all corners of the earth (almost). After reading this collection, we hope that you will see the amazing diversity and passion that emanates from each of these scenes. Metal scenes are places, like metal music, which can bring people together who share a love for metal music, and they can act in many ways for the members. Places to develop close friendships, support systems in times of need, ways to expose people to different cultures, to support and nurture local music, to feed the members new ideas and new music, to mentor and train, to learn about where the members are from, to expose members to various types of metal, to bring people from a variety of social, economic, cultural, and ethnic groups together, and even to be in places where disagreements or arguments are played out. Regardless, metal scenes can act, in many ways, like a home for some people much like the music they love can bring enjoyment and passion into their lives. Through the metal scenes discussed in these pages, a more detailed understanding of metal culture and the relationships that exist in these communities is addressed. This research sheds more light on an aspect of metal scholarship that hasn't yet been given its due, and which provides rich material for further study. Looking at metal scenes is an important first step in a wider examination and analysis of other scenes around the world. By continuing this research, more people will be exposed to the diversity that exists in the world of metal, and in so doing gain a better understanding of metal music and culture.

REFERENCES

Bennett, Andy, and Peterson, Richard A. (eds.) (2004), "Introducing music scenes," in *Music Scenes: Local, Translocal and Virtual*, Nashville: Vanderbilt University Press, pp. 1–15.

Mortensen, T. (2014), "The shared values of authenticity in northeast Ohio cover music scene," MA thesis, Kent: Kent State University.

Straw, Will (1991), "Systems of articulation, logics of change: Communities and scenes in popular music," *Cultural Studies*, 5:3, pp. 368–88.

Wallach, Jeremy, and Levine, Alexandra (2013), "'I want you to support local metal': A theory of metal scene formation," in T. Hjelm, M. LeVine, and K. Kahn-Harris (eds.), *Heavy Metal: Controversies and Countercultures,* Sheffield: Equinox Publishing Ltd, pp. 117–35.

1

From the Ashes of the Fallen Empire: Heavy Metal and Community in Postapartheid South Africa

Edward Banchs

Since overcoming apartheid, one of the more tumultuous periods of modern history, South Africa's identity has slowly transitioned into one of promise. As a result, a myriad of subcultures is awakening, including the niche heavy metal subculture. Finding their impetus under an authoritarian rule, metal acts in South Africa performed away from the lenses of peering authorities as the music found itself increasingly stigmatized. Today, however, the metal subculture is finding its way through the postapartheid era, enjoying the benefits of a dedicated fandom from many throughout the nation, including the province of Gauteng.

This chapter discusses the post-authoritarian metal scene in the greater Johannesburg area by presenting a discussion of what the scene looks like today and how the scene is embracing the communal aspect around metal music. The principal research for this chapter is a result of a scene survey that was conducted online in 2017. Responses were then followed up with interviews to select respondents to gain a better understanding as to what these participants observe in the contemporary scene and the community that has blossomed around this subculture.

Black, white, and red all over

Heavy metal in South Africa came to life under one of the most restrictive political mechanisms in modern history. The evolution of the genre in South Africa into a formidable musical presence rose from a passionate fan base who reached toward the west for a musical expression that best reflected their lives. However, their reach toward this western import was constantly slapped, pulled, and cut away during a period of political, economic, and cultural boycotts in response to their country's oppressive regime. Thus, the first metal acts in the country, including the bands Black Rose, Suck, Retribution Denied, and Metalmorphosis, formed with limited western influences.

While some western artists including AC/DC, Van Halen, and Led Zeppelin were heard and enjoyed in a similar fashion to their western contemporaries, the "other" western scenes, including death and thrash metal, were promoted through an intricate network of underground word-of-mouth, letter writing campaigns, and emigrant/immigrant exchanges, all under the structures of a church-led authoritarianism—a deterrent to the promotion of the genre.

This restrictive mechanism was a product of the Calvinist tradition that has been embroidered into the South African cultural map beginning with the arrival of the Dutch and French Huguenots in the late 1600s. Yet, it was during the 1948 elections when the National Party (NP), campaigned on promises to the white minority, including a perfervid policy of segregation and land rights to the nation's white minority who numbered less than 10 percent of the population. By virtue of birth, whites were granted the full privileges of citizenry, including voting, property, and movement rights, as well as the benefits of stronger financial privileges. For 46 years, South Africa was officially a racist state.

The NP needed to enforce their policy of racial separation in a manner that could not be compromised. Thus authoritative institutions were constructed. As a result of the attachment to Calvinism, religious authorities were also able to hold sway and control challenges to its philosophy through a variety of means.

Ways of influencing what the population consumed for entertainment, including inculcations against heavy metal, came to fruition during apartheid. Not only did the mandating of the Publications Act of 1974 assist censors in monitoring what was being broadcast on television and radio,[1] but the government was also helped by personal crusaders or moral entrepreneurs (Goode and Ben-Yehuda 1994: 154). One of the more notable figures leading these moral crusades was a former police officer named Rodney Seal whose personal mission was to dissuade school-aged youth away from the dangers of rock and metal music owing to their purported links to Satanism.

The quixotic Seal often presented a list of known "Satanists and homosexuals," complementing his presentations with rock and metal music and videos from artists he deemed to be perpetuators of immorality. Seal also published a book called *Rock Music and the Right to Know*[2] (1988), which allowed his message to reach larger audiences. However, as metal fans who grew up during the latter portion of apartheid attest, Seal's plan to deter potential listeners by playing heavy metal to students had a reverse effect: his tactics introduced new fans to the genre.

Promoter and blogger Patrick Davidson recalls attending school with an interest in metal during this era:

> The government had a strong tie with the white Afrikaner church, and it was compulsory in government schools that there were Bible classes in the curriculum. They would sometimes screen these Christian documentary-style films in Bible class about how evil (metal) bands were supposed to be. So it's no lie to say that school introduced me to metal at the age of ten or eleven or thereabouts.
>
> (Davidson 2012: n.pag.)

Metal's entrance into the dialogue of conservative leadership was propitious—it stepped into the dialogue of desperate leaders as apartheid was coming to an end. As Falkof posits, "[t]he Satanism scare was a response to social change, a consequence of the fear of apartheid's end" (Falkof 2012: 7). "The possibility of blaming Satanism for personal and communal ills was only available to those who inhabited the spaces of privilege" (Falkof 2012: 19). Metal had stepped into mainstream relevancy in the 1980s, existing in South Africa under difficult circumstances. However, as a result of a passionate fealty, metal bands formed, established live performance spaces, and worked adroitly with limited resources—all under a poisonous police state. Moreover, unlike their erstwhile counterparts, the next generation of South African metal fans would define their scene in a liberal, desegregated democracy.

Gauteng's metal scene today

In their study of heavy metal scene formation, Jeremy Wallach and Alexandra Levine define scenes "as *loosely bounded functional units* containing a finite number of participants at any one time [...] (acting) as *conduits* to the global circulation of metal sounds and styles." Scenes also "provide gathering places for the *collective consumption* of metal artifacts [...] *sites for local performance and artifactual production*,"—noting that scenes must interact with the larger economic order of society—and "*promote local artists* to the larger network of scenes" (Wallach and Levine 2011: 119, original emphasis). Notably, their research indicates that metal scenes "are always found in a metacultural context of modernity" (Wallach and Levine 2011: 120), which is what best defines the Gauteng province.

Home to over 13 million people (South African Government Census 2016: n.pag.), Gauteng is, geographically, the smallest province of South Africa's nine, boasting of not only the nation's political capital, Pretoria, but also the country's largest city, Johannesburg. Formed on April 27, 1994,[3] Gauteng today serves as the nation's economic center producing one-third of South Africa's GDP, 10 percent of the sub-Saharan GDP, and—incredibly—7 percent of Africa's GDP (IMF; see Brinkhoff 2017). Given its significance as a financial and cultural center, a survey was conducted with the intent to gather a better understanding of the scene from the participants themselves and to further discuss themes relevant to metal's place in the current setting, Gauteng, South Africa: home to numerous bands, fans and spaces for performance, as well as a sizable fan base.

This survey asked: How old is the average metal fan? What is their occupation? Are they educated? Are they male? Female? Since the fall of apartheid, has the metal scene become more diverse? What are the popular bands of the scene today? What are the frustrations and aspirations of the fans in today's metal scene? What drives fans to metal shows in the first place? And, if applicable, what are the challenges facing the metal scene today? What follows is the result of a survey constructed in order to answer these questions, which assisted in formulating a more constructive hypothesis to assess whether the corresponding scene shows signs of viability.

Methodology

The survey used to research the scene in Gauteng was based on a draft written by Dr. Bardine for his survey of the Dayton, Ohio, metal scene. The original survey results were presented as part of a panel comparing the Gauteng metal scene to the scenes of Dayton, Ohio, and Hull, United Kingdom, at the *International Association for the Studies of Popular Music Conference* (IASPM-US) in March of 2018 at Vanderbilt University in Nashville, Tennessee. In order to better reflect the intended correspondents, the original survey was augmented with two additional questions that best embody South Africa's diversity: What is your home language? And, what is your race?

The survey was posted on two Facebook pages in South Africa—Krank'D Up (5,492 followers) and Metal4Africa (6,675 followers)[4]—by the administrators of each page. The former represents a festival held annually in Gauteng, featuring a multiple-stage setup composed of local acts along with two international headliners. The latter is a page representing a webzine, *fanforum*, and an eponymous biannual metal festival based in Cape Town. Both pages are curated by the respective festival's promoter. The popularity of these forums within South Africa led to my decision to contact the purveyors of each page as they are both considered "go-to" sites for fans to promote music from local and international bands. Once the survey was posted, the site administrators encouraged visitors to complete the survey if they lived in the Gauteng province, or frequently visited the province. The prospective respondents were informed of the survey's purpose.

The survey was activated via Google Drive and was live for the duration of several weeks before the response function was shut off on October 19, 2017, at 15:39 EST. A total of 342 responses were compiled and studied. In some surveys, not all of the questions were answered. Once the answers were reviewed, I set about composing interviews with several of the participants by way of email to follow up on specific aspects of the survey,[5] notably the responses regarding gender, community identity, and the diversity of the scene. Follow-up interviews were chosen with individuals based on their involvement within the Gauteng scene; whether as promoters, musicians, or journalists, they are active participants who have acquired a significant amount of acuity of their local scene.

Age, scene participation, and the communal experience

A strong indication that metal is translating well to the current generation of South Africans is noted from the 69.9 percent of respondents who indicated their age to be between 19 and 30 years old. One positive reflection would be that heavy metal has continued to inspire new generations of fans globally because of its overwhelming appeal to young audiences, not just from the well-established acts of the genre's treasured history, but also from a wave of acts that continue to expand metal's appeal.

While it is difficult to obtain the necessary information as to what exactly served as each respondent's introduction into heavy metal or how old they were when they transitioned into metal fandom, there is a strong correlation between age and metal fandom in this era. Fans are not only coming into metal in the modern South African state, a liberal democracy, but they are also utilizing the internet to access new music from the world around them. Heavy metal bands have benefitted greatly from the promotion of their music in this internet era as acts are able to reach larger audiences at home and abroad. Thus, the correlation of youth and the internet generation are strongly linked. In Gauteng, 26 percent of respondents have identified as being metal fans for between two and five years. While it may be presumptuous to assume everyone in South Africa has access to the internet, the advent of this technology has assisted immensely as "[i]nternet and personal computer use [has] catalyzed the spread of metal into new countries and to a lesser degree intensified the adoption of metal within countries" (Mayer and Timberlake 2014: 41).

James Irving, guitarist of the Johannesburg-based metalcore band Facing the Gallows, cited a number of reasons, notably, "content and the free access people have online" (Irving 2018: n.pag.), that have assisted in metal's recent explosion in the nation among millennial audiences. Wayne Boucher, a promoter and musician based in Johannesburg, says that not only the internet, but also an increase in the number of live performances has assisted the local metal scene immensely:

> In South Africa we get little to zero radio support for rock and metal, so it seems to me a lot of it has to do with word of mouth among friends and the power of the internet. Never before in history have we been exposed to so many different kinds of music from all over the world, all accessible at the touch of a smartphone or PC. Chances are that our live music scene has helped a lot, too. There's nothing like seeing a great metal band live to change your mind about the genre should your ears have enjoyed mainly pop music in the past. There's something special about watching a band performing everything 100 percent live.
>
> (Boucher 2018: n.pag.)

The live performance aspect that Boucher discusses is crucial in understanding the growth and prosperity of a scene as this survey indicates that 35.9 percent of respondents say they attend more than nine shows a year. Also, it must also be noted that the survey indicates that 24.4 percent of the respondents claimed to

FIGURE 1.1: Fans at the 2018 Krank'D Up Festival, in Gauteng. Photo credit: Nathan Ferreira.

have attended between five to eight shows a year, thus 60 percent of the respondents are attending more than five shows a year.

One salient reason the respondents cited a higher number of concerts attended may be correlated with those that noted, overwhelmingly, a satisfaction with their local scene. When asked "What do you like most about the Gauteng scene?" 59.2 percent of the respondents cited "community" as their number one choice, while another 48.3 percent cited their local (South African) bands.[6]

As is commonplace with the culture of music fandom, regardless of genre, fans have long enjoyed attending live performances: the visceral reaction of experiencing the songs one enjoys being performed live directly from the artists, sharing this reactionary moment with others, pulled away—even if briefly—from the surrounding world. As Thomas Turino explains, "[p]eople go out to concerts and clubs because they like to be with other like-minded people [...] [as] presentational events can connect individual and identity groups" (2008: 61).

This experience not only serves to reinforce fans' passions for their favorite acts; live settings are also spaces of reinforcement for metal fans as a center of community, as a metal fan in a live setting can find themselves surrounded by others linked to their favorite music style. As Snell and Hodgetts describe, these types of settings are "central to the construction of a heavy metal community," as one can find others with similar attire, symbolic displays, and even willful participants in "headbanging [...] the practice of moving one's head, usually violently, in time to music" (2007: 434). These examples highlight the importance of shared experience for fans of the genre, whether tacitly or verbally. Furthermore, participants are now included into a group that they are responsible for maintaining, which would have greater benefits to not only the scene but also the individuals involved, as "research has shown that feeling part of a community has a significant positive impact on a range of outcomes for both individuals and groups" (Davidson and Cotter in Varas-Díaz et al. 2015: 91).

Responses indicating a strong sense of community encompass the shared identity that fans attribute to their local bands as well as local spaces. This bond is what links the identity of metal fans to the ownership of their respective scene. Attending live metal concerts not only creates synergy between the amalgam of fans gathered but also validates that sense of belonging.

In her essay "Communities of metal," Deena Weinstein declares that the idea of community or the communal experience in metal relies on four commonalities: notably a shared set of values, mutual identification, interaction, as well as solidarity—qualities that also enable a sense of trust among participants (Weinstein 2016: 10). The latter characteristic she describes is the antitheses of the experience of alienation: "As an emergent feature of community, solidarity is instrumental to community, constituting it, and maintaining it" (Weinstein 2016: 11).

These four commonalties are what connects the Gauteng scene to the rest of the world, enabling a member of another scene or an actor in the local scene, such as a band, to travel to Gauteng and easily assimilate into its existing state and vice versa. This is what has allowed Gauteng acts such as Deity's Muse, Vulvodynia, and Facing the Gallows to enter western markets with the same familiarity that western bands such as Metallica, Iron Maiden, and Trivium have entered Gauteng. As such, scenes exist as familiar entities for those who do not occupy a specific scene on an everyday basis. Highlighting Wallach and Levine's research, Weinstein states that their model provides an emphasis rooted in locality: "As their model indicates, 'scene consciousness' is achieved through places such as stores and venues, that can be used regularly by, and for metal fans" (Wallach and Levine 2011: 121 quoted in Weinstein 2016: 9); yet none of these requires or indicates exclusivity for members of a specific local scene. What is necessary is the shared experience of metal fandom.

Community building through metal is a vital component of creating scene viability; Gauteng's, as well as the rest of South Africa's, heavy metal scene has grown substantially since the turn of century as a result of people making a shift from complacent to proactive movers. During my first trip to South Africa in 2007, I noted a severe lack of spaces for metal fans and musicians to perform or congregate. What transpired in the years since was a movement led by those with limited acumen and resources. Wayne Boucher was one such individual who took to creating the scene he imagined while observing the working habits of promoters and bands when performing in the United States and Europe with his band, Deity's Muse. Along with his working partner, Duncan Bell, they began organizing the Krank'D Up Festival in Gauteng in 2011. The event has become an annual success. Likewise, in Cape Town, the biannual Metal4Africa Festival has also grown into a positive space that celebrates metal fandom.

Irving describes the recent surge in festivals and positive spaces over the past ten years as benefiting the collective scene as a platform that allows for the sharing of knowledge:

> What promoters are doing is raising the game here. Besides the fact it's awesome watching your favorite internationals play on your home turf, you get the opportunity to meet and learn from them—how they approach their live shows, how they built up their following or what worked for them in terms of promoting their band—invaluable information that you don't freely get anywhere else. It's getting stronger each year. The bands are pushing the limitations musically and the promoters are putting together world-class events. We have access to the same tools and equipment as overseas, which makes everything sound professional.
>
> (2018: n.pag.)

Boucher states that this was what he wanted all along:

> It's an ongoing plan. It seemed to me that the best way to help our scene grow and to get an international audience's attention is to bring the bands we look up to so much to our shores and get them to play alongside our very own bands. By watching a world-class experienced international act on a regular basis you get to see first-hand what makes them successful and what sets them apart from you. By so doing, you as an upcoming musician in your local scene get to take mental notes and learn from the best in the business. It also helps with your confidence to know that a large chunk of our local acts can share the stage with an established international act and even match them in the talent department.
>
> (2018: n.pag.)

As discussed, the community of metal fans has emerged among those with the desire to surround themselves with like-minded souls. However, does this ideal of community encapsulate everyone? Is the metal scene in Gauteng truly inclusive toward people of color and women?

Race and gender

While the continent's sub-Saharan metal scenes are almost entirely composed of non-white populations, within South Africa the rock and metal scene is primarily made up of the nation's white minority, which accounts for less than 10 percent of the population. A total of 339 of 342 survey respondents replied to the question "What is your race?": 318 identified themselves as white (93.8 percent), 5 as Black, 4 colored (a term used by South Africans to describe people of mixed race), 6 Asian, and 1 Indian. The remaining 3 chose ambiguous designations: "cyborg," "other," "soul."

But has the South African metal scene, whose nascence came under the control of an authoritarian, racist government, moved on from the past into including those who would not previously have been allowed to participate legally? The scene's non-white members are few. While a few acts including Facing the Gallows, Deity's Muse, and 11th Hour feature mixed-race lineups, the numbers are too few to interpret as successful progress. However, in recent years, a vibrant scene has awoken in Soweto, a township that was once known globally as a center of resistance during apartheid. Acts such as TCIYF, Ree-burth, and Demogoroth Satanum have received national press—notably Demogoroth Satanum, whose meteoric rise in the extreme metal scene has placed them as one of the more notable metal bands in Gauteng (Monnakgotla 2017: n.pag.). Yet, as Hoad argues,

FIGURE 1.2: Dayton, Ohio's Miss May I at Krank'D Up Festival. Photo credit: Nathan Ferreira.

metal in South Africa today "offers a starting point for mapping the desire to remold a white South African identity [...] problematizing any attempts to speak for a unified South African nation" (2014: 193).

Mary Robertson also argues that music in today's South Africa is instrumental in affirming racial identities; an aspect drawn in by the distinctions that South Africans have made between the image of the performers, or "Black music" and "white music." She posits, "For many, division in music taste according to 'race' was interpreted as evidence of the racially determined nature of the experience in post-apartheid South Africa" (Robertson 2011: 460). Furthermore, the lived experiences of the entertainers were also what was at the center of the lyrical structures of the music being performed, such as *kwaito* music, a style of music born in the nation's townships during apartheid. Thus, the music served as a reflection of shared experiences for Blacks, their political and historical experiences, as well as the structure of support (Robertson 2011: 460). While no form of music is exclusive in South Africa, the labeling of such forms of music as "Black" or "white" music may be hindering specific genres' fecundity.

Metal, however, has long prided itself on being a medium that is an open invitation to those who have a genuine interest in the expressiveness of the genre's visceral aggression—thus, the ease at which the genre has globalized and the reason,

FIGURE 1.3: Soweto's Demogoroth Satanum. Photo credit: Christelle Duvenage.

FIGURE 1.4: Gauteng's Facing the Gallows. Photo credit: Mike Bell.

perhaps, why this genre has appealed to a wide array of fans regardless of nationalities (Clinton and Wallach 2015: 275). The genre is defined less by the skin color of the performers or the fans and more by how one defines the music; how one allows it to shape their identity; what one can contribute; and how one is able to recognize the structures, history, and interpretations of the genre. These are the markers that have constructed the shared identity of heavy metal fans worldwide.

But it would be irresponsible to just state that the genre is an all-encompassing panacea of colorblindness, or a form of sameness in which all semblances of racism or privilege disappear (Rodriguez 2006: 646), as the visibility of the genre's superstars are palpably white. Catherine Hoad argues that whiteness in heavy metal is so entrenched into the norm that "whiteness itself is largely rendered invisible, while difference is made hypervisible" (2014: 190–91). This form of whiteness, whether physical or emotional, ostracizes any inclinations of incorporating more Black African influences as the main objective of South African metal fans and acts to reinforce their place in the global, European, American, and male-dominated metal world. Thus the proclivity of local musicians to adhere to the codes of sounds established by the genre's leading acts and forefathers. However, would a white dominated scene in South Africa welcome in fans and emotions from outside of the genre's traditional rubrics?

Regarding the Gauteng scene, Roushan van Niekerk[7] of the Johannesburg-based metalcore band Riddlebreak states:

> The philosophy surrounding metal speaks to people who fall on the outskirts of society, people who are marginalized. The current scene in theory is welcoming to people who have been "otherized." Metal in South Africa has definitely become more welcoming. It wasn't always so, and this is apparent through the lack of attendance of those outside of the "white-male" rubrics and comparing it to the current increase in attendance. South African metal is a small community as is; the crowds desperately need to expand. Gauteng is a diverse place to begin with and I feel that the metal scene definitely allows for inclusion of this diversity.
>
> (2018: n.pag.)

Claire Martens, a freelance music writer, adds that in today's South Africa, a nation named the most unequal in the world in 2018 (World Bank quoted in Baker 2019: n.pag.), one aspect that is likely a stronger factor in hindering the metal scene is a perfervid economic inequality:

> I think we are too comfortable with what we have and don't have much of a drive to change. The scene is still white-male dominated and all the people of color in the scene come from similar socio-economic backgrounds (as the survey results

> support, the respondent average professions requiring some form of educational training).[8] South Africa is a country with a social and cultural hangover, one that is not going away very easily [...] The economic policies that came after the democratic elections in 1994 only resulted in deepening inequality, despite the country's wealth and resources no longer being solely controlled by whites.
>
> (Martens 2018: n.pag.)

Martens's assessment reflects what becomes palpable with immersion into the local scene, that heavy metal is not immune to the lingering vestiges of apartheid, whether or not participants are even aware of the damage that previous generations left without compunction: a country rooted in institutions of privilege, income disparity, and patriarchy that will take generations to transform. The heavy metal scene in Gauteng is very much a microcosm—"a white enclave" (Martens 2018: n.pag.)—of this divide as it may be viewed as a place for reinforcing an "us-ness" (Roy and Dowd 2010: 190).

Metal and masculinity

While women have long played roles of significance in the heavy metal industry, the marginalization of their contributions and the notion that women in metal are continually assumed as a "plus one," whose appreciation and enjoyment of the music cannot be authentic, have been driving issues in the dialogue of just how diverse the genre truly is.

While the end of apartheid put legal racism to bed, the onerous task of displacing a salient vestige, patriarchy, remains difficult in the era of confronting perceptions. For some, these biases linger as the country's citizenry still adheres to its patriarchal religious past. Yet metal can serve as a bridge "to reinterpret the power imbalance between men and women in patriarchal societies [...] a transgressive discourse to promote equality among genders" (Varas-Díaz et al. 2017: 69). But has this postapartheid generation moved on from the patriarchal structures of the past as well as its societal norms? Or are the problems rooted in the heavy metal subculture as a whole? Gauteng-based musician Natalie Cowling posits:

> I think the reason women were excluded from the heavy metal subculture in the past is because they didn't see women as being capable of possessing the characteristics associated with heavy metal (aggressiveness and independence) and behaving in a manner which is distinctively masculine. I think these elements are localized aspects within the sociology of the heavy metal subculture. I believe women just needed to put themselves out there and show how amazing metal music can sound with a

> female vocalist and that female metal musicians are just as capable of writing and performing metal music as any male metal musician is.
>
> (Cowling 2018: n.pag.)

Cowling's observation of the genre's embodiment of characteristics of masculine behavior serves as a template for much of the research being conducted in academia today. While metal may be ahead of societal trends in its varied settings, there is space to advance. As van Niekerk attests, perhaps the difficulty for women is the attribution to many of the stereotypes attached to the genre:

> Metal has been posed as unfeminine in the past; headbanging and moshpits are seen as male activities because of the roughness [...] the characteristics of the music itself could be seen as masculine in the loudness and aggression, which are seen as male characteristics.
>
> (van Niekerk 2018: n.pag.)

Martens contextualizes that the issue of female participation in metal is emblematic of the larger picture for women. She argues:

FIGURE 1.5: Roushan van Niekerk. Photo credit: Wayde Flowerday.

> Metal is a microcosm of society at large and I think it as welcoming to women as any other space in society. We are fighting to carve out spaces in male-dominated arenas and sometimes succeeding and sometimes not succeeding because we are still undervalued.
>
> (Martens 2018: n.pag.)

According to Walser, metal's place in any scene, regardless of the local culture attached, is always at a crossroads of identity and sexism:

> Metal replicates the dominant sexism of contemporary society but it also allows a kind of free space to be opened up by and for certain women, performers and fans alike. Female fans identify with a kind of power that is usually understood in our culture as male—because physical power, dominance, rebellion and flirting with the dark side of life are all culturally designated as male prerogatives. Yet women are able to access this power because it is channelled through a medium—music—that is intangible and difficult to police.
>
> (2004: 364)

This power, as described by Walser, is what has allowed some female fans to find a form of safety in heavy metal, and as Martens says, this embrace of certain masculine traits allows her to express herself in a manner that confronts gender norms:

> Personally, I love the masculine element of metal and that it allows me to step into this other role (the Doc Marten-wearing, powerful looking role) [...] It's a form of role playing that is safe, fun and inclusive. I know that quite a few female musicians are lesbian, so I think it also speaks to their need to straddle gender roles and assert more of themselves into what they wear, listen to and give a shit about. Having said that, I think metal in (South Africa) is not a very masculine place specifically not in a way that makes you feel excluded.
>
> Beyond metal, there is not much else that offers South Africans an "alternative" space—so it attracts a lot of diverse people who may not love metal as much as they love the inclusive nature of it—that you can exist outside the norm, but be normal or even too normal in metal [...] and so the metal scene captures many of these types of people. So I think it offers a haven for a lot of young women, some even of the LGBTI[9] crowd, who don't feel like they can be masculine, hard or different elsewhere.
>
> (Martens 2018: n.pag.)

Yet, there remains the pervasive issue with how women are valued in metal, both inside and outside of South Africa—what van Niekerk calls "the 'groupie' or 'girlfriend' stigma" (van Niekerk 2018: n.pag.), which she describes as the questions surrounding your attendance to metal concert and the assumption that a woman is only in attendance for an ulterior motive. "Even female musicians are assumed to be "plus ones" of the band. Females in the scene are often met with surprise as their presence is unexpected" (van Niekerk 2018: n.pag.). For men in patriarchal societies, the unexpected place of women in metal stems from entitlements of exclusionary roles in metal, one that has long dominated the image and discourse of the genre. Yet, these norms merit a challenge, not only in South Africa, but also the rest of the world. As Rosemary Lucy Hill writes:

> Deeper consideration of women's pleasure in hard rock and metal music is vital in challenging assumptions about the genre and its fans [...] It is necessary in order to challenge the orthodoxy of the genre as masculine and therefore the naturalized hierarchy that places men upon the stage and/or positioned in the audience as the "real fan" whilst women are relegated to the subordinate role of the groupie.
>
> (2016: 290–91)

Thus, female participants tend to deal with horrendous objectification and unparalleled ostracizing, as objectifying women has long been a cottage industry within the male-dominated music industry, one "permeated with sexism" (Weinstein 2000: 66). But are these aspects of marginalization localized within the sociology of the scene's setting? Or, is heavy metal to be defined by its masculinity? Says van Niekerk:

> I definitely think there are elements in metal as a genre, sociology and within the masculinity of metal that ostracized women in the past. I think it is more apparent in certain subgenres than others. For example, within lyrical content the female body is often posed as abject and other. It is used for shock value. There has been an underlying tone of disdain towards women.
>
> Musically, in some of the lyrical content in certain subgenres, female body parts and functions are used to demonstrate the abject and referred to in order to garner shock value. This is counteractive towards inclusion and often makes women uncomfortable and poses women as inferior, disgusting and their bodies as material objects.
>
> (2018: n.pag.)

The inclinations to subject the female body are driven by a male-centered identity in metal as the genre "validated the use of women as sexual accessories in videos, song lyrics, and even by ignoring their musical abilities [...] often ignored or belittled in male-dominant cultures" (Varas-Díaz et al. 2017: 61). In terms of viewing the female body as a novelty, Lucinda Viljoen, a thrash metal drummer, argues that the inculcation is societal as a constructed gender norm: "A lot of people still think that way, in terms of being a novelty, or just trying to show their bodies. People need to stop this thing about, "girls can't do it'" (Viljoen 2012: n.pag.). At the time of our meeting, Lucinda was drumming for thrash metal band Junkyard Lipstick. Explaining that the patriarchy of South African society is deeply rooted, Lucinda said that while the metal scene was open to seeing her perform with three other female musicians in their band, greater society was not as accepting. For female headbangers, heavy metal was a step away from these norms. She adds:

> With South Africa, we already have a very conservative heritage (and) our music is already seen as the devil's music. We aren't in the kitchen barefoot and pregnant; we are actually doing something that makes us feel independent and powerful.
>
> (Viljoen 2012: n.pag.)

Conclusion

Gauteng's metal scene and the South African scene as a whole crossed a broken barrier: a system of authority and obedience that was complicit in subjugating over 45 million people. Today's Gauteng scene has progressed well beyond the previous generation's expectations, validating itself into a viable scene that fosters and facilitates professional, touring acts who are able to earn a living through their art. A scene in which musicians in the past chose to emigrate from for entry into the global metal scene is today home to acts that realize this is no longer necessary, as the current generation is pursuing the acumen necessary to step onto the global heavy metal market.

Metal in Gauteng and South Africa will be viable for generations to come as a result of the community that has grown around its fans and the safe space it could provide for those who feel marginalized, including metal fans of color. However, the scene for now is "noticeably white and centered in urban areas" (Hoad 2014: 193). Yet, its existence and presence is what is necessary for any growth to occur, including the acceptance of non-white, non-male identities and voices.

Furthermore, metal has remained viable for quite some time because it is a constant evolution. The ethos of the scene has already begun to unpack itself outside of the middle-class and white rubrics and into townships with fans of varying backgrounds, whether racial or economic, slowly embracing a form of music that would otherwise be seen as "white," likely because of the increase of musicians of color—a boundary that was not possible a generation ago. Its roots remain strongly embedded in its core foundation, yet it absorbs whatever it is being fed by its perspicacious performers.

Acknowledgments

The author wishes to thank the editors of this book for their constructive feedback in shaping this chapter. To Lewis and Bryan for realizing this idea was worth pursuing. Brad Klypchak and Stacey Campbell for the extra set of eyes and absolutely wonderful input. The staff and librarians at the Gumberg Library at Duquesne University and Carnegie Library of Pittsburgh for their assistance and support. And a very special thanks to the metal fans and musicians of beautiful Gauteng, one of my favorite places on earth, who took the time to respond to the survey and my email inquiries. South Africa rocks!

NOTES

1. Censors were provided a set of thirteen guidelines by the South African Broadcast Company which informed them of the necessary criteria for banning music (Drewett 2003: 154; Reitov 2004: 82–83).
2. Title translated from Afrikaans: *Rock Musiek: Die reg om te weet.*
3. Formerly known as Pretoria-Witwatersrand-Vereeniging (PWV), the province—once a part of the Transvaal Province—was renamed Gauteng in December of 1994.
4. These were the number of followers from Krank'd Up and Metal4Africa's Facebook pages as noted at time of the survey's posting.
5. Similar surveys of various scene studies have also been conducted and published. See: Gertenbach 2017; Guibert and Guibert 2016; Mirabella 2017; Ury-Petesch 2016; Varas-Díaz et al. 2015.
6. Participants were asked to choose at most three responses of five and were able to include their own answers as well.
7. Roushan also performs with the all-female metal "all-star" group Sistas of Metal, a band composed of female members of other Gauteng area bands.
8. Martens had no knowledge of the results of the survey when interviewed.
9. In South African English, "I" is used to refer to "intersex" in LGBTI.

REFERENCES

Baker, Aryn (2019), "What South Africa can teach us as worldwide inequality grows," *Time*, May 2, https://time.com/longform/south-africa-unequal-country/. Accessed June 10, 2019.

Boucher, Wayne (2018), email to author, February 25.

Brinkhoff, Thomas (2017), "Major agglomerations of the world—Population statistics and maps." City Population, January 1, www.citypopulation.de. Accessed December 8, 2017.

Clinton, Esther, and Wallach, Jeremy (2015), "Recoloring the metal map: Metal and race in global perspective," in T. M. Karjalainen and K. Kärki (eds.), *Proceedings from Modern Heavy Metal: Markets, Practices and Cultures,* International Academic Conference, Helsinki, Finland, June 8–12, pp. 274–82.

Cowling, Natalie (2018), email to author, February 3.

Davidson, Patrick (2012), in-person interview, Cape Town, South Africa, November 24.

Drewett, Michael (2003), "Music in the struggle to end apartheid: South Africa," in M. Cloonan and R. Garafolo (eds.), *Policing Pop*, Philadelphia: Temple University Press, pp. 153–65.

Falkof, Nicky (2012), "Satan has come to Rietfontein: Race in South Africa's satanic panic," *Journal of Southern African Studies*, 38:4, pp. 753–67.

Gertenbach, Ian (2017), "Lack of audience attendance within the live metal music industry in South Africa," specialized project dissertation, Johannesburg: Campus of Performing Arts.

Goode, Erich and Ben-Yehuda, Nachman (1994), "Moral panics: Culture, politics, and social construction," *Annual Review of Sociology*, 20, pp. 149–71.

Guibert, Christopher, and Guibert, Gérôme (2016), "The social characteristics of the contemporary metalhead: The Hellfest survey," in A. R. Brown, K. Spracklen, K. Kahn-Harris, and N. W. R Scott (eds.), *Global Metal Music and Culture: Current Directions in Metal Studies*, New York: Routledge, pp. 167–89.

Hill, Rosemary Lucy (2016), "Masculine pleasure?: Women's encounters with hard rock and metal music," in A. R. Brown, K. Spracklen, K. Kahn-Harris, and N. W. R Scott (eds.), *Global Metal Music and Culture: Current Directions in Metal Studies*, New York: Routledge, pp. 277–93.

Hoad, Catherine (2014), "Ons is saam—Afrikaans metal and rebuilding whiteness in the Rainbow Nation," *International Journal of Community Music*, 7:2, pp. 189–204.

Irving, James (2018), email to author, February 5.

Martens, Claire (2018), email to author, January 29.

Mayer, Adam, and Timberlake, Jeffrey (2014), "The fist in the face of god," *Sociological Perspectives*, 57:1 (Spring), pp. 27–51.

Mirabella, Marita (2017), "Heavy metal and globalization: Reception study on the metal community in the global south," master's thesis, Stockholm: Stockholm University.

Monnakgotla, Motlabana (2017), "Money, witchcraft and beer. This is metal from Soweto," September 25, *Forbes Africa*, https://www.forbesafrica.com/life/2017/09/25/money-witchcraft-beer-metal-soweto/. Accessed January 15, 2018.

Reitov, Ole (2004), "Encounters with a South African censor: Confrontation and reconciliation," in M. Korpe (ed.), *Shoot the Singer!: Music Censorship Today*, London: Zed Books, pp. 82–87.

Robertson, Mary (2011), "The constraints of colour: Popular music listening and the interrogation of 'race' in post-apartheid South Africa," *Popular Music*, 30:3 (October), pp. 455–70.

Rodriguez, Jason (2006), "Color-blind ideology and the cultural appropriation of hip-hop," *Journal of Contemporary Ethnography*, 35:6 (December), pp. 645–68.

Roy, William, G., and Dowd, Timothy, J. (2010), "What is sociological about music," *Annual Review of Sociology*, 36, pp. 183–203.

Seal, Rodney (1988), *Rock Musiek: Die reg om te weet*, 2nd ed., South Africa: M.F.Y.

Snell, Dave, and Hodgetts, Darrin (2007), "Heavy metal, identity and the social negotiation of a community and practice," *Journal of Community and Applied Social Psychology*, 17:6, pp. 430–45.

South African Government Census (2016), http://www.statssa.gov.za. Accessed July 2, 2021.

Teppo, Annika (2009), "My mouse is protected by a dragon: White South Africans, magic and sacred spaces in post-apartheid cape town," *Suomen Anthropologi: Journal of the Finnish Anthropological Society*, 34:1 (Spring), pp. 19–41.

Turino, Thomas (2008), *Music as Social Life: The Politics of Participation*, Chicago: University of Chicago Press.

Ury-Petesch, Jean-Philippe (2016), "The numbers of the beast: surveying iron maiden's global tribe," in A. R. Brown, K. Spracklen, K. Kahn-Harris, and N. W. R. Scott (eds.), *Global Metal Music and Culture: Current Directions in Metal Studies*, New York: Routledge, pp. 145–66.

van Niekerk, Roushan (2018), email to author, February 26.

Varas-Díaz, Nelson, Mendoza, Sigrid, Rivera, Eliot, and Gonzalez, Osvaldo (2017), "Metal as a vehicle for critical culture in Latin America and the Caribbean: Challenging traditional female gender roles through music," in B. Bardine and M. Elovaara (eds.), *Connecting Metal to Culture: Unity in Disparity*, Bristol: Intellect, pp. 57–79.

Varas-Díaz, Nelson, Rivera-Segarra, Eliut, Rivera Medina, Carmen L., Mendoza, Sigrid, and Gonzalez-Sepulveda Osvaldo (2015), "Predictors of communal formation in a small heavy metal scene: Puerto Rico as a case study," *Metal Music Studies*, 1:1, pp. 87–103.

Viljoen, Lucinda (2012), in-person interview, Cape Town, South Africa, November 24.

Wallach, Jeremy, and Levine, Alexandra (2011), "I want *you* to support local metal: A theory of metal scene formation," *Popular Music History*, 6:1–2, pp. 116–34.

Walser, Robert (2004), "Forging masculinity: Heavy metal sounds and images of gender," in S. Frith (ed.), *Popular Music: Critical Concepts in Media and Cultural Studies*, London: Routledge, pp. 343–72.

Weinstein, Deena (2000), *Heavy Metal: The Music and Its Culture*, rev. ed., Boston: Da Capo Press.

Weinstein, Deena (2016), "Communities of metal: Ideal, diminished and imaginary," in N. Varas-Díaz and N. Scott (eds.), *Heavy Metal Music and the Communal Experience*, New York: Lexington Books, pp. 3–22.

2

Polar Fate: Mapping Metal at the Southern Edge of the World

Catherine Hoad

Introduction

In this chapter, I explore the notion of the "South" as a response to primacy of the "North" in heavy metal's structuring discourses and consider how a critical examination of the "South" might emerge as an antipodean alternative to the conditions, cultures, and symbols of metallic "Northernness." This response concerns how the aesthetics of "Antipodean Gothic" might be considered as a mode of attending to the distinct nuances of metal music and cultures situated at the Southern edge of the world. In doing so, I respond to two key discourses of heavy metal identity: first, that of the "North" as a central form of spatial, territorial, and symbolic capital within metal, and second, the "edge" as a symbolic spatial metaphor which underscores an emphasis on isolation, alienation, and marginality. In this discussion, I focus on metal bands from the southernmost regions of Australia and Aotearoa/New Zealand—Tasmania, Otago, and Southland. In doing so, I aim to unpack what "South" means in the context of metal music and practices—not simply as an antipodean counterpart to the "North," but rather to open up the possibilities of seeing how metal which emerges in the atmospheres of the extreme South might be imagined within the dimensions of place, gender, and history which have informed metal music scholarship.

Metal's pronounced interest in the symbolism and masculinities of the "North" has meant that such imaginings have reproduced hegemonic notions of "Northernness " as commensurate with "metalness." In response, I argue for the importance of engaging with the symbolic capital of the "South" within the spatial polemicisms of metal. This chapter thus acknowledges how discourses of the

North have potentially shaped and infiltrated metal at the Southern "end of the world," yet also considers how an alternate sense of "Southern" space and territory has been reflected in metal performed in these places. Metal's texts, practices, and aesthetics, as realized within the following examples from Tasmania, Otago, and Southland, must be considered first as products of a particularly geolocalized "heaviness," rather than immediately positioned as sites which respond to the hegemony of "global" metal. The notion of "metal on the edge" is a central structuring discourse for the North, and I argue that this notion of "edgeness" is even more pronounced for metal communities in Australia and Aotearoa/New Zealand. A sense of extremity and wilderness has been central to the nuanced ways in which Tasmania, Otago, and Southland have positioned themselves as places which exist at the "edge" of the world.

Through an application of critical discourse analysis and textual analysis, I thus situate this chapter as a (by no means exhaustive) critical response to the primacy of the discourse of Northernness as a mode of articulating metal's ostensibly transferrable values, and instead point to the ways in which entanglements of metal and locality emerge at the Southern edge of the Earth. The chapter hence canvasses three main sections. In the first section, I give an overview of the dominance of "Northernness" as a discourse and aesthetic within both metal cultures, and metal music studies as an academic field. From here, I consider the limited ways in which the notion of the "South" has been represented in metal's narratives, and introduce the notion of the Antipodean Gothic as a mode through which to present an alternative model for mapping the entanglement of polar identities with metal symbolism. However, as I contend here, the notion of the Antipodean Gothic itself is one which relies on colonialist constructions of Australia and Aotearoa/New Zealand, and often precludes Indigenous knowledges from circulating through such spaces. In the final section, I consider how such "Gothic" modes are articulated and performed in disparate ways through select examples of metal bands in the southernmost points of Australia and Aotearoa/New Zealand: Tasmania, and Otago and Southland, respectively.

In approaching these sites, I focus specifically on how artists articulate a sense of geographic and territorial identity as it occurs within and in response to particular discourses, spaces, and stylistic structures. This research, then, is not entirely a study of a "scene," in a sense of the contexts in which producers, musicians, and fans "collectively share their common musical tastes and collectively distinguish themselves from others" (Bennett and Peterson 2004: 1). These factors—of collective identification, commonality, and the interaction of multiple musical practices—are undoubtedly vital for research, but in seeking to propose a critical alternative to a particular theoretical modelling in metal music studies, I take "scene" here in Mark Olson's sense, where scenes are "territorializing machines" (Olson 1998: 281) which create and mobilize particular kinds of relationships in geographic locations. The relationship I explore here is that between the bands as their music is shaped by territorialized sentiments toward space and identity, and the wider international context in which metal is situated.

The examples here are by no means wholly exemplary of the metal produced within Southland, Otago and Tasmania at large, nor is it a conclusive study of metal that emerges at these "Southern edges" as they manifest worldwide. This chapter is also, importantly, not a comparison, but a deliberately messy mapping of types of difference which emerge from ostensible commonalities, from which I hope to spark a wider push toward problematizing some of the universalizing rhetoric that has emerged in metal discourses around space and place. This chapter thus considers how the identity of the "South" has emerged as an expression of particular kinds of regional "heaviness." This metallic "Southernness" emerges as a discourse which has multiple, complex manifestations, which realize the distinct geo-local politics, histories, and identities of Australia and Aotearoa/New Zealand in specific ways. However, I remain cognizant of how these places have been immediately shaped by violent colonial contexts and gender relations, a factor which cannot, and must not, be overlooked. This, I argue, anchors these strands of Southern metal within the wider questions of hegemony, centers and peripheries which plague metal at large, realized here in metal from the Antarctic ends of the Earth.

Northernness meets metalness

Metal's relationship with the "North" has become a key area of interest for both popular and scholarly accounts of heavy metal as the genre has rapidly expanded in the region. The ready association of metal with Northern Europe has been well-documented in both academic and popular press. Such associations have at once been focused on the relative popularity of metal in the region, wherein the Nordic countries currently boast the highest rate of metal bands per capita in the world (Grandoni 2012). However, further to this, since the mid 2000s, metal scholars have displayed an accelerated interest in the "cultural aesthetics and identity politics" of metal in Northern Europe (Brown 2015: 261). Academic work in this period has explored the cultural economy of Vikings in hard rock and metal music (Trafford and Pluskowski 2007; Heesch 2010): the relationship between metal and Old Norse mythology, sagas and "native art" (Von Helden 2010, 2017), the attempts to locate (or imagine) a distinctly Nordic "sound" (Hagen 2011), and the revitalization of Nordic Paganism through metal (Weinstein 2014). Invocations of the North in metal music are of course not a particularly new phenomenon, nor have such allusions been strictly limited to Northern European artists. However, the relatively recent surge in metal music studies as a somewhat-consolidated academic field has invited a plethora of research into metal's entanglements with the symbols, traditions, and politics of Northern Europe in ways that have centralized the region as a key site for constructions of metallic identity.

Within both scholarship and the music at large, metal's obsession with the symbolism and masculinities of the "North" has meant that such imaginings have reproduced hegemonic notions of "Northernness " as commensurate with metalness. Narratives of Northern masculinity, liberty, and heathenry have become central to heavy metal's foundational discourses, and they point to the ways in which "Northernness" becomes mobilized as a particular symbolic category. The Northern branding of musical styles is apparent in the use of "Nordic," "Scandinavian," and the "North" as interchangeable frameworks for the marketing of particular styles of heavy metal. This branding strategy has become increasingly apparent in the American and European metal festival circuits,[1] and in the branding power of "North" itself across multiple regions.[2] "Nordic metal," Von Helden argues, "is a trademark and a best seller" (2010: 33). In addition to such explicit branding of the "North" as inherently "metal," the emphasis on externality, isolation, and extremity further emerges as a key form of capital for the "North" in metal discourses. The focus on Nordic metal existing "outside" the mainstream is commensurate with understandings of extreme metal as "on the edge of music" (Kahn-Harris 2007: 5); moreover, such sentiments are situated within a wider regional narrative which sees the Nordic region at the geographic Northern "edge" of Europe and the world, as remote and isolated (Grimley 2006: 2).

The production of an "imagined community of Northernness," as Lucas et al. (2011) have shown in their discussion of the extrapolation of Nordicness into "Northernness," has thus created problematic boundaries of who, or what, may be represented in such categories. However, as I have argued elsewhere (Hoad and Whiting 2017), metal's "Nothernness" cannot be considered as a uniform, essential category, but rather one marked by tensions and paradoxes that undercut the possibility of any singular understanding of the "North." Just as metal itself is "exceptionally diverse" and "constantly developing and reconfiguring" (Kahn-Harris 2007: 6–7), so too is the category of the "North." This need to engage with metal's obsession with the "North," as it becomes a synecdoche for an array of cultural symbols standing in for notions of masculinity, strength, liberation, and ethnonational belonging, thus underscores the critical task I wish to undertake for the remainder of this chapter. In drawing attention to how the "North" has dominated within the spatial polemicisms of metal, I now turn to the "South" as a way of providing an alternate to such symbolism. Nonetheless, just as I have argued that metal music studies faces the vital need to move beyond an essentialist understanding of the North, and look toward a critical mapping of the way in which

"Northern" might be given different value in different contexts, here I argue that the same principles must be applied in articulating an understanding of the value and meaning of the "South" in metal.

Looking to the Southern edge of the world

Whilst metal's imagining of the "North" is a well-researched area, manifestations of the "South" have been largely unexplored. This, I must emphasize, is not to say that metal scenes in the world's geographic "South" have not been analyzed. The Caribbean, Central, and South America have provided rich sites for the study of metal: Varas-Díaz et al. have shown the ways in which metal communities in Cuba, Puerto Rico, and the Dominican Republic have "integrated and displaced local racial and ethnic discourses in light of their particular socio-political contexts" (Varas-Díaz et al. 2014: 291); Idelbar Avelar's 2003 work on Sepultura focuses on the specific sociocultural conditions of Brazil from the 1960s onwards, which he argues gave shape to a particular aesthetic for pioneering Brazilian acts. In looking to sub-Saharan Africa, Edward Banchs's work (2016) has been vital in documenting the rich identities of scenes in Botswana, Kenya, and Madagascar, amongst other nations. Annie Klopper (2011) has also examined metal in South Africa within the context of the burgeoning postapartheid Afrikaans punk movement, while my own work has explored the Afrikaans metal scene (Hoad 2014). Scenes in Malaysia and Indonesia have been contexts for diverse academic work (Baulch 2007; Wallach 2011; Yin and Khiun 2017), as have those in Oceania, where this current chapter emerges alongside a body of work exploring metal in Australia and Aotearoa/New Zealand (cf. Phillipov 2008; Overell 2014; Hoad 2019; Heath 2015). Certainly, as these examples show, scholarship has engaged with scenes located in the geographic South. However, what I contend here is that the "South," as a cultural imaginary, has not been mobilized as a site of sematic and symbolic meaning in the same way that the "North" has; what I wish to propose in this chapter, then, is a way of theorizing through the discourse of "Southernness," and the identities which may be imagined and critiqued therein.

Metal's relationship to the "South," as a discourse of identity, has emerged, thus far, largely in relationship to the American South, where "Southern metal" is a term used largely to refer to the New Orleans, or NOLA, scene which produced Exhorder, Down, Eyehategod, and Crowbar, and which pioneered sludge and groove metal. This iteration of "Southern metal" has been documented sporadically, in texts such as the documentaries *Slow Southern Steel* (2010) and *NOLA: Life, Death, and Heavy Blues from the Bayou* (2014), and Michael

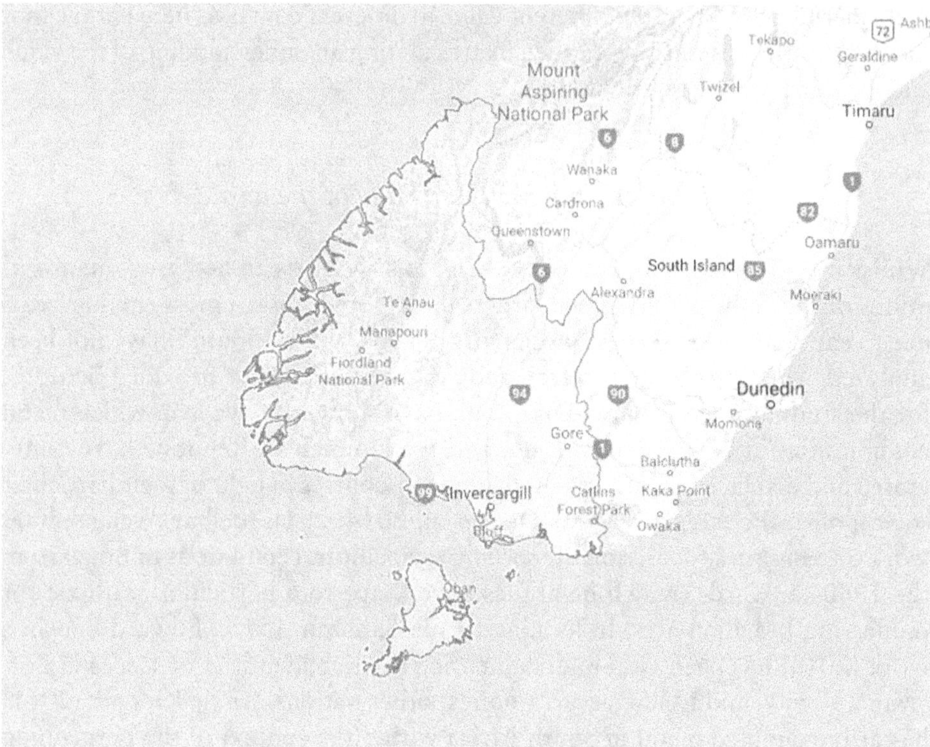

FIGURE 2.1: Map of Murihiku/Southland, 2019, Google Maps [online]. Copyright Google.

McDowell's thesis (2016) on the "heavy south." Here "Southernness" signals a mode of rural, "authentic" masculinity marked by working class belonging, fierce regionalism, and strong sense of insular community bonds (Eastman 2012; McDowell 2016). Any unpacking of what the rhetoric of the "South" might mean beyond its American contexts, however, is largely absent from studies of metal. Moreover, engaging with the South as a polar zone or "edge," in the same way the north is oft-situated as the "Northern edge" of the international metal community, and indeed the world, necessitates a shift considerably beyond the southern regions of the United States. Here, then, I want to take the opportunity provided by this book to go roughly another 13,000 kilometers south, to the southernmost points of Australia and Aotearoa/New Zealand—Tasmania, Australia's southernmost state, and Southland and Otago, the southernmost regions.

Southland (Figure 2.1) occupies the lower western corner of Aotearoa/New Zealand, with a population of 102,000; Otago (Figure 2.2) represents the eastern corner and coast, with a population of 236,000; and Tasmania (Figure 2.3) is an

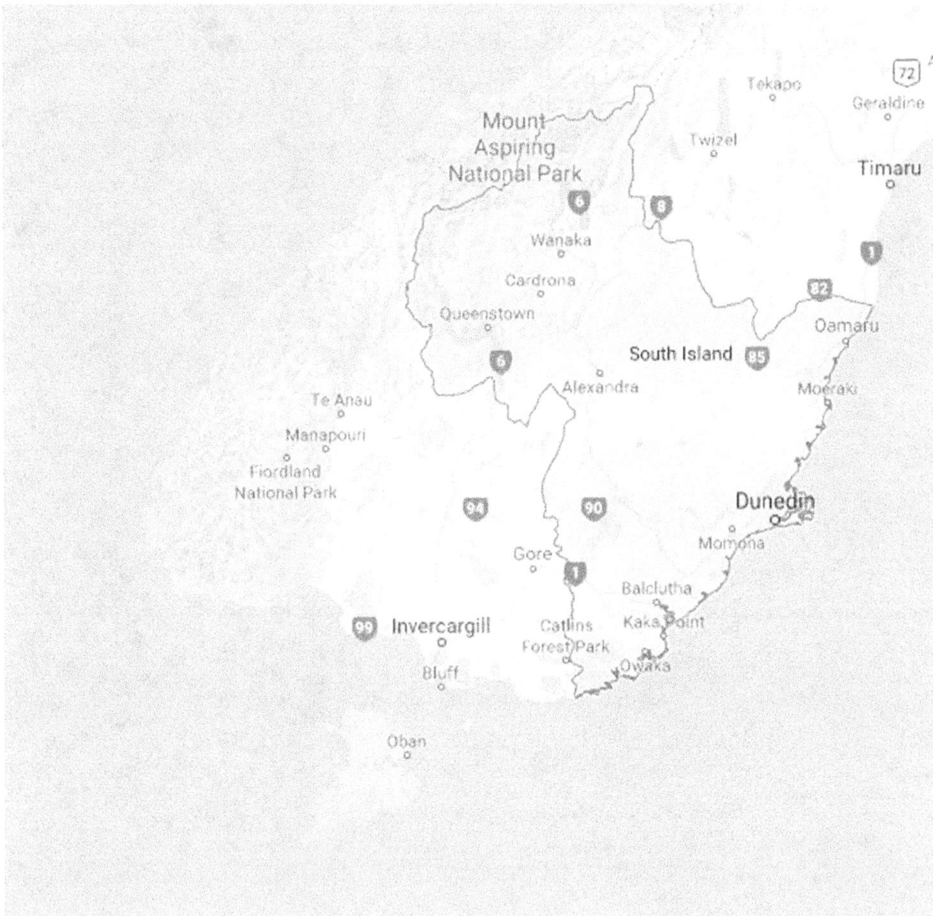

FIGURE 2.2: Map of Otago, 2019. Google Maps [online]. Copyright Google.

island state 240 kilometers south of the Australian mainland, with a population of just over 540,000. All three regions are home to relatively small but stable metal scenes supported by local infrastructure; these regions are generally overlooked in international touring schedules, but all have some form of semi-regular nights for local bands in smaller venues and active online presences. All three regions have metropolitan centers and sparsely populated rural towns as well as huge tracts of national parkland, the "wilderness" of which has become core to the ways in which these places are branded and form identities.

Just as the notion of "metal on the edge" is a central structuring discourse for the North, I contend that this notion of "edgeness" is even more pronounced in Australia and Aotearoa/New Zealand. A sense of extremity and wilderness has

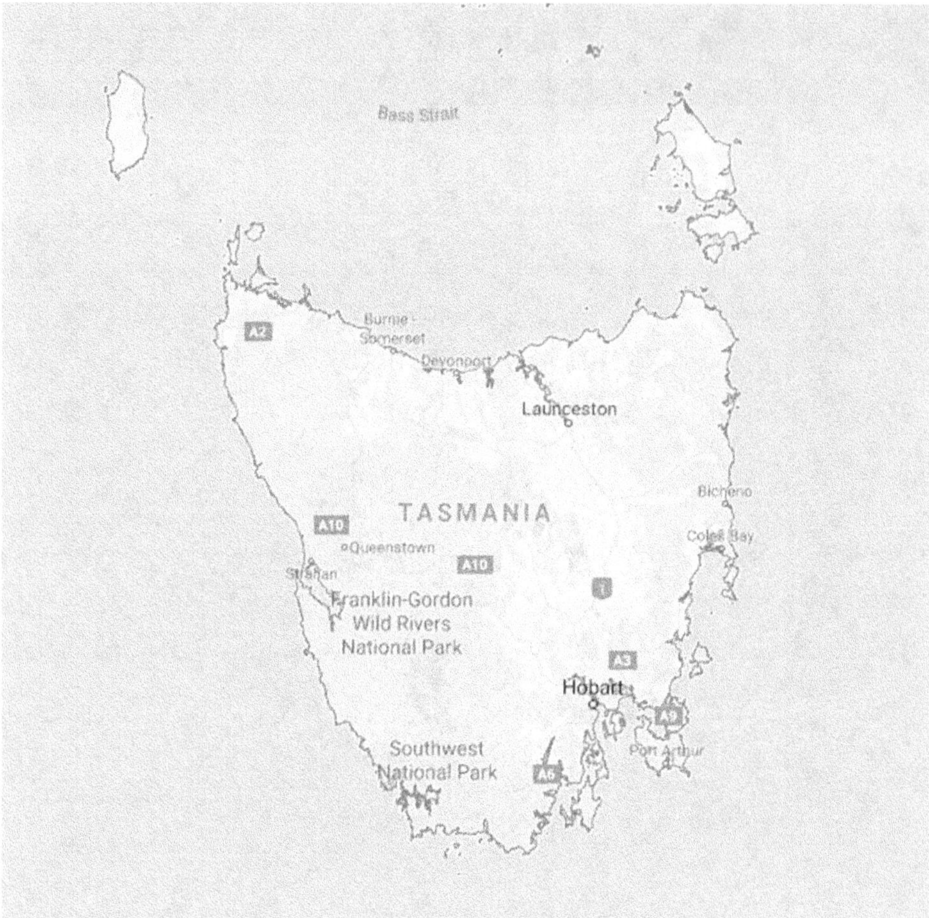

FIGURE 2.3: Map of Tasmania, 2019. Google Maps [online]. Copyright Google.

been central to the nuanced ways in which Tasmania, Otago, and Southland have positioned themselves as places which exist on "the edge" of the world. For Stewart and Hopcroft, Tasmanian music exists at "the end of the world," where Tasmania is "the final stopping point before the frozen wastes of the South Pole, an outpost remote even from the already remote continent of Australia" (Stewart and Hopcroft 2009: 134); Doug Heath, in his work on Invercargill, calls this "heavy metal from the Antarctic ends of the earth" (Heath 2015: 230). Such discourses, in some ways, replicate the Northern notion of Nordic metal existing on the extreme edge of both the international metal scene and the northern hemisphere. That both north and south regions, in this context, are characterized by climates of harsh extremity and mythologies of frontier masculinity surviving in such conditions is an important precondition for engaging with colonial discourses of "polar" masculinity. I also note that the wider scenic populations in which these bands are also represented as largely male and white, with some exceptions in Southland which I speak to. All of these three regions are, however, marked by internal differences which are crucial to acknowledge within any discussion of a "Southern" aesthetic. Just as hegemonic notions of Northern metal reproduce exclusionist notions of whiteness and ethnonationalism which fail to attenuate to the distinct differences between the Nordic countries, here I reiterate that attempts to situate Tasmania, Otago, and Southland within similarly encompassing polar frameworks ignores the ways in which these regions' histories are structured in complex and nuanced ways.

For the remainder of this chapter, I introduce three kinds of "Southernness" articulated by metal bands in Southland, Otago, and Tasmania. In Southland, there has developed a self-titled "Southern metal" tradition which emphasizes rural, working-class masculinity; in Otago, black metal bands emphasize individualism, misanthropy, and abjection; in Tasmania, a distinct brand of "lo-fi forest black metal" is characterized by themes of isolation and the dark pastoral. I loosely position these different iterations of metallic "Southernness" as variants within the Antipodean Gothic, an aesthetic which Jennifer Lawn (2006) expands upon to refer to the "heaviness" of land in the far-south Antipodes. The Antipodean Gothic is a mode which emerges from Australia and Aotearoa/New Zealand, marked by its entanglement of gothic traditions of darkness, the supernatural and the sublime, with the isolated, and often hostile, rural landscapes, identities, and tensions of the antipodes.

Such an entanglement is inescapably marked by the legacies of colonialism; the very notion of Australia and Aotearoa/New Zealand being consolidated as the "Antipodes" emerges from an Anglo- and Eurocentric perspective. The concept of the Gothic itself, moreover, is a distinctly European philosophy of the aesthetic and ecological beauty which obfuscates the much longer histories of Indigenous relationships to and custody of these lands. Tasmania, Otago, and Southland, furthermore, have been the sites of long-term colonial brutality in both countries, and further marked by modern massacres, natural disasters, and crippling deindustrialization. As such, I mount the following critique of metal and the Antipodean Gothic aesthetic, as it has emerged in Southland, Otago, and Tasmania, to come to a critical understanding of how this term has been used to conflate a set of Australian and Aotearoa/New Zealand experiences which are shaped by the trajectory of colonial masculinity and imperial violence. The Antipodean Gothic is a term that nonetheless is unable to attend to how such trajectories have held varied implications for Australian Indigenous and Aotearoa/New Zealand Māori communities, histories, and identities.

Slaughterhouse gothic: Metal in Southland

Southland's name in Te Reo Māori is *Murihiku*, meaning "the last part of the tail." Southland is one of Aotearoa/New Zealand's most sparsely populated areas, and its metropolitan center of Invercargill is one of the most isolated cities in the world. Southland nonetheless boasts what Doug Heath has referred to as a "culturally significant level of heavy metal musical groups" (Heath 2015: 230), with more than 50 metal bands in Invercargill alone, making it one of Aotearoa/New Zealand's most "metal" regions. The metal of Southland, Heath argues, is immediately shaped by the interweaving of several geo-localized factors: the biculturalism of Aotearoa/New Zealand, the isolation of the region, the epic scenery of Fiordland and the Queenstown lakes and, crucially, heavy industrial-scale agriculture and a lingering "hauntology" (Mitchell 2016) underscored by the region's troubled history of infanticide. Southland was the home of possibly Aotearoa/New Zealand's most infamous murderer Minnie Dean, a nineteenth-century baby farmer who was the only woman to ever be hanged in Aotearoa/New Zealand.[3] Southland, furthermore, boasts the southern hemisphere's largest livestock killing and processing plants. Grueling work in the meat industry has been a key source of both income and influence for metal bands from Southland. Long days in abattoirs are thus seen as vital to the aesthetic of Southland metal:

> We all met in 2000 at the Alliance meat freezer [...] we were all in the boning room or killing yards [...] yeah it had an effect on us [...] you kinda get used to the sight of death every minute [...] it's a soul destroying job. The freezing works was also a source of depression, which also transposed into our music, making it much darker and aggressive.
>
> (D. Rodgers in Heath 2015: 235)

The South, in this sense, is a site of violence and industrialized death. Southland's "Southernness" is underpinned by mischance, despair, and the desensitizing realities of the industrialized agriculture which continues to represent Southland's main industry. This iteration of Southland's Antipodean Gothic is one which laments the industrial death which permeates the region, "min[ing] a deep vein of the dark underbelly of rural society along with a kind of melancholy nostalgia" (Bishop in Benson 2008). Groove metal band Osmium, for example, in a track about their hometown of Invercargill, "Forsaken City" (*The Misery Harvest* 2012), tell the story of the population decline of the city, and the resultant landscape of a depressed, gray, weathered, dying region. Of further note, however, is how the lexicon of the American South and Southern metal has been mobilized in this context. Osmium is a "Southern metal" band in the groove-laden, sludge tradition that McDowell sees as a characteristic of metal produced in the American South—"Slayer with a swamp sickness" (McDowell 2016: 12). Beyond Osmium, who refer to themselves as a "southern groove metal" band, the Southland scene at large refers to itself as "Southern metal"; and the collective which organizes and promotes metal shows in this region is named the "Southern metal confederacy." This rhetoric is also articulated spatially: touring bands from Christchurch (the northernmost city of the South Island) mention playing in the "Deep South" of Southland: "We've had sic[k] shows down in the deep south! [...] I know many metal bands have had more successful shows with way more support and fans in Invercargill than gigs in scarfie Dunedin" (Sheppard in Heath 2015). This positioning of Invercargill as superior to "scarfie" Dunedin ("scarfie" is a pejorative term for University of Otago students, drawn from the practice of wearing scarves in the university rugby team colors) is significant, I argue, because it draws on a similar lexicon of "Southern" masculinity that Jason Eastman identifies in American Southern rock. Here, by "embracing a self-declared 'southerness,' poor and working class men reject the presumably northern, middle-class definitions of manhood built upon the institutions of work and education" (Eastman 2012: 272).

Southland metal represents a particularly intriguing case for studies of metal and glocalization. In many ways, Southland's performance of the Antipodean Gothic, which emphasizes the soundscapes of slaughterhouses, regional solidarity, and a distrust of outsiders, echoes the practices Eastman identifies in the Southern metal scene of the United States, in which "which men claim their masculine honour and mastery by defining themselves in opposition to the middle class and presumably northern power elite" (Eastman 2012: 279). However, to move toward a straightforward conflation of the performance of "Southernness" in the United States and the performance of Southernness in Southland is a precarious task given the vastly different social and political histories of the United States and Aotearoa/New Zealand, and furthermore, the ways in which austerity, marginality, and colonialism have been felt in these disparate regions. That the rhetoric of the "deep South" and the "confederate" has been mobilized in Aotearoa/New Zealand, when the terms have traditionally connoted troubled racial dynamics underpinned by white, colonial violence, makes Southland a place marked by distinct tensions and complexities. That such power-laden terms have been deployed in these contexts is notable, particularly given that one of Southland's most renown metal acts, Hatred, are descendants of Ngāi Tahu, the principal Māori Iwi of the South Island, and the band has included Māori themes and symbolism in their music (Heath 2015:232). Southland metal thus offers an intriguing example of what McDowell has called the performativity of Southern metal, where emphasis is placed on the *concept* of the South and the *performance* of Southernness and how these concepts and performances are negotiated within a scene, rather than one's physical position south of the Mason-Dixon line (McDowell 2016: 3); albeit, in this case, roughly 13,000 kilometers south of said line.

Protestant gothic: Metal in Otago

Southland's particular iteration of Southernness, with its emphasis on bloody, industrial masculinity, sits in contrast with that of the neighboring region of Otago. Otago was the site of rapid commercialization throughout the late nineteenth century in the wake of the Otago goldrush and was, for a period, Aotearoa/New Zealand's cultural and economic center, producing Aotearoa/New Zealand's first daily newspaper and its first university. The legacies of this period are immediately visible in Otago's largest city of Dunedin, one of the Southern hemisphere's best-preserved examples of Victorian and Edwardian architecture. Dunedin's wealth of grand basalt-stone buildings and history of political conservatism have made it a steady fixture of the landscape of the Aotearoa/New Zealand gothic, where the city's character, argues Lawn (2004: 126), has derived from a combination of religious protest, colonial idealism, commercial wealth, and subsequent slow decline. Dunedin is, she claims, a "living Victorian and Edwardian cityscape signifying not the ebullience of empire, but decay and the gravity of time" (Lawn 2004: 126). Such heaviness has become mobilized into the city's branding, where Dunedin is imagined as "the most intriguing city in New Zealand"—intelligent, opinionated and conservative; its dark gothic architecture is emphasized in the gothic font which greets airport arrivals, and has been steadily used in the city's advertising and tourism material.

Otago at large, Lawn (2004) contends, is furnished by a specifically Protestant gothic matrix which emphasizes self-help, self-discipline, and self-advancement. Such staunch matrices of power are present in the lingering violence of Otago's colonial history—in the nineteenth century, Otago Harbour's island Kamau Taurua was used as a quarantine station; in the same period, Dunedin made steady use of Māori prison labor. Otago's position as Aotearoa/New Zealand's "utopian New World" (Lawn 2004) declined with the end of the Gold Rush boom and the subsequent movement north of much of its population. In the words of Erik Olssen, Dunedin's sunless days now match a "stagnating region" watched by "the mocking relics of a prosperous and proud past" whose Calvinist force is still felt in the city's cultural production (Olssen 1984: 215). "South," in this context, is thus realized through the entanglement of individualism and morbid decay, sentiments which are expressed by members within Otago's black metal acts in particular. Otago's Antipodean Gothic emphasizes an individualist conservatism, yet is also underpinned by a morbid fascination with the grotesque and abject (Lawn 2004). This wider fascination with the abject and grotesque lurking under Dunedin's staunch exterior, for Lawn, expresses a desire to threaten the boundaries that regulate social order (Lawn 2004: 133); a sentiment well-situated within metal's wider generic performativity of the abject and subversive (cf. Kahn-Harris 2007). This is a sentiment evident in the output of Methchrist, a Dunedin three-piece who describe their music accordingly:

DANIEL: A rejection of religion. A vile misanthropic abject expression. Nihilism. Hate.

OLLIE: The name merely identifies a gateway to that which is virulent, abject, filthy, diseased.

(Thompson 2017)

Methchrist's emphasis on misanthropy and the abject narratives are again not unique within the globalization of heavy metal. Both Keith Kahn-Harris and Ross Hagen recognize these discourses as ubiquitous to black metal's sense of self: black metal fans and musicians value individualism and isolation as a key characteristic of scene identity, argues Hagen (2011). This sense of remoteness is a central feature of the way in which the genre articulates its own history and identity, where black metal understands itself as a scene which exists on the extreme "edge" of metal (Kahn-Harris 2007), entailing within it a misanthropic and self-conscious elitism based on contempt for the assumed "weakness" of most humans (Kahn-Harris 2007: 40). Such contempt however emerges in Dunedin's black metal acts, I argue, both within black metal's wider narratives of death and misanthropy, as well as from a particular geo-localized matrix. Libertarianism and self-advancement are also themes for the black metal act Sul Ad Astral, whose 2014 album *Afterglow* laments "comfortable ignorance," with repeated motifs of "free to decide which rights are wrong" and "now I am free to create my own world." Misanthropy and abandonment again emerge for the band Strife Machine, who tie their identity to the rural macabre. The cover of their 2014 release *Atrophy*, for example, is a photograph of the site of the Hinterkaifeck murders (Germany's most infamous unsolved domestic murder). For the aforementioned Methchrist, their brand of black metal is a rejection of the worldwide scene, which they see as watered down and inauthentic (Thompson 2017); such rejection also attends to an aggressively individualistic narrative, where the band members assert that they "don't see us as being part of anyone's scene" (Thompson 2017). Methchrist's approach, I contend, mirrors the dual individualism and insularism of the Otago Gothic—"don't support Southern Warmetal," they assert (in Thompson 2017)—"it's not for you."

The dark pastoral: Metal in Tasmania

These brief case studies from Aotearoa/New Zealand's South highlight the ways in which "Southernness" has divergent meanings, even within the space of the same nation. As a final example of the nuances of the Antipodean Gothic, I then cross the Tasman to Tasmania, Australia's southernmost state. Tasmania, Stewart and Hopcroft argue, is a place of extremities, "the southernmost outpost of the southernmost continent, whipped by icy winds from the pole; it is also a place of isolation, the final banishing point for the convicts whose bloody punishment marks the island's history" (Stewart and Hopcroft 2009: 131). Maria Tumarkin (2001: 202) argues that Tasmania functions as the "geographic unconscious" of Australia, a place beyond the edge of the known world on which anxieties and fantasies are displaced and contained. The strangeness, disorientation, and darkness of Tasmania has been relatively successful in mobilizing the state as a site of "dark tourism," which, Marchant and Edmonds (2015) argue, is explicit in the branding of Dark Mofo, Tasmania's winter festival, a self-consciously occult and avant-garde event that regularly attracts international extreme metal bands. Much in the same way that Tasmania at large is renowned for its sinister colonial past and has an enduring reputation as a land set apart from the rest of Australia (Bullock 2014: 84), so too have Tasmania's metal acts asserted themselves distinct from notions of "Australian" metal. Here there has emerged a particular brand of "lo-fi forest black metal" characterized by bands such as Dissonant Winds (from Margate) and Striborg (from Maydena).

Tasmania's sense of remoteness and disjunction, coupled with this regional emphasis on the ecological, is realized in Dissonant Winds' 2017 album *Forestial Transcendence*, which emphasizes silence, isolation, and the omniscient stoicism of the Tasmanian forest, represented by frostbitten gumtrees on the cover. For Striborg—arguably Australia's most cult black metal act—the music the act produces within this paradigm mimics the elements and essence of the Tasmanian landscape: "[T]he guitars would be the mist, the frost, the snow [...] drums would be the heart of the land, the trees and the rocks [...] the vocals are just the voice of the forest" (*One Man Metal* 2012). Russell Menzies, the man behind Striborg, lives virtually in rural isolation; he lives in the town of Maydena, population 240, where none of his neighbors knows that he has a global cult following. Menzies, the documentary One *Man Metal* claims, is a man who does not just play the music, "but also embodies what it reflects: isolation, misanthropy, and anger" (2012: n.pag.). Such discourses reify Tasmania's marginality, and the wider discourse of metal, and particularly black metal, on the "edge." However, while Tasmania's "gothic" mode is a troubling challenge to the symbolic depictions of Australia, it does so by alluding to the same violent colonial pasts and discourses of "outposts" which have shaped Tasmania's, and indeed Australia's, artistic and social histories.

Tasmania's "Southernness," as it is realized through bands such as Striborg, is a site of lingering colonial anxieties of the hostility of the environment, and the impotent colonial violence which has attempted to control it. Such heaviness has in turn become a component in the strategic branding of this region, wherein the "Tasmanian gothic" has emerged to refer to the ways in which the "relatively outdated way of life and the vast unspoiled natural beauty in Tasmania makes it seem gothic, very different from modern mainland Australia" (Davidson 1989: 307). "Tasmanian gothic," for Bullock, adapts the gothic mode to geographic locale and responds to local cultures, becoming a byword for the unsettling combination of Tasmania's colonial histories and its harsh landscapes (Bullock 2014: 71). The long tradition of "Tasmanian gothic" and "Tasmanian grotesque" linking the island's convict past and sites of Aboriginal massacres with its rugged, sometimes treacherous, landscape (Mitchell 2009: iv) is a relationship which has found expression not only in metal music, as the above examples show, but also in the region's sound cultures more generally. For Stewart and Hopcroft, Tasmanian music emerges at "the end of the world," where Tasmania is "the final stopping point before the frozen wastes of the South Pole, an outpost remote even from the already remote continent of Australia" (Stewart and Hopcroft 2009: 134). Tasmania's landscape of "dripping greenness and harsh extremity" (Stewart and Hopcroft 2009: 134) is thus a fitting context for the development of a particular iteration of the Antipodean Gothic, here realized through a manifestation of the dark pastoral which is often at odds with wider parochial imaginings of Australia. As Stewart and Hopcroft note,

> in contrast with the sunburnt desert landscapes that are the dominant representation of the Australian geographical environment, Tasmania has a landscape of dripping greenness and a climate of harsh extremity. Bitterly cold and raging winds traverse the globe before slamming into the island's west coast, and gales race up across Antarctic waters and hurl themselves against the south. In some parts of the island, trees grow pretty much parallel to the earth.
>
> (2009: 134)

This imagining of Tasmania as a place "apart" from Australia, dangling perilously at the southern edge of the world, attests to the ways in which the rhetoric of liminality and extremity has accompanied the ways that the southernmost regions of the Antipodes articulate their sense of self. This "Southernness," however, as I have argued, does not occupy the "edge" in the same way, in the same places. In leading toward an end for this discussion, and point to where future research can build, I wish to revisit Mark Olson's understanding of a scene as a "territorializing machine" (Olson 1998: 281). Here a musical scene creates and mobilizes particular kinds of relationships in geographic locations. "Southernness" is a commonality for Southland, Otago, and Tasmania, but it is mobilized in particular ways concordant with the interlocking colonial, industrial, and institutional histories which have shaped each region. Moreover, such "territorializing" here has specific colonial overtones; in looking to a slaughterhouse gothic, a protestant gothic, and dark pastoral Tasmanian gothic, each mode potentially obscures and erases Indigenous histories with complex and differing implications. The "territorializing" function of a scene is then a process which, on one level, binds people and practices to space and shapes their relationships therein. "Southernness" too, however, is a territorializing term, which must be unpacked with the same critical eye that has started to be cast toward the territorializing functions of "Northernness" as it has emerged in metal's discourses and practices.

Conclusion

In many forms, I concede, the flows and themes of heavy metal from the "north" have infiltrated and shaped the trajectories of metal as it is performed in Otago, Southland, and Tasmania. I am intrigued, as I have noted, by the currency of "Southern metal" and the vocabulary of confederacy and the "Deep South" in Southland. The misanthropy, individualism, and self-conscious elitism of Dunedin black metal harks back, in many ways, to the foundational narratives of Norwegian black metal. The similarities between Tasmania's forest black metal and the Cascadian black metal of the Pacific North West is likewise an area to pursue further. Nonetheless, there are also many tensions that emerge in seeing bands (and their associated scenes) in the extreme south of Australia and Aotearoa/New Zealand as the antipodean counterparts of metal bands, communities, and practices in the northern hemisphere. "Southernness" here relies on a semiotic relationship to the "North," where the colloquialism of "things going South" very literally connotes the narratives of brutality, despair, and fierce individualism which have accompanied these three regions, in markedly varied ways. Moreover, seeing both Australia and Aotearoa/New Zealand as shaped by a "shared history" ignores the ways in which such histories were experienced by Indigenous populations prior to colonial engagement in the region. The rhetoric of the "Antipodean" itself is also one which conflates such histories in ways that do not, and cannot, attend to the traumas and complexities which have followed European colonization. Naming is political: the naming of Australia and Aotearoa/New Zealand as the "Antipodes" is a reminder that "Australasia" emerged as a political and cultural entity with European settlement (Mein-Smith and Hempenstall 2003: 1), and is an act of territorialization which continues to reinscribe Eurocentric notions of sovereignty and ownership in the region.

These Antipodean Gothic imaginings of the "South," in metal, emerge as discourses with multiple, complex manifestations, which realize the distinct geolocal politics, histories, and identities of these regions in specific ways. What I wish to start to move toward here is a mode of responding to the ubiquity of "Northernness" in heavy metal's structuring discourses and consider how the identity of the "South" has emerged not only in response to this hegemony, but also as an expression of a particular kind of regional "heaviness." I am intrigued by the potentialities of the Antipodean Gothic as a tool for critically engaging with metal's aesthetics in Australia and Aotearoa/New Zealand which have, until very recently, been largely occluded from the scope of "global metal." In doing so, however, I remain cognizant of how the notion of the "Antipodean Gothic" is itself one immediately shaped by violent colonial contexts, a factor which cannot, and must not, be overlooked. This, I argue, anchors this strand of Southern metal within the wider questions of hegemony, centers and peripheries which plague "global metal," realized here in the misty atmospheres of the "Other" edge of the world.

NOTES

1. This is seen in touring festivals such as Paganfest, and localized festivals including Noctis Valkyries (Canada), Ragnarock Festival (Germany), Flight of the Valkyries (United States), Heathen Crusade (United States), Warhorns (United Kingdom), and Midgardsblot (Norway).
2. See events such as North Dissonant Voices (Portugal), North of the Wall (Scotland), Northern Invasion (United States), and Defenders of the North (Mexico).
3. Minnie Dean is the subject of a track by Wellington black metal band Bulletbelt.

REFERENCES

Avelar, Idelber (2003), "Heavy metal music in postdictatorial Brazil: Sepultura and the coding of nationality in sound," *Journal of Latin American Cultural Studies*, 12:3, pp. 329–46.

Banchs, Edward (2016), *Heavy Metal: Africa: Life, Passion and Heavy Metal in the Forgotten Continent*, Tarentum: Word Association Publishers.

Baulch, Emma (2007), *Making Scenes: Reggae, Punk and Death Metal in 1990s Bali*, Durham: Duke University Press.

Bennett, Andy, and Peterson, Richard A. (2004), "Introducing music scenes," in A. Bennett, and R. A. Peterson (eds.), *Music Scenes: Local, Translocal and Virtual*, Nashville: Vanderbilt University Press, pp.1–16.

Benson, Nigel (2008), "Southern gothic," *Otago Daily Times*, November 20, https://www.odt.co.nz/entertainment/arts/southern-gothic. Accessed March 18, 2019.

Brown, Andy R. (2015), "Everything louder than everyone else: The origins and persistence of heavy metal music and its global cultural impact," in A. Bennett and S. Waksman (eds.), *The Sage Handbook of Popular Music*, London: Sage, pp. 261–77.

Bullock, Emily (2014), "Rumblings from Australia's deep south: Tasmanian gothic on-screen," *Studies in Australasian Cinema*, 5:1, pp. 71–80.

Davidson, Jim (1989), "Tasmanian gothic," *Meanjin*, 48:2, pp. 307–24.

Dissonant Winds (2017), *Forestial Transcendence*, Paris: T2.

Eastman, Jason (2012), "Southern masculinity in American rock music," in S. Harrison, G. Welch, and A. Adler (eds.), *Perspectives on Males and Singing*, Dordrecht: Springer, pp. 271–86.

Grandoni, Dino (2012), "A world map of metal bands per capita," *The Atlantic*, March 29, https://www.theatlantic.com/entertainment/archive/2012/03/world-map-metal-band-population-density/329913/. Accessed March 18, 2019.

Grimley, Daniel M. (2006), *Grieg: Music, Landscape and Norwegian Identity*, Woodbridge: Boydell Press.

Hagen, Ross (2011), "Musical style, ideology, and mythology in Norwegian black metal," in J. Wallach, H. M. Berger, and P. D. Greene (eds.), *Metal Rules the Globe: Heavy Metal Music Around the World*, Durham: Duke University Press, pp. 180–99.

Heath, Doug (2015), "Heavy metal from the Antarctic ends of the Earth: Investigating the metal music identity from Invercargill, Southland, New Zealand," in T. Karjalainen and K. Kärki (eds.), *Modern Heavy Metal: Markets, Practices and Cultures*, Helsinki: Aalto University, pp. 230–39.

Heesch, Florian (2010), "Metal for Nordic men: Amon Amarth's representations of Vikings," in N. W. R. Scott (ed.), *Metal Void: First Gatherings*, Oxford: Inter-Disciplinary Press, pp. 71–80.

Hoad, Catherine (2014), "'Ons is Saam': Afrikaans metal and rebuilding whiteness in the rainbow nation," *International Journal of Community Music*, 7:2, pp. 189–204.

Hoad, Catherine (ed.) (2019), *Australian Heavy Metal: Scenes, Practices, Identities*, Bingley: Emerald Books.

Hoad, Catherine, and Whiting, Samuel (2017), "True Kvlt? The cultural capital of 'Nordicness' in extreme metal," *M/C Journal*, 20:6, http://journal.media-culture.org.au/index.php/mcjournal/article/view/1319. Accessed March 18, 2019.

Hubbard, J., and Pessaro, F. (2014), *NOLA: Life, Death, and Heavy Blues from the Bayou*, USA and Canada: Vice.

Kahn-Harris, Keith (2007), *Extreme Metal: Music and Culture on the Edge*, New York: Berg.

Klopper, Annie (2011), "In ferocious anger I bit the hand that controls: The rise of Afrikaans punk rock music," in A. Grundlingh and S. Huigen (eds.), *Reshaping Remembrance: Critical Essays on Afrikaans Places of Memory*, Amsterdam: Rozenberg Publishers, pp. 179–89.

Lawn, Jennifer (2004), "Scarfies, Dunedin gothic, and the spirit of capitalism," *Journal of New Zealand Literature*, 22, pp. 124–40.

Lawn, Jennifer (2006), "Warping the familiar," in M. Kavka, J. Lawn, and M. Paul (eds.), *Gothic NZ: The Darker Side of Kiwi Culture*, Dunedin: University of Otago Press, pp. 10–23.

Lipke, David, and Terry, Chris (2010), *Slow Southern Steel*, USA: Gonzo Metal.

Lucas, Caroline, Deeks, Mark, and Spracklen, Karl (2011), "Grim up north: Northern England, Northern Europe and black metal," *Journal for Cultural Research*, 15:3, pp. 279–95.

Marchant, Alicia, and Edmonds, Penelope (2015), "The aesthetic of Dark Mofo: Emotion, darkness and the Tasmanian gothic," *Histories of Emotion*, July 26, https://historiesofemotion.com/2015/07/26/the-aesthetic-of-dark-mofo-emotion-darkness-and-the-tasmanian-gothic/. Accessed March 18, 2019.

McDowell, Michael (2016), "Heavy south: Identity, performance, and heavy music in the southern metal scene," master's thesis, Florida: University of South Florida.

Mein-Smith, Philippa and Hempenstall, Peter (2003), "Australia and New Zealand: Turning shared pasts into a shared history," *History Compass*, 1:1, pp. 1–10.

Mitchell, Tony (2009), "Music and the production of place: Introduction," *Transforming Cultures eJournal*, 4:1, pp. i–vii.

Mitchell, Tony (2016), "'Hatbox, horror, and hanging': Southland hauntology in songs about Minnie Dean," *The International Association for the Study of Popular Music (Australia/New Zealand Chapter) Annual Conference*, CQ University Ooralea, Mackay, December 7–9.

Olson, Mark J. V. (1998), "'Everybody loves our town': Scenes, spatiality, migrancy," in A. Herman, J. M. Sloop, and T. Swiss (eds.), *Mapping the Beat: Popular Music and Contemporary Theory*, Oxford: Blackwell, pp. 269–89.

Olssen, Erik (1984), *A History of Otago*, Dunedin: John Mclndoe.

Osmium (2012), *The Misery Harvest*, independently released.

Overell, Rosemary (2014), *Affective Intensities in Extreme Music Scenes: Cases from Australia and Japan*, New York: Springer.

Phillipov, Michelle (2008), "Metal 'downunderground': Mapping the terrain of the Great Southern wasteland," in S. Homan and T. Mitchell (eds.), *Sounds of Then, Sounds of Now—Popular Music in Australia*, Hobart: ACYC Publishing, pp. 215–30.

Redaelli, Jordan, and Rabinowitz, Michelle (prods) (2012), *One Man Metal*, USA and Canada: Vice, https://www.vice.com/en_us/article/wdp77m/one-man-metal-part-1. Accessed March 18, 2019.

Stewart, Keryn, and Hopcroft, Helen (2009), "A band without walls at the end of the world: The Green Mist, Next Stop Antarctica and the Tasmanian geographic imaginary," *Transforming Cultures eJournal*, 4:1, pp. 131–48.

Strife Machine (2014), *Atrophy*, independently released.

Sul Ad Astral (2014), *Afterglow*, independently released.

Thompson, F. (2017), "Methchrist discuss their new album and more," *Dunedin Sound*, http://dunedinsound.com/blog/methchrist-interview/. Accessed March 18, 2019 [no longer available].

Trafford, Simon, and Pluskowski, Aleks (2007), "Antichrist superstars: The Vikings in hard rock and heavy metal," in D. W. Marshall (ed.), *Mass Market Medieval: Essays on the Middle Ages in Popular Culture*, Jefferson: McFarland, pp. 57–73.

Tumarkin, Maria (2001), "'Wishing you weren't here...': Thinking about trauma, place and the Port Arthur massacre," *Journal of Australian Studies*, 25:67, pp. 196–205.

Varas-Díaz, Nelson, Rivera-Segarra, Eliut, Mendoza, Sigrid, and González-Sepúlveda, Osvaldo (2014), "On your knees and pray! The role of religion in the development of a metal scene in the Caribbean island of Puerto Rico," *International Journal of Community Music*, 7:2, pp. 243–57.

Von Helden, Imke (2010), "Scandinavian metal attack: The power of Northern Europe in extreme metal," in R. Hill and K. Spracklen (eds.), *Heavy Fundamentalisms: Music, Metal and Politics*, Oxford: Inter-Disciplinary Press, pp. 33–41.

Von Helden, Imke (2017), *Norwegian Native Art: Cultural Identity in Norwegian Metal Music*, Zurich: LIT Verlag Münster.

Wallach, Jeremy (2011), "Unleashed in the east: Metal music, masculinity, and 'Malayness' in Indonesia, Malaysia and Singapore," in J. Wallach, H. M. Berger, and P. D. Greene (eds.), *Metal Rules the Globe: Heavy Metal Music Around the World*, Durham: Duke University Press, pp. 86–105.

Weinstein, Deena (2014), "Pagan metal," in D. Weston and A. Bennett (eds.), *Pop Pagans: Paganism and Popular Music*, New York: Routledge, pp. 58–75.

Yin, Kelly Fu Su, and Khiun, Liew Kai (2017), "From folk devils to folk music: Tracing the Malay heavy metal scene in Singapore," in G. Bloustien (ed.), *Sonic Synergies: Music, Technology, Community, Identity*, New York: Routledge, pp. 115–23.

3

The Enemy Within: Conceptualizing Turkish Metalheads as the Ideological "Other"

Pierre Hecker and Douglas Mattsson

> *I think [the present political situation] is a great opportunity for black metal in Turkey because I think people are finding their sounds, they are starting to find their own sounds, not copying the Norwegian bands [like] back then. They have started their own sounds because of this hatred [against the pious conservatism of president Recep Tayyip Erdoğan's regime]. So it's a good thing for black metal, bad thing for us, the people.*
>
> (Eren, vocalist of a Turkish black metal band, Ankara, November 2017)[1]

What makes this quote so staggering is the fact that it is tantamount to claiming that political Islam, as represented by Turkey's governing power bloc, elicits creative impulse to black metal, thereby prompting it to develop its own "authentic self" in distinction from the dominant norm of pious conservatism. This might come as a surprise to those who have been observing how Turkey's new ruling elite has been striving to establish a cultural hegemony of pious conservatism over state and society; a new hegemony that is both monistic in scope and repressive in character.

By holding power uninterruptedly since November 2002, President Recep Tayyip Erdoğan's Adalet ve Kalkınma Partisi (AKP; Justice and Development Party) has set a record of being the longest-serving government in modern Turkish history. Over these past eighteen years, Turkey's pious conservative elite has succeeded in consolidating its power by establishing control over the state institutions and paralyzing civil society, including the country's almost entire mediascape. Only a few years ago, Erdoğan's "New Turkey" was still highly praised for achieving the supposedly impossible, namely freeing Turkey's democracy from military tutelage and reconciling political Islam with the principles of secularism, human rights, and a free market economy (Özbudun 2006: 547–48; Yavuz 2006). From today's perspective, the early phase of AKP rule must be seen as the successful attempt to establish authoritarian rule by means of abusing democratic discourse and state institutions. This process has only recently resulted in a constitutional change to Turkey's political system, from a parliamentary democracy to an authoritarian presidential system that no longer operates on the basis of the functional separation of powers (Öztürk and Gözaydın 2017; Yılmaz 2018). Within the context of this "authoritarian turn," Turkey's new ruling elite has branded those sections of society who are being different as the ideological enemy (see Toprak et al. 2009; Hecker 2014).

This chapter is based on extensive fieldwork conducted by the authors individually between 2002–09 and 2014–18 (and an additional month between January and February 2020), respectively. The study relies on qualitative data (field notes, interview transcripts, fanzines, flyers, recordings, etc.) gathered through participant observation at dozens of metal festivals and concerts, more than a hundred in-depth and biographical interviews, as well as a vast number of casual conversations with scene protagonists throughout the years. This chapter examines how the Turkish metal scene, since its early days in the late 1960s, has functioned and been conceptualized as the cultural and ideological other in relation to Turkish majority society. This process of otherization has, however, also granted the metal scene the possibility to position itself in a dialectic relationship of opposition to the hegemonic discourse brought forth by the state and as such harvest what Keith Kahn-Harris (2007) refers to as transgressive subcultural capital. Although the scene, at times, resisted to be portrayed as the ideological other, it commonly positions and conceptualizes itself today as the ideological and cultural other to Erdogan's "New Turkey." In this sense, metal represents a cultural challenge to the new hegemonic project propagated by Turkey's pious conservative elite.

First encounters with the unknown

The roots of heavy metal music in Turkey date back to the late 1960s, when a group of young musicians, namely Erkin Koray (b. 1941), Barış Manço (1943–1999), Cem Karaca (1945–2004), the band Moğollar, and some others started what came to be known as Anadolu Rock ("Anatolian Rock"). Anadolu Rock stands for the fusion of modern rock music with Anatolian folk traditions. The classical rock lineup of electric guitar, bass, and drum kit was merged with instruments such as the *ney*, the Anatolian form of the reed pipe, or the long-necked seven string *saz*, which, in the process of blending both music traditions, was also amplified and popularized as the *elektro saz*. In the 1970s, Anadolu Rock received considerable international acclaim for its new and unique psychedelic sounds. Some European and North American musicians even traveled to Turkey in order to take inspiration from their Turkish counterparts (e.g., the German progressive rock band Embryo). The psychedelic years of Anadolu Rock music (see also Erkal 2014) are perhaps most prominently represented in Erkin Koray's 1974 album *Elektronik Türküler* ("Electronic folk songs"). Only one year after *Elektronik Türküler*, in 1975, Tünay Akdeniz ve Çığrışım released a 45 single named *Salak* ("Stupid"), which is commonly referred to as Turkey's very first punk rock recording (Boynik and Güldallı 2007). *Salak* not only marks the birth of Turkish punk rock, it furthermore anticipates the emergence of a vital DIY underground rock scene that also spawned Turkey's metal subculture in the 1980s and 1990s.

The cultural representations of 1970s Anadolu Rock were, however, not confined only to the music. Men started to grow their hair and beards long. Music magazines, radio programs, and even a number of movies gradually popularized the genre among the younger generation. The 1975 musical comedy *Baba Bizi Eversene* ("Give us permission to marry, Daddy"), starring a charmingly sweet Barış Manço, or the Turkey-made Western *Kralların Öfkesi* ("Anger of kings"), featuring Cem Karaca, contributed significantly to the popularity of rock music and culture in Turkey. Sociologist Ozan Eren, in a recently published article, argues that this development was only possible due to the liberal political atmosphere of the time, which helped to unleash certain internal dynamics and create the nucleus for an autonomous artistic consciousness in Turkey. This, Eren argues, was not only limited to the field of music but also included other forms of cultural production such as the performing arts, fine arts, and literature (Eren 2017: 143).

The popularity of some rock artists, first and foremost of Barış Manço, who in the 1980s hosted several highly popular TV shows on state-owned TRT, was accompanied by a process of otherization and stigmatization at the same time. Today, Barış Manço and Cem Karaca are loved and admired even among conservative sections of Turkish society. This admiration of the popular artist should, however, not be confused with Turkish majority society being commonly sympathetic to rock music and culture. The long-haired rocker did not and still does not correspond to what is seen as the commonly accepted norm and is frequently contrasted to other dominant national identity constructions. Well-known caricaturist Adülkadir "Aptülika" Elçioğlu, in a conversation with one of the authors, recalled a teenage boy from his neighborhood who desperately wanted to grow his hair long. While the boy's parents apparently liked Aptül (long hair included), it was an absolute no-go for them to allow their boy to wear his hair long. When the boy pointed out that "Aptül abi" ("Brother Aptül") also had long hair, the parents surprisedly replied: "But Aptül's an artist!" This brief anecdote reveals how limited and volatile the space for cultural deviance is. Deviance from dominant cultural norms goes unsanctioned only if it successfully incorporates significant elements of dominant culture as, for instance, in the case of Barış Manço, and moreover remains confined to the realm of artistic production. Visibility of cultural deviance in everyday life is a different story.

What certainly also contributed to the evolvement of rock music and culture in Turkey was the European and North American hippie movement. From the late 1960s onward, the overland hippie trail from Europe to India brought thousands of soul-searching, unkempt, young travelers to the country. The first major stop on their way to the East was certainly Istanbul's Sultan Ahmet district. The area, which is home to Istanbul's great mosques, the Ottoman Sultan's Topkapı Palace, as well as the antique remnants of Byzantine Constantinople, quickly adapted to this new wave of foreign travelers. Cheap backpacker hostels and coffeehouses welcomed the newcomers from the west, of whom many decided to extend their stopover to several weeks and months. An iconic figure of the time was Hippi Perihan, a teenage runaway from Izmir who had joined Sultan Ahmet's international hippie community in the late 1960s and died from an overdose in early 1970. The death of the beautiful young girl ("Hippie queen Perihan") drew considerable attention from the Turkish media. An outraged Necmettin Erbakan (1926–2011), who (decades later) would become Turkey's first Islamist prime minister, even warned his followers of an impending "hippieization" of the Turkish nation (see Bengi 2012). The death of Hippi Perihan was not the only controversy associated with rock music and culture. In 1969, Cem Karaca Ve Apaşlar ("Cem Karaca and the Apaches") incorporated a poem from Aşık Mahzuni Şerif (1939–2002), a controversial but all the more popular Anatolian folk musician and poet, into their song "Oy Bana Bana" ("Oh, pity me pity me") The line of the song "I do not differentiate between people's values. East, West, infidel, Muslim. It's all the same to me" resulted in accusations of showing disrespect toward religion. The song was consequentially banned from Turkish national radio programs (Bengi 2012).

The further development of Anadolu Rock was brought to an abrupt halt by the Turkish military coup d'état of 1980. The coup, which first and foremost was directed to quell the country's increasingly successful socialist movement, affected Turkish rock music on several levels. Cem Karaca and other musicians who had openly supported the political left went into exile to Western Europe. Out of fear of prosecution, many people destroyed their records and cut their long hair because these were seen as alleged proof of being a communist and therefore an enemy to the state. The first Turkish heavy metal bands emerged in this environment, which, for many families, was also a time of economic hardship. Throughout the 1980s, it was highly difficult to get access to international rock and metal albums on the Turkish market. Turkish rockers and metalheads, therefore, established their own networks in order to import music from abroad. The period from the 1980s to the early 1990s was the era of *korsan* or pirate cassettes. Underground street sellers and small record shops recorded LPs from their archive onto cassette tapes and sold them for moderate prices to a quickly growing audience in Istanbul, Ankara, Izmir, Bursa, and other urban centers of Western Turkey. Since the late 1980s, an increasing number of Turkish metalheads also got involved in tape trading; a global analogue network that connected metalheads from around the world. Based on these connections, an early concert with the Norwegian band Mayhem was organized in Izmir on December 9, 1990. The event took place only months before Mayhem's vocalist Per Yngve Ohlin (aka Dead) blew off his own head with a shotgun and the band became internationally recognized in connection to a series of church burnings in Norway. Mayhem, who apparently had travelled to Turkey by Interrail, were only the second international metal band to play live in Turkey. German thrash metal band Grinder had taken the stage with Turkish Pentagram and Akbaba in Istanbul on May 12 of the same year (Hecker 2012).

The late 1980s was also a period when the first coffeehouses evolved into rock bars—as, for instance, the legendary Kemancı "köprü altı" ("The fiddler 'under the bridge' "), one of the first hangouts for Turkish metalheads under the old Galata Bridge—and caricaturist Abdülkadir "Aptülika" Elçioğlu invented his famous comic strip Grup Perişan ("Group of losers"), which was published in the satirical magazine *Hıbır*. Grup Perişan told the story of a young metalhead and thus had a huge impact on the emergence of the Turkish metal underground. Aptülika not only told the story of Grup Perişan, thereby also featuring real-life metalheads and bands from Turkey, but also used the margins of the magazine's pages to add additional caricatures and information on international rock and metal bands as well as their latest releases. Shortly after, the first metal fanzines and even independent record labels began to emerge. Since then, Turkey's metal scene has seen continuous evolution, fragmentation, and, more than anything, contestation by state and society. From the early 1990s onwards, Turkish metal has experienced a series of moral panics over Satanism, teenage suicides, and murder.

Satanic scare

Throughout the 1990s, metal culture was subjected to a gradual process of otherization which eventually ended in a societal moral panic over metal in Turkey

(Hecker 2012). Although metal culture constituted a new public visibility in Turkey by the end of the 1980s, it was not until the autumn of 1990 that "metal culture" made it into mainstream media. Following a metal concert in Istanbul, the Turkish daily newspaper *Sabah* published a photo report and a commentary by the popular journalist Engin Ardıç. In this polemic, Ardıç concluded that "metalheads" are the new plague of the land. According to Ardıç, the young metalheads at the concert all suffered from moral deprivation, leading them to indulge in sexually, religiously, and morally subversive behavior, including, black masses, orgies, homosexuality, and apostasy. Ardıç's polemic piece would come to act as a blueprint for future depictions of metal in Turkish media.

Consequently, when a young woman was found murdered and raped in a cemetery in Istanbul's Ortaköy neighborhood in September 1999, the country immersed into a full-scale moral panic (for details see Hecker 2012: 91–128). The young woman, Şehriban Coşkunfırat, was on her way back home from a rock bar in Beyoğlu, Istanbul, when three youths, who had accompanied her that night, murdered and raped her in an act they later described to have been "ordered by Satan." Days later, pictures of them posing with a beheaded cat began to circulate in the media. What followed in the aftermath of the media reporting of the incident could be described as a moral panic on its own. Pressure arose to find the source of this deprivation and, unsurprisingly, metal music was portrayed as the main protagonist. The "witch hunt" on metal that followed was intense: metal bars were raided and closed down, bands dissolved, fanzines went bankrupt, parents quit their children's guitar-lessons and burned their metal albums, and some even cut their long hair because of the fear of reprisals. Black clothes, metal music, long hair and earrings were, and still are, somewhat associated with Satanism and the Turkish newspaper *Milliyet* even published a manual for parents on how to detect a "Satanist" (Hecker 2012: 79–107).

Because no substantial evidence surfaced that a "Satanic terrorist organization" existed in the country, most of the media lost interest after ten days. Another suicide in 2002 would, however, once again surface the issue of Satanism in Turkey, only this time the government became more involved in the "Satanic problem." A police unit that specialized in combating Satanists was formed and the Emniyet Genel Müdürlüğü (Security General Directorate) released a report claiming that there existed 3,500 Satanists in Turkey aged between 14 and 25 and that "rock bars" were the places where they recruited new members. A Turkish parliamentarian even compared the threat from Satanists to that of Hizbollah or PKK (Hecker 2012: 106–08). During the Satanic scare, Turkey's main body of religious affairs, the Diyanet İşleri Başkanlıgı (Presidency of Religious Affairs) took notice. Mehmet Nuri (head of the Diyanet at the time) said that the reason behind the youths' delinquency was a consequence of "moral emptiness," and he encouraged Turkish families to provide religious education for their children and teach them the values of Islam.

A central argument that distanced "metalheads" from the average Turk revolved around religion. Although the Kemalists strongly enforced their version of secularism at the founding of the republic, Sunni-Islam, the majority religion of the country, became central to the Turkish national identity. This was even further emphasized during the 1950s and after the1980s coup d'état when the government propagated a "Turkish-Islamic synthesis" designed to combat socialist movements and to reduce the influence of non-Turkic Islamic groups (Şen 2010). In that regard, the struggle over what constitutes Turkey's national identity should not necessarily be seen as one between "secularism" over "Islam," but rather (as Umut Azak argues) between what constitutes a "good" or a "bad" Muslim (Azak 2010). To therefore be portrayed as someone who has renounced Islam in favor of a Satanic cult that is in direct opposition to Islam effectively distanced metalheads from the Turkish majority society, be it secular or conservative alike.

In addition to religion, metalheads were also described as sexually subversive, with an uncleansed thirst for sex outside of marriage and homosexuality. This is problematic in so far as large portions of Turkish society's understanding of proper sexual conduct derives from a traditional *Hanafi* interpretation of Islam, in which both premarital sex and homosexuality are considered to be grave sins (Ali 2006).

Lastly, metal culture was described as "western," and thus foreign to Turkish culture. Young Turkish metalheads had supposedly degenerated into the point of cultural betrayal, proven by their renouncement of Islam and illicit sexual behavior. In a country where many have a strong sense of national and cultural pride, involvement with metal culture would, in the worst-case scenario, effectively brand a person as non-Turkish, at best as a deviant who, through proper religious and social education, could be brought back into the fold. The cultural otherization of metal has received new attention in recent years, not least during the Gezi Park protests.

"The final resistance?"

The Turkish protest summer of 2013 saw many metalheads participate in the nationwide anti-government demonstrations. The so-called Gezi Park protests (named after the small Istanbul park close to the city's iconic Taksim Square where the initial protests took off) are considered by most observers as the country's largest pro-democracy movement since the foundation of the Turkish Republic in 1923 (e.g., Ayat et al. 2013; Özkırımlı 2014; David and Toktamış 2015). The protests, which lasted from the end of May until the second half of August before finally being quelled by the police, were a reaction to the government's increasingly authoritarian stance toward Turkish civil society and its the-winner-takes-all mentality, which came to dominate the political atmosphere since the governing party's renewed success in the general elections of 2011. Public discontent arose not only as a result of the steady erosion of basic human rights but also from the government's intervention in the private sphere of people's everyday lives. President Recep Tayyip Erdoğan's plan to create a "New Turkey" based on an authoritarian presidential system and a political ideology inspired by pious conservatism was regarded by many as an imminent threat to their personal lifestyle choices. In particular, the secular sections of Turkish society were on high alert because of the government's attempt to reverse the secular achievements of the republic. Establishing creationism as the commonly accepted norm in Turkish schools, stigmatizing the consumption of alcohol, or publicly questioning the principles of gender equality were only some of the measures that gave evidence to this process (Şen 2010; Yazıcı 2012; Kaya 2015; Lüküslü 2016; Karakaya-Stump 2018).

Even though metal did not function as a driving force behind the protests, it certainly provided the adequate means to challenge the government's authoritarian rule; in a similar way as so many other forms of cultural resistance did—be it dance performances, protest songs, theater plays, public lectures, graffiti, comic books, stand-up comedy, TV game shows, and so on. On July 26, Turkish metalheads used Iron Maiden's Istanbul concert as an opportunity to stage protest against police violence during Gezi by, for instance, wearing gas masks or shouting pro-democracy slogans. When Bruce Dickinson, in solidarity with the Gezi movement, recasted the band's famous song "Fear of the Dark" into "Fear of the Park", Turkish fans experienced a heyday of passion and self-empowerment. This euphoria was, however, only short lived after a "thumbs up" photo of Steve Harris and Janick Gers with two Turkish policemen went viral the other day.

Certainly the most striking example of cultural resistance in Turkish metal as related to the Gezi Park uprising is Murder King's album *Gürültü Kirliği* ("Noise pollution"). Released in the spring of 2014, only months after the mostly peaceful demonstrations had come to a violent end, the album starts off with an instrumental named "Bu Daha Başlangıç" ("This is only the beginning"), a statement of defiance used by many protesters in the face of authoritarian oppression. The album ends with a similarly defiant statement, an instrumental entitled "Mücadeleye Devam" ("Continue the fight"). The album cover depicts the torso of a muscular young man engulfed in a cloud of smoke, his face protected by a gas mask (see Figure 3.1). Due to the excessive usage of tear gas by the police, the gas mask has turned into an icon of resistance, a cultural representation of defiance, freedom, and the struggle for democracy. It was worn by numerous activists during Gezi Park protests as, for instance, the iconic female ballet dancer or the

FIGURE 3.1: Murder King, *Gürültü Kirliği* (2014). On Air Müzik.

whirling dervish whose photographs have been widely popularized and reproduced on social media.

The official music video of the song "Demokrasi" ("Democracy") also evolves around the Gezi Park uprising.[2] Combining multiple scenes from the protests with snippets of historical events, Turkish leftist activists, and well-known politicians, the video clip suggests a meaningful connection between the events surrounding Gezi uprising and other historical incidents and concepts that do not necessarily relate to each other. In doing so, the producers of the Murder King video create an alternative interpretation of political events. Scenes of police violence during Gezi protests do, for instance, take turns with (historical) TV footage of Kenan Evren, the leader of the Turkish military coup d'état of 1980; Fethullah Gülen, the Islamic preacher and former close ally of Turkey's present government who, today, is made responsible for organizing the latest coup attempt on July 15, 2016; or Adnan

Menderes, Turkey's 1950s prime minister who is hailed as a martyr by Turkey's conservatives and despised by the political left for his pro-Islamic, authoritarian rule. The music video also contains images of the US presidents George W. Bush and Barack Obama who are apparently meant to signify imperialist oppression. Further visible are multiple scenes of the Second World War, including footage of Nazi soldiers with swastikas and Adolf Hitler himself. What makes this highly subversive is the fact that the only politician who is shown in "Demokrasi" not only once but twice is Turkey's president, Recep Tayyip Erdoğan. The music video thus creates a direct connection between him and the concepts of oppression and fascism. In other words, it expresses the opinion that the Turkish government's actions against the Gezi Park protesters represent an act of fascism. This is further emphasized by the song's lyrics which also draw a clear connection between Erdoğan's government, fascism, and oppression:

Demokrasi	**Democracy**
[...]	[...]
Bizm ampul gelir aşka	Our "light bulb" flares up
Oynar götü başı her gün başka	Contradictory conduct every day
Kana doymuş, gözü dolmuş, olan olmuş	Blood-stained, tear-filled eyes, the damage done
Habire yasta	Incessant mourning
Faili meçhul işler, görmez bürokrasi	Unresolved issues, unseen by bureaucracy
Saltanat olmuş hitler, sözde demokrasi	Hitler in power, so-called democracy
Her yeri satmış yetmez, doymaz ki ecnebi	Sold everything to greedy foreigners
Kabus olmuş gitmez, nerde demokrasi	A never-ending nightmare, where is democracy?
[...]	[...][3]

The "light bulb" in this song appears to be a reference to the political emblem of the governing AKP of Erdoğan, which depicts a light bulb on orange ground. The metaphor of Erdoğan as Hitler is also present; as well as the reference to an enormous corruption scandal that has rocked Turkey only briefly after Gezi uprising, but, since then, has completely disappeared from public discourse due to a general gag order imposed by the government. The phrase "kimi ümmet, kimi mafya"—"partly Ummah, partly Mafia," which is also part of the song and apparently equates the community of Muslim believers (*Ummah*) with the mafia, polemicizes the ruling elite's public image of piety and moral superiority. The video clip furthermore contains numerous references to Turkey's left wing resistance movement. It depicts scenes of commemoration of the Marxist-Leninist revolutionaries Deniz Gezmiş, Yusuf Aslan, and Hüseyin İnan, who were executed for their activities in 1972; Uğur Mumcu, a critical journalist who was assassinated in 1993; Turkish Armenian intellectual Hrant Dink, who was shot and killed by an ultra-nationalist teenager in 2007; and, finally, Mehmet Ayvalıtaş, Ali Ismail Korkmaz, and Ethem Sarısülük, three out of several young activists who were killed by the police during the Gezi Park uprising. Accordingly, the producers of "Demokrasi" imply that the Gezi Park protests must be seen in this particular, meaningful line of events; they are depicted as part of the same story and connected to each other. This alternative narrative, which depicts the event as an uprising against oppression and fascism, openly contradicts the ruling elite's official narrative, which labels the protest movement as an attempted coup d'état against Turkey's democratically elected government instigated by foreign powers and the "international finance lobby."

Critics might say that Murder King's "Demokrasi" only represents one particular album of one particular band and, therefore, cannot, by any means, be used to represent Turkey's multi-faceted metal scene as a whole. What appears safe to say, however, is that for Turkey's pious conservative elite, which today controls virtually every domain of the Turkish state and society, metal represents the "perfect" other. Over the past ten years or so, Turkish society has become highly polarized. Politics is increasingly driven by an "us" against "them" mentality that is propagated by the country's pious conservative government in order to keep its followers on high alert and rally support in the face of a constant state of crisis. This polarization has been accompanied by the reemergence of "classical" Islamist discourses that see Islam as the essence of Turkish culture, thereby demonizing whatever is seen as un-Islamic or, in this view, the result of "western" imperialism. The ruling elite's uncompromisingly essentialist worldview has significantly contributed to the tense political atmosphere in Turkey today. Turkish metal culture is deeply rooted in the tradition of Turkish secularism and therefore the undeniable "other" to Erdoğan's idea of a "New Turkey." This, however, goes for numerous other cultural representations in Turkish society as well.

Thus it should be emphasized that Turkish metalheads are not alone in their defiance to authoritarian rule. The song "Eyvallah" ("Bring it on") composed by the alternative rock band Duman at the height of the Gezi Park protests, for instance, became something of a countercultural anthem of resistance and remembrance for many of those who took to the streets in the summer of 2013.

Its lyrics and visual translation into various DIY music videos on YouTube and other social media channels have helped to keep alternative narratives on the political events alive:

Eyvallah	**Bring it on**
[...]	[...]
Saldır bana utanmadan, sıkılmadan	Attack me without shame, relentlessly
Gözlerim yanar ama ezilmedim, azalmadım	My eyes are burning but I didn't break I didn't falter
Özgürüm dedim hala	I am still free I told [you]
Haklıyım dedim hala sana, sana	I am still right I told you, I told you
İnsanım dedim hala	I am still a human being
Vazgeçer miyim söyle bana, oooh [...]	Am I giving up? You tell me! Oooh [...]
Biberine gazına	To your pepper and your gas
Cobuna sopasına	To your batons and your sticks
Tekmelerin hasına	To your harsh kicks
Eyvallah, eyvallah	[I say] Bring it on! Bring it on!
Kaldırın eli çekinmeden ve korkmadan	Raise your hands without hesitation, without fear
Meydanlar bizim unutmayın bu vatan bizim	Don't forget! These squares belong to us. This country belongs to us
Özgürüz dedik hala	We are still free we told [you]
Haklıyız dedik hala sana, sana	We are still right we told you, we told you
İnsanız dedik hala	We are still human beings
Vazgeçer miyiz söyle bana, oooh	Are we giving up? You tell me! Oooh
[...]	[...]

More recently, in September 2019, "Susamam" ("I can't remain silent"), a joint music video by sixteen Turkish hip-hop artists (including well-known rappers Şanışer, Fuat, Ozbi, and Miraç), literally broke the silence that appeared to have spread across Turkey's popular music scenes in the wake of state repression and activist exhaustion. The song critically engages with various topics, such as environmental pollution, homelessness, fascism, women's rights, animal's rights, legal and educational injustice, and suicide. With their rhymes, the rappers complain why "they" don't care about what is happening in present-day Turkish society. In recent years, many sociopolitical issues have practically disappeared from public discourse due to government pressure on broadcasters, journalists, and civil society actors. While it did not address Erdoğan and the country's ruling power bloc directly, "Susamam" scored a direct hit on the government. Especially among Turkey's younger generation, the song has become extremely popular. At the time of writing this chapter, it has been watched by more than 40 million viewers on YouTube. Pro-government loyalists were quick to label the music video as terror propaganda and the German public international broadcaster Deutsche Welle was officially admonished by Turkish authorities for streaming an interview with several of the rappers shortly after the song's release. However, the artists themselves appear not to have suffered from any legal consequences yet, but at least one of the artist, Defkhan, backed out of the project after the song received too much political attention (*BirGün* 2019).

This may give the impression that Turkish musicians are still free to publicly express their opinion and criticize the political situation in their country. However, this is not the case. Artists who critically voice their opinion about government policies take considerable risk as, for instance, the case of the Turkish pop singer and actress Zuhal Olcay shows. In July 2019, Olcay was given jail sentence for eleven months and twenty days for allegedly insulting President Erdoğan during a concert almost two years earlier. Another drastic example involves several musicians of the political activist band Grup Yorum. As a popular, self-professed Marxist-Leninist band that in the past publicly voiced sympathies for Devrimci Halk Kurtuluş Partisi-Cephesi (DHKP-C; the Revolutionary People's Liberation Party/Front) and, furthermore, criticized the government's political agenda on many occasions, Grup Yorum has frequently faced legal prosecution (Way 2018: 94). In February 2018, six musicians of the band were put on the state's wanted list for allegedly being members of an illegal organization and participating in terrorist activities. Subsequently, they were remanded in custody. Legal prosecution, however, was solely based on the statements of anonymous witnesses (as has been the case in other political situations in the past). Only after going on an indefinite hunger strike did the criminal court rule to release the musicians in late 2019 and place them on house arrest in early 2020.

Turkish law allows pretrial detention for a period of seven years. The case of Turkish philanthropist Osman Kavala shows that the legal remedy of pretrial detention can be also used with regard to countercultural activities. Kavala, who is best known for being the founder of Anadolu Kültür, a highly influential nonprofit institution that supports (politically controversial) culture and arts projects all over Turkey, was detained in October 2017 for allegedly having organized the Gezi Park protests in an attempt to overthrow the government. He has been in pretrial detention since then. Only hours after a court in Istanbul ruled for his full acquittal and release in February 2020, the public prosecutor's office issued a new detention warrant on the claim that he also orchestrated the military coup attempt of July 15, 2016. Kavala's case not only demonstrates the breakdown of the rule of law in Turkey but also the importance that can be ascribed to countercultural activities by the government. The fear of prosecution and punishment without trial appears to be an effective weapon in the struggle for political power and cultural hegemony, despite the fact that (subcultural) exceptions can still be found. In the present political context, Turkish metalheads assume the role of the ideological other not only in terms of cultural resistance to authoritarianism and fascism (e.g., Murder King) but also in terms of challenging the ruling elite's ideas of pious conservatism. This becomes particularly clear with regard to Turkey's black metal community.

Internal otherization

In addition to being subjugated to a process of ideological and cultural otherization, the Turkish black metal community in particular also partakes in the construction of internal hierarchical categories of what constitutes "true metal" (Williams 2011). This "true metal" discourse is meant to exclude other metalheads by ascribing them values and opinions that declares them as nonmetal, and as such subjugating them to a form of otherization. Not least is this prominent within the black metal scene. Needless to say, many factors are at play in the construction of a subcultural identity. Empirical evidence, as discussed elsewhere (Mattsson forthcoming 2021), points to the fact that the question of what constitutes "true" metal, or more precisely, "true black metal," is often defined in relation to a band's or scene member's attitude toward religion. The following quote from an interview by Mattsson with a Turkish black metal protagonist makes this obvious. The interviewee's comments on another Turkish black metal band are as follows:

> They don't, they don't play black metal. [...] because first of all, they are Muslims, they are Muslim guys and that's just unacceptable. There is this shit called un-black metal, it's basically black metal music with Christian lyrics and stuff, I see that [...] I see them as the same as the band from that genre actually because there [...] well you know there must be some authenticity, you know at some point and when you play with these things like you're [...] well if you're not anti-religious, I use a very broad term yeah, but if you're not anti-religious or anything or if you are in favor of religion at any point of your lifetime then you shouldn't be doing any black metal or even metal maybe.
>
> (Mattsson forthcoming 2021)

Besides enforcing strong restrictions on what could be considered to be black metal, the quote also reveals an important change in how parts of the Turkish metal community relate to religion. Many Turkish metalheads do indeed happen to be Muslim (similar to how Slayer's Tom Araya by circumstance was born and raised a Catholic). However, there does not seem to be a single Islamic metal band in Turkey—at least, not to the knowledge of the present authors. "Islamic," in contrast to "Muslim," is used here to designate religiously motivated cultural activities in terms of, for instance, doing metal in order to spread the word of God or promote Islam (similar to what "white metal'" refers to in a Christian context). Down to the present day, Turkey's metal community has established itself as a staunchly secular culture that is defiant to all forms of political Islam (see also Hecker 2012).

The quoted metalhead, however, questions whether someone can "do metal" if he or she lacks an anti-religious discourse. Indeed, since over a decade, parts of the Turkish black metal community have, allegedly, actively distanced themselves from what they perceive to be Muslim metalheads:

> Yeah that's right, in the beginning we were, I, actually I never hang out with such Muslim people in metal, because I was ok to be alone. I just [...] it was very wrong to me you know? [It is] still the same. I am asking if they [the metalheads] are believing in Islam. If they say yes, I am saying that "never talk to me again, never say hello to me." I have been doing it for fifteen years or more.

Not all protagonists of the black metal scene go as far as refusing to socialize with Muslims, but a significant section appears to actively differentiate between themselves and "regular metalheads." Concerts are one of those occasions where the apparent split within the metal community becomes visible and where many in the black and extreme metal community refrain from attending concert venues and metal bars who host cover bands. Some are even disturbed by the possibility that people might associate them with "regular rock guys" who listen to Metallica:

> like when they see my beard, or hair, or earring, which I don't have now, they all say "oh you're a Metallica listener?" or these regular Turkish society guy, "oh this is a Metallica guy" or "you listen to rock I guess?" or "you look like a rocker or something," and I really don't like it because I don't want to be included in those stereotypes.

This desire to distinguish oneself from "ordinary metalheads" is quite common in black metal (Kuppens and van der Pol 2014) and is therefore nothing new. Important to note, however, is that in the Turkish context it serves an additional purpose since many in the black metal community perceive the average Turkish guys, even the "metalheads," as Muslims.

This process of intra-scenic otherization, in which "Muslim metalheads" are expelled from the black metal community's definition of what constitutes "real metal," reveals many of the discourses that the Turkish metal scene is currently subjugated to.

For parts of the black metal community, to clearly distance themselves from Muslim metalheads is perceived to be an important aspect in communication with international record labels or concert organizers. Some bands feel a need to prove themselves as authentic explicitly, through lyrics, artworks, and actions, and exemplify that they really are an anti-religious black metal band. Relating to this, there has also been a surge of explicit anti-religious and blasphemous expressions within the black metal scenes' cultural production in the last decade, not least against Islam. It is still too early to say if this constitutes a general shift within the scene but based on a current sample of over 100 records, demos, and EPs stretching from 1993 to 2018, a substantial shift seems to have occurred since the last decade where a more explicitly anti-religious discourse is produced (Mattsson forthcoming 2021).

To date, no legal action has been taken against Turkey's black metal community. Yet, there are several laws that pose a potential threat to the freedom of speech in black metal. Although Turkey lacks a clear-cut blasphemy law, article 216, entitled "Provoking the Public to Hatred, Hostility, or Degrading," under the fifth section, "Offenses Against Public Peace," of the Turkish penal code has practically functioned as such since it regulates hate crimes, blasphemy, and religious insults. The third and last paragraph of article 216 states thus:

> A person who publicly degrades the religious values of a section of the public shall be sentenced to a penalty of imprisonment for a term of six months to one year, where the act is capable of disturbing public peace.
>
> (The European Commission for Democracy through Law 2016: 4).

Articles 213, 215, and 217 may also be used in a case regarding blasphemy. The European Council of Human Rights has leveled critique for the way article 216 is formulated and applied, stating that it should "not be applied to punish blasphemy, but [be] limited to cases of religious insults that intentionally and severely disturbs public order and calls for public violence" (The European Commission for Democracy through Law 2016: 13)."[4] That critique is yet to be accommodated.

At the time of writing, the cultural production of the Turkish metal and black metal scene has so far gone unnoticed by public prosecutors, or at least failed to trigger a legal response from the Turkish state. Important to note is that same is not true for other cultural representations or personalities in Turkey, the most famous being the case against Fazıl Say.

In 2012, the Turkish world-renowned pianist and composer Fazıl Say tweeted lines attributed to the eleventh-century Persian poet Omar Khayyam, in which religious hypocrisy is targeted (Şirin 2014). Say (a vocal critic of the AKP government) was brought to court and sentenced under charges of having insulted the values held sacred by religion (Şirin 2014). That the values of a *religion*, rather than the values of its practitioners, were found to be the victim of Say's slandering is, according to the human rights scholar Kerem Altıparmak, important to note since the former does not enjoy any protection under human rights, whereas the latter does (Şirin 2014: 77–78).[5] The court initially sentenced him to ten months in prison but on October 26, 2015, the Supreme Court in Turkey acquitted Say of the charges by a majority vote, stating that his tweets should be regarded as freedom of thought and expression (Şirin 2014).

Although unsuccessful, the persecution of Say elucidates the contemporary climate for critique against religion in Turkey and, as the jurist Tolga Şirin notes, "especially in recent years, the limits of tolerance for critiques towards Islam [...] have been enormously narrowed," and, "the religion of Islam is virtually protected in Turkey" (Şirin 2014: 76). What should be added to the case of Fazıl Say is that one of the nine tweets he was persecuted for simply stated that he was proud to be an atheist (Şirin 2014).

Blasphemy and transgressive subcultural capital

The trend to pursue an increasingly blasphemous cultural production could also be read as an effort by the Turkish black metal community to counter (both perceived and real) assumptions of metal music in Muslim majority societies. While touring abroad in Europe, several Turkish black metal bands apparently have had similar experiences of meeting concert attendees and organizers who were having a hard time to fathom that black metal music actually exists in Turkey. From a black metal perspective, in which "metal," at its core, is anti-religious, it makes perfect sense to distance oneself from what is perceived to be "Muslim metalheads," and should be seen as representing an effort by parts of the scene to claim authenticity on a national and international level.

In addition to receiving extra attention at festivals abroad, many music reviewers also stress the bands country of origin to an extent beyond biographical information. Consider the following quote from a review of the album *Towards the Ultimate Extinction* by the Turkish band Persecutory:

> Ok, let's move to our band for this review: PERESECUTORY [*sic*]. This band came [*sic*] from Turkey. Yes, you read right, from Turkey. And if I say to you that this band plays black/thrash metal, you believe me? You must, because I'm not kidding.
> (*Metal Maniack* 2017: n.pag.)

The reviewer in *Metal Maniack* is obviously so surprised by the band's country of origin that he sees himself obliged to emphasize to the reader that this is not a joke. Besides reproducing the worldview that black metal is incompatible with Muslim majority societies, the review also highlights another interesting consequence for the Turkish metal scene that derives from that understanding—namely, the possibility that, through their exoticization, they claim transgressive subcultural capital.

In his book *Extreme Metal* (2007), Keith Kahn-Harris distinguishes between two forms of scenic capital: mundane and transgressive. At its core, mundane subcultural capital can be gained through a long-term commitment to the scene and working hard for scenic institutions, whereas transgressive subcultural capital can be obtained by transgressing and challenging "accepted norms within and outside the scene" (Kahn-Harris 2007: 126). As such, transgressive subcultural capital is often gained through extreme individuality, musical and artistic innovation, or by criticism of the metal scene itself. As previously investigated, as part of portraying an authentic anti-religious identity, Turkish black metal bands now deliberately target Islam in their cultural production (Otterbeck et al. 2018; Mattsson forthcoming 2021). In conversations with one of the authors, numerous Turkish metalheads stated that they were impressed and supportive of these new scenic expressions, but that they would not have dared to produce it themselves due to their extreme transgressive quality. By making use of explicit expressions targeting Islam, the black metal scene clearly transgresses national social norms regarding religion and is thereby ascribed transgressive capital by the Turkish metal scene.

In the review above, however, it is not the band's music that is awarded the most attention, but the fact that they originate from Turkey. As such it is important to acknowledge that in the realm of global metal, a band's possibility to gain transgressive subcultural capital, both nationally and internationally, is not only limited to a band's level of musical and artistic innovation, but in addition can, as in the Turkish case, be awarded because of the geographical circumstances a band operates in. If Turkey is perceived to be hostile to metal, or more specifically, to black metal, engaging with these subcultures, regardless of their artistic production, seems to automatically grant Turkish bands transgressive subcultural capital within global metal. However in the national context, a more transgressive production is required.

The emergence of an intra-scenic process of otherization that pays particular attention to the religious identity is hard to solely explain through an ambition to claim transgressive subcultural capital. Rather it must also be understood, as Eren points out in the introductory quote of the chapter, as a response to the present political and social situation in Turkey and as a reaction to the AKP's politics of pious conservatism, and where Islam and Muslims are increasingly perceived to constitute a threat to many of the metalheads' way of life. Therefore, to be Muslim and metal at the very same time are for many in the extreme metal milieu two mutually exclusive categories, and Muslim metalheads are constantly labelled as "posers," unfaithful to the "true" underground ethos of metal, which at its core, is supposed to be against religion. Important to note is that the ideological split within the Turkish metal community is not necessarily limited to genres, since many in the extreme metal milieu socialize with bands and persons from the punk community for example. Rather, the line seems to be drawn between those who adhere to the "true" (anti-religious) ethos of metal and the underground scene, and those who do not, and Muslim metalheads are constantly placed in the latter category.

Concluding remarks

This chapter argues that the Turkish metal scene, since its inception, has been conceptualized as the ideological and cultural other in Turkish majority society. In contrast to previous controversies over metal ("hippieization of the Turkish nation," "satanic scare"), during which metal usually functioned as the widely passive scapegoat for social and cultural change ("westernization") or contentious social issues ("teenage suicides"), metal in "New Turkey" now seems to stand in open opposition to political Islam as represented by the governing pious conservative power bloc under the leadership of Recep Tayyip Erdoğan. Metal, which is deeply rooted in the tradition of Turkish secularism, thus can be seen as the "natural enemy" of "New Turkey's" pious conservatism. To this day, Turkey has not seen the emergence of any religiously inspired Islamic metal bands as has been the case in some Southeast Asian Muslim majority societies (James and Walsh 2019).

In present-day Turkey, popular culture functions as a key site of this ideological struggle (Hecker et al. forthcoming 2021) involving cultural resistance from various oppositional groups and individuals who, despite their differences, unite in the struggle against "New Turkey." In this sense, metal might one day come to represent the "true spirit" of the Turkish nation provided that the vision of "New Turkey" proves unsuccessful.

The present situation in Turkey has also provided a climate, in which the division of what constitutes "true metal" is centered around religion and Turkish black metal band's ability to transgress norms regarding religion is an important aspect of this construction. By transgressing social norms about religion, the

Turkish black metal community actively engages in the enjoyment of their own exclusion and "otherization" thereby not only defining their own identity toward Muslim majority society and the other within the Turkish metal community, but also obtaining subcultural capital in terms of being acknowledged and becoming visible on an international level while at the same time receiving proof of authenticity from within the global black metal community. Two final and illustrative examples of how Turkish metalheads conceptualize themselves as the ideological other by humorously appropriating popular stigmata assigned to them by Turkish majority society are provided by, first, the following quote from a self-description of *Delikasap*,[6] one of Turkey's longest existing rock and metal magazines[7]:

> *Delikasap* is not [just] a rock magazine [...] Because it is the incarnation of rock n roll itself! The most flashy, heavy rock, totally loose and lithe groovy roll [magazine]! Sweaty leather-gloved, smoothly hardening [*sic*] metal! Bare-chested piss punk! [...] The number one orgasmic, intellectual rock platform for perversion, disobedience, hooliganism, paganism, and barbarism.[8] The world's first shamanism-bound music magazine! *Delikasap*, [the magazine for] pagan, pot-smoking,[9] depraved rock n roll warriors! The enemy number one of all [traditional] big shot bullies! The heavy metal representative for the lust for life. *Delikasap* is a magazine for rock n roll culture. Because rock n roll is not just a musical genre [...] [*Delikasap*] has indeed been a vivacious, rebellious, anti-war, impertinent, and undisciplined [magazine] for the past 13 years.[10]

A second recent example of the Turkish metal scene's continued defiance happened in Istanbul (February 1, 2020). The Turkish hard-core band Radical Noise opened their song "Colors of Hate" with a videoclip from an interview with the famous anarchist Emma Goldman. In the clip, Goldman is asked by one of the reporters if she would change her speeches about anarchism if the American government would object to them. Her reply, which resulted in ecstatic cheering and massive applauds from the audience, was as follows: "I would leave the country rather than deny my ideas. I prefer to stick to my guns."

NOTES

1. Due to the controversial nature of Turkish black metal, the authors have deicide to anonymize direct quotes from Turkish black metal protagonists and provide them with alias instead of using their real name.
2. For Murder King's "Demokrasi" [official video], see https://www.youtube.com/watch?v=lv8UZ8wlTGQ (Accessed September 16, 2019).
3. Translations by Pierre Hecker.
4. English translation provided by the European Commission for Democracy through Law.

5. It should be mentioned here that in 2008 the Human Rights Council adopted a resolution where religion *de facto* enjoyed protection. This resolution was accepted in the UN in 2010 during the 65th meeting of the general assembly, in which 76 delegates voted in favor of the resolution, 67 against, and 40 delegates passed on voting on the bill. In 2011, following an extended discussion on freedom of speech, freedom of consciousness, and blasphemy, jurists from the HRC vetoed the resolution. For more info, see Otterbeck (2011) on United Nations.
6. *Delikasap* (literally "Mad Butcher") named itself after Destruction's 1987 *Mad Butcher* EP.
7. The following quote has been taken and translated from YouTube clip produced by Murat Arda for *Delikasap*: https://www.youtube.com/watch?v=6EpPTJxiZJE. Accessed July 2, 2021.
8. *Delikasap* literally speaks of the "Scandinavian sledge hammer" (*iskandinav balyozu*) and the "land of the Huns" (*hun diyari*) here, which is most likely a reference to Norse mythology (Thor's hammer), as frequently used in global metal culture, and the Turkish nation's supposed pre-Islamic barbarian ancestors, the Huns.
9. *Delikasap* actually uses "Zoroastrian" (*zerdüşt*) and "Assassin/Hashishin" (*haşhaşi*) here. *Zerdüşt* is still frequently used in Turkish political discourse to denounce political opponents as pagan and, therefore, apostates from Islam. *Haşhaşi* originally is a reference to the medieval Nizari Ismaili order that, due to its military tactics, became eponymous for "assassin"; the group was furthermore mistakenly said to have smoked hashish.
10. Translation by Pierre Hecker.

REFERENCES

Ali, Kecia (2006), *Sexual Ethics and Islam: Feminist Reflections on Qur'an, Hadith, and Jurisprudence*, Oxford: Oneworld Publications.

Ayata, Gökçe Çiçek, Burcu, Yeşiladalı, Cansu, Muratoğlu, İdil, Elveriş, İdil, Işıl Gül, Lami, Bertan Tokuzlu, Pınar, Çağlı, Sevinç, Eryılmaz, and Ulaş, Karan (2013), *Gezi Parkı Olayları: İnsan Hakları Hukuku ve Siyasi Söylem Işığında Bir İnceleme*, Istanbul: İstanbul Bilgi Üniverrsitesi Yayınları.

Azak, Umut (2010), *Islam and Secularism in Turkey: Kemalism, Religion and the Nation State*, London and New York: I. B. Tauris.

Bengi, Derya (2012), *Uzayda bir elektrik hasıl oldu: 1960'larda müzikli Türkiye*, exhibition, Depo İstanbul, September 15–October 24.

BirGün (2019), "Defkhan 'Susamam' projesinden ayrıldı," September 18, https://www.birgun.net/haber/defkhan-susamam-projesinden-ayrildi-269104. Accessed March 2, 2020.

Boynik, Sezgin, and Güldallı, Tolga (eds.) (2007), *An Interrupted History of Punk and Underground Sources in Turkey 1978–1999*, Istanbul: BAS.

David, Isabel, and Toktamış, Kumru F. (eds.) (2015), *"Everywhere Taksim": Sowing the Seeds for a New Turkey at Gezi*, Amsterdam: Amsterdam University Press.

Demirkol, Gökhan (2018), *Gırgır: Bir Mizah Dergisinde Gündelik Hayatın Dönüşümü (1972-1989)*, Istanbul: İletişim.

Eren, Ozan, (2017), "Türkiye'de 1960'larda Müzik Alanı ve Protest Müziğin İlk Nüveleri: Anadolu Pop Akımı," *Sosyoloji Dergisi*, 38:1, pp. 131–62.

Erkal, Güven Erkin (2014), *Türkiye Rock Tarihi 1: Saykodelik Yıllar*, Istanbul: Esenkitap.

Hecker, Pierre (2012), *Turkish Metal Music, Meaning, and Morality in a Muslim Society*, Aldershot and Burlington: Ashgate.

Hecker, Pierre (2014), "A clash of lifestyles?: Jugendliche Lebensstile im politischen Diskurs der Türkei," in J. Gertel and R. Ouaissa (eds.), *Jugendbewegungen. Städtischer Widerstand und Umbrüche in der Arabischen Welt,* Bielefeld: Transcript, pp. 326–52.

Hecker, Pierre, Furman, Ivo, and Akyıldız, Kaya (eds.) (forthcoming 2021), *The Politics of Culture in Contemporary Turkey*, Edinburgh: Edinburgh University Press.

James, Kieran, and Walsh, Rex (2019), "Religion and heavy metal music in Indonesia," *Popular Music*, 38:2, pp. 276–97.

Kahn-Harris, Keith (2007), *Extreme Metal: Music and Culture on the Edge*, Oxford and New York: Berg.

Karakaya-Stump, Ayfer (2018), "The AKP, sectarianism, and the Alevis' struggle for equal rights in Turkey," *National Identities*, 20:1, pp. 53–67.

Kaya, Ayhan (2015), "Islamisation of Turkey under the AKP rule: Empowering family, faith and charity," *South European Society and Politics*, 20:1, pp. 47–69.

Kuppens, An H., and van der Pol, Frank (2014), "'True' black metal: The construction of authenticity by Dutch black metal fans," *Communications*, 39:2, pp. 151–167.

Lüküslü, Demet (2016), "Creating a pious generation: Youth and education policies of the AKP in Turkey," *Southeast European and Black Sea Studies*, 16:4, pp. 637–49.

Mattsson, Douglas (forthcoming 2021), "'Spreading VX Gas over Kaaba': Islamic semiotics in Turkish black metal," in P. Hecker, I. Furman, and K. Akyıldız (eds.), *The Politics of Culture in Contemporary Turkey*, Edinburgh: Edinburgh University Press.

Metal Maniack (2017), "Persecutory—Towards the ultimate extinction," *Metal Maniack*, http://www.metalmaniack.com. Accessed July 29, 2017.

Otterbeck, Jonas (2011), "Blasfemi Som Problem För Mänskliga Rättigheter," in D.-E. Andersson and J. Modée (eds.), *Mänskliga rättigheter och religion*, Malmö: Liber, pp. 228–40.

Otterbeck, Jonas, Mattsson, Douglas, and Pastene, Orlando (2018), "'I am Satan!': Black metal, Islam and blasphemy in Turkey and Saudi Arabia," *Contemporary Islam*, 12:3, pp. 267–86.

Özbudun, Ergun (2006), "From political Islam to conservative democracy: The case of the Justice and Development Party in Turkey," *South European Society and Politics*, 11: 3&4, pp. 545–57.

Özkırımlı, Umut (ed.) (2014), *The Making of a Protest Movement in Turkey: #occupygezi*, Hampshire and New York: Palgrave Macmillan.

Öztürk, Ahmet Erdi, and Gözaydın, İstar (2017), "Turkey's constitutional amendments: A critical perspective," *Research and Policy on Turkey*, 2:2, pp. 201–24.

Şen, Mustafa (2010), "Transformation of Turkish Islamism and the rise of the Justice and Development Party," *Turkish Studies*, 11:1, pp. 59–84.

Şirin, Tolga (2014), "Freedom from religion in Turkey," in H. Ç. Özgür, and M. Yıldırım (eds.), *Freedom of Religion and Belief in Turkey*, Newcastle: Cambridge Scholars Publishing, pp. 59–88.

The European Commission for Democracy through Law (2016), "Opinion on articles 216, 299, 301, and 314 of the penal code of Turkey," http://www.venice.coe.int/webforms/documents/default.aspx?pdffile=CDL-AD(2016)002-e. Accessed February 3, 2020.

Toprak, Binnaz, İrfan, Bozan, Tan, Morgül, and Nedim, Şener (2009), *Being Different in Turkey: Religion, Conservatism and Otherization*, Research Report on Neighborhood Pressure, Istanbul: Boğazici University.

Way, Lyndon C. S. (2018), *Popular Music and Multimodal Critical Discourse Studies: Ideology, Control, and Resistance in Turkey since 2002*, London: Bloomsbury.

Williams, J. Patrick (2011), *Subcultural Theory: Traditions and Concepts*, Cambridge: Polity Press.

Yavuz, Hakan M. (ed.) (2006), *The Emergence of a New Turkey: Democracy and the AK Parti*, Salt Lake City: University of Utah Press.

Yazıcı, Berna, (2012), "The return to the family: Welfare, state, and politics of the family in Turkey," *Anthropological Quarterly*, 85:1, pp. 103–40.

Yılmaz, Battal (2018), *The Presidential System in Turkey: Opportunities and Obstacles*, Hampshire and New York: Palgrave Macmillan.

4

"*Métal noir épique patriotique*": Analysis of Historical, Sociological, and Cultural Discourses Uniting *métal noir québécois* and Québec Society

Mei-Ra St. Laurent

Unlike in many Northern European countries, black metal did not develop until later in the Province of Québec (Canada). Even if the first Québécois black metal bands appeared in 1993, it is only at the beginning of the 2000s that the style gained momentum. From this period, a specific community—known under the moniker of *métal noir québécois* (MNQ)—emerged within this black metal scene and became the focal point of attention locally and internationally. Indeed, its main bands (e.g., Forteresse, Chasse-Galerie) are characterized by French lyrics and historical references specific to the province. However, the unifying feature of MNQ groups remains the fact that all the members advocate a nationalist ideology, while scarcely mentioning the actual discourse on nationalism held by the different political parties in Québec. More specifically, their songs are almost uniquely oriented toward the Patriots Rebellion of the nineteenth century, where the French settlers sought to gain independence from the British Empire. By doing so, the MNQ bands are voluntarily ignoring the most recent attempts (e.g., the referendums for the independence of 1980 and 1995). Thus, for most black metal fans, MNQ remains remote from any kind of political reality and is seen as a nostalgic representation of these past conflicts.

However, even if this marginal community often seems to function according to its own codes, values, or networks, it remains intrinsically linked to the present Québec society; numerous sociopolitical events that have influenced Québécois from the last 30 years have had a huge impact on the development of a nationalist stance for the first black metal bands of the 1990s, and have contributed to the emergence of the MNQ community. To better understand how these sociopolitical events had an impact on the nationalist discourse for the MNQ, I will use the concept of *eventialization* developed by French philosopher Michel Foucault. It can be described as a way to "find the connections, the meetings, the supports, the blockages, the games of force, the strategies, etc., which have, at a given moment, formed what will then function as an evidence, a universality, a need" (Foucault 1994: 23).[1] In other words, this concept refers to the analysis of the different discourses surrounding key events in a society. In the context of this chapter, its use will allow me to draw parallels between the development of black metal (and MNQ) and the advent of major political, cultural, and social events of the province.

Moreover, the way the historical elements used by the MNQ bands are entangled in the music, images, and discourse can be understood as narrative identity, a concept elaborated by the French philosopher Paul Ricoeur. Indeed, Ricoeur affirms that our personal and collective identity is better understood when it is ordered through a chronological narrative. However, this restitution is never completely objective, and the way in which these elements are understood by a group of people in a given society can be viewed as narrative identity. Indeed, not only the discourse used by the members of the community can be interpreted as pieces of a wider narrative, but also the images included in album booklets and several musical elements.

Throughout this chapter, I will use different tools; first, in order to draw links between the MNQ and the various societal debates that have marked the Province of Québec since the 1990s, I will rely on the annual publications entitled *L'annuaire du Québec* and *L'état du Québec*. Second, in order to define the discourse of the community, I will dwell upon 21 ethnographic interviews conducted with members of the Québec black metal scene between 2014 and 2018.[2] Third, I will rely on booklet images, on lyrics, and on distinctive musical characteristics of the first albums of the main groups of the MNQ community—namely, Forteresse (*Métal noir québécois* 2006), Brume d'Automne (*Fiers et victorieux* 2005), and Chasse-Galerie (*Ars Moriendi* 2010)—to better explain how the nationalist stance is understood in the repertoire and how it can be seen as a narrative identity. Finally, I will also use different data emanating from *Metal Archives* database[3] (e.g., the years of group formation), which will provide a quantitative support to the discourse gathered in interviews.

This chapter will be structured as follows: I will first define the concept of nationalism while linking it to the history of the province. Then, I will examine how the main sociopolitical events that have occurred in the province over the last 30 years have shaped the black metal scene. In this middle section, I will also linger on the interpretation of historical elements reused by the bands and illustrated though images, lyrics, music, and discourses. Finally, I will demonstrate how the MNQ narrative identity, and their perception of the province history, is both distinct and similar to the narrative identity held by most of Québécois.

Defining the concept of nationalism in the sociohistorical context of the province

Since the nineteenth century, the nationalist question remains a central issue in Québec. However, before explaining in what ways nationalism has been influential for the province, it is important to define this highly connotated concept. First, for political scientists Danic Parenteau and Ian Parenteau, "nationalism" refers to a deep attachment to its own nation. Indeed, they specify that this notion is based on the belief that the nation constitutes the "center of the world" (Parenteau and Parenteau 2008: 159). In this instance, "nation" is understood as "the object of all concerns." The authors also specify the following: "As a political program ensuing, any nationalist action takes the form of a project, with multiple dimensions depending on the context, which aimed at awakening, developing, glorifying, stimulating, protecting and defending the national interest" (Parenteau and Parenteau 2008: 159).

However, this notion is also linked to negative connotations. As the authors add, nationalism also remains linked to the purity of the race, as it is visible with Nazism (Parenteau and Parenteau 2008: 167). In addition, they point out that in Europe, nationalism is perceived more as a phenomenon anchored on the extreme right wing. This can be explained by the excess of fascists and Nazis during the Second World War, which directly affected the European countries. On the contrary, in North and South America, nationalism can be understood as a left-wing oriented ideology for historical reasons. Indeed, the various decolonization movements that have marked these countries have favored the emergence of ideologies linked with the national liberation of oppressed populations (Parenteau and Parenteau 2008: 154).

This last conception of nationalism is visible in Québec. Indeed, in this province, nationalism has been often liked to a left-wing ideology, while being generally seen as a desirable outcome. As explicated by political scientists Daniel Béland and André Lecours,

> [o]ne of the most interesting aspects of Québec nationalism since the 1960s is its anchorage on the left. Compared to Flemish and Catalan nationalism [...], Québec nationalism is most often associated with egalitarian social democratic policies. However, long before the 1960s, nationalism in Québec had been viewed as a tool

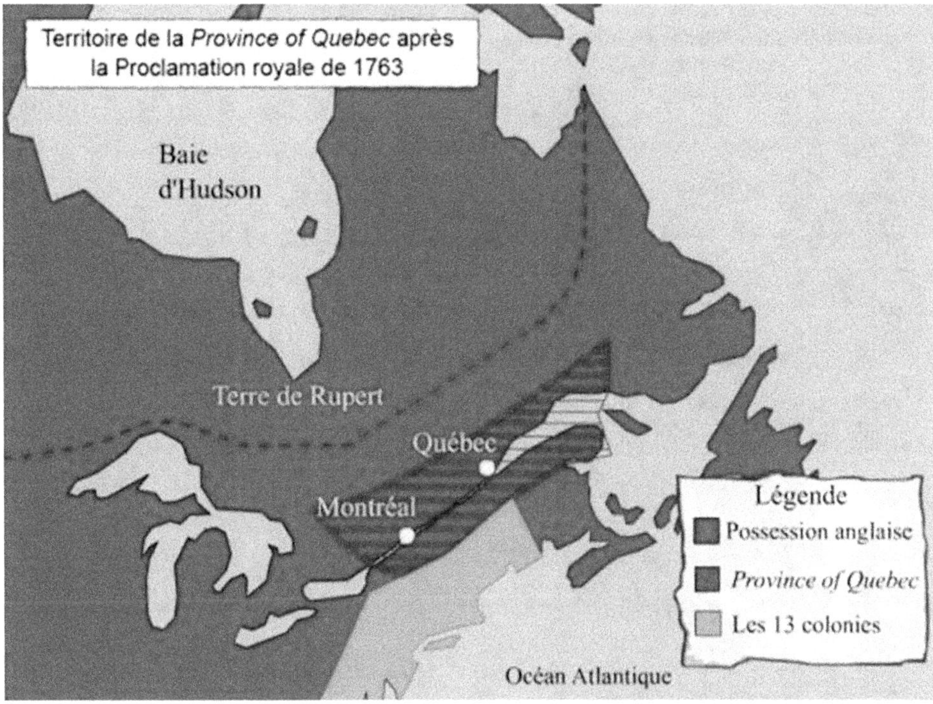

FIGURE 4.1: Territory of New France around 1745. Creative Commons Licence (cc).

> allowing French Canadians to conserve their culture, language and identity in a context where neither the British Empire or the English Canadians government wanted to fully recognize their specificity.
>
> (Béland and Lecours 2011: 37)

More specifically, Québec—or Nouvelle-France, as it was named at the time—was a French colony from 1534 to 1763 (Figure 4.1), before becoming a British territory in 1763 (Figure 4.2).

From 1791 (Figure 4.3), French Canadians were given a specific territory (Low Canada), as well as a political representation in the government (Balthazar 2013: 54). However, in the wake of the nineteenth century, and influenced by French and American Revolutions, French Canadians realized soon that they had no political or economic power inside the British Empire. Influenced by the Patriot Party[4] and its leader Louis-Joseph Papineau, French-Canadians became conscious that the goal of the British Empire was to assimilate them. This acknowledgment led to a series of armed conflicts between the French settlers, named the patriots, and the British soldiers between 1837 and 1838. These armed conflicts, known

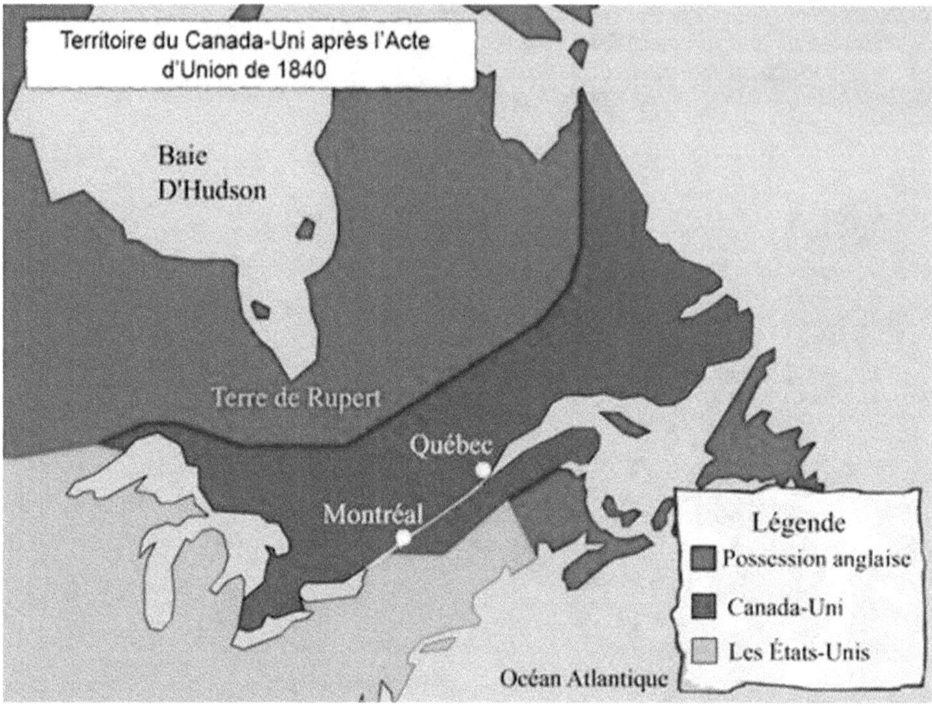

FIGURE 4.2: Territory of Province of Québec after the royal proclamation of 1763. Creative Commons Licence (cc).

under the designation of the "Patriots Rebellion," ended with the hanging of twelve leaders of the resistance movement on February 15, 1839 (Buckner 2013).[5] Indeed, despite an initial win of the patriots at the Battle of St. Denis on November 23, 1837, the five other confrontations were lost in the favor of better armed and trained British soldiers.

The following period (roughly between 1840 and 1960) was characterized by a willingness to survive, where the French Canadians tried to protect their culture, traditions, and language in a context where the English Canadian minority imposed its political, economic, and cultural power over the French Canadian majority (Balthazar 2013: 32–34). In the 1950s, in the wake of the decolonization process in Asia and Africa, a Québécois sovereigntist conscience, breaking with the tradition, was crystallized. During the next two decades, the Québec society was characterized by a deep reorganization of its social structure; the provincial government—in the manner of a Nation-State—became more and more involved in many spheres of the society (e.g., education, health care, and communication) that were previously controlled by the Church and the federal government. This

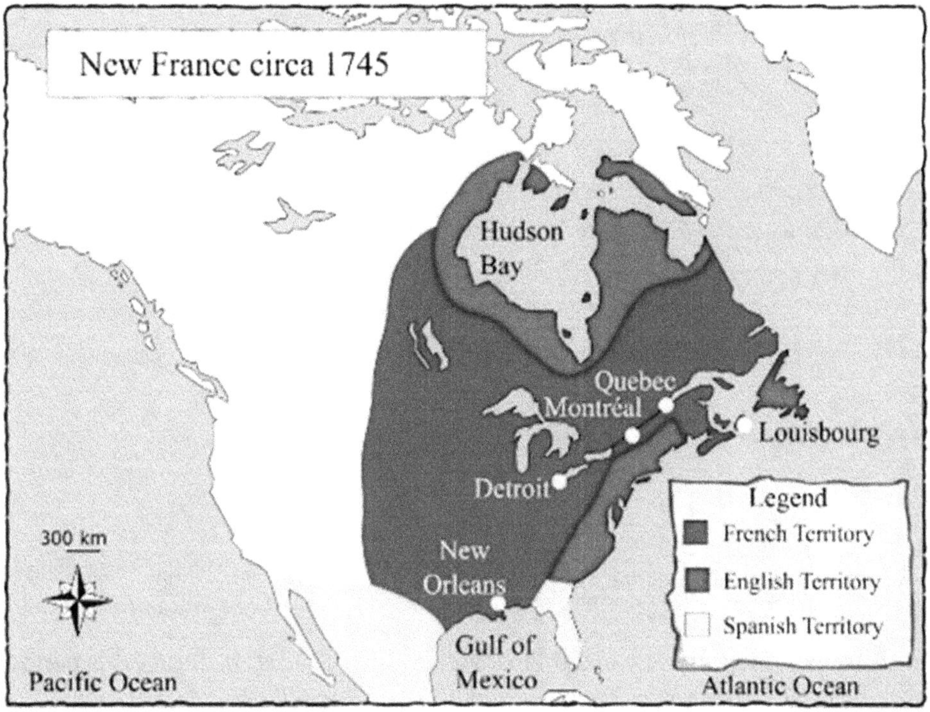

FIGURE 4.3: Division of the territory after the Union Act. Creative Commons Licence (cc).

nationalist stance was also shared by feminist movements and unions, and it led to a first referendum on independence in 1980. More specifically, this referendum was an initiative of the Parti Québécois (PQ), a progressive left-wing party, which (unsuccessfully) attempted to make a country out of a province.[6] After this defeat, the support to the sovereigntist movement decreased drastically. However, in 1990s, many events led to the recrudescence of this sovereigntism, which had a decisive impact on the development of the new black metal scene. These elements will be explained below in the next section and linked with the growth of a new black metal scene.

The first period of the scene: The rise and development of black metal in the Province of Québec (1993–2000)

Before putting forward a nationalism claim, the new black metal scene had to build its core of bands and define its ideological and aesthetical concepts. Yet,

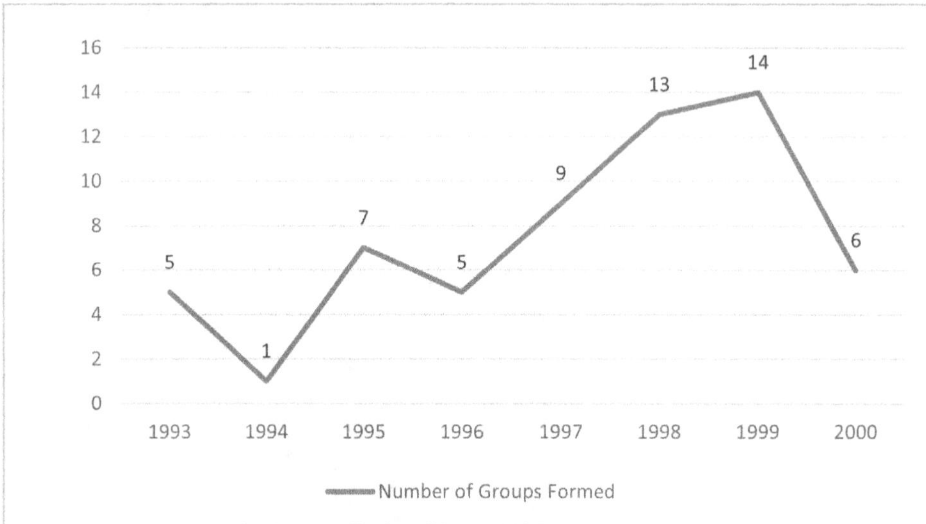

FIGURE 4.4: Annual formation of black metal bands in Québec (1993–2000).

at the same time, very few metal fans were aware of the style during this period, and the groups themselves had not yet developed a specific bond with each other.

According to Myrkhaal (former band member of Tenebrae and Frozen Shadows, and records label owner), we cannot really speak of a black metal scene in Québec before the 2000s (Myrkhaal 2016). The data we can find in *Metal Archives* website mirrored Myrkhaal's comment (see Figure 4.4). Indeed, according to this website, it was in 1993 that the first five black metal bands[7] were formed in Québec—Tenebrae being the one to which the interviewees referred the most. However, it was not until 1998 that the number of new black metal bands formed annually increased significantly; to the 27 existing groups (formed between 1993 and 1997), thirteen new ones were added in just one year (Figure 4.4).[8]

This late interest for the style was noticeable according to four elements: (1) at first, black metal remained unknown by metal fans; (2) when it was known, it was not valued or (3) it caused a deep misunderstanding; and (4) there was little communication between the members of the scene.

More specifically, this lack of knowledge was reflected in the way metal fans reacted when they learned about black metal for the first time. For example, Myrkhaal shared the following anecdote:

> It must have been in [19]92. I went to see the show of Deicide and they were playing music between the bands. At one point, they put on "Kathaarian Life Code," the first [song] from *A Blaze in the Northern Sky* [1992]. And when my friends realized that

> I knew what was playing, they ask me what the band's name was. When I answered them that it was Darkthrone, another guy that had heard the first album told me: "No, it can't be Darkthrone!"[9] I answered him: "Yes, it's Darkthrone. Now they are into black metal." Then, people around me responded: "What is black metal?" (Myrkhaal 2016: n.pag.).

On the other hand, when metal fans knew the style, it was usually viewed negatively. Indeed, thrash and death metal remained, at that moment, the most popular metal styles in the province, where the technical skills and hi-fi productions were valued. As Sébastien (member from Sorcier des Glaces and sound engineer) recalled: "My friends were laughing at me because I was listening to this [Darkthrone]. 'Darkthrone! What a shitty band!' For them, it was not technical, and it was poorly played" (Sébastien 2016: n.pag.). Still others simply did not know how to consider black metal when exposed to it. As Myrkhaal evoked:

> I remember the stunned reaction of the crowd at the last show I did with the group [Tenebrae] in 1994 [...] When the public saw us entering the stage with our war tackle (nails, corpse paint, ceremonial dresses) and flanked by two followers holding torches, people did not know how to react and seemed overwhelmed by this event. (Quoted in Asakku 2012: n.pag.)

For Myrkhaal, a certain incomprehension was felt when it came to this style, given the ideological and aesthetic distinctions marking it as fundamentally different from death metal or thrash metal. Thus, it took some time before it was appreciated by fans.

Finally, as reported by Winterthrone (member of Dépérir and Hak-ed-Damm, and chronicler), this first period was also characterized by the difficulty to communicate between the scene members, since no social media platforms were yet created (Winterthrone 2016). Thus, this lack of communication did not allow the members to establish contact with each other, which would have led to the creation of a scenic unity.

The musical and thematic characteristics of the groups

As Myrkhaal explains, two types of black metal sounds can be found among the first Québec's bands. The first musical trend, which was more common, emanated from bands influenced by the melodic sound of Cradle of Filth and Dimmu Borgir. These groups (e.g., Blinded by Faith and Magister Dixit) valued virtuosic musical lines, English lyrics, and they used universal scope subjects, such as Satanism, death, or depression. The second trend was characterized by groups, such as Frozen Shadows, Esker, or Akitsa, that were inspired by the aesthetic of the first Norwegian black metal bands. Their sound, highly distinct from the first trend, was exemplified by monolithic harmonies, simple melodic lines, and a continuous blast beat. Moreover, these latter bands referred to themes related to the province and some even used French lyrics, such as Frozen Shadows (the most cited bands by the interviewees).

Formed in 1996, Frozen Shadows was—according to Myrkhaal (2016)—the first black metal band to use French in its lyrics. From the beginning, Myrkhaal's intention was clear: to affirm his Québécois identity by using his mother tongue. However, the band goes much further than the simple use of the French; it expresses its affiliation with Québec in its album cover art. This is visible from the first album *Dans les bras des immortels* (1999), where a Québec flag appears on the back page of the booklet (Figure 4.5) with the following inscription below: "These odes to evil are primarily dedicated to Molière's language lovers endued with a black soul. Frozen Shadows is and will always be a pure Québec Black Metal band."

On the same album, the song "Lune funèbre" ("Funeral moon"), with its mention of "Nouvelle-France" in the lyrics, was one of the first songs written by a black metal band from Québec to evoke the province territory. Thus, as indicated by Myrkhaal, although the purpose of this indication was to situate the action (Myrkhaal 2016), its use reinforced the link with the identity discourse of this new scene.[10]

During the same period, other groups, such as Sombre Nostalgie, Esker, and Akitsa, also used French, as well as imagery and themes linked with the province. The influence of Norwegian bands was not the only reason explaining these references. Indeed, this interest also arose from the persistence of the independence question in Québec society during the 1990s.

The independence question in the Québec society in the 1990s

Even if the sovereigntist project seemed to be set aside after the defeat of the 1980s referendum, tensions remain present between the French-speaking province and the rest of Canada. Indeed, to protect the francophone culture from the English influence, the Province of Québec adopted specific laws (such as unilingual French signage in the province). However, the province's desire to focus on distinctions instead of similarities with the rest of Canada highly displeased the federal government. Yet, one event revived the nationalist debate and generated extremely high rates for independence in the early 1990s in Québec: the failure of the Meech Lake Accord. This accord, which was to be signed by all provincial governments at Meech Lake in 1990, aimed to review the Canadian Constitution in order to increase the powers attributed to the provinces, and to recognize Québec as a

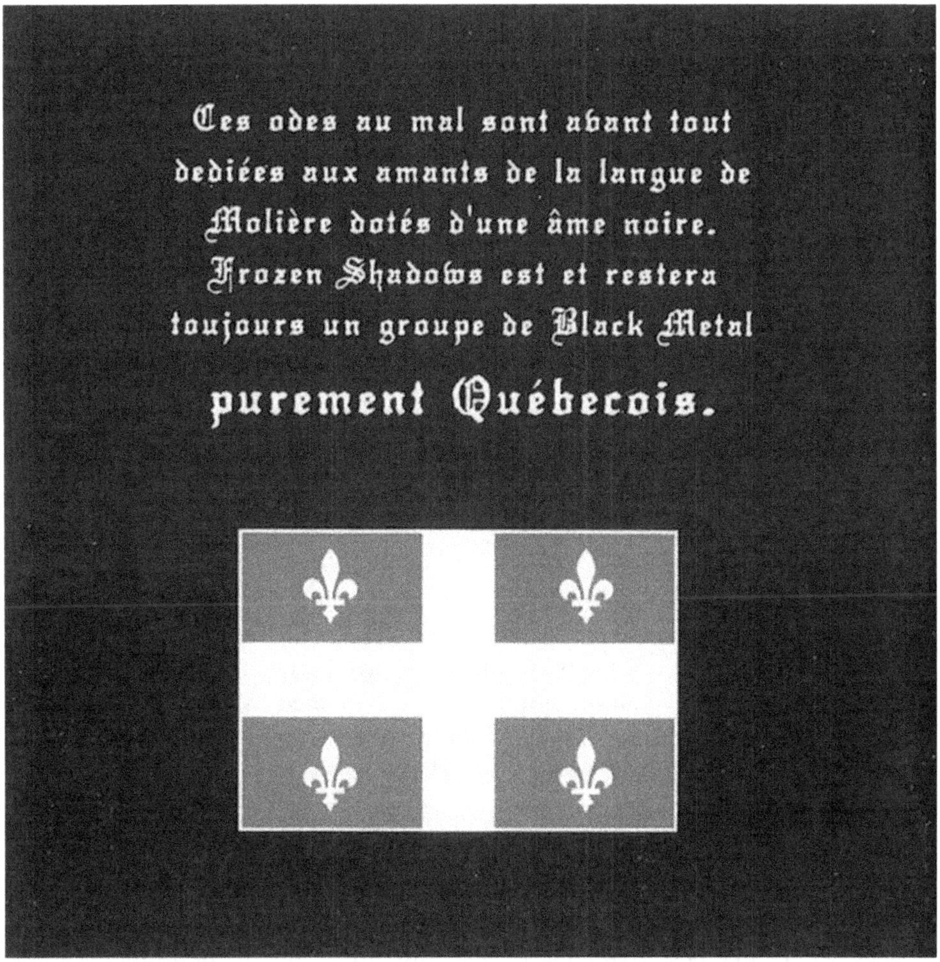

FIGURE 4.5: Back cover of the album *Dans les bras des immortels* (Frozen Shadows, 1999). © Sepulchral Productions 1999.

distinct society. However, the provinces were not able to agree on the content of the agreement, leading to its failure (Gall 2006).

This event triggers a significant loss of Québécois confidence in the federal government, which refuses (once again) to recognize the distinction of Québec's society (Monière 1999).[11] This dissatisfaction lead to a new referendum on the separation of Québec, held on October 30, 1995. Thus, despite very high polling results in favor of separation (50 percent of Québécois were in favor), the media and political arsenal deployed by the federal government against the dismemberment of the country resulted in a second failure.[12] Following the second referendum defeat, the federal government no longer considered separation a possibility, since it perceived Québécois as not having the courage of their convictions. Rather, the federal government promotes the equality of individuals and provinces, which results in the refusal to recognize the distinctiveness of Québec society (Monière 1999).

As explained by Myrkhaal, given the propensity of Norwegian black metal bands to idealize the past and the heritage, the inclusion of cultural references emanating from Québec black metal bands seemed to flow naturally. However, in light of events presented, it was normal that Québécois' concerns about their identity reverberate in the music of the first black metal bands. Therefore, the fact that the black metal groups were dealing with these elements (even in a superficial way) demonstrates that they were very aware of the political upheavals of this period. Then, to a certain extent, music was used by the bands to share their opinion on those issues.

The second period of the scene: The growth of the scene and the formation of the MNQ (2001–09)

In the early 2000s, the expansion of the black metal scene that began at the end of the 1990s became even more important. As explained by Matrak (member of Chasse-Galerie and Forteresse) and Monarque Helserkr (member of Monarque and Forteresse), even if black metal was still a marginal phenomenon, this second period was a booming one. In Québec society, the interest for nationalist themes was gaining momentum due to the rise of a new generation. Indeed, having only known the second referendum, this new generation did not feel the despondency nor the lack of interest in the nationalist question characteristic of previous generations.

The data from *Metal Archive* site (Figure 4.6) illustrates an important rise at the beginning of this second period. Indeed, a total of 199 new groups were formed between 2001 and 2009, which far exceeded the figures presented previously. In addition, the years 2002 and 2004 remain the most important ones, with the formation of, respectively, 26 and 27 groups. However, a decrease is also visible over the years and reached the lowest point at the beginning of the third period, as it will be further demonstrated.

This significant scenic growth characterizing the beginning of this second period is primarily attributed (1) to the advent of social networks; (2) to the higher demand for black metal shows; (3) to the maturation of the scene's members; and (4) to the creation of local labels supporting the emerging local bands. Moreover, this second period also corresponds to the advent of a new community which grew up inside the black metal scene: MNQ. All those elements contributed to the increase of live performances and the annual records production.

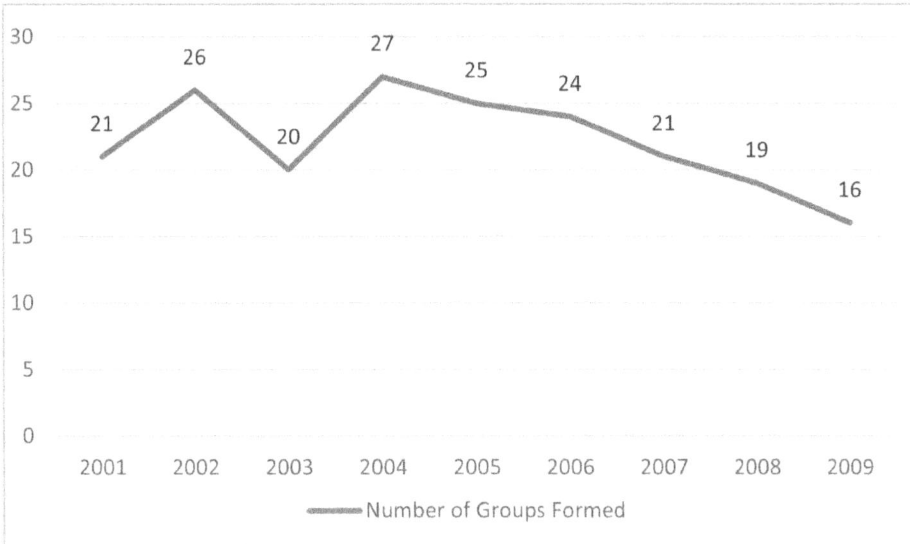

FIGURE 4.6: Annual formation of black metal groups in Québec (2001–09).

As revealed by many interviewees, the main factor explaining this increase in the scene activity remains the greater accessibility to the internet; it allowed Québécois fans to get acquainted with Norwegian groups, while inspiring them to build their own scene. More specifically, the advent of MySpace (2003) had a huge impact on the scene. As Sion Daus (member of Neige et Noirceur) explains, "even if the MySpace phenomenon only lasts for 3 years, it made it possible to contact everyone in one click; you could upload your songs, send links, speak to [real] people" (Sion Daus 2016: n.pag.). In addition, as Myrkhaal (2016) mentions, it is thanks to this platform that he heard Forteresse's music for the first time. The more elaborate musical and conceptual content as well as the use of French of the new black metal bands drew Myrkhaal's attention. In 2006, he resumed the activities of his label, Sepulchral Productions (founded in 1999), and signed three emergent bands, Forteresse being one of them. Other black metal labels (e.g., Tour de garde) were also launched during this period.

Concurrently with the growth of this scene, Monarque Helserkr and Moribond (member of Forteresse) mention the desire of the scene's members to create bands that were influenced by the aesthetic of the first Norwegian black metal bands, which in turn increased the black metal shows offered (Monarque Helserkr 2016; Moribond 2016). For Matrak, this period could also be considered as an opportunity for the new scene members to develop their skills and specific aesthetic. Therefore, among the new bands formed, many could be understood as the first incarnation of black metal bands that would gain recognition afterwards.[13]

It was also during the second period that most groups associated with MNQ are formed. MNQ first referred to groups which in the early 2000s consciously decided to orient their artistic concept around the Province of Québec, from including references to folk music (the use of reels or traditional instruments), to various historical events that have marked the province, or to symbols representing Québec's cultural heritage (e.g., the Québec flag). More specifically, the first groups claiming MNQ appellation were Brume d'Automne (2003), Forteresse (2006), and Chasse-Galerie (2007). More specifically, as Winterthrone (2016) explains, it is when Nordet, with his album *Fiers et victorieux* launched in 2005, decided to combine his Québec heritage with the black metal sound that he created the first MNQ album (Winterthrone 2016). Despite Nordet's initial uncertainty as to how this name would be received (Nordet 2016), it was soon borrowed by Forteresse, which launched the album *Métal noir québécois* in 2006.

Moribond explains that MNQ was originally considered "as a grouping of bands from the Province of Québec who found it important to express themselves in French" (Moribond 2016: n.pag.). According to him, MNQ is born of a mutual aid between different groups of the scene between 2004 and 2006, where one can witness the birth of a community feeling. In terms of musical characteristics, MNQ is mostly based on the musical aesthetics of Norwegian and Québécois groups of the 1990s, while being influenced by the French and the Swedish black metal scenes. These first groups—still active today—are mainly interested in the period surrounding the Patriots Rebellion of 1837–38, in terms of imagery, lyrics, and music—elements we will now examine more closely.

The rise of MNQ community: Nationalism expressed through a narrative identity

The Québécois identity is reflected in many ways by the MNQ bands through the use of iconography and lyrics found in the booklets as well as through musical characteristics. For example, the first albums of Brume d'Automne (*Fiers et victorieux* 2005), Forteresse (*Métal noir québécois* 2006), and Chasse-Galerie (*Ars Moriendi* 2010) represent the way the theme of the Patriots Rebellion is expressed in their subsequent albums.

In terms of iconography, the cover of the first album of Brume d'Automne (Figure 4.7) characterizes the themes addressed by the groups in different ways. First, the album cover presents an autumnal landscape—which resembles a landscape in the province—and a forest along a body of water. Regarding the use of landscape in booklets, Monarque Helserkr (2016) and Blanc Feu (2016) explain that the Québécois identity does not limit itself to Émile Nelligan (a French-Canadian poet) or to the battles of the patriots; the nature can also be a representative element from Québec. Therefore, for interviewees, the use of this kind of landscape is a marker of their identity and refers to their deep attachment to nature and the land.

Second, the landscape is also juxtaposed a drawing (entitled *Saint-Denis*) created by the French-Canadian artist Henri Julien in 1887. It represents the patriots feasting around a British cannon seized during their victory at St. Denis on November 22, 1837. Thus, this representation of the only victory of the patriots is reinforced with the album title *Fiers et victorieux* ("Proud and victorious").

FIGURE 4.7: Front cover of the album *Fiers et victorieux* (Brume d'Automne 2005). © Winter Forest 2005.

Third, above the image, we can also see two characters armed with musket and framing the logo of the group. These characters are also taken from Julien's artwork entitled *Un vieux de '37* or *An old from '37* (*c.*1904) (Figure 4.8).

FIGURE 4.8: Henri Julien, *Le vieux de '37*, *c.*1904. Gouache on paper. Royalty free image, private collection.

Even if this figure was first considered as tribute to the patriots of 1837–38, from the 1960s, it has been ascribed a revolutionary meaning by many nationalist scholars (e.g., Joseph Costisella) and political groupings (e.g., Front de libération du Québec) (St-Jean 2009: 117). Today, it appears at different occasions (e.g., the National holiday of the province or Patriot Remembrance Day). In the context of the MNQ, the use of this figure seems to express the willingness to continue the fight and to remember the great deeds of their ancestors. Finally, we distinguish in the group logo a small lily flower, which is yet another symbol of the independence movement since it refers to the flag of the province. These three iconographic elements (the Québec landscape, the representations of the Patriot through two artworks from the province's artistic heritage, and the lily flower) are also used extensively by other MNQ groups.

Moreover, the songs of the three targeted groups are often constructed in the form of a "phonographic narrative." Developed by musicologist Serge Lacasse, this concept aims to consider a recorded song (or a "phonogram") as a narrative, where both compositional elements (e.g., harmony, melody, form), and sound effects added to a song (e.g., reverb, sampling) or the singer's vocal timber (e.g., growl voice, scream voice) are combined with lyrics. In this context, the vocalist can be considered as a narrator transmitting a narrative comprising a spatiotemporal frame (place, time) and a speech (dialogue, monologue), where the various musical elements mentioned influence the understanding of this narrative.

Thus, when examining the songs of the first MNQ albums, one realizes that the titles and lyrics refer mainly to the various battles fought by the patriots in the nineteenth century against the British Empire. The songs "La mort d'un patriote" ("The death of a patriot") from Brume d'Automne, "La patrie des sans-âme" ("The homeland of the soulless") from Chasse-Galerie, and "Une nuit pour la patrie" ("One night for the fatherland") from Forteresse all bear on this subject and address it in different ways.[14] More specifically, "La mort d'un patriote" presents the fight of the patriots as already over, where a narrator encourages the current generation to resume the battle. For its part, "La patrie des sans-âme" narrates an ongoing battle preceding the surrendering of the American French territories to England. Finally, "Une nuit pour la patrie" relates to a battle about to unfold, where a narrator urges the patriots to stay strong for the fight that will take place the next day.

Finally, various musical elements are used by the groups to stage the period in which these narratives take place. For example, in Brume d'Automne's songs "La mort d'un patriote" and "Quand les morts s'agitent" ("When the dead are waving"), one can note the presence of traditional instruments, such as Irish flute, wooden spoon, or foot tapping. In addition, the Forteresse's songs "La moisson de la liberté" ("The harvest of liberty") and "Métal noir québécois" ("Québécois black metal") feature sampling of traditional music that became popular in the nineteenth century, and recorded in the 1930s by the famous French-Canadian fiddlers Joseph Allard and Tommy Duschesne. More specifically, "La moisson de la liberté" comprises an excerpt of the "Reel des forêts" ("Reel of the forest") and "Métal noir québécois" presents an excerpt of the "Gigue de Barnabé" ("Barnabé's jig").

These elements, although they do not refer to combat, still anchor narratives in the nineteenth century.[15] Indeed, even if the French-Canadian musical folklore stems in part from the traditional French tunes transmitted orally by the first French settlers, it was also influenced by Irish and Scottish immigrants who settled on the territory between 1815 and 1870. The reels and jigs emanating from these newcomers were included in the French-Canadian music (Bizzoni and Prevost-Thomas 2008: 508). Today, the traditional tunes of the nineteenth century that remain are used mainly during the holiday season, due to their dancing and light rhythms.

For many interviewees, the integration of traditional instruments in MNQ songs is not anecdotal. For Will (member of the Sombre Nostalgie) and Geneviève (sponsor of metal events), the presence of these tunes in the songs of the repertoire of the MNQ adds a certain nostalgia. Geneviève adds thus: 'Our grandfathers and great-grandfathers, they all gathered around a fire and they played [reels and jigs]. I think it reinforces even more the historical side and the Québécois roots' (Geneviève 2016: n.pag.).

Therefore, the discourse of MNQ groups presented through the images, lyrics, and music can be seen as a narrative identity, where the members choose to highlight the moment of history that they find the most glorious. As shown once again, the high interest in the nationalist question for the MNQ bands during this second period remain intimately linked with the way the nationalist question was treated at that moment in the society.

The revival of the independentist question in Québec society (2001–09)

In Québec society, the first decade of the new millennium is characterized foremost by reflections on the sovereignty project, but in a pan-Canadian context (Maclure 2000: 92). More specifically, in 2003, the victory of the Québec Liberal Party (PLQ), a non-sovereigntist party led by Jean Charest, brought the province more closely aligned politically to the federal government. However, despite the desire for change that motivated Québécois to vote for the PLQ, certain decisions taken by the Charest government (regarding the environment or cuts in government budget) led to a great dissatisfaction among union members and the general population (Venne 2004: 18). This period also marked the fragmentation of the left-wing. More specifically, a new citizen left, less oriented toward separation, but supporting the protection of the environment and the defense of cultural diversity, gave birth to the Québec Solidaire Party in 2006 (Parenteau 2004: 438). On the federal level, the election of Stephen Harper's conservative government (which remained in power until 2016) also set the sovereigntist movement back. Indeed, in 2006, this government was the first to recognize that 'Québécois form a nation within a united Canada' (Chevrier 2012: 137). This statement, even if it is considered as a recognition of the specificities of the Francophone province, was overtly criticized by academics and politicians—as well as many Québécois (MNQ members included)—who considered this comment as one more attempt to demonstrate the subjection of the province by the federal government (Bock-Côté 2007: 16).

It is also interesting to note that the year 2003, which corresponds to the election of a provincial government opposed to the project of sovereignty, was marked by the advent of several popular music groups that prioritized Québec folklore and identity. In this regard, the musicologist Luc Bellemare comments that groups like Loco Locass, Mes Aïeux, and Les Cowboys Fringants turned to folklore in order to transmit a sovereigntist message, which was similar to that of the 1960s. This message was articulated around the desire "to master its economy and institutions, to be open to other cultures, but to remain attached at the same time to its traditional values" (Bellemare 2008: 40). However, as the historian Éric Bédard explains, groups like Mes Aïeux or Les Cowboys Fringants advocated values that could also be associated with a conservative right, such as the return to the land, the importance of transmitting traditions, and so on (Bédard 2011: 27). Then, for the philosopher Christian Nadeau, this new conservative nationalism expressed the will of Québécois to reconnect with their traditions and to acknowledge the great battles of the history of the province (Nadeau 2012: 199–200).

Thus, the arrival of MNQ at this specific period seemed to echo the desire of Québécois to reconnect with their culture and folklore. Indeed, it gained momentum at a time where the sovereigntist project was no longer on the government's agenda, where the dissatisfaction of citizens with the government (provincial and federal) was at its height, and where Québécois feared they would lose their culture and values due to the greater mobility of peoples.

The third period of the scene: Between the stagnation and the professionalization of the black metal scene (2010–17)

As mentioned previously, a decline in the formation of new black metal bands characterizes the last period. Indeed, only one MNQ band was formed (Cantique Lépreux) and was constituted of the same line-up as Chasse-Galerie. However, this decline was not necessarily linked with a scene in peril; black metal and MNQ bands were performing on stage more than before. In Québec society, less attention was drawn toward the independence issues, which were reflected in the rise of new concerns in Québec society.

When examining data from *Metal Archives* (Figure 4.9), we see that only 77 bands were formed between 2010 and 2017, including only 5 in 2017, a figure similar to the first years of the scene. Moreover, *Metal Archives* reports that of the 123 new groups formed between 2002 and 2006 (the most thriving period), only 55 are still active today. Musically, this third period can be understood as a reinforcement of the aesthetic presented earlier.

This almost continuous decrease in the formation of new black metal groups (since 2006) has also been noticed by some interviewees (among others, Winterthrone 2016; Monarque Helserkr 2016; and Matrak 2014, 2018). For them, it can be explained by the average age of the scene members. Indeed, many turned 30 around this period, which also signifies that their personal obligation (study, work, family) took over the time they previously had for their band. Moreover, Monarque Helserkr and Matrak argue that the bands that are still active today[16] are often constituted by the same members.[17] Thus, the latter indicates a certain lack of succession and a stagnation of the scene, especially in recent years. Nevertheless, according to another portion of the interviewees—notably Nordet (2016) and Blanc Feu (member of Chasse-Galerie and Cantique Lépreux)

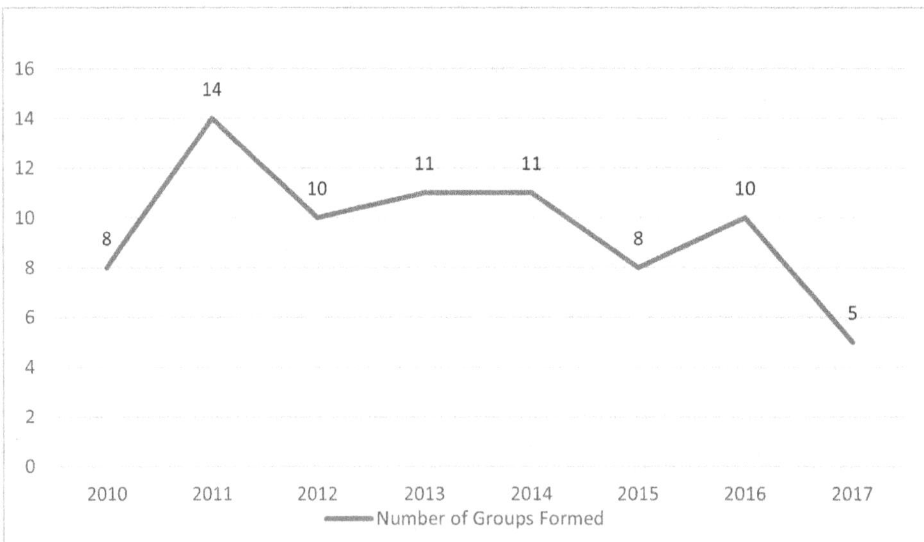

FIGURE 4.9: Annual formation of black metal bands in Québec (2010–17).

(2016)—the scene is seen as healthy. Indeed, groups such as Forteresse and Brume d'Automne, which were originally intended as being studio projects, also carry their nationalist discourse on stage (both on North American and European tours) during this last period.

Thus, we note that the decline in the formation of new groups in the scene is not necessarily synonymous with a decrease in the organization of activities and black metal shows. This willingness by the members of the community to continue spreading the nationalist message, even if fewer bands are joining the ranks, is also present in the Québec society of the last two decades.

The decline of the sovereigntist question in Québec society (2010–17)

This decade is marked by the rising of citizen political action. Indeed, several important measures of the provincial Charest government (such as the rising of tuition fees at the university level) has caused a strong dissatisfaction among the population (Côté 2011: 163). This civic protest materializes during the spring 2012 students' strike, which brought the province more closely aligned politically and culturally to the federal government. Indeed, this strike mobilized 300,000 students and led to the takeover of the PQ, with Pauline Marois at its head (Hurteau 2017: 1).

In 2012, influenced by the social movement for the destitution of the Charest government, the MNQ community allied themselves behind Option Nationale, a new left-wing party that gave a central place to the sovereigntist project. In an official statement written by Matrak and published on the Facebook page of Chasse-Galerie on August 18, 2012, the latter voices his exasperation toward the paternalistic policies, the disproportionate exploitation of nonrenewable natural resources, and the proven corruption of the PLQ government. The text ends with a support statement for Option Nationale signed by several MNQ groups (e.g., Chasse-Galerie, Brume d'Automne, and Forteresse). This is the only moment in the history of black metal in Québec where a portion of the scene is directly associated with a political party. In this case, the triggering element undeniably remains the political context of Québec at this point in time as well as the rise of citizen action, which probably influenced the members into this mobilization.

Even if this event allows us to better understand the direct influence that the Québec society has on the development of black metal, and afterwards of the MNQ, a question remains: to what extent is the narrative identity presented by the MNQ different or similar to the identity transmitted by Québec society? The last section of this chapter will deal with this aspect.

The distinctions and similarities characterizing the narrative identity of the MNQ and of Québec society

The narrative identity constructed by the MNQ members stems both from the black metal ideology, insofar as a majority prefers to perceive their musical creations as being independent of current political questions. However, this same narrative is also intimately linked with the way most Québécois interpret their own history.

More specifically, for many interviewees, the music from MNQ bands is perceived as being cut off from contemporary politics. Antoine (drummer from Monarque and Délétère) explains thus: "There is a difference between talking about one's cultural roots and cultural nostalgia, and the current political situation" (Antoine 2016: n.pag.). In this respect, as argued by Blanc Feu (2016), Athros (member of Forteresse) (2016), and Outre-Tombe (2016), current social issues remain deliberately omitted from the texts of the majority of groups, or otherwise treated as allegory (as it is the case with Chasse-Galerie), in order to avoid any comparison with a left-wing or right-wing political ideology. Indeed, Outre-Tombe stated,

> [o]n the political level, métal noir québécois doesn't really have a stature since [the groups] are not the representatives of any political party. What métal noir québécois does is simply remind us of what was going on in Charlevoix or in Estrie. They take *Les belles histoires des pays d'en haut*[18] and they put them into music in a metal way. (2016: n.pag.)

However, as stated by Winterthrone (2016) and Moribond (2016), the fact that the MNQ groups do not mainly talk about these contemporary aspects does not mean that they pay no attention to them; it means that the ideological and aesthetic concept of these groups is not oriented in this direction.

For the sociologist Keith Kahn-Harris (2004), this willingness to dissociate the music with the political context has also been described by as a fundamental characteristic of black metal. Indeed, he explains that in the black metal context, "[s]cenic discourses and practices attempt to assert that good music must be 'autonomous' from social structure. This is part of a long tradition of idealistic western musical discourse that has obscured the connections between music and society" (Kahn-Harris 2004: 107). In this sense, this separation between politics and music is directly linked with the black metal ideological codes.

Nevertheless, other interviewees (like Blanc Feu and Matrak) argue that MNQ remains linked with the current political situation. For example, Matrak claims that the political aspect is implicitly present in group music and manifests itself through the use of French lyrics. He also adds that the majority of the groups choose to sing in French since they believe that, even today, their language and culture are threatened by the inaction of the government and the disinterest of most of Québécois concerning the independence of the province (Matrak 2014, 2018). Thorleïf[19] (member of Délétère) even argues:

> From the moment we sing in French, we are aware that we are a Québec band, that we are part of a thing called métal noir québécois, that we give ourselves a certain coherence—whether lyrical or musical—whether we stand together in community [...] yes, we make choices. I will say that these are cultural and social choices, but ultimately, it has a political impact in Québec.
>
> (2016: n.pag.)

Yet, the perception held by the members of the MNQ regarding the valiant patriots fighting for freedom does not only stem from black metal and its attraction to the ancestors' fights; on the contrary, it also comes from Québécois' collective imagination. Indeed, as specialists in Québec literature Daniel Vaillancourt and Marilyn Randall indicate, over the years, a certain reinterpretation of the figure of the patriot has taken place in Québec and is now shared by several Québécois. First, by "figure" Vaillancourt and Randall (2001: 452) refer to the way in which the patriot, as an iconographic, literary or historical figure, is understood in the collective imagination of Québec. As Vaillancourt indicates, both in historical works and artworks following the defeat of the rebellion and afterwards, the typical patriot is often represented as the one on Julien's artwork (see Figure 4.8): a peasant warrior from the countryside, armed with a musket and about to repel the British invaders. However, even if the term "patriot" is usually associated with the love of the country, in early-nineteenth-century Canada, it had a completely different meaning. It related to a member of the Patriot Party and a city orator (Vaillancourt and Randall 2001: 462). Nevertheless, the failure of the rebellion leads to the downfall of these city orators who were initially idolized (such as Papineau).

Therefore, for Vaillancourt, this defeat is not only military; it is also a major political failure, where the hope of establishing a republic in Lower Canada had to be abandoned. According to Vaillancourt, it can explain "why, after the events of 1837, the figure of the patriot will be reactivated by retrenching the city orator" (Vaillancourt 2001: 465). This fall from the pedestal is visible in the iconography used, especially with the artwork *Un vieux de '37* by Julien.[20] Indeed, it is no longer the educated orator from the city who is represented, but the constructed vision of valiant patriot of the countryside (Vaillancourt 2001: 467). Moreover, this artwork remains an eloquent example of the revolutionary meaning that has been inscribed to it from the 1960s (as previously explained in the section dedicated to the second period of the scene).

Thus, a parallel can be drawn with the way in which the MNQ members perceive the struggles for independence. Indeed, just as the erasure of the role of the city orator after the Patriots Rebellion, the impact of politicians in the recent sovereigntist movement is generally omitted by MNQ groups. On the contrary, the latter—who regard the recent efforts of the independence movement as failures—prefer to draw on the past from inspiration which they consider to be more heroic. Thus, the ideological postures present in the discourse of the interviewees, such as the idealization of the peasant warrior who defended the nation, rather stem from this historical reinterpretation process coming from Québec society (Maclure 2000: 20). Even if, both in the nineteenth and in the twentieth century, the fight for the independence was mainly led by politicians, it was the failure of the latter that led, not only MNQ members, but also French-Canadians and Québécois, to draw on the past to build a more edifying version of their history. Then, in this sense, MNQ can be understood as being intimately linked with the actual society.

Conclusion

This chapter aimed to establish an *eventialization*—of the different sociopolitical events that have influenced Québec society since the 1990s—in order to demonstrate the intimate link between the MNQ community (emanating from the Québec black metal scene) and Québec society. In addition to drawing on the history of the province by adapting it to the black metal aesthetic, the groups remain influenced by the various political and social events that have shaped Québec society over the past 30 years (e.g., the two referendums on independence). Thus, even if the groups are not usually evoking any of the actual political conflicts in their songs, it would hardly be possible for such a community to exist if Québec was sovereign. Indeed, it is in response to a current dissatisfaction with the actual government that members of the MNQ groups are writing songs about the great deeds of their ancestors who fought for their recognition.

This chapter also demonstrated that the iconographic and musical elements used by the groups can be understood as a narrative identity. More specifically, by relating to the Patriots Rebellion and idealizing the past, the members are offering a *re*-narration of the history of Québec. However, this narrative remains intimately linked to that of a majority of Québécois, where the meanings attributed to the various symbols, images, or musical extracts used by MNQ groups reflect those of the culture and society from which they originated.

Therefore, the present political context plays a major role, even though community members do not always want to admit it. Indeed, this refusal to recognize the importance of the political context in black metal (shared notably by Winterthrone, Moribond, and Antoine) stems—as was previously presented through the discourse of Kahn-Harris—from a desire shared by black metal fans to cut the bridges between music and politics. Then, since the bands are not addressing actual society debates in a concrete way, MNQ is understood by many interviewees as having an "autonomous" status.

Finally, even if the interviewees all share their love for Québec and their desire to achieve independence, I discovered through interviews that their individual political positions remain distinct and fall within a private sphere; some advocate a left-wing as well as a right-wing political ideology. Thus, even if the discourse of the groups contributes to spread the nationalist claim, the individual political positions remain separate from the artistic productions of the groups. Indeed, despite the fact that MNQ's bands allied themselves to the Option Nationale Party in 2012, this affiliation has to be understood as punctual, as well as contextual. It could be argued that the absence of a clear political position regarding nationalism expressed by the MNQ remains intimately linked to the way in which nationalism has been perceived in Québec as a whole since the early 2000s: both as a right-wing and a left-wing movement.

NOTES

1. Unless otherwise stated, all French translation are from St. Laurent.
2. Throughout the 21 ethnographic interviews, I spoke with 25 members of the black metal scene, which were involved as musicians, music producer, sponsor, record label owner or fans. Most of them are male (three females were interviewed), are in their thirties, and have other careers to help them sustain their activities in the scene.
3. https://www.metal-archives.com. Accessed July 2, 2021.
4. Formed in 1804, this party is the first political party from Lower Canada. More specifically, it advocates "the equality of all citizens before the law" and therefore "the abolition of social privileges," which denounces the advantages reserved for certain members of society (often English-speaker) (Buckner 2013: n.pag.).
5. Papineau had already left the country at that point and was not hanged in 1839 (Buckner 2013: n.pag.).
6. The two main elements that led to the defeat of the first referendum were (1) the absence of consensus between the PQ members (concerning a possible economic partnership between the new country and Canada) and which generated numerous tensions; (2) the election of a new Canadian prime minister (Pierre Elliott Trudeau), who gained a lot of popularity in the province by promising to revaluate the decisional power of the province, but only in case of a winning vote against the separation.

7. Anhkrehg, Malvery, Slaotvean, Soulseasons, and Tenebrae are the first black metal groups that were formed in Québec province in 1993.
8. The *Metal Archives* data on the dissolution of the groups have not been considered. Indeed, they often remain incomplete (the year of dissolution is not always written), which did not allow a reliable graphical representation.
9. The first album of Darkthrone (*Soulside Journey*, 1991) was a death metal album.
10. Regarding the song "Lune funèbre," the subject of this song is not linked with nationalism, since it is about lycanthropy. However, the fact that the story is evolving in New France is to be mentioned for its originality.
11. For the federal government, to recognize Québécois people as a distinct society is a first step toward the recognition of a specific nation within Canada and another toward the separation of Québec, which is unacceptable (Monière 1999).
12. One of the strategies employed by Jean Chrétien's federal government was to discredit Québec's national assertion by transforming it into "congenital racism" (Monière 1999).
13. Heretic Blood (formed in 2005) can be considered as the version 1.0 of Forteresse (formed in 2006).
14. To listen to these three songs, please follow these YouTube links: "La mort d'un patriote" (https://www.youtube.com/watch?v=Y64E_Yzm3Vk&list=PLJ7MGcw79UQ5Mfm5Tnd4kSRL0DtPhrLW6&index=4&t=44s); "La patrie des sans-âme" (https://www.youtube.com/watch?v=Kr4J35wOJKQ&list=PLJ7MGcw79UQ5Mfm5Tnd4kSRL0DtPhrLW6&index=12); and "Une nuit pour la patrie" (https://www.youtube.com/watch?v=vTBfGNk2bjU&list=PLJ7MGcw79UQ5Mfm5Tnd4kSRL0DtPhrLW6&index=27). All accessed July 2, 2021.
15. To listen to these three other songs, please follow these YouTube links: "Quand les morts s'agitent" (https://www.youtube.com/watch?v=6A3ZNXyB-ro&list=PLJ7MGcw79UQ5Mfm5Tnd4kSRL0DtPhrLW6&index=6); "La moisson de la liberté" (https://www.youtube.com/watch?v=lILbCE-3yCs&list=PLJ7MGcw79UQ5Mfm5Tnd4kSRL0DtPhrLW6&index=26); and "Métal noir québécois" (https://www.youtube.com/watch?v=3HFtZ7Up5aY&list=PLJ7MGcw79UQ5Mfm5Tnd4kSRL0DtPhrLW6&index=29). All accessed July 2, 2021.
16. The interviews were done mostly in 2016. Then, the "current state" refers to this period.
17. Indeed, members of Chasse-Galerie also play in Cantique Lépreux, members of Délétère play in Monarque, just as members of Monarque and Chasse-Galerie are part of Forteresse.
18. *Les belles histoires des pays d'en haut* designates a Québec television series broadcast between 1956 and 1970, a series set at the end of the nineteenth century in the Laurentians region.
19. Thorleif is a PhD candidate in medieval history in Université Laval (Québec).
20. A similar figure of the patriot is also presented in the work from the historian François-Xavier Garneau (*Histoire du Canada depuis sa découverte jusqu'à nos jours* 1848) and in the novel of Pierre-Joseph-Olivier Chauveau (*Charles Guérin*, 1846) (Vaillancourt 2001: 468–69).

REFERENCES

Antoine (2016), in-person interview, Brûlerie St-Roch, Québec city, October 31.

Asakku, Asag (2012), "Entrevue avec Martin Marcotte (Sepulchral Productions)," *Métal obscur*, October 15, http://metalobscur.com/2012/10/15/entrevue-avec-martin-marcotte-sepulchral-productions/. Accessed November 19, 2015.

Athros (2016), in-person interview, La Source de la Martinière, Québec city, June 17.

Balthazar, Louis (2013), *Nouveau bilan du nationalisme*, Québec: VLB éditeur.

Bédard, Éric (2011), *Recours aux sources*, Montréal: Éditions du Boréal.

Béland, Daniel, and Lecours, André (2011), "Le nationalisme et la gauche au Québec," *Globe: À courant et à contre-courant: Les gauches québécoises depuis 1960*, 14:1, pp. 37–52.

Bellemare, Luc (2008), "Le Folklore, arme de persuasion dans la musique populaire québécoise avant et après l'âge d'or des chansonniers," in L. Bizzoni, and C. Prevost-Thomas (eds.), *La chanson francophone engagée*, Montréal: Triptyque, pp. 39–64.

Bizzoni, Lise, and Prevost-Thomas, Cécile (eds.) (2008), *La chanson francophone engagée*, Montréal: Triptyque.

Blanc Feu (2016), in-person interview, Nektar Caféologue, Québec city, September 27.

Brume d'Automne (2005), *Fiers et victorieux*, Winter Forest.

Bock-Côté (2007), "De la reconnaissance du Québécois à celle des Québécois: Retour sur la reconnaissance de la nation par le gouvernement de Stephen Harper à l'automne 2006," *Institut de recherche sur le Québec*, http://irq.quebec/wp-content/uploads/2015/03/ReconnaissanceNation.pdf. Accessed February 14, 2020.

Buckner, Philip A. (2013), "Rebellions of 1837–38," in A. Wilson-Smith (ed.), *The Canadian Encyclopedia*, July 15, https://www.thecanadianencyclopedia.ca/en/article/rebellions-of-1837. Accessed February 25, 2019.

Chasse-Galerie (2010), *Ars Moriendi*, Québec: Productions Frères Chasseurs.

Chasse-Galerie (2012), "Déclaration officielle," Facebook, August 18, https://www.facebook.com/profile.php?id=100034733666479, Accessed March 13, 2019.

Chevrier, Marc (2012), "La famille souverainiste en crise," in M. Fahmi (ed.), *L'état du Québec 2012*, Montréal: Éditions du Boréal, pp. 134–42.

Côté, Catherine (2011), "Les citoyens Québécois: Du cynisme à l'indignation," in M. Fahmi (ed.), *L'état du Québec 2012*, Montréal: Éditions du Boréal, pp. 163–68.

Darkthrone (1991), *Soulside Journey*, Dewsbury: Peaceville Records.

Darkthrone (1992), *A Blaze in the Northern Sky*, Dewsbury: Peaceville Records.

Daus, Sion (2016), in-person interview, Le Saint-Bock, Montréal, November 27.

Forteresse (2006), *Métal noir québécois*, Montréal: Sepulchral Productions.

Foucault, Michel (1994), *Dits et écrits, 1954–1988* (ed. D. Defert, and F. Ewald), Paris: Gallimard.

Frozen Shadows (1999), *Dans les bras des immortels*, Montréal: Sepulchral Productions.

Gall, Gerald L. (2006), "Meech Lake Accord," in A. Wilson-Smith (ed.), *The Canadian Encyclopedia*, February 7, https://www.thecanadianencyclopedia.ca/en/article/meech-lake-accord. Accessed March 12, 2019.

Geneviève (2016), in-person interview, Théâtre Plaza, Montréal, November 26.

Helserkr, Monarque, (2016), in-person interview, La Barberie, Québec city, August 24.

Hurteau, Philippe (2017), "Le mouvement étudiant a-t-il creusé son tombeau?," *Institut de recherche et d'information socioéconomique*, February 14, https://irirecherche.qc.ca/publications/gr%C3%A8ve2012. Accessed March 10, 2019.

Kahn-Harris, Keith (2004), "The failure of youth culture: Reflexivity, music, and politics in the Black metal scene," *European Journal of Cultural Studies*, 7:1, pp. 95–111.

Maclure, Jocelyn (2000), "Le projet nationaliste en transition: La fin des vaches sacrés?," in R. Cote (ed.), *Québec 2001: Annuaire politique, social, économique et culturel*, Montréal: Éditions Fides, pp. 91–97.

Matrak (2014), in-person interview, Café au Temps Perdu, Québec city, October 24.

Matrak (2018), in-person interview, Starbucks, Québec city, March 2.

Monière, Denis (1999), "Les débats idéologiques," in R. Boily (ed.), *L'année politique au Québec 1997–1998*, Montréal: Presse de l'Université de Montréal, https://pum.umontreal.ca/apqc/97_98/moniere/moniere.htm. Accessed March 1, 2019.

Moribond (2016), in-person interview, La Source de la Martinière, Québec city, June 17.

Myrkhaal (2016), in-person interview, McKibbins Irish Pub, Montréal, July 3.

Nadeau, Christian (2012), "Quel projet pour la gauche et la social-démocratie au Québec?," in M. Fahmi (ed.), *L'état du Québec 2012*, Montréal: Édition Boréal, pp. 164–70.

Nordet (2016), in-person interview, L'Anti Bar & Spectacles, Québec city, April 9.

Outre-Tombe (2016), in-person interview, St-Viateur Bagel, Montréal, November 24.

Parenteau, Danic, and Parenteau, Ian (2008), *Les idéologies politiques: Le clivage gauche-droite*, Montréal: Presses de l'Université du Québec.

Parenteau, Ian (2004), "La gauche en effervescence," in M. Venne (ed.), *L'annuaire du Québec*, Montréal: Éditions Fides, pp. 438–44.

Sébastien (2016), in-person interview, L'Archibald Microbrasserie, Québec city, December 9.

St-Jean, France (2009), "L'iconographie rébellienne, la face cachée de l'historiographie des rébellions de 1837–1838: Quelques études de cas," *Revue d'histoire intellectuelle de l'Amérique française*, 101:1, pp. 95–138.

Thorleïf (2016), in-person interview, Café Fou Aeliés, Québec city, December 16.

Vaillancourt, Daniel (2001), "Les têtes à Patriote: Une figure retorse au XIXe siècle," *Voix Et images*, 26:3, pp. 456–73.

Vaillancourt, Daniel, and Randall, Marilyn (2001), "Présentation: Généalogies de la figure du Patriote 1837-1838," *Voix et images*, 26:3, pp. 451–55.

Venne, Michel (2004), "Le Québec en ébullition," in M. Venne (ed.), *L'annuaire du Québec État du Québec 2005*, Montréal: Éditions Fides, pp. 18–19.

Winterthrone (2016), in-person interview, Café Sobab, Québec city, April 12.

Will (2016), in-person interview, Nacho Libre, Montréal, November 26.

5

Living Sonic Knowledge in South-Eastern Austria: The Sound History of the Metal Scene in Graz and Styria, c.1980 to the Present

Peter Pichler

Introduction

The authors of the case studies collected in this volume aim at shedding more nuanced light on the factors that keep metal scene communities alive or make them flourish, or conversely on the factors that contribute to the demise of a scene. Concepts from cultural history as an since the 1990s established academic discourse (Burke 2004; Hunt and Biersack 1989; McCaffery and Marsden 2014) and more specifically from "sound history" as a recent sub-discourse with its innovative approach to popular music cultures (Garrioch 2003; Hendy 2013; Paul and Schock 2013; Schrag 2011) can be helpful in analyzing such factors.

A very recent strand of historical scholarship, researchers from sound history look at the cultures of scenes as distinct but "glocally" (Robertson 1998) connected spheres of sonic experience and learning (for an analysis of metal's "musical language," see Elflein 2010). Defined by their own practices and rules, scenes (Bennett and Peterson 2004; Baulch 2007; Brown et al. 2016; Nohr and Schwab 2011; Wallach et al. 2011) form distinct "units" (Wallach and Levine 2011: 29–30) of hearing and listening to metal in varying local and regional contexts. Diachronically, scenic communities are structured by distinct patterns of local "sonic knowledge" that comes from the specific experience in each individual scene. Hence, understanding the sound history of a scene can help understand why and how some scenes stay alive or flourish while others stagnate or even dissolve.

Drawing on this recent approach, in this chapter I discuss the sound history of the metal scene in the Austrian *Bundesland* (i.e., the German-language notion for states in the Austrian federal system) of Styria with its capital town Graz, for the period from 1980 to the present. The members of this regional scene in South-Eastern Austria developed a distinct inventory of sonic knowledge. How they did so since the early 1980s affected their Styrian way of "living metal."

In my discussion of this sound history, I take three steps. In a short *first* part on "sound history" and "sonic knowledge," I introduce the theoretical lens through which I look at this scene. Methodologically, this is necessary to familiarize readers with the used theoretical framework.

Plunging right into this sound history, the *second* step is giving a chronological overview of the three phases of the Styrian metal community's history since the early 1980s. Herein, we can identify the history of the scene's networks and institutions. However, at this point this still will be a structural overview that cannot accurately identify this scene's distinctness as a community of sonic knowledge.

Hence, in my *third* and last substantial part, at the base of an analysis of the Metal on the Hill festival in Graz as a paradigmatic recent scene event, I will address the question of how exactly the community's sonic knowledge contributed to shape the scene's distinctness and helped the community flourish in a new "digital age" since the turn of the millennium.

The theoretical lens: The sound history and the sonic knowledge of local metal scenes

Some years ago, Kahn-Harris (2016; for Kahn-Harris's important discussion of the subgenres of extreme metal, Kahn-Harris 2007) called for self-reflexive memory-building by both the metal scenes and by the scholars in metal studies. Despite this call for reflexive memory-building and history-building, so far the academic history of metal scenes has been written by sociologists, culturalists, philosophers, and musicologists (Brown 2011; Hickam 2015; Kahn-Harris 2011; Klypchak 2016; Masciandaro 2011; Weinstein 2011, 2016).

Of course, this is not "wrong." However, sociologists write in the academic style of sociology, cultural studies scholars use their own theories, philosophers employ the philosopher's gaze, and musicologists analyze the structures of the music itself. Conversely, historians ask their own questions on scene-building. Their answers have the potential of theoretically and empirically enriching existing scholarship. Written by a trained cultural historian, this scene case study also is an intervention into these emerging debates.

In current metal research, the concept of "scene/s," however polymorphically utilized (Baulch 2007; Bennett and Peterson 2004; Diaz-Bone 2010; Kahn-Harris 2007; Wallach and Levine 2011; Varas-Díaz et al. 2016), is used to describe metal communities in a supposedly "holistic" way (Kahn-Harris 2007: 11–13). From a trained historian's point of view, these current scene community theories do not reflect satisfyingly the *longue durée* dimension characteristic of scene histories, as they usually virtually isolate those scenes in history in a "presentist" mode of analysis (Pichler 2020). Crucially, metal communities develop over longer periods and thus require us to focus on their diachronic knowledge processes over decades. Commonly, a scene's distinct archive of local metal practices and knowledge is developed, established, and disseminated within the regional cultural landscape over years and decades. Scenes have elementary diachronic patterns (Pichler 2016, 2020). In order to better grasp this cultural-historical dimension, these diachronic patterns (i.e., the individual culture and identity a of scene, that is what I call a scene's "sonic knowledge" in the following sections) deserve closer attention.

To familiarize my readers with this approach, it makes sense discussing this problem at the base of Wallach and Levine's (2011) theory of scene transformation. This theory has grown influential since its first publication. In many ways, it is representative of current paradigms in metal studies. Wallach and Levine defined metal scenes as follows:

> We regard metal scenes as loosely bounded *functional units* containing a finite number of participants at any one time. [...]
> 1. They act as *conduits* to the global circulation of metal sounds and styles.
> 2. They provide gathering places for the *collective consumption* of metal artefacts and the display of metal-related fashion and expertise.
> 3. They *provide sites for local performance and artefactual production*. At this point some interaction with the larger economic order of society becomes unavoidable, and *scenic institutions* become vital.
> 4. They *promote local artists* to the larger network of scenes. These promotional aims are not usually oriented towards commercial interests and are rarely focused on one single, exceptional band.
>
> (2011: 29–30, original emphasis)

That is a helpful starting point for scene research. Yet, this notion of scenes implicates an analytical presentness. The authors look only at the always present spaces of scenes, seemingly restricting themselves to looking foremost at the synchronic dimension of history, for example, the historically isolated scenes of the 1980s or of the 1990s (Walser 1993; Weinstein 1991). They approach scenes in their present moments, rather oddly isolated from history. Not isolated in a sense that there is no historical thinking in metal research at all (Coenen 2014; Varas-Díaz et al. 2016; Zaddach 2019), but in a sense that there could be a much more thorough historicity in metal studies when it would take full advantage of the expertise of history as a scientific discipline. Current "scene histories" do so only in a limited sense. Thus, this paradigm lacks a clearer sense of historicity, despite the call for reflexive memory-building (Kahn-Harris 2016; Pichler 2020). I suppose that the expertise of historians broadly and of sound historians in particular can help addressing this issue and refining our theoretical treatment of scene-building processes.

This said, I conduct my research on Styria under a theoretical framing of what I call the sonic knowledge of a scene community (Pichler 2018, 2020). For this purpose, the (never fully reachable) meta-theoretical ideal would be completely unwrapping the diachronic patterns that rendered this community distinct from its direct environment and from other metal culture communities around the globe (Nohr and Schwab 2011; Wallach et al. 2011). My starting point is the above-mentioned recent research discourse of sound history (Garrioch 2003; Hendy 2013; Paul and Schock 2013; Schrage 2011). This sub-discourse of cultural history already produced fresh conceptual insights into the history of musical cultures. In an important special issue of the German-language journal *Zeithistorische Forschungen* (*Studies in Contemporary History*) devoted to the sound history of the twentieth century, Dominik Schrage characterized sound history's grasp of music like this:

> The musical mode of hearing enables us as subjects to experience comprehensibly the effects of sounds and rhythms, be it contemplatively or expressively—plunging into music or dancing to it. Like images, sounds cannot be transferred to linguistic meaning without fractures; but both are experienced as being in harmony with each other, correspond with moods, affections, and emotions in the experiencing subject. Sounds, melodies, chords, and rhythms share a fundament across cultures, but in different musical cultures they are encoded, systematized and linked to harmony theories in different ways.
>
> (Schrage 2011: 269–76, author's translation)

A fruit of the "the new cultural history" (Burke 2004; Hunt and Biersack 1989; McCaffery and Marsden 2014), sound history scholarship (Garrioch 2003; Hendy 2013; Paul and Schock 2013; Schrage 2011) offers a sophisticated theoretical approach to music history. Sound-historical research thematizes the ways how acoustic sense-making—that is, hearing and listening—influenced history. Sound historians examine how hearing and listening changed over periods of decades during the twentieth and twenty-first centuries. They ask for the history of the patterns that influenced the "cultural ear."[1] For instance, the dramatically changing acoustic worlds of big cities in the first decades of the twentieth century, when the automobile conquered the cities, affected immensely how people constructed their view of the industrialized world (Garrioch 2003; Hendy 2013; Paul and Schock 2013; Schrage 2011).

Following this approach, I suggest that also metal music discourse in general and local metal scenes in particular have their distinct sound histories (Pichler 2018 2020). Drawing on sound history, one can assume that the historically varying settings, in that people have heard metal and listened to metal since the inception of metal around 1970, affected how scenes were constructed. The varying local contexts of scenes around the world seem to have produced varying local spheres of acoustic sense-making (Berger 1999, 2009; Brown et al. 2016; Diaz-Bone 2010; Nohr and Schwab 2011; Wallach et al. 2011; Weinstein 1991). For historians, it is crucial to ask how the acoustic sense-making in the scenes changed patterns or persisted over periods of years and decades.

In metal history, there is a well-known paradigmatic example of such processes. The cultural setting of hearing and listening in 1970, when Black Sabbath's self-titled debut was released, differed eminently from the one in 2013, when their last LP *13* was issued. In 1970, fan communities listened to music recordings on vinyl or on the radio. Nowadays, we listen to the debut and to *13* on the global Spotify platform. Today, if one does not want to listen to Black Sabbath anymore, he or she can jump to Rihanna or Kanye West in a second, or even to another medium like YouTube. There is much more fluidness, and there are many more cross-genre jumps. Overwhelmingly, we face massively more music to choose from. Hence, in 2020 and beyond we experience very different forms of hearing and listening and have a very different "cultural metal ear." These drastic changes need to be studied over periods of decades. From a sound-historical view, these changes are the diachronic backbone of the development of scenic communities, as well in the Styrian case.

Thinking along these lines, I introduced the notion of "sonic knowledge" to get a theoretical grip on such long-lasting processes (Pichler 2018, 2020). Sonic knowledge is the (intuitive) knowledge of the cultural concepts (e.g., "heaviness," the "riff," "loudness," "speed," significant narratives, metaphors, idioms, etc.) that have characterized metal in the long run since around 1970. The notion is thought to capture the ways these concepts have changed or have persisted over long periods. Locally varying and globally shared forms of such knowledge keep scenes together in the long run (Berger 1999, 2009; Diaz-Bone 2010; Elflein 2010; Walser 1993). Most scenes seem to have sonic knowledge archives that feature both local and global patterns—they are "glocal" in such a sound-historical sense (Robertson 1998).

It is "sonic" knowledge because all cultural categories in question (i.e., heaviness) depend on music and sound. In the long temporal range, scenes are structured by the knowledge of these categories. Indeed, the scene communities Wallach and Levine (2011: 29–30) described as "loosely bounded functional units" normally are very densely bounded diachronic temporal units. Scenes crystalize over time around those categories. Applying this view, I now turn to a chronological overview of the Styrian case as an example of such a scene sound history.

The sound history of the Styrian metal scene since the early 1980s: A chronological overview

The early 1980s were the years when first institutions and networks of an independent scene emerged in the Austrian *Bundesland* of Styria with its capital Graz. To suppose, this corelated with European and global trends of scene-building (Wallach et al. 2011; Weinstein 1991).[2] Having a population of about 1.2 million, Styria is located in the South-Eastern "corner" of Austria and borders Slovenia. Since the Habsburg Monarchy, the southern parts of Styria are closely connected to Slovenia (Pickl 2004). With about 300,000 inhabitants, Graz is the cultural and economic heart of Styria, thus also the most important place for the regional metal scene. The scene is most dense there. However, also the northern and more mountainous areas with smaller industrial towns such as Kapfenberg and Leoben have been taking part in scene-building activities since 1980. The eastern areas with the towns of Weiz and Gleisdorf have played a role in this history, too. Furthermore, Deutschlandsberg in the west has artists and scene networks. These networks and structures formed the realm in which the sonic knowledge of the scene was developed, evolved, and exists until today.

Today, the Styrian metal community is alive and well, and it seems to flourish in Graz in particular. With Wallach and Levine (2011), it is a structural "functional unit." However—as I will try to show—it is more than this; it is a historically grown community of distinct sonic knowledge. The scene, in terms of preferred styles of subgenres and the social composition with respect to gender, sex, age, and class of the members, seems to reflect global trends of diversification in metal scenes around the globe (Pichler 2016; Nohr and Schwab 2011; Wallach et al. 2011). The distinctness of this scene comes from a hybridization of local traditions and local patriotism with global streams of metalness. This hybrid "bricolage" (Weinstein) of Styrian-ness and global metalness renders the scene distinct. Providing building-blocks for this distinctness, local hearing and listening experiences within the scene helped integrating the scene in the long run. However, current scene theories, such as Kahn-Harris's (2007), Wallach and Levine's (2011), or also Bennett and Peterson's (2004), cannot explain this. As we will see, looking at this "glocal" hybridization of global metal with local culture through the lens of sound history and sonic knowledge can help us understand the scene's individuality.

Besides a rather small number of qualification works (Edlinger 2017; Sackl 2010, 2014), there is few scientific production on the history of metal in Graz, Styria, and Austria. But predominantly on the web, there is a large corpus of media works that deal with metal and metal history in this area (Kleine Zeitung 2015; Kronen Zeitung 2017; Music Austria 2018; Orf 2014). In addition, there is a dense discourse of webzines (*Blackmetal.at* 2019; *Darkscene* 2019; *Metalunderground Austria* 2019; *Stormbringer* 2019), fan-sites, Facebook groups (Der Metal Ferdl 2019), and even a metal travel guide to Graz and Styria (Metal Travel Guide 2018). A book and online project called *Styrian Metal History*, initiated and written by local musician and author Andreas Krammer (2019) aims at codifying a historical encyclopedia of Styrian metal artists. Locally, this reflects global metal culture's trends of the building of cultural memories. Already here, we see that the sound history of the scene moved on from analog and "real" spheres to the digital spheres of the web. This has consequences for the scene's identity. On balance, the Styrian metal scene history since 1980 consisted of three phases.

A *first* pioneering phase in the 1980s saw the foundation and establishment of first scene sites and structures. The local history of "Club Q," a subcultural club, concert location, and pub established in Graz in 1981, is an important example (Club Q 2019). It has been an institution of the scene since then, where, even today, many young metalheads have their initiation to the scene in this club with its unique environment of sonic experience. Concert venues like "Explosiv Jugend- und Kulturzentrum Graz" (Explosiv 2019), supported by the local communist party, and other youth clubs are examples, too. In Northern Styria, there have been venues and youth clubs like Jugendzentrum Bunte Fabrik ("Youth center colorful factory," founded in Kapfenberg in 1982) (Bunte Fabrik 2019) and Jugendzentrum Spektrum ("Youth center Spektrum," already founded in Leoben in 1978) (Spektrum 2019)—this is what Wallach and Levine would call "scenic institutions" (Wallach and Levine 2011: 29–30). The *Styrian Metal History* project shows instructively that, with countable numbers of new artists, this was the decade of the breakthrough of metal culture in this region (Krammer 2019), and hence it was also the decade of the emergence of the scene's first patterns.

That period was followed by a *second* phase of the intensification, diversification, and consolidation of the metal scene in the 1990s. Seen through the prism of Wallach and Levine's (2011: 29–30) theory, this was the point when "interaction with the larger economic order of society becomes unavoidable." Again, only looking at that one point of this history cannot explain the long-range evolvements. As said, this phase lasted the whole decade of the 1990s and brought a growing number of artists, festivals, gigs, and networks—which became important structural spaces, in which the scene's sonic knowledge could be practiced and learned. As the scene grew denser over a period of ten years, extrapolating one individual point out of this structural process appears reductionist.

A part of this process, the history of the globally operating record label Napalm Records (2019a) started in Eisenerz in 1992. Artists like death and thrash metal group Darkfall (formed in Graz in 1995) (Darkfall Official Website 2019) or black metal band Asmodeus (formed as Diabolus in Graz in 1996) (Asmodeus Official Website 2019) have been active since that phase. The concert venue and club Nachtexpress (Nachtexpress 2019), led by local musician Kurt "Mr. Voice" Haid, is an important part of the rock and metal scene since 1992. Again, those were scenic institutions. Yet why they persisted or changed in the long run, and how were they able to integrate the scene is not explainable with Wallach and Levine (2011). One has to look more closely at the diachronic history (Pichler 2020) as a distinct enculturation of the "metal ear" in a local context.

Since about 2000, the scene is in a *third* period, in which (as in practically all other local or regional scenes in the world) "real" and digital patterns of scene-construction and scene-transformation happen in interrelation (Bennett and Peterson 2004; Kahn-Harris 2016). In this phase, the local concert venue project Pop Culture (PPC) (Project Pop Culture Official Website 2019) was established in Graz in 2002, with the support of the local government. With artistic projects like symphonic metal group Visions of Atlantis (Visions of Atlantis 2019), pagan metal band Heathen Foray (Heathen Foray 2019), heavy metal band Apis (Apis 2019) or black metal band Ellende (Ellende 2019), the scene flourishes until today. Digital scene media like the webzines *Blackmetal.at* (2019), *Darkscene* (2019), *Metalunderground Austria* (2019), and *Stormbringer* (2019) are recent developments characterizing this phase. It is one of the most pressing questions to find out how this shift from the analog and "real-life" production of the scene's shared sonic knowledge to learning and practicing it (also) in digital discourse modified or influenced this sound history.

Hence, in this phase in the new millennium, the Styrian metal community is alive and well because its infrastructure and knowledge forms have been modified and adapted to the context of digitalization. Now, music, merchandize, and several other kinds of identity-constructing elements of the culture predominantly circulate on the web. The mentioned webzines form a "glocal," hypertextual hub of such purposes. The hub is a structural hinge where the global streams of metalness and local aspects can flow into each other. With social media, they help the scene to keep integrated in this new period.

Also, the crucial commercial stakeholders of the scene (e.g., Napalm Records) started to heavily intervene into this digital yet (somehow) still Styrian sphere. It was that digital realm that made Napalm Records (2019a), with its large webstore, become a "global player" of metal. Yet the company retains its "home-base" in the local area and keeps in touch with scene actors. Also, practically all the venues, pubs, and clubs I spoke of before (see Club Q 2019; Explosiv Official Website 2019; Nachtexpress 2019; PPC 2019) as well as local artists (Apis 2019; Darkfall 2019; Heathen Foray 2019) use this huge sphere to promote themselves and make themselves visible. In short, since 2000 the scene advanced to the digital sphere and adapted its infrastructures accordingly.

To recap, the history of the local heavy metal scene in this South-Eastern Austrian region developed over three discernable phases since the 1980s. The scenic structures and networks can be grasped using current scene theories, but only so rather oddly isolated in history. What cannot be explained when employing current theories is how the history of the shared sonic knowledge of the scene developed. Because the sociological look at the structures only gives a rather reductionist historical interpretation, it is not clear how exactly these structures and networks were spaces of the production of the scene's knowledge. Hence, in my final substantial section, I analyze a paradigmatic key event of the scene's community under the concept of sonic knowledge. My aim is to illuminate how this approach can produce new insights.

"How exactly does this sound history work?": The Metal on the Hill festival in Graz as a recent example of the Styrian scene's sonic knowledge

In the previous section, we developed first a chronological account—a macro-narrative—of the sound history of the Styrian scene. In this, the structures and networks of the local Styrian scene shined through as important structural institutions. These structures build something like a form-like social "vessel," in that the sonic knowledge of this community was established. Yet, this knowledge itself cannot be revealed when limiting the analysis to the scene as a "functional unit" in Wallach and Levine's sense (2011: 29–30). In order to grasp what happened within this vessel, one must dig deeper and ask how exactly the shared knowledge of this community was developed, learned, and further evolved within it.

In the following, I look at a the Metal on the Hill festival as a recent key event of the processes within the vessel. This provides us with the occasion of identifying one of the recent definitional patterns of the community: the current narrative that the scene constructs of its position in the cultural landscape of Graz and Styria. Examining this example cannot unwrap the entire identity of this scene. However, it can show where the scene stands at the moment as an individual community of sonic knowledge.

Metal on the Hill is a festival which the big genre label Napalm Records (2019a, 2019b) organizes in Graz since 2016. Taking place in the center of the town each year, the festival has become a crucial event for scene. It is two days of practicing, reestablishing, and further developing the local community's identity. At Metal on the Hill, the scene's shared sonic knowledge—as the most recent result of the almost four decades of the sound history we already saw—is staged, practiced, and celebrated. Growing from a one-day event to a two-day event since 2017, this festival takes place in the venue of Kasemattenbühne ("Casemates stage") on the Schlossberg ("Castle mountain"), the hill in the center of the city. Kasemattenbühne is an old vault of reddish brick walls, which had been used for storage as a part of the town's castle in Renaissance times (City of Graz Official Website 2016). Under historical auspices, also looking to practices of historic reenactment (Braun et al. 2014), it had been modified into a *Freilichtbühne* ("a small open-air arena"). The atmosphere of the event—as witnessed also by the author in 2016 and 2017—reflects an at first glance peculiar, but in fact perfectly working hybridization of Styrian tradition and global metal culture.

On the one hand, this seems to be another indication that global metal culture touches on areas of the cultural mainstream (Pichler 2018, 2020). On the other hand, much more significant for our research, is the fact that, spatially and semiotically, the culture of (extreme) metal has reached the very heart of an Austrian and European city. As mentioned earlier, Graz is the second largest urban agglomeration in Austria with 300,000 inhabitants and has so integrated extreme forms of heavy metal into its municipal culture. To be sure, the fact that Napalm Records is based in Eisenerz in Northern Styria did help smooth this process. This means that the scene's sonic knowledge is recodified each year in the heart of Styria.

Within the cultural vessel of this event, the global stream of metal discourse (represented by the headliners of the festival since 2016: Arch Enemy, Satyricon, Blind Guardian, Paradise Lost, Powerwolf, and Hammerfall) (Napalm Records 2020) is taken in by the Styrian community in their local context. In this process, both the global of metal and the local of metal are (re-)forged into something new and unique: the distinct sonic knowledge of this scene. For this scene, Styrian traditions, semiotics, and dialect language, put into the context of the global metal discourse, are the fundaments for its own imagined community.

So, a restrengthening of the distinct sonic knowledge of the Styrian metal scene takes place each year at Metal on the Hill. The shared identity, which keeps the scene together, is a strange brew of the global imaginaries, sounds, and practices of metal juxtaposed with Styrian language, dialects, spaces, and history. The venue of the festival (the Kasemattenbühne as a spatial representation of the history of

FIGURE 5.1: Audience, Metal on the Hill, Graz, August 13, 2016. Photo credit: Peter Pichler.

Graz and Styria since Renaissance times) already paradigmatically illustrates this juxtaposition. Figure 5.1, which shows the audience in 2016 practicing the "metal horns" as global metal code in this local setting, captures the hybridization of local tradition with global metal culture.

For an in-depth analysis of the event's specific role in the Styrian scene sound history, the "blazon," which Napalm Records created to promote the festival in 2019 (see Figure 5.2), makes a paradigmatic semiotic example. Metaphorically, the picture perfectly captures how the festival "works" as a historical event.

The image displays the official blazon of the Republic of Austria, the *Bundesadler* ("federal eagle"). In addition, the traditional symbol of Styrian identity—a white panther on green ground—is standing right behind the *Bundesadler*, the panther's head with the flame-like red tongue well visible. The original Austrian blazon's hammer and sickle have been replaced by two swords. Here, the local metal scene is imagined in a specific semiotic way. The original Austrian *Bundesadler* and the Styrian panther stand for the sovereignty of the community of the state.

FIGURE 5.2: Metal on the Hill "blazon" 2019. Image source: Napalm Records 2019b.

Both represent the state community's prerogative of making and enforcing the law. By transforming the blazon into a metalness version of both, the image tells that now the Styrian metal scene could (or even *should*) make and enforce their own scene-laws at Metal on the Hill. Hence, the scene is imagined as having the power of living metal in Styrian ways. It is imagined as being a community in Graz of its own.

Allegorically, this picture depicts exactly how the sound history of the local scene works currently. Over the two days of the festival, about 2,500 scene members and the above-mentioned scene stakeholders (e.g., artists, pubs, labels, shops, journalists) take part in a big event, in which global metal culture (in the allegory of the image: the swords; in the lived practice at Metal on the Hill; the forming of mosh-pits; wearing battle vests and band t-shirts; showing the "metal horns"; discussing globally important records; and so on) is employed as a weapon-like tool in "conquering" Styria and Graz. The playful aggressiveness in the metaphorical act of the blazon describes perfectly how the scene uses metal's global language to fortify its own local standing: Metal claimed and received Styrian cultural space.

Each year, Schlossberg and Kasemattenbühne are "conquered" as Styrian metal spaces. The community and its shared sonic knowledge are on the way to becoming an even-more established and respected part of the local cultural life—perhaps even a mainstream one.

Now, how exactly does the theory of sonic knowledge help us in understanding this scene? If we interpret the discussed event as an annually repeated reperformance and recodification of the sonic knowledge that has been encultured in the Styrian scene since the early 1980s, over four decades now, then it is much more than an isolated event. Under the theory of sonic knowledge, Metal on the Hill is a quintessentially historical event, which continues each year to write the sound history of *this* metal community. I think the crucial point is that the notion of sonic knowledge allows us to describe how exactly the collective knowledge of the scene is to be seen against the backdrop long-term developments. Currently, the scene members together, as a community of Styrian metalheads, are enculturing a shared narrative of "conquering" Styria and Graz at Metal on the Hill.

This narrative of an "usurpation" of the Styrian identity—perfectly staged and exploited in Napalm Records' marketing campaign (see Figure 5.2; Napalm Records 2019b)—characterizes the present state of affairs. Seen historically, the "usurpation" narrative is a logical symptom of the current period of the digitalization of the scene since the turn of the millennium. Sonic knowledge theorizing sharpens our view on the historicity of the scene in this phase. It shows us that the "real" and "analog" event of Metal on the Hill in fact has benefitted from the opportunities of the digital age—it is worth noting that the metaphorical image we discussed above was retrieved from the web. Also, the marketing campaign for the 2020 edition of the festival follows this strategy (Napalm Records 2020).

As the result of this in-depth analysis, Metal on the Hill thus should be interpreted as an event deeply rooted in history and as having far-reaching consequences. The successful "conquest" of a well-respected place in the local cultural landscape is Metal on the Hill's function as an individual event in this sound history. Sound history and sonic knowledge theorizing help us recognize the "conquest"/"usurpation" narrative as one of the patterns that currently stabilize the scene and keep it vital in a phase of the "abundance" of metal-related information on the world wide web (Kahn-Harris 2016).

Conclusion

I have argued that drawing on theories from recent sound history scholarship (Garrioch 2003; Hendy 2013; Paul and Schock 2013; Schrage 2011), understood as an innovative approach to popular music cultures, makes an exciting enrichment for metal studies. Above all, drawing on theories that ask for the development of scenes over long periods of the late twentieth and early twenty-first centuries could nurture scholarship's self-reflexivity (Kahn-Harris 2016). My theory of sonic knowledge—understood as the (intuitive) knowledge of the cultural concepts that keep metal scenes integrated in the long run—is a proposal in this respect.

Applying this theory to studying the local heavy metal scene in the South-Eastern Austrian region of Styria, with a focus on the capital city Graz, helped us identify three distinct periods of metal history there. In a *first* pioneering phase in the 1980s, first scene structures and networks appeared: subcultural pubs, venues, record stores, and labels that supported local artists and connected them to the global flux of metal discourse.

A *second* phase, beginning around 1990, brought about the diversification, intensification, and consolidation of the local metal community—in terms of structures and networks, but also in terms of countable numbers of artists. Several local bands that started out in this period are still active and successful. As an example of the interwovenness of local and global metal discourses, the globally operating Styrian label Napalm Records started in this era.

The *third* period of this scene's sound history, which began around 2000 and lasts until the present, deserves our closest attention. This is not only the case because this is the ongoing era of the scene; having happened around the turn of the millennium, we can see a structural shift in the scene's modes of sonic knowledge production. Its sonic knowledge began to be produced, learned, and circulated in new ways: As in practically any local scenes across the globe, the new digital age brought about an almost overwhelming availability of digital metal spaces—a new phase of an "abundance" (Kahn-Harris 2016) of metal-related contents.

As my analysis of the Metal on the Hill festival has illustrated, in this current phase it was crucial that the scene learned to creatively and playfully combine the "real" and analog aspects of metal life (e.g., concerts, pubs, venues, shops) with the digital metal spheres (e.g., webzines, web-projects like *Styrian Metal History*, web-shops, social media). This was necessary in order to successfully keep the scene integrated. Historically, the "usurpation" narrative cultivated around this festival is a paradigmatic symptom of this. The Styrian way of living sonic knowledge today is both: analog and digital. So maybe it is real in a new, digitally transformed way. This result also makes the decisive matter to reflect upon forthcoming conceptual and empirical research.

If we see the sound history of this scene as a knowledge history, which was culturally structured by the scene members' shared urge to keep alive their common knowledge, then the "glocal" digitalization of Styrian metalness is revealed as the scene's main challenge of the last twenty years. For today's digital age, the case study of Styria and Metal on the Hill seems to be a paradigmatic one, in which a local scene learned to creatively and playfully take the opportunities of the new age. In this new age, the "real" and the digital, thus even more than before also the local and the global (a new intensity of the "glocal"?), are to be combined. With the constitution of the "usurpation" narrative, the Styrian metalheads faced this challenge successfully—at least for the moment.

Acknowledgments

This research was made possible through generous funding from Austrian Science Fund (FWF) [P 32982-G].

NOTES

1. I thank all the participants and discussants at the panel "History" at the ISMMS conference in Nantes on June 19, 2019, for their thoughts on this.
2. I thank Prof. Dr. Anita Ziegerhofer for providing reflections on the chronology of my examination. I also thank Prof. Dr. Hiebaum for his feedback.

REFERENCES

Apis (2019), "Startseite," Facebook, https://www.facebook.com/pg/apismusic/. Accessed April 18, 2019.

Asmodeus Official Website (2019), "Home page," https://www.asmodeus.at/. Accessed May 28, 2019.

Baulch, Emma (2007), *Making Scenes: Reggae, Punk, and Death Metal in 1990s Bali*, Durham: Duke University Press.

Bennett, Andy, and Peterson, Richard (eds.) (2004), *Music Scenes: Local, Translocal, and Virtual*, Nashville: Vanderbilt University Press.

Berger, Harris M. (1999), *Metal, Rock, and Jazz: Perception and the Phenomenology of Musical Experience*, Hanover: Wesleyan University Press.

Berger, Harris M. (2009), *Stance: Ideas about Emotion, Style, and Meaning for the Study of Expressive Culture*, Middletown: Wesleyan University Press.

Black Sabbath (2013), *13*, Santa Monica: Vertigo Records.

Blackmetal.at (2019), "Home page," http://www.blackmetal.at/. Accessed May 27, 2019.

Braun, Micha, Heeg, Günther, Krüger, Lars, and Schäfer, Helmut (eds.) (2014), *Reenacting History: Theater and Geschichte*, Berlin: Theater der Zeit.

Brown, Andy R. (2011), "Heavy genealogy: Mapping the currents, contraflows and conflicts of the emergent field of metal studies, 1978–2010," *Journal for Cultural Research*, 15:3, pp. 213–42.

Brown, Andy R., Spracklen, Karl, Kahn-Harris, Keith, and Niall W. R. Scott (eds.) (2016), *Global Metal Music and Culture: Current Directions in Metal Studies*, New York: Routledge.

Bunte Fabrik (2019), "Startseite," Facebook, https://www.facebook.com/buntefabrik/. Accessed May 7, 2019.

Burke, Peter (2004), *What Is Cultural History?*, Cambridge: Cambridge University Press.

City of Graz Official Website (2016), "Home page," https://www.graz.at. Accessed August 2, 2019.

Club Q (2019), "Startseite," Facebook, https://www.facebook.com/pg/ClubQGraz/. Accessed May 7, 2019.

Coenen, Ekkehard (2014), "Headbanging in Nairobi: The emergence of the Kenyan metal scene and its transformation of the metal code," *Metal Music Studies*, 1:1, pp. 105–25.

Darkfall Official Website (2019), "Home page," http://www.darkfall.at/. Accessed May 28, 2019.

Darkscene (2019), "Home page," http://www.darkscene.at/. Accessed May 27, 2019.

Der Metal Ferdl (2019), "Startseite," Facebook, https://www.facebook.com/der.metal.ferdl/. Accessed May 27, 2019.

Diaz-Bone, Rainer (2010), *Kulturwelt, Diskurs und Lebenssti: Eine diskurstheoretische Erweiterung der Bourdieuschen Distinktionstheorie*, Wiesbaden: Verlag für Sozialwissenschaften.

Edlinger, Christoph C. (2017), *Louder Than Hell: Über die Rezeption von Heavy Metal Musik im Kontext biografischer Lebensbewältigung im Jugend- und jungen Erwachsenenalter*, master's thesis, Graz: University of Graz.

Elflein, Dietmar (2010), *Schwermetallanalysen: Die musikalische Sprache des Heavy Metal*, Bielefeld: Transcript.

Ellende (2019), "Startseite," Facebook, https://www.facebook.com/ellende.official/. Accessed April 18, 2019.

Explosiv Official Website (2019), "Home page," http://www.explosiv.at/. Accessed May 7, 2019.

Gardernour Walter, Brenda, Riches, Gabby, Snell, Dave, and Bardine, Bryan (eds.) (2016), *Heavy Metal Studies and Popular Culture*, Houndmills: Palgrave Macmillan.

Garrioch, David (2003), *Sounds of the City: The Soundscape of Early Modern European Towns*, Cambridge: Cambridge University Press.

Heathen Foray (2019), "Startseite," Facebook, https://www.facebook.com/HeathenForay0/. Accessed April 18, 2019.

Hendy, David (2013), *Noise: A Human History of Sound and Listening*, London: Profile Books.

Hickam, Brian (2015), "Amalgamated anecdotes: Perspectives on the history of metal music and culture studies," *Metal Music Studies*, 1:1, pp. 5–23.

Höpflinger, Anna-Katahrina (forthcoming), *Von Repräsentation zu Emotion: Die Rezeption religiöser Codes in vestimentärer Populärkultur am Beispiel der Black Metal-Szene*, habilitation thesis, Luzern: Universität Luzern.

Hunt, Lynn, and Biersack, Aletta (eds.) (1989), *The New Cultural History*, Berkeley: University of California Press.

Kahn-Harris, Keith (2007), *Extreme Metal: Music and Culture on the Edge*, New York: Berg.

Kahn-Harris, Keith (2011), "Metal studies: Intellectual fragmentation or organic intellectualism?," *Journal for Cultural Research*, 15:3, pp. 251–53.

Kahn-Harris, Keith (2016), "Introduction: The next steps in the evolution of metal studies," in B. Walter Gardernour, G. Riches, D. Snell, and B. Bardine (eds.), *Heavy Metal Studies and Popular Culture*, Houndmills: Palgrave Macmillan, pp. 1–15.

Kleine Zeitung (2015), "'Within the ruins': Gleisdorf im Metal-Fieber," Kleine Zeitung, April 5, http://www.kleinezeitung.at/steiermark/landleute/4655578/Within-the-Ruins_Gleisdorf-im-MetalFieber. Accessed March 7, 2018.

Klypchak, Brad (2016), "Same as it never was: Machinations of metal memory," in B. Walter Gardernour, G. Riches, D. Snell, and B. Bardine (eds.), *Heavy Metal Studies and Popular Culture*, Houndmills: Palgrave Macmillan, pp. 82–98.

Krammer, Andreas (2019), "Styrian metal history," Facebook, https://www.facebook.com/mm.andikrammer/. Accessed May 7, 2019.

Kronen Zeitung (2017), "Metal on the Hill: Die Metal-Szene erobert den Grazer Schloßberg," Kronen Zeitung, August 12, http://www.krone.at/583260. Accessed March 7, 2018.

LeVine, Mark (2008), *Heavy Metal Islam: Rock, Resistance, and the Struggle for the Soul of Islam*, New York: Random House.

Masciandaro, Nicolas (2011), "Metal studies and the scission of the word: A personal archaeology of headbanging exegesis," *Journal for Cultural Research*, 15:3, pp. 247–50.

McCaffery, Peter, and Marsden, Ben (eds.) (2014), *The Cultural History Reader*, London: Routledge.

Metal Travel Guide (2018), "Austria," http://www.metaltravelguide.co.uk/europe/austria/. Accessed March 8, 2018.

Metalunderground Austria (2019), "Home page," http://www.metalunderground.at/. Accessed May 27, 2019.

Music Austria (2018), "Die österreichische Metal-Szene im Porträt," September 30, https://www.musicaustria.at/die-oesterreichische-metalszene-im-portraet-2/. Accessed March 7, 2018.

Nachtexpress (2019), "Startseite," Facebook, https://www.facebook.com/Nachtexpress-Graz-207474569264327/. Accessed May 28, 2019.

Napalm Records (2019a), "Official website," https://www.napalmrecords.com/. Accessed May 28, 2019.

Napalm Records (2019b), "Metal on the Hill 2019," https://www.metalonthehill.at. Accessed May 27, 2019.

Napalm Records (2020), "Metal on the Hill 2020," https://www.metal-on-the-hill.com/. Accessed January 28, 2020.

Nohr, Rolf F., and Schwab, Herbert (eds.) (2011), *Metal Matters: Heavy Metal als Kultur und Welt*, Münster: LIT.

Orf (2014), "Dissertation: Metal-Musik nicht mehr männlich," Orf, http://steiermark.orf.at/news/stories/2594681/. Accessed March 7, 2018.

Paul, Gerhard, and Schock, Ralph (2013), *Sound der Zeit: Geräusche, Töne, Stimmen—1889 bis heute*, Göttingen: Wallstein.

Pichler, Peter (2016), "Metal on the Hill 2016: A thick description of a cultural historian's imagination at an extreme metal festival," *Blog Stahl*, August 20, http://www.peter-pichler-stahl.at/uncategorized/metal-on-the-hill-2016-a-thick-description-of-a-cultural-historians-imagination-at-an-extreme-metal-festival/. Accessed February 2, 2018.

Pichler, Peter (2018), "Homo Ludens Metallicus: On Huizinga, the historian's gaze and sonic knowledge in metal music studies," *Blog Stahl*, February 26, http://www.peter-pichler-stahl.at/artikel/homo-ludens-metallicus-on-huizinga-cultural-history-and-sonic-knowledge-in-metal-music-studies/. Accessed May 20, 2018.

Pichler, Peter (2020), *Metal Music, Sonic Knowledge, and the Cultural Ear in Europe since 1970: A Historiographic Exploration*, Stuttgart: Franz Steiner.

Pickl, Othmar (ed.) (2004), *Geschichte der Steiermark*, 10 vols, Graz: Historische Landeskommission für Steiermark.

Project Pop Culture (PPC) Official Website (2019), "Home page," https://popculture.at/. Accessed May 28, 2019.

Robertson, Roland (1998), "Glokalisierung: Homogenität und Heterogenität in Raum und Zeit," in U. Beck (ed.), *Perspektiven der Weltgesellschaft*, Frankfurt am Main: Suhrkamp, pp. 192–220.

Sackl, Susanne (2010), "Männerbilder im musikalischen Genre Heavy Metal: Eine Videoclipanalyse," master's thesis, Graz: University of Graz.

Sackl, Susanne (2014), "Gender—Metal—Videoclips: Eine qualitative Rezeptionsstudie," dissertation thesis, Graz: University of Graz.

Schrage, Dominik (2011), "Erleben, Verstehen, Vergleichen: Eine soziologische Perspektive auf die auditive Wahrnehmung im 20. Jahrhundert," *Zeithistorische Forschungen (Studies in Contemporary History)*, 8:2, pp. 269–76.

Spektrum (2019), "Startseite," Facebook, https://www.facebook.com/juz.spektrumleoben/. Accessed May 7, 2019.

Stormbringer (2019), "Home page," https://www.stormbringer.at/. Accessed May 27, 2019.

Varas-Díaz, Nelson, Mendoza, Sigrid, Rivera-Segarra, Eliut, and González-Sepúlveda, Osvaldo (2016), "Methodological strategies and challenges in research with small heavy metal scenes: A reflection on entrance, evolution and permanence," *Metal Music Studies*, 2:3, pp. 273–90.

Visions of Atlantis (2019), "Startseite," Facebook, https://www.facebook.com/visionsofatlantisofficial/. Accessed April 18, 2019.

Wallach, Jeremy W., and Levine, Alexandra (2011), "'I want *you* to support local metal!': A theory of metal scene transformation," *Popular Music History*, 6:1&2, pp. 116–34.

Wallach, Jeremy W., Berger, Harris M., and Greene, Paul D. (eds.) (2011), *Metal Rules the Globe: Heavy Metal Music Around the World*, Durham: Duke University Press.

Walser, Robert (1993), *Running with the Devil: Power, Gender, and Madness in Heavy Metal Music*, Hanover: Wesleyan University Press.

Weinstein, Deena (1991), *Heavy Metal: A Cultural Sociology*, New York: Lexington Books.

Weinstein, Deena (2011), "How is metal studies possible?," *Journal for Cultural Research*, 15:3, pp. 243–45.

Weinstein, Deena (2016), "Reflections on metal studies," in A. R. Brown, K. Spracklen, K. Kahn-Harris, and N. W. R. Scott (eds.), *Global Metal Music and Culture: Current Directions in Metal Studies*, New York: Routledge, pp. 22–31.

Zaddach, Wolf-Georg (2019), *Heavy Metal in der DDR: Szene; Akteure, Praktiken*, Bielefeld: Transcript.

6

Heavy Metal Scene in Osaka: Localness Now and Then

Kei Saito

Introduction

Located at 34°41′38″N and 135°30′8″E, Osaka is the third largest city in Japan, with a population of over 2.6 million. It also forms the metropolitan area *Kei-han-shin* along with its neighboring cities Kobe and Kyoto. This region is considered as the counterpart of the dominant Japanese culture which is represented by Tokyo. *Kei-han-shin* is roughly similar to Kansai (the western), and it is also regarded as the opposite of Tokyo and Kanto (the eastern) culturally, economically, and in all other aspects.

Like any second- or third-tier city elsewhere, Osaka has also been compared to the capital city Tokyo. For example, the people of Osaka are often considered to be more "friendly" and "straightforward," in contrast to the "bureaucratic" Tokyo. Novelist Ango Sakaguchi once stated that "the self-consciousness of Osaka is not based on objective facts, but formed by the rivalry with Tokyo" (Sakaguchi 1947: 21).[1] As I elaborate later, the narrative of the Osaka heavy metal scene has a similar structure, although it is changing in line with globalization.

Many recent studies on local heavy metal scenes have dealt with problems of identities in connections with ethnicities and the global market (Banchs 2016; Mansfield 2014; Fox et al. 2013; Fu and Liew 2008). In this chapter, however, focusing on relatively more domestic issues, I would like to illustrate how this local identity or localness was formed and expressed when the Japanese heavy metal (or *Japa-meta* in short) movement began in the 1980s, and how it has changed in today's internet era.

Statistics and current musical situation

As I elucidate in the next section, Osaka was once the most active city for heavy metal music, and it triggered the Tokyo-Osaka rivalry in the 1980s. However, the situation has changed, with the heavy metal scene in Osaka declining in the last 30 years.

Although the rivalry has been mentioned often, there is a huge difference between the two cities, according to statistics. Figures from the *All Japan Concert & Live Entertainment Promoters Conference* (ACPC) showed that Tokyo held 4,686 concerts (all genres) from January to June 2019, while Osaka hosted almost half as much as Tokyo at 2,338. The proceeds from concerts in the Kanto area during the same period was approximately 76.8 billion yen, whereas the Kinki (Kansai) area earned 24.9 billion yen (ACPC 2019). Considering that the population in the Tokyo metropolitan area is around 3.4 times higher than in Osaka, these statistics do not seem to be very unreasonable, but it is obvious that Tokyo provides more opportunities for people to enjoy live music compared to Osaka. The number of heavy metal bands also vary. One of the most comprehensive heavy metal online archives, Encyclopedia Metallum,[2] states that 816 bands are registered as based in Tokyo, while on the contrary, Osaka only has 268 music groups.

As these numbers elucidate, the heavy metal market in Osaka is much smaller than in Tokyo. Therefore, this chapter deals with how Osaka has been struggling in a relatively small market to retain its identity which was formed in the 1980s and maintained through the years.

Japa-meta *movement from/in Osaka and* live-houses *in the 1980s*

The phrase "west high, east low" was often used to describe the Japanese heavy metal scene in the 1980s. Many major bands were from the west (Osaka and Kansai), and one of the earliest and the most successful ones among them was Loudness.

The early musical career of Loudness is complicated. The band was launched as Lazy in 1973, which included the two main members of Loudness, Akira Takasaki and Munetaka Higuchi, and they played hard rock and other pop music when they started performing in schools, at several local venues, and TV show auditions. However, when they decided to move to Tokyo with support from Hiroshi Kamayatsu, a member of a famous rock band from the earlier generation[3] called The Spiders, they were forced to change their musical style and appearance to more pop and *idoru*[4]-like. They also had to change their names to Michell (Hironobu

Kageyama), Suzy (Takasaki), Pocky (Shunji Inoue), Funny (Hiroyuki Tanaka), and Davy (Munetaka Higuchi), in line with current trends.

Takasaki confesses to a dilemma he experienced when Lazy was treated as an *idoru*-band. According to him: "When it's worse, half of our job was the one without the instruments" (Takasaki 2015: 46), because Lazy was often featured on a variety of TV shows, not music programs.

In the Japanese music industry at that time, the measure of success for rock bands was going to Tokyo, winning a contract with a major record company, and appearing in the major show business (*Geinoukai*[5] in Japanese), which sometimes demands that the bands appear on TV shows without playing any music.

Masashi Okagaki, who was the lead player and keyboardist of the Osaka-based Terra Rosa, launched in 1982, and is presently with Jill's Project and Aphrodite, had known Lazy before they debuted and performed hard rock in local venues, so he says he was shocked when he saw them playing pop songs on TV and assumed that "[o]nce we enter the major show business, we will be ordered to do THIS" (Okagaki 2019: n.pag.).

Lazy changed its music into a heavy metal-oriented style in 1980, and the new approach was adopted by Loudness, which was formed by two main members of Lazy and ignited the first heavy metal movement in Japan. The success of Loudness was an epoch-making phenomenon for local bands in Osaka. Their contribution to the Japanese heavy metal scene was, or still is, considered enormous. However, Lazy/Loudness was a band "from" Osaka, not a band "in" Osaka. Takasaki says that he had not connected with other guitarists from Kansai until they went to the United States (Takasaki 2018: 11).

The local heavy metal scene in Osaka and Kansai comprised bands that intended to follow Loudness' success in a few years, such as X-Ray, Earthshaker, Marino, 44 Magnum, Terra Rosa, and Dead End.

For these bands, live venues functioned not only as places to perform, but also to communicate with each other and to make the arena more active.

Small halls are called "*live-houses*" in Japanese-English. It is considered that the earliest *live-houses* also started in Kansai. Bahama in Osaka and Jittoku in Kyoto were regarded to be the origins of *live-houses*. To use the English word "live" to indicate "live music" was popular among blues and folk musicians in Kansai, and Jittoku was one of the main venues for blues music.

Among the many important *live-houses* in Osaka such as the Bourbon House, Candy House, and Yanta Rokumeikan (later Nishikujo Brand New), Bahama, which was located in the Shinsaibashi area in Osaka from 1963 until 2006, was considered to be one of the most legendary ones for heavy metal music. Bahama was initially launched as a jazz club and the owner reopened it as a *live-house* in 1972. Later, it became the central venue for the hard rock/heavy metal music in

Osaka. The owner, Toshiko Fujita, explains the reasons as to why she was interested in hard rock/heavy metal.

> I felt pity for those hard rock bands, for they were in a vulnerable position in Osaka then. They had been excluded from other venues [...] Luckily, the bands were hard-working people. The members of Earthshaker and 44 Magnum are aware of the feeling of being isolated when nobody is interested in listening to their music [...] Loudness, from Osaka was very influential, but they were professional musicians from the beginning, while Earthshaker had been an amateur band. For other amateurs in Osaka, a band whose performance they had been watching had debuted in the domestic scene. Then they came to think that "We are the next" and they debuted too [...] They were like "team-Bahama."
>
> (Fujita 2018: 94)

In an interview, she explains why the heavy metal scene in Osaka/Kansai was very active at that time, comparing it to the one in Kanto. She points out that the sound was also different. According to her, the bands from Tokyo sounded neat and square, while those from Osaka did dirtier and more original tunes, even though the styles were similar (Fujita 2018: 95).

It is obvious that the *live-houses* were not just venues but literally the "scene" itself, and it was enlivened by the sense of belonging of the members in the community, staff at *live-houses*, audiences, and musicians.

Bahama also had a record label called After Zero. It released several *Visual-kei*[6] albums and contributed to the music scene. As I explain later, genre conflict between heavy metal and *Visual-kei* has been complicated, but when focusing on the venue and its label, they were not so separated but often collaborated with each other.

Bahama was closed in November 2006, because of the owner's health issues. The newspaper which reported this wrote that Bahama was "synonymous with rock music" and the owner has been loved by many musicians who call her an "elder sister" (Anon. 2006: 35).

Other *live-houses* also contributed toward maintaining the quality of heavy metal music in Osaka. Okagaki, although he rarely played for Bahama, because his musical equipment was too large to enter the venue, recalled thus:

> The earlier bands from Osaka, such as Novella and Loudness, showed us an example; you cannot be on the stage if you are not well-trained [...] If your band's performance was not good enough, staff at *live-houses* would tell you "You can never be on the stage again if you perform like you did today" [...] There were a lot of *live-houses* where auditions were very severe. But once you performed there,

> people would look you up. I was very proud of myself, when my band passed the audition at one of those venues.
>
> (Okagaki 2019: n.pag.)

According to Okagaki, half of the audience comprised musicians at that time. They came to the venue to check their rival bands. "If we find a good guitarist, we ask him to join our band. That's the reason why there were only good bands in the Osaka scene" (Okagaki 2019: n.pag.)

As Okagaki mentioned, the skill and the technique of performing live were two of the most important conditions for being part of the Osaka heavy metal scene. As will be discussed later, this attitude contributes to distinguishing the setting from other areas, especially Tokyo.

Osaka/Tokyo narrative in Japanese heavy metal scene

In this "west high, east low" scenario, the Osaka/Tokyo or Kansai/Kanto narrative was often used to highlight the rivalry.

In the early 1980s, releasing compilation albums was popular among the Japanese heavy metal bands. One of the albums highlights the tension between the two areas is *Kanto vs Kansai Sensenfukoku: Fighting Rock Revolution!!* which was released in 1985. *Sensenfukoku* means a declaration of war in Japanese. As highlighted on the album's cover, the songs are from three bands from Tokyo (Slayer, Rei's, and Storm Bringer), one from Osaka (Virginkiller), and one from Kobe (Pandora), the neighboring city of Osaka. The cover suggests that this is the first volume, although the second one was never released, so probably the label aimed to continue this Kanto vs Kansai structure.

Another example is a concert series which invited bands from Kansai to several venues in Tokyo in 1983. It was named Kansai Nagurikomi Gig, which means "a raid from Kansai." This also shows how the concept of the Kansai/Kanto structure was highlighted in the scene.

Musicians also experienced this rivalry. Shinichiro "Shara" Ishihara talks about his experience soon after his Earthshaker's debut in 1983 with the self-titled album, which was released by King Records, a popular record company in Tokyo.

> The reaction from the audiences in Osaka was unexpected. I had believed they would have a blast with our triumphal show, but they didn't. Later, I heard that it was because of their sense of rivalry. They believed that we had betrayed *Kansai*.
>
> (Shinichiro "Shara" Ishihara 2018: 25)

This episode shows the strong loyalty displayed by fans toward their locality. In this movement, the identity of being Osaka/Kansai meant being "from" Osaka/Kansai. However, this also states that it was necessary for the bands to visit Tokyo when they wanted to push their career, even though their identities were Osaka/Kansai. Once this was achieved, the next step was to go outside Japan.

Global connection

As the movement progressed, several bands started performing across the globe. Bow Wow from Tokyo and Loudness from Osaka were the most recognized performers, followed by E・Z・O (formerly Flatbacker) from Hokkaido. They performed in several European countries and the United States, and they considered those places as the "world" at that time. Undoubtedly, as Niihara of Loudness writes, language had always been a major issue (Niihara 2018).

While performances by these bands were gaining popularity in the global market, underground bands and their fans had their own means to connect with the international heavy metal scene—a tape-trading based on fanzines. Shoji Nakamura, the vocalist of Riverge, a thrash metal band based in Osaka, recalls that he used to receive "chainmail" demo tapes in the late 1980s. "Chainmail" is a box containing ten demo tapes, and the recipient has to select one and replace it with another and forward the box. According to Nakamura, the US setting was colossal, so he often exchanged information with Germany where the scene was relatively small. He said he received demo tapes by Sodom and Kreator through this "chainmail," adding "that's how we communicated with the global scene back then without the internet or SNS." (Nakamura 2018: n.pag.)

The transitional period: 1990s

Like many other countries, the 1990s was a period of hardship for heavy metal bands. E・Z・O and Earthshaker broke up in 1990 and 1994, respectively, while Loudness changed its members drastically and began focusing on the domestic market from around 1992. The Japanese heavy metal scene was facing a low. Instead of heavy metal, *Visual-kei* came to be recognized as a popular genre, and a magazine for the genre *Shoxx* was first published in 1990.[7]

Anchang, a singer and guitarist from the Tokyo-based Sex Machineguns, narrates how his band was prevented from playing at *live-houses* just because it played heavy metal, and he decided to apply make-up to become a *Visual-kei* band to attract more people (Anon. n.d.).

According to Syu, a guitarist from the Osaka-origin Galneryus, even in 2001, when he formed with the band after leaving the *Visual-kei* band Valkyr, the heavy metal scene was "Barren, just barren" (SYU 2018: 134).

This is what Okagaki had to say about this era.

> The rise of *Visual-kei* once destroyed the heavy metal scene [...] In the 90s, most of the heavy metal bands stopped performing, even though they didn't break up [...] All the bands became redundant after releasing three or four albums, and *Visual-kei* appeared exactly at a time when the heavy metal scene had become weaker.
>
> (Okagaki 2019: n.pag.)

Although sonic characters of the *Visual-kei* bands are similar to those of heavy metal, its fan communities were very different. *Visual-kei* fans share concepts with girls' comics and most of them were female, unlike the past heavy metal bands, which were supported mostly by male audiences (Inoue et al. 2003).

Meanwhile, *Visual-kei* appealed to females and relatively younger audiences, and extreme metal became much more popular in the underground scenes. Thrash and death metal, which first started in Tokyo in the late 1980s, were becoming bigger genres in the local scene in Osaka.

These two genres (*Visual-kei* and extreme metal) which succeeded the *Japameta* movement can be considered as parallel cultural phenomena. When *Visual-kei* gained fans of different communities to remain in the forefront, extreme metal bands started to create a more specific scene for the narrower hardcore fans. In Osaka, Raging Fury, Riverge, Vexation, Beleth, Disgust, Goats, and Narcotic Greed were the main acts of such extreme metal bands (Asai 2019).

Music schools/lessons in Osaka

Music schools also have functioned as important institutions for the local scene. Although they had not specialized in heavy metal music, in Osaka, students seemed to be familiar with the genre.

Shimataro, a bassist who was a member of the Osaka-based instrumental band D_Drive, was also a staff member at CAT Music College, one of the largest music schools in Suita city, Osaka, which was founded in 1979. He describes his experience in the school, comparing it to the scene in Tokyo.

> In Tokyo, music is considered as entertainment. So your appearance is important. In Kansai, musicians are often too fat or too thin, but they turn it to their advantage, by saying, for example, "I may look uncool, but my play is awesome, isn't it?" They are proud of their musical skills. The old heavy metal bands in Osaka were very skillful and people copied those songs. It is still played in music schools and colleges. Even if they have retired, they succeed the bloodline of the Kansai heavy metal in instrument shops and studios, or as independent teachers [...] I think this is the unique culture of Kansai [...] If you are from Kansai, and your play is sloppy, you will be disappointed.
> (Shimataro 2019: n.pag.)

It is obvious that Shimataro refers to *Visual-kei* when he mentions about musicians' appearances. His chat also reveals that playing skills are indispensable in Osaka, and it has become one of the primary characteristics of music, as I mentioned before.

Another major music school in Osaka is Musicians Institute Japan (MI Japan), which is a sister concern of the Musicians Institute in California, United States. It opened colleges in Tokyo, Osaka, Nagoya, and Sendai in 1995, followed by colleges in Sapporo and Fukuoka in 1997.

Basically, these colleges have a common curriculum for instrument players, but some musicians believe that somehow Osaka has its own characteristic which is related to heavy metal. Leda, the guitarist of Far East Dizain and one of the special lecturers at MI Japan, describes his experience when he taught at different colleges.

> In Tokyo, a lot of students are like "I relish these stylish chords" [...] when they shred, they try to play altered notes. There are many students who love Allan Holdsworth. But in Osaka, students just play melodic minor or harmonic minor scales and they're like *trrrrrrrrrrr* [...] It was very impressive.
> (Leda and Hizaki 2018: 35–36)

Midori, the guitarist of Lovebites, also recalls "I went to MI Japan Osaka. There were far more metalheads than in Tokyo or other places" (Miyako and Yuki 2018: 46).

MI Japan is being run by ESP Music School since 2018, and it has produced many musicians in heavy metal as well as other genres. It became a part of the heavy metal culture in Osaka.

Japanese scene after 2000

Through the 1990s, despite the shrinking global heavy metal market, Japanese audience continued to listen to foreign heavy metal bands (Kawano and Hosokawa

2011). In 1997, *Burrn!* magazine, which mainly focuses on bands outside Japan, marked their highest sales. However, as we have seen, many Japanese heavy metal musicians remained in a stagnant zone. Temporary projects such as Animetal and other similar records[8] recorded steady sales, but those were mainly consumed as comical gimmicks.

However, from around 2000, the scene started to change gradually. First, classic bands reunited or reformed with past members: Bow Wow (1998), Earthshaker (1999), Loudness (2000), 44 Magnum (2001), and X-Japan (2005). The bands' reunion made it possible to gain a larger audience compared to the 1990s.

Second, the gap between heavy metal and *Visual-kei* narrowed to a certain extent, although it still exists. New bands which were recognized by both markets made an appearance. One of the leading bands in such genre is Onmyo-za formed in Osaka in 1999. Their heavy music and their arrival in traditional Japanese costumes appealed to both heavy metal and *Visual-kei* fans. The global success of Dir En Grey also lowered the barrier between the two genres.

The internet contributed to the revival of Japanese heavy metal too. Similar to other places in the world, people started to enjoy relatively unpopular music around the world in the internet era, and it need not be necessarily sung in English. The internet has changed the geographical context radically and the concept of localness in the heavy metal scene also shifted to the next phase.

Current problem

Specifically, the internet has changed the situation of local extreme metal bands. Nakamura from Riverge says "Going to Tokyo from Osaka, then to the world from Tokyo. It doesn't happen in our scene" (Nakamura 2018: n.pag.). It is easier for the bands in relatively smaller markets to directly connect with different local scenes in the world without ever leaving the community.

However, the situation is different in the mainstream hard rock/heavy metal segment. Shimataro insists that if a musician wants to pursue their professional career, not in the underground scene, they must go to Tokyo, considering that the population is much larger, and accordingly, job opportunities are greater than in Osaka (Shimataro 2019).

There is another problem. Mikitoshi Matsuo, the owner of the record shop Rock Stakk Records in Osaka, mentioned in an interview that he is concerned about the waning interest of younger people in this genre. Lately, heavy metal shows are mostly held on weekends, because musicians and audience have gotten older and they have to work harder during the weekdays. Naturally, several bands play on the same day, making it difficult for people to attend different shows (Matsuo 2019). Okagaki also feels the same way; the scene is getting older, and it is becoming increasingly difficult to attract younger audiences (Okagaki 2019).

Shimataro says that most of the younger heavy metal bands do not play only in an authentic style, but use the format of the old-school heavy metal and add certain other elements, such as other genres, *idoru* appearances, and comical lyrics, because they often realize that it is difficult to enter the closed community of older heavy metal music (Shimataro 2019).

Heavy metal record shops in Osaka

Despite these problems in the current scene, some people in the heavy metal community in Osaka try to maintain and energize the scene. One of the intents to revive the scene has been led by local record shops.

The internet has changed the behavior of music consumers, with online shopping in the early years, and downloading later. People tend to buy fewer CDs, LPs, or other audio materials. Although Japan is known for its obsession with CDs (McIntyre 2014), sales in 2018 declined to one-third compared to its peak in 1998 (RIAJ 2018). In Osaka, there were several record shops that dealt with heavy metal but most of them have since closed.

However, some stores continue to be active. For example, Tower Records still has two outlets in Osaka, while Disk Union, one of the major record chains in Japan that opened in 2015, continues to have a vast heavy metal collection. But when it comes to stores which specialized only in heavy metal, there are only two in Osaka: Rock Stakk Records and S. A. Music.

Rock Stakk Records, which opened in the Doyama area of Osaka in 2006, is now one of the centers of heavy metal culture in the city. It has a record label by the same name and has released around 30 CDs and DVDs. This is the only local label which focuses on heavy metal music.

Rock Stakk Records deals with both new and second-hand records and has brick-and-mortar as well as online stores. However, the online store sells only new records. Used materials can be purchased only at the physical store, and this is the intention of the owner Mikitoshi Matsuo.

> When I first started this job as a part-time staff at the other outlet in 1991, there was no internet and I learned from other staff members how exciting it is to work in a brick-and-mortar shop. And when I opened this store in 2006, I was aware of the importance of selling online, so I decided to run this shop as if it were two shops;

> the shop here and an online store. If I sold used ones online, it would be unavoidable for me to focus only on the web.
>
> (Matsuo 2019: n.pag.)

His aim to maintain the significance of a physical shop in the internet era made this place more rooted to the location. Especially, collectors of old vinyl records, cassette tapes, and VHSs must visit these outlets to browse and purchase them.

S. A. Music, which opened in 2010, also intends to keep the place lively. The owner of the shop, Ryosuke Asai explained thus:

> Physical stores always come first. This is where I mainly deal with major works for various customers. But the online shop displays rare and attractive items, which other shops don't. On the internet, when I do the same thing as Amazon or other large shops, it doesn't work. It's impossible anyway […] I try to make the physical shop easier to access.
>
> (Asai 2019: n.pag.)

Asai emphasizes that he learned the importance of physical shops when he was just a heavy metal fan. According to him, during the 1980s and 1990s, one of the staff members at Waltz-do, a record shop in Osaka, started regular meetings with people at other shops which deal with heavy metal, and he was the only customer who was allowed to attend. Then they started to issue a fanzine called *Suckerpunch*, and it turned into a magazine that represented the local culture. After he worked at Disk Heaven Osaka, which closed in 2010, he opened his own shop. He continues to publish his own fanzine as his "lifework" (Asai 2019).

While the number of stores has decreased, owners' intention to maintain the significance of physical shops has kept the local scene alive.

True Thrash Fest since 2009 and Asian connections

In today's heavy metal scene in Osaka, one of the highlights is the True Thrash Fest, an attempt to invigorate the scene, which Matsuo and his store Rock Stakk Records have been organizing as an annual event since 2009. It is an international live festival that specializes in thrash metal and similar genres. He usually invites popular bands from Europe or America, young bands from Asian countries, and Japanese bands. The first True Thrash Fest featured Hirax as a main performer. Matsuo describes how it started.

> In the autumn of 2007, I made a business trip to a metal festival in Germany. Hirax was performing there [...] I went to the backstage and spoke with the members and told them that I would like to invite them to Japan someday, although it was just my resolution. I had a small shop and had no budget to organize such a major event back then.
>
> A year later, at the post-event party of Riverge's show, we talked about how the band and the scene should be expanded. While releasing CDs is definitely one of the strategies, we also desired to hold a unique event which hosts one or two foreign bands and several active bands in the Japanese underground scene. Then Nakamura of Riverge pointed at me and said "You do it." I remembered Hirax and replied "I have an idea" [...] About Japanese bands, Riverge had more connections with other bands than I had at that time, so I asked the members of Riverge to put together bands. True Thrash Fest is not a business but a celebration in a sense.
>
> (Matsuo 2019: n.pag.)

Nakamura of Riverge also recalls when he told Matsuo that "[i]t's boring to do anything normal. You, invite bands from outside Japan to our releasing event. I'll take care of Japanese bands" (Nakamura 2018: n.pag.). As is evident from both the interviews, the first True Thrash Fest was organized through face-to-face interactions of the staff and the bands.

When he launched this festival, Matsuo was quite aware of Osaka's rivalry with Tokyo. In Tokyo, there was an event that specialized in thrash metal already: Thrash Domination started in 2004. It had invited major acts, such as Overkill, Death Angel, Flotsam and Jetsam, Testament, Kreator, Exodus, Forbidden, and Sodom. Matsuo confesses how he felt when he decided to name his event "True." "To tell the truth, I had a strong sense of rivalry against it [Thrash Domination]. If they do it, we should name ours 'true' [...] Since we call it 'Fest,' I want to keep it exclusive [...] I want people from across Japan to gather in Osaka" (Matsuo 2019: n.pag.). Nakamura had a similar opinion too. When he discussed the plan regarding the True Thrash Fest with Matsuo, he told him to "gather cool bands, which business-oriented promoters in Tokyo have never ever imagined" (Nakamura 2018: n.pag.).

Another characteristic of the True Thrash Fest is the inclusion of bands from other Asian regions. Since 2011, eleven Asian bands have been invited. It was, or still is, a very rare occasion for the Japanese audience to see them perform live, since Japanese fans have been familiar with music from Europe and the United States. Matsuo provides two reasons as to why he decided to invite bands from Asia. First, he was a fan of music from non-English-speaking regions. He had collected demo tapes from Asian countries. Financial problem is the second reason. Matsuo noted thus:

> The True Thrash Fest 2011 was the third time the event was being held, and I already knew how much it would cost. It takes more money to invite bands from Europe, the US, and South America. South East Asia is not very far and the bands there were very eager to perform here. Some of the bands said they would pay the travel fee on their own. And Lobotomy from Malaysia was the first Asian band which signed up to perform at the event. It was very original and innovative then. No other event had organized such an item.
>
> (2019: n.pag.)

The rivalry with Tokyo, the limited budget, and the connections among the bands, both domestic and global, have made this event very unique.

It is still not very popular for Japanese heavy metal bands to perform in other Asian regions, but some bands have successfully accomplished it. One of the earliest examples is Sabbat from Mie Prefecture, which has been recognized as one of the most influential Japanese underground black/thrash metal bands globally, which started to expand their market by playing in Southeast Asian countries. When Riverge was invited to the Philippines for their first show outside Japan in 2013, Nakamura asked Gezol, the vocalist and the bassist of Sabbat, about their experience in Southeast Asia. "It was Gezol of Sabbat who gave me a supportive push" (Nakamura 2018: n.pag.), he says.

After their first show in the Philippines in 2013, Riverge has performed almost every year in various Asian countries: Malaysia and Thailand in 2014, Bangladesh in 2016, Seoul in 2017, and Singapore in 2018. Nakamura adds a comment about his local identity which reflects this recent situation of the band.

> Musically, I have never considered ourselves as a local band. I feel a little disappointed when I see a promoter mention "from Osaka" after the band's name in a flyer or a poster. However, we behave as if we are in Osaka at the after-party. When we perform outside Japan, it's OK to add "from Japan," for we don't expect to be well-known there.
>
> (Nakamura 2018: n.pag.)

This implies that the rivalry between the cities does not always matter and the connections outside the country affected the identity of the band more.

Conclusion

As we have seen, Osaka became the focal point of the Japanese heavy metal scene in the 1980s. Musicians, *live-houses*, staff members, and audiences were strongly connected with each other and formed a steady cultural sphere to dominate the main scene in Tokyo. Clearly, technique-oriented musicianship which had been cultivated in this movement was inherited by today's heavy metal musicians in Osaka, and it has contributed to the success of the scene.

Indeed, it seems quite unlikely that a similar movement would happen at the same level as it was in the 1980s within a few years. Musical genres have been subdivided much more than before and consequently each market has shrunk. As mentioned earlier, the problems caused by generation gaps and ageing cannot be ignored. In addition, compared to Tokyo, a smaller population is a major disadvantage for Osaka to develop its musical market constantly.

However, endeavors such as True Thrash Fest show that adverse geographical and financial conditions can make the scene more unique. The current heavy metal scene in Osaka is not thriving as it was from the economic point of view, but it redefines what "localness" is in this information-oriented society, where physical and geographical significance has decreased and communication between remote local areas has become easier. A new sense of localness is formed directly through face-to-face interactions. For example, bands from other Asian regions are not Osaka bands but they are now a part of the local heavy metal culture of the city. This became possible by combining the internet and direct communication. There is also a balance between physical and online communications to sustain the scene. This multisided communication is producing a new localness; it does not only mean "from" Osaka, like in the 1980s, but "in" or "to" Osaka, and it can be regarded as the reason to expect more advancement of the scene in the future.

Acknowledgement

I would like to thank Mr. Ryosuke Asai, Mr. Mikitoshi Matsuo, Mr. Shoji Nakamura, Mr. Masashi Okagaki, and Shimataro-san (alphabetical order), for their cooperation and valuable advice.

NOTES

1. For historical argument on the identity formation of Osaka, see Cronin 2017.
2. https://www.metal-archives.com/ (Accessed January 28, 2020).

3. The rock movement in the late 1960s was called Group Sounds movement, which was influenced by The Beatles, The Ventures, and other foreign rock bands. The Spiders, which debuted in 1965 and broke up in 1970, was one of the most popular bands at that time. They performed as an opening act for Peter & Gordon (1964), The Animals (1965), The Beach Boys (1966), and other musicians from abroad.
4. *Idoru* (derived from English "idol") is the specific Japanese term to indicate young entertainers who attract fans with not only their music and dance, but also with their appearance in TV shows and public images. The term started to be used in 1960s and formed larger market in 1970s and 1980s. When rock music was not popular in the mainstream media, many rock musicians were produced as *idoru* singers to gain an audience which was not familiar with the genre.
5. For further information on the relationships between Japanese music industry and each genre, see Mitsui 2015.
6. *Visual-kei* is a term which indicates bands whose costumes are flamboyant and often feminine. It was started in the 1980s by bands that had been inspired by the UK new-wave music such as Bauhaus and The Cure. The genre name began to be used in the early 1990s. Their sound varies from standard J-pop to extreme metal, but most of them employ heavy metal/hard rock styles. Despite its sonic similarity with heavy metal, it has been considered a different (or even opponent) genre, for its strong consciousness toward how they look.
7. Some *Visual-kei* bands playing heavy metal music, such as X-Japan and Dir En Grey, are now recognized as the leading heavy metal bands in the global market. However, they were not regarded as a part of Japanese heavy metal culture on most occasions. As Mirai Kawashima of the black metal band Sigh talks about the difference between heavy metal and *Visual-kei* in Sam Dunn's famous documentary film *Global Metal* (2007), *Visual-kei* was not considered as "cool" genre by heavy metal fans. But as mentioned, it was not always separated in Osaka. For example, Gargoyle from Osaka, which performed often at Bahama, won popularity among fans of both genres.
8. Animetal was a project which debuted in 1996 and played classic Japanese anime songs in a heavy metal style. Their first album released in 1997 sold around 300,000 copies. Similar projects such as Drametal performed songs from TV dramas and Enka-metal played *enka* (Japanese schlager) songs. Most of the members of the projects were heavy metal musicians who had been famous in the 1980s.

REFERENCES

All Japan Concert and Live Promoters Conference (ACPC) (2019), "Market survey (From January to June 2019)", https://www.acpc.or.jp/marketing/transition/stagehold.php. Accessed January 28, 2020.

Anon. (2006), "Earthshaker ya Scanch: Band sodateta shinise ga shushifu" ("Long-established venue closed: Earthshaker and Scanch played there"), *Yomiuri Shinbun* (Osaka), November 21, p. 35.

Anon. (n.d.), "Director T shi no ura banashi" ("The back story of the director T"), http://ent2.excite.co.jp/music/special/sexmachineguns/bio_t.html. Accessed March 13, 2019.

Asai, Ryosuke (2019), interview by the author via email, March 6.

Banchs, Edward (2016), *Heavy Metal Africa: Life, Passion, and Heavy Metal in The Forgotten Continent*, Tarentum: Word Association Publishers.

Cronin, Michael P. (2017), *Osaka Modern: The City in the Japanese Imaginary*, Harvard East Asian Monographs, vol. 403, Massachusetts: Harvard University Asia Center.

Fox, K. M., Riches, G., and Dubnewick, M. (2013), "Juxtaposing aboriginal hip hop, local heavy metal scenes, and questioning public recreation/leisure services," *MUSICultures*, 38:1, https://journals.lib.unb.ca/index.php/MC/article/view/20203. Accessed October 15, 2020.

Fu, S. Y. Kelly, and Liew, K. K. (2008), "From folk devils to folk music: Tracing the Malay heavy metal scene in Singapore," in G. Bloustien, M. Peters, and S. Luckman (eds.), *Sonic Synergies: Music, Technology and Community Identity*, Aldershot: Ashgate, pp. 115–23.

Fujita, Toshiko (2018), interview by Shinkichi Saito, *Young Guitar*, 746, pp. 94–95.

Inoue, Takako, Murota, Naoko, Morikawa, Takuo, and Koizumi, Kyoko (2003), *Visual-kei no Jidai: Rock, Kesho, Gender* ("The age of Visual-kei: Rock, make-up, and gender"), Tokyo: Seikyusha.

Kawano, Kei, and Hosokawa, Shuhei (2011), "Thunder in the Far East: The heavy metal industry in 1990s Japan," in J. Wallach, H. M. Berger, and P. D. Greene (eds.), *Metal Rules the Globe: Heavy Metal Music Around the World*, Durham: Duke University Press, pp. 247–67.

Leda, and Hizaki (2018), interview by Kyosuke Tsuchiya, *Young Guitar*, 746, pp. 34–39.

Mansfield, John (2014), "Listening to heavy metal in Wadeye," in A. Harris (ed.), *Circulating Cultures: Exchanges of Australian Indigenous Music, Dance and Media*, Canberra: ANU Press, pp. 239–62.

Matsuo, Mikitoshi (2019), interview by the author, Osaka city, March 4.

McIntyre, Hugh (2014), "85 percent of music sales in Japan are CDs," *Forbes*, September, https://www.forbes.com/sites/hughmcintyre/2014/09/21/85-percent-of-music-sales-in-japan-are-cds/. Accessed March 13, 2019.

Mitsui, Toru (ed.) (2015), *Made in Japan: Studies in Popular Music*, London: Routledge.

Miyako, Midori, and Yuki (2018), interview by Takayuki Murakami, *Young Guitar*, 746, pp. 44–47.

Nakamura, Shoji (2018), interview by the author, Ibaraki city, December 19.

Niihara, Minoru (2018), *Niihara Minoru Jiden: Shinga-Singer* ("Minoru Niihara autobiography: Singer"), Tokyo: Rittor Music.

Okagaki, Masashi (2019), interview by the author, Osaka city, March 22.

Recording Industry Association of Japan (RIAJ) (ed.) (2018), *Statistics Trends: The Recording Industry in Japan*, https://www.riaj.or.jp/f/pdf/issue/industry/RIAJ2018.pdf. Accessed March 13, 2019.

Regev, Motti (1997), "Rock aesthetics and musics of the world," *Theory, Culture and Society*, 14:3, pp. 109–23, https://journals.sagepub.com/toc/tcs/14/3. Accessed October 15, 2020.

Sakaguchi, Ango (1947), *Yokubo Ni Tsuite* ("On desires"), Tokyo: Hakuto Shobo.
Shimataro (2019), interviewed by the author, Kyoto city, March 18.
Shinichiro "Shara" Ishihara (2018), interview by Shinkichi Saito, *Young Guitar*, 746, pp. 22–25.
SYU (2018), interview by Yosuke Hayakawa, *Hedoban*, 17, pp. 133–43.
Takasaki, Akira (2015), *Raijin-Raising: Takasaki Akira Jiden* ("Akira Takasaki autobiography: Raising"), Tokyo: Rittor Music.
Takasaki, Akira (2018), interview by Shinkichi Saito, *Young Guitar*, 746, p. 813.

7

Heart of Sadness: Fieldwork in the Copenhagen Black Metal Undergrounds

Tore Tvarnø Lind

The black metal band Solbrud ("sun breach") is seminal to the reinvigoration of black metal in Denmark in the 2010s, the sprouting of an unforeseen variety of black metal expression, and formations of new bands and festivals.

In this chapter, part of a larger work in progress, I draw on my experiences and encounters with actors in the black metal scene in Copenhagen, the capital of Denmark, during (an ongoing) ethnomusicological fieldwork initiated in 2014. There have been black metal bands around since the early 1990s, also in Denmark; yet, the aim here is to address some of the recent developments in the black metal undergrounds. When musicians, fans, and media speak about black metal, they use the terms "underground(s)" and "scene" interchangeably, which is why I readily adapt them in my ethnography.

The scene-focus in the present collection alludes to the omnipresence of the concept in metal music studies, but what a scene comprises remains a compelling discussion for each case. Initially, "locating the scene" seemed to me to be a straightforward task. However, speaking to people, listening to the music, and going to shows made me realize how very-far-from-homogenous the scene in Denmark is. Fieldwork has left an unequivocal impression of a black metal scene highly fragmented and differentiated in terms of aesthetics and style of performance, production ethics and sound, global network, and ways of social organization. This experience speaks volumes about the importance of meeting people where they produce, perform, listen, and talk about their music.

Giving primacy to experience, dialog, and reflexivity aligns with what ethnomusicologists Timothy Cooley and Gregory Barz term the "new fieldwork"

(Cooley and Barz 2008), and an emphasis on experience in metal music sound and sociality (Berger 1999) and affective belonging (Overell 2014).

During fieldwork, I interact with many people. Some agree to participate in interviews, yet brief exchanges of words are commonplace at concerts. Typically, interviews are rather formal to begin with; I record them and follow common semi-structured research interview practices. Interviews—with individuals or entire bands—take place at venues, in sound studios and peoples' private homes, and other places. As I get to know people, "research encounters" turn into *hanging out* together, chatting, listening to music, and so on. Relations change over time, also in fieldwork. Verbal and other kinds of interaction are valuable sources of information that tell something about musical practices, understandings, and ways of socializing. Participant-observation (see, for example, Cooley and Barz 2008: 4) is a conventional musico-anthropological term covering all sorts of intersubjective interaction during fieldwork: I attend concerts and studio recording sessions, share posts on Facebook, and on occasion help the bands selling merchandize and carrying gear. I engage in writing press material for a few bands and participate as a festival volunteer. A contribution of a more personal kind has been a piece of poetic calligraphy, which I made for the rerelease of Orm's album *Ir*.

Becoming part of the scene one studies is inevitable, I believe. In fact, *getting involved* is crucial to the process of becoming. Relations are not observable; I can only speak about relations in the scene by *relating* to people (and their music) myself in the various ways that opens along the way. *Hanging-out* is what metal people do; it is an inevitable part of playing shows and making records. There is a lot of waiting, rehearsing, sound checking, and guitar tuning on top of miles on end covered on the road. Hanging out covers a variety of social practices such as small talking, cracking jokes, and exchanging news about an upcoming black metal release or whatever. The Danish vernacular, *at hænge ud*, is a straightforward translation of the English. The band Morild and some others use the term *at chille* ("to chill")—a positive word for having a good time with a group of friends taking it easy. At first glance, chilling or hanging out doesn't seem to really produce anything, and in a way, it implicitly opposes the industrious production mode of capitalist society, which many black metal bands despise. Sure, the scene is very productive, but hanging out is crucial. Morild let me know one day that they appreciate that I seem to be a person who takes his time and understands how to chill. A rare and fine compliment—if they only know how busy I am transcribing interviews—and one that emphasized the importance of taking part in the ways scene members meet.

In letting myself known to others, it is my ambition to make sustainable relations built on mutual trust and a shared (albeit not identical) interest in the music. While I am—as a musical anthropologist—both influenced by my (changing) conceptions of scene and black metal, etc., *and* by other scene actors' (varying) understandings, the outcome of the intersubjective encounter "is never a synthesis of all the various points of view taken together, but an arbitrary view that demands further dialogue and engagement" (Jackson 2013: 261). In following Harris Berger, I understand "the constitution of meaning in music as an open-ended process, something that people discover as they perform, listen to, and reflect on music over time" (Berger 2008: 72).

Each encounter with people in the black metal scene has offered new insights into what black metal is; consequently, the black metal scene invoked in this ethnography is an *emerging* scene. It emerges in an *ontological* sense, as I get to know the music and meet people where they do black metal. This aspect deals with what black metal is, which makes sense only when considering the question: to whom? Second, the black metal scene emerges *epistemologically* as my ethnographic writing takes shape: scene, as an ontogenetic concept, shaped my preunderstanding, and guided me to pre-construct "the black metal scene" (whatever that is in the singular). However, my *black metal fieldwork experience* soon came to challenge this point of departure, and the question arose: Where is it, this scene? Allowing fieldwork experience to feed back on the theoretical framework and the work of pre-constructing, I could see how "locating" the scene turned out to be a matter of constructing it. The scene is not merely out there, "ready to be mapped," and hence the ambiguity concerning its topography and ontology is an inevitable part of "locating" it. As post-representational thought in cartographic theory has it, maps are not "truth documents" (Kitchin et al. 2009: 4). Applying this idea to the field of music, the act of mapping or locating a scene provides unstable, multiple, and selective stories and produces the scene as much as it describes it, which is true for any account including this one, of course. The point is that scene, in ways similar to a map, becomes a space for reflection in which "meaning is constructed by linking present information with past knowledge" (Kitchin et al. 2009: 14)—in this case concerning black metal.

This study, therefore, is as much about understanding black metal as a scene constantly in a process of becoming, as it is about reflecting on how concepts like scene and underground are active agents in forming this understanding. In following Georgina Born's use of Manuel DeLanda's theory of assemblage (DeLanda 2006), black metal's ontology is that of a plural, ever shifting, conflicting, and distributed socio-material being (Born 2012: 268). Therefore, black metal can have no essence but only exist in what Born (2012: 268) calls "multiple simultaneous forms."

I will mainly refer to two black metal undergrounds. First, the atmospheric black metal vein is underground music that occasionally thrives on the fringes of the larger metal scene. Second, the raw black metal from the Korpsånd scene is born out of a specific location, the Mayhem venue in Copenhagen, an "ultra-marginal underground" (Graham 2016: 3–4). Black metal, I argue, emerges in terms of "affective alliances" that are more or less shared across fragments (the various undergrounds) such as these two and others. Below, I refer to "the oceanic," old weapons, and *vemod* ("sadness") as examples of *affects* crucial to the forming of both virtual as well as translocal and immediate socialities of black metal practice (cf. Born 2012: 266).

The ethnomusicologist and the mediation of black metal

Participation in black metal conversations and concerts in the Danish black metal underground positions me within the scene. As I take part in the exchange of knowledge of bands and records that take place among black metal fans and musicians, I may point to black metal previously unknown to people, just as I get to know black metal, I never heard of. I become a mediator of local black metal knowledge, which simultaneously alters my relations to the people whose music I am studying. Although the impact of a single scholar is limited, it might affect others all the same. In ethnomusicology, the idea that researchers are active participants in transmitting the musical traditions they study is not new. They become mediators, or "meddlers" (Shelemay 1996: 49). The same dynamics hold true for fieldwork in the black metal undergrounds. With an effort, I can imagine myself a "black metal-meddler" and keep up appearances. Kay Kaufman Shelemay discusses how the ethnomusicologist "while seeking to document the transmission process, becomes part of it" (Shelemay 1996: 35). Adjunct to the scholarly goals of this study, then, is the perpetuation of black metal in Denmark, which happens every time I quote or paraphrase conversations with scene members (cf. Shelemay 1996: 36, 49). Mediation entails not only "an intermediary zone between the community and outsiders," but also "participating in raising awareness of the tradition within the community itself" (Shelemay 1996: 49–50).

The atmospheric black metal underground

When Solbrud formed in 2009 in Copenhagen and started breathing, strumming, and blast-beating new life into black metal, they inaugurated the "atmospheric turn" in Danish black metal music (Solbrud 2017, 2014, 2012). To some, this "turn" relates to the influence of atmospheric USBM bands such as Wolves in the Throne Room, the so-called third wave. Yet, Solbrud mention American black metal only when I ask directly. The Norwegian black metal bands and Pink Floyd come first.[1]

In the black metal undergrounds, there is a shared understanding of do-it-yourself musical production, festivals, and tours. Underground black metal music production does not resemble the corporate musical industry. Album production aims at a "break even" in the sense that record company and band share the production expenses. This is practiced for example by the independent label Indisciplinarian from Copenhagen, and the Berlin-based DIY-label Vendetta Records, who signed Danish bands such as Solbrud (2017), Afsky (2018), Orm (2017), Morild (2019), and Sunken (2018), all in the atmospheric black metal vein. This practice resembles what Peterson and Bennett (2004: 5) call a "scene-supporting industry," or what Spracklen identifies with an "alternative" scene, which is able to resist "the hegemony of the instrumentality of corporate mainstream" (Spracklen 2018: 251), first and foremost because black metal musicians (and label owners) value the freedom to make their own music the way they want it. All actors in the scene I met share this view. The black metal undergrounds are very productive, yet the word "industry" seems a bit off considering the limited number of physical albums produced, typically between 35 and 300, although numbers vary.

Welfare system support

Unlike "the scene," venues exist at a socio-practical level. Most public venues in Denmark enjoy municipal and state support, and the welfare system is a benefit to the underground scenes. One of the ways funding works is by securing a small but regular staff (typically booking, security, sound production) and by way of the so-called tariff-system (pay rates), which helps bands with transportation and other expenses. Most venues, though, still rely on steady transactions over the bar counter, and would not be able to run without loyal support of volunteers (such as bartending and wardrobe). When a band establish themselves as an association, it is exempt from taxes as long as no money is taken out. For example, Solbrud members take no money out, which means that they cannot make a living out of it, but as a band, they make enough to cover the costs of the next tour and the next batch of t-shirts.

The Youth House holds a unique position in the musical underground, not least in relation to punk and extreme metal music. The Youth House runs according to an agreement of operation with the Copenhagen municipality. All activities at the Youth House observe a strong commitment to a do-it-yourself/nonprofit ethics. The tradition of combining volunteer work with municipal and other support is crucial to the underground scene and its organization.

One night, I fell into conversation with two musicians from New York-based black metal band Yellow Eyes. They spoke enthusiastically about the hospitality of the Youth House and like-minded places in Germany, the offering of food and a place to stay standing out as a new and welcome experience to them.[2]

The Youth House hosts a number of festivals, such as the triannual Kaldet fra Dybet ("the call from the deep," since 2012), organized by members of Solbrud with the aid of volunteers working for a festival ticket and a vegan meal. The festival mixes black and doom metal under the label "dark metal," presenting local bands primarily. The 2015 *mørk metal* ("dark metal") festival Bornhell at the island of Bornholm enjoyed support from the neighboring restaurant and were able to sell draft beer at cheerful prices because of local sponsorships. The annual Northern Discomfort festival (since 2016), housed by the Youth House, has not only black metal, but also doom as well as sludge acts in the line-up. The 2019 version includes local acts and bands such as Vanum (New York) and Ultha (Germany).[3] Night of the Black Attack is a one-day festival focusing exclusively on black metal. After three years in Albertslund, a suburb west of Copenhagen, the 4.0-version (2019) of the festival relocated to central Copenhagen. According to one of the organizers from the webzine *heavymetal.dk*, Cecilie Roos (2018), the format has potential: "Our ambition for the festival is to include international acts at some point."

Oceanic black metal

Despite demanding song lengths, atmospheric black metal by Solbrud, Sunken, Morild (phosphorescence) and others has a relative broad appeal. The music is melodic in character and shows prevalence for hi-fi production quality. These bands are indifferent to Satanism and limit theatrical expression to smoke and strobe lights, and do not use corpse paint. The bands give primacy to sound and sonic-affective atmosphere. Solbrud, for example, favor a relentless "storm sound" (Lind 2019a) while performing in their everyday attire.

The bands support each other at concerts and festivals, such as Kaldet fra Dybet. Morild do not hide their gratitude to Solbrud for accepting to play together, "they invited us in with open arms." Danish black metal bands tour Scandinavia and Germany mostly, but also visit other European countries. Vendetta Records, central to the European underground black metal network, facilitate contact between bands. Sunken, originating from Aarhus, emphasize how important their bonds to bands in Germany, Italy, and France are, while adding thus: "There is a black metal scene in Copenhagen, which we are very proud to be part of."

Morild set up their latest release show at Den Blå Planet ("The Blue Planet"), the aquarium in Copenhagen. In setting the scene in front of the oceanic basin with UV-painted faces, an alternative to corpse paint, Morild created a new kind of otherworldly atmosphere. The inhabitants of the oceanic basin did their usual routine, swimming around calmly during show[4] as if to emphasize the insignificance of human struggle.

FIGURE 7.1: Morild live at Den Blå Planet. Photo: Jacob Dinesen, Devilution.dk. Used with permission.

In Morild's and Sunken's music, the ocean is a dominating theme, and in my studies of it, the notion of "oceanic black metal" has become meaningful to pursue (Lind 2019b). Both bands emphasize in conversations that their music deals with pain, depression, desertion, and desperation. To Sunken, the ocean is meaningful to work with:

> Simon Skotte Krogh (guitar): Black metal is inspired by the local surroundings, and Denmark has no mountains, almost no forest, but a very long coast line. I grew up close to the sea, and it is under my skin. But also metaphorically.

Martin Skyum Thomasen (vocals) continues:

> I kind of bought Simon's idea of the ocean and worked it into the lyrics [...] the lyrics are very personal [...] to me [...] Our music is very atmospheric, introvert [...] It felt like a straightforward way to express some of my thoughts on depression. I guess most people who engage with this genre have personal experiences of depression. It wasn't complicated to tie a music that plays metaphorically with the ocean together with a lyrical universe of melancholy and depression. In these *streams of thoughts*,

> you can get this feeling of drowning [...] or of the immense pressure from the world around you; it feels like crushing waves, or like the pressure at the bottom of the sea. If the depression runs suicide deep, you *want* to go out into that overwhelming oceanic territory [...] and lose yourself.
>
> (Sunken 2018: n.pag., author's translation)

Showing preference for hi-fi sound production, blast beats, and long passages of lingering guitar riffing and power chords, Morild (2016, 2019) and Sunken (2017) add ambience, sea sounds, and a dynamic way of playing; Morild, especially, employ long shoegaze-style crescendos. Sunken use a "wet reverb" sound effect, which creates a "wet sound," or "background sound," in some song passages. Yet, they do not want to stretch the oceanic component too far. One metaphor Krogh uses for describing his guitar sound is gastronomic: "On my guitar parts, there is always plenty of 'sauce', as we call it [...] and sometimes I get comments like, *oh, you put less sauce on today*" (Sunken 2017: n.pag.).

In a conversation with Morild,[5] they told me how they experienced glowing plankton at a beach in Cambodia, and stayed in the water for hours, until their skin literally started dissolving.

> It was psychedelic, we felt like being one with nature. The idea is [...] we *are morild* (glowing plankton). It is a social thing; we regret that we wrote our names on Facebook; we are a unity; we want to drag out the ego of the project [...] to dissolve [...] turn into a liquid.
>
> (Morild 2018–19: n.pag.)

Not devoid of self-irony and humor, cliché-like phrases such as "yeah, become one" and "let go of your earthly tether" are uttered jokingly in a free-and-easy way during our conversation.

> We create music out of atmospheres [*stemninger*], we don't think in *songs*, we think in *atmospheres*. Solbrud started something new, and we thought [...] it hurt [...] we could feel it! It is important that the music has this trance-like character; it allows you to *zone out*.

When I asked to comment on a phrase in their EP *VI* (2017), "give your body back to the open waters," Morild answered thus:

> It points to a way of being restored in the earthly biomass, become part of the new life that will inhabit the planet. It's about drowning, about taking your own life.

> It's about fear and desperation facing the climate crisis, our dying planet [...] we express our personal pain, our suffering.
>
> (Morild 2018–19: n.pag.)

The oceanic feeling, "is a [transient] feeling of dissolution of the psychological and sensory boundaries of the self," as in both Sunken's and Morild's conception of dissolving. But it is also a "world-disclosing feeling" (Saarinen 2014a, 2014b), or "relatively permanent feelings of unity [and] embracement" (Saarinen 2015: 4), as in Morild's devotion to the collective orientation. The concept of the oceanic feeling has been widely discussed within the field shared by psychoanalysis and the psychology of mysticism. Recent studies points out that Freud "misrepresented" Romain Rolland's central meanings of the oceanic feeling "within the received view of a regressive primary narcissism" (Kripal 2000: 374; Parsons 1998). Taking the concept in a new direction, one of particular interest here, psychologist Jussi Saarinen understands the oceanic feeling as an "existential feeling" (Saarinen 2014a; Ratcliffe 2008). Saarinen notes how the oceanic feeling in painterly creativity describes the artist feeling "at one with his work," which reminds me of Morild's way of working, but also that "artistic work need not merely aim at producing artworks; it can also involve the conscious reorganization of one's existential orientation" (Saarinen 2014b). Thus, the oceanic feeling may denote a change in existential orientation, as when a depressed world, drained of life is "shaken up to reveal" new paths, at least it is one possible appreciation of Sunken's *Departure* and Morild's *Så kom mørket* (Morild 2019). The potential usefulness of the oceanic feeling to the study of black metal calls for a darker version of the oceanic feeling to complement the joyful ones. Morild's concert at The Blue Planet—the choice of venue was not coincidental—is a compelling example of how the affective alliance of the oceanic, as in the dissolution of the self, or the feeling of oceanic embrace expressed musically, is a driving force in forming and organizing shows.

Underground on Facebook

The black metal underground is present on mega-tech social media such as Facebook and Instagram, which at first seems to contradict the underground's generic defiance of mainstream media and commercial industries. Understanding the scene in terms of assemblage, though, changes on the institutional plane does not automatically affect the other planes (such as sound, locality, community), because the various parts of an assemblage are attached to one another via "relations of exteriority" (DeLanda 2006: 2, 10; Born 2012: 268), rather than transforming into some organic entity. This allows underground bands a social media presence without necessarily compromising their underground status. As Graham shows in his study of global underground music, the web "is crucial as a tool of marketing and distribution for underground labels" (Graham 2016: 127).

Almost all bands announce concerts, records, and new merchandise on Facebook. It is practical, everybody is online, and a profile does not add to the expenses. Virtual platforms are also important to my fieldwork, as I communicate with musicians via Messenger, and Facebook updates help me in keeping track of activities as well as expanding my network. Not everything you want to know about underground music is available online, a point similar to the secrecy that Ross Hagen identifies with the black metal "kvlt" (Hagen 2014: 227). The digital life of underground black metal has facilitated access to (some) information about the music, but as Graham notes, "one must *go to* the underground instead of it coming to you" (Graham 2016: 10, original emphasis), "admittedly lines are blurrier that they used to [be], but there's still a distinction, to anyone who cares to notice" (Graham 2016: 11).

Stadium black

That black metal has gone mainstream might seem to be a contradiction in terms. Ross Hagen notes that already around the turn of the millennium, black metal became one of the most profitable genres within extreme metal (Hagen 2011: 223). This has caused much lament not among only fans and musicians, but also among scholars claiming that black metal will never be part of a cultural mainstream (see, for example, Michalewicz 2007: 214). In a review of a Behemoth show in January 2019 at Vega, a venue in central Copenhagen, a Danish music critic launched the term "stadium black" (Hansen 2019) to describe the choreographed stadium-rock attitudes of Behemoth. Live Nation organized the show, which sold out despite astronomical ticket prices in comparison to entrées for black metal shows at the Youth House, Loppen (at Freetown Christiania), Mayhem, and others. This is not per se a critique of black metal for the masses, though; the heterogeneity of the black metal scene that I speak of includes black metal as part of mainstream metal music entertainment industry, and makes the notion of a fragmented scene all the more imperative.

Danish black metal bands have performed at the Copenhell metal festival, also organized by Live Nation. Since 2010, Copenhell is the biggest Nordic metal festival, hosting 27,000 guests in 2019. Devoted black and doom metal fan Torben Sloth, whom I often meet at black metal concerts, finds Copenhell to be dominated by "mainstream rock" and "heavy metal," calling for more extreme "underground stuff" in the line-up. Bands such as Solbrud, Slægt (lineage, 2018,

2017, 2015, 2013), and Orm have performed at Copenhell, thereby showing their interest in playing for the more diverse audience at Copenhell, fringing with the mainstream hard rock scene, and taking part in the celebration of everything metal in the global nation of live music. The "global black metal nation" includes Mayhem, Immortal, Watain, Taake, Primordial, Dimmu Borgir, Batushka, Myrkur, and others. Copenhell and the much bigger, nonprofit Roskilde Festival have showcased many of them. That black metal is part of the mainstream metal entertainment hardly marks the end of the black metal world. Two observations are important here: First, some black metal bands seem to thrive on the fringes between the undergrounds and the above-grounds, such as Solbrud, Sunken, Morild, and Slægt, while retaining their identification with the undergrounds. Second, Copenhell has inspired others to make alternative, more narrow or more extreme festivals. The Korpsånd underground scene at the Mayhem KBH venue is such an alternative.

The Korpsånd scene at Mayhem

Established in 2009, Mayhem, or Mayhem KBH (short for København), is a place for "extreme and experimental sound, music and performance" (Mayhem 2010: n.pag.), in the beginning mostly within noise, avant-garde, freeform, and other narrow genres outside the repertory of well-established venues. Mayhem is located in the old "KTK" (Kommune Teknik København) buildings of the former municipality of Copenhagen's technical service unit, together with other nonprofit social activities. Although governed by the municipality of Copenhagen's culture- and leisure management (Københavns Kommunes Kultur- of Fritidsforvaltning), Mayhem is run by the users. Under the banner of "Korpsånd" a group of twelve to thirteen people has since 2016-ish established a community and forming a number of black metal bands. These include Lesion, Gabestok (2019, 2018), Blot & Bod (2019, 2017, 2016), Vaabnet (2017), Fanebærer (2017, 2018, Jordslået (2019, 2018), Ærekær (2019), Seiðr (2019, 2018, 2017), Ascendency (2020, 2018), and others. Releases come out on different local underground labels such as Nattetale, Hævngær, and Night Shroud Records, as well as on translocal labels such as Iron Bonehead (Germany), Profound Lore (Canada), Fallow Field (United States), and Tour de Garde (Canada). A few earlier, pre-Korpsånd black metal bands Garotte (2009, 2010), Sexdrome (2009), and Sejr (2013, 2014) are featured on the compilation *DOKUMENT #1* (2013), as part of the wider Mayhem community's "genre-disrespectful" musical projects. The word "Mayhem" was painted on a wall in the concert room, so the story goes, and it stuck with it. Whether or not it initially was a reference to Mayhem (the band), remains unclear.

The rehearsal facilities are adjacent to the concert room. A Mercyful Fate banner decorates the wall—a tribute to the King's influence on black metal in the forming years (Merciful Fate will reunite for the 2021-version of the Copenhell festival); instruments and equipment are stacked everywhere. I notice a red plastic tape recorder, a signal-colored reminder of the early lo-fi days of black metal. On the wall behind the drums, the word *Korpsånd* ("body-spirit") reads in big black gothic letters.

As musician, producer, and manager of Mayhem, Jesper Bagger Hviid, points out that "the Korpsånd-scene is a bunch of friends making music together" (Hviid 2019: n.pag.). Describing the community in terms of "friendship" suggests a close proximity between its members. Volunteer enthusiasm thrives: everybody helps each other out when running a show. Entrées and drinks are inexpensive. "Mayhem is for all, and everyone is welcome." The bands who perform "split the door and whatever is gained on beers" (Hviid 2019: n.pag.).

In most parts of the Danish metal scene, bands favor vinyl editions; few make CDs for the German market. The Korpsånd bands have predilection for the cassette tape, and they admire cassette labels such as Fallow Field for their effort. The music is stream-able via Bandcamp, Soundcloud, Spotify, and Discogs. To Emil Toft and Hviid, the cassette tape exceeds the positives of the vinyl, as "it easily slips into any pocket." Collecting tapes is a way to remember one's musical path, a souvenir of a great night. "The cassette tape was never out of circulation in the undergrounds," they contend, contrary to how so-called retromania-theory (Reynolds 2011) has it; only, today "awesome quality cassette players such as the

FIGURE 7.2: Korpsånd. Copyright Korpsånd. Used with permission.

Nakamichi BX-300E has become affordable" (Hviid 2019: n.pag.). Musical presence on the web is not contradictive to being underground, but if you want the cassette tape, you still have to go to the show.

The music from the Korpsånd constellations are often termed "raw black metal." What does raw mean? Black metal bands all have their differences and, as Cohen points out, "the relationship between sound and the local is not straightforward" (Cohen 1999: 247). For Korpsånd, "raw" is not about creating a distinct sound. Take a few examples: Fanebærer is a duet, drums and guitar, both musicians on vocals. Their songs are short, mid-tempo, as on the album *Fra hånd til jord* (Fanebærer 2018). The style of playing (and producing) portrays a lo-fi aesthetic approach with mildly distorted and high-pitched power triads and chords; vocals are shrieking, snarling, and occasionally growling. By contrast, the band Blot & Bod ("sacrifice and redemption") is a trio with furious drums, heavily distorted guitar, and bass. Again, songs are short and played fast; power chords and riffing are frequent. The three vocals range from shrieking to low-pitch growling (Blot & Bod 2019, 2017, 2016).

"Raw," then, refers to "a rather straight forward lo-fi and low budget production practice" that is "neither too time consuming," according to Hviid, reminiscent of black metal's "old days" (Reyes 2013: 242, 250; Hagen 2011). In this way, the Korpsånd scene upholds a distance to black metal bands that do time-consuming studio work with hi-fi quality sound. Toft, member of Fanebærer, Ærekær, and Jordslået, have not many nice words to say about "listener friendly" black metal (Christensen 2018). Hviid maintains that Korpsånd is not ambitious about making great sound; rather, they favor "immediacy in recording sessions," and usually, they produce the records within the day "without too many preconceptions standing in the way" (Hviid 2019: n.pag.). Toft says that the Mayhem-people show only little interest in other Danish black metal bands if any. Later, though, it turned out that he is good friends with Morild. Moreover, Sunken frequently mention the Korpsånd bands and attend their shows, despite their differences in black metal. Heterogeneity need not generate enmity.

"There is no lounge comfort" and not even a stage at Mayhem. Performances are "raw floorshows" on the concrete floor, with red lights and scene smoke only. Sometimes candles are placed on the floor in front of the mics, or by the keyboard at dungeon synth shows. Scene points to the theatricality of musical performance and the scene of Mayhem is stripped down. The demon-like vocals and a "guitar sound stripped of humanity" add a sense of the inhuman other, or otherworldliness, that "black metal need in order to work." This is the "return of the raw" in Danish black metal, and on a compilation album, it was boldly launched as an introduction to "The New Wave of Danish Black Metal," or NWDKBM (Korpsånd 2018, 2019). The word Korpsånd points to the simultaneity of unity and disruption, in the sense that the brutal sonic elements express bodily desire (corps, body), whereas melody and lyrics describe the need to exceed these desires (spirit, mind).

Mayhem/Korpsånd is associated with other parts of the underground such as the local death metal label, Extremely Rotten Productions, and the people behind Kill Town Death Fest, an underground death metal festival. Several of the musicians also play in death metal and hardcore bands.

Strange Aeons Records from Aarhus, a newly established black metal label, rereleased Copenhagen band NyreDolk's first album that initially came out on Caligari (NyreDolk 2018, 2019b). NyreDolk ("kidney-dagger") seems to be inspired by the aesthetics of the Korpsånd scene, but a review in the online magazine *Passive/Aggressive* spelled out how the sound differs from the "raw, Scandinavian black metal of Mayhem"; it is much more "atmospheric" and "international" (Nielsen 2019), sharpening the stylistic boundaries within the expanding underground. At their first live performance in April 2019, NyreDolk wore masks to maintain their anonymity and performed an aggressive hardcore-style show: jumping out into the crowd, throwing drums around, a spectacle foreign to the Mayhem bands. There is not much to find online about NyreDolk, but, as the drummer explained to me, "our music is *not really* black metal, we call it 'true Danish slow duka' [...] it's doom-like and atmospheric." A review on *Cult Nation* uses the phrase "blood-soaked, blackened punk" while announcing the release "the black metal demo of the month" (Reveron 2018: n.pag.).

I met the founders of Strange Aeons; they did not know the members of NyreDolk as they had been corresponding electronically and never met in person. Andreas Trillingsgaard and Quentin Nicollet have been active in the black metal undergrounds since the 1990s; they know many people from the older part of the scene, including Afgrundsvisioner ("visions of the abyss"), a black metal project from the region of Djursland, north of Aarhus. It turns out that the musicians in Gabestok, one of the Korpsånd bands, are old friends, too. Their new album is released on Strange Aeons (Gabestok 2019).

The Vort Fatum Festival

The Korpsånd scene has developed ties to global underground black metal bands and record companies via digital correspondence and by sharing music. In March 2019, Hviid organized a two-day black metal festival called *Vort Fatum* ("our destiny") for members of their global network to finally meet "in the flesh." Among the featured bands were Akitsa and Verglas (Canada), Carved Cross (Australia), and others, including local Korpsånd bands.

It was Akitsa's first show in Europe, and to the "ultra-marginal" underground crowd, Vort Fatum was something out of the ordinary. Akitsa was initially Pierre-Marc Tremblay's one-man band project, and he has been running the underground label Tour de Garde since 2001, which released Slægt's *DEMO* (2013), Seiðr's *Frostbreed* (2017), and Grifla de la Secta's *Dyrs Føde* (2018), among others.

The Vort Fatum Festival became a scene of a hitherto unseen tumult and physical violence, as the presence of infamous German neo-Nazi Hendrik Möbus among the audiences attracted the attention of Antifascistisk Aktion (AFA or ANTIFA). They interrupted Akitsa's concert by overthrowing the merch booth and pepper spraying the venue, forcing everybody outdoors, where a balaclava-clad AFA squad were standing in formation and ready to beat everybody up. The crowd that Saturday night was unusually diverse for a Mayhem show, as the festival attracted many new and curious audiences. Far from a melee-combat kind of audience, people were "coughing pepper," and were genuinely confused and upset by the interruption. I saw people lighting cigarettes, going back inside to get more beers; others were leaving; and the AFA split. Eventually, Akitsa picked up the guitars and finished the set for the remaining crowd.

In the following week, the media were eager to get statements. The Facebook community—counting several opinionated contributions from people who never visited Mayhem and never listened to the music—demanded explanations, while insisting on debating black metal, neo-Nazism, the "righteous AFA-violence," sexism, and audience policies. My own fieldwork expanded to participating in interviews on the metalzine *Devilution* and at *Radio24syv* (radio24seven) as an eyewitness. The Facebook community, and the metal media (who were absent that night), thrives well with the Nazi-narrative, and I found it important to counter the verbally aggressive attempts at blowing the story out of proportions.

Ross Hagen (2011) discusses the blurred boundaries between the wider black metal and the NSBM scenes. As Benjamin Olson shows, "in western culture, few things are more transgressive, alienating and provocative than neo-Nazism" (Olson 2011: 136), and is a controversial, gray-zone issue within the black metal scene itself, as well as the wider musical community. That the borders of scene activities are not always easy to define (Wickström 2009: 26; Straw 2004: 412)—and may be subject to heated negotiation—is a point of particular value for understanding the underground scene as the one at Mayhem.

After talking it over within the Mayhem community, Hviid offered a public apology for the mistake they made (selling Möbus a ticket), and new standards for future audience policies stated that violence and callous behavior, such as racism, will not be tolerated. Not that it ever was, but the wider community needed to hear it spelled out that all-who-welcomes-all are (still) welcome at Mayhem. The profound impact that the heated discussion in the media and on Facebook had on audience policy changes at Mayhem shows that what black metal in the undergrounds can and cannot be does not remain unaffected by the wider identity politics, the public imaginary, and the institutional planes.

Heart of sadness

I have gradually become to think of my fieldwork in the fragmented scene as a path leading to the heart of sadness, perhaps because sadness often strikes me in the field when at concerts. Sadness is a ubiquitous affective state. Most black metal express different measures of misanthropy, depression, aggression. *Vemod*, the Danish equivalent to the German *Wehmut*, means sadness, a translocal vernacular of melancholy. My argument is that *vemod* in musical form spawns "affective alliances" (Straw 1991: 374) in black metal, which are "folded into musical experience" (Born 2012: 267), and the formation and organization of black metal communities. Hviid speaks explicitly about *vemod*:

> *Vemod* is a fantastic word. It's about finding comfort in longing, in loss, in grief. *Vemod* is the most Nietzschean, life-affirming concept I can possibly think of. We share this with all other black metal bands.
>
> (Hviid 2019: n.pag.)

The word *vemod* can be seen as an actor in the scene. Etymologically speaking, *vemod* in its Danish vernacular contains the two words "pain" (*ve-*) and "sind" (*-mod*, from the German *Mut*), meaning "mind" or "disposition." Hviid's reading points to the potentiality of that disposition to inspire action. *Vemodig*, or *wehmütig*, is an affective state of mind having a bearing on the social context of black metal. Etymology is helpful, but does not exhaust the meanings of words.

Solbrud's third album is entitled *Vemod* (2017). When I mentioned this in a conversation with Hviid, he told me he did not know the album, but he also showed interest. Exchanging *vemod* references made me realize my role as an occasional meddler *within* the scene. Thinking of *vemod* as reference to both raw and atmospheric black metal made me wonder about the word *alliance*. Could affective alliances not work across the various undergrounds or scene fragments *without* these mutating into the same socio-material form of black metal?

I met a black metal fan, musician, and photographer known as Skoggangr on a rainy day at Farum Lake, north of Copenhagen. He embodied an intense kind of sadness and restrained aggression, compressing his voice, clenching his fists so hard they turned white. When I asked him, if he wanted to talk about it, he refused. Moments before I got on the train, he turned to me and said: "Take a good look at my self-portrait, and see what it reads on the wall [...] '*svigtet*' (let down). That is as far as I will go in terms of explaining myself."

Could the scene be "organized" around affects such as these? Or is organization something different? The notion of some kind of "affective belonging" (Overell 2014), and affective investment, is what makes the notion of a black metal (underground) scene meaningful in the first place. Vernacular terms such as *vemod* (sadness) and *svigt* (desertion, letdown) animate experience, assuming "balancing functions" for the individual as "creative violence" (Mørk 2009: 172–73). Various constellations of violence are ingrained in how we relate others (Kolnar 2003: 13). Kolnar sees violence as part of self-maintaining mechanisms; thus, he deals with violence beyond violence as unambiguously negative and destructive focusing on how violence works in the individual.

Creative violence is a way to open up violence for investigation, which Kolnar studies in conjunction with discourses of masculinity (Kolnar 2003: 14). Consumption, consumerism, and choice of lifestyle permeate modern life (Kolnar 2003: 196), pervading "our entire way of desiring, feeling, thinking, acting and choosing. And it is [...] because of the forceful and violent way it [...] is constantly being impressed into people's body and mind, that it has to be [...] "drained out"

FIGURE 7.3: Skoggangr, self-portrait, https://www.deviantart.com/skoggangr. Courtesy of Skoggangr.

by way of aggressive [...] strategies" (Mørk 2009: 192). The anti-aesthetic ideal taken up anew by Korpsånd and others may be understood in terms of an "energetic attempt to hold one's own against what may seem as a constant outer threat" (Mørk 2009: 195); in Mørk's analysis of the Burzum song "War," the threat is consumerism, the "commodified world of corporate rock" (Spracklen 2010: 91). In Skoggangr, desertion is the threat.

Mørk discusses the use of "weapons of some old-fashioned and primitive kind," for sale and worn in the Norwegian scene, suggesting "what it means for humans to be in a 'natural state.'" She argues that the "majestic, harsh and willful character of nature is taken as a model of authentic being. In this sense, "the waging of war is natural and great," and one's natural feelings of hate and frustration "ought to be released through aggression" (Mørk 2009: 181). Cover art and t-shirts by Jordslået, Seiðr, NyreDolk, Ascendency and others portray technical museum drawings of weapons from the Danish Bronze Age. Band names such as Vaabnet ("the weapon") and Fanebærer ("banner carrier"); song titles like "Knogler og skjold" ("bones and shield;" Jordslået 2018) and "Mit blodbad" ("my blood bath"; Blot & Bod 2017)—all these communicate that a war is waged as part of human nature. It is a battle for masculine vigor in the face of the watered-out consumer-masculinity and "Hollywood-greatness."

Many of the bands mentioned here take Danish words as band names and write lyrics in Danish, often in archaicized poetic styles to invoke grandeur, a sense of belonging, and as a creative way of making personal experiences publicly relevant. As the band Orm ("worm") has it, "the fundamental problems in life are the same as always, but instead of singing about private stuff, we dress the mundane in ancient Norse mythology, and perhaps we'll learn something about being human" (Orm 2017, 2019). Recourse to ancient mythology, indigenous language, the ocean, and historical weaponry are ways of insisting on a sense of immediate belonging and existential engagement and are vehicles for retelling painful and violent, personal stories.

Conclusion

As Mark Olson notes, scenes are themselves productive of a sense of locality and belonging as they mobilize people (Olson 1998). The Mayhem/Korpsånd scene has created a name for the black metal friendship, and the community has been able to maintain, in their own words, a strong "no-bullshit" and "raw" musical profile. The Korpsånd scene is almost synonymous with the Mayhem location. Although the Mayhem scene is still a very diverse scene, it is telling that most would speak of the "Mayhem scene" when referring to Korpsånd black metal.

FIGURE 7.4: Jordslået, cover art, *EP II* (2019). Courtesy of Emil Toft/Jordslået.

The idea of creating a sense of belonging is also taking place on the virtual level. As Olson notes for the Seattle scene, it was based "not upon already being there [...] but in terms of a common desire to be there, a common belonging to a trajectory of investment towards a particular place: a movement" (Olson 1998: 283 quoted in Kahn-Harris 2007: 20). A similar dynamic describe the exterior relations between the plural forms of black metal discussed here. There is a sense of a common belonging to a trajectory of investment toward affective alliances expressed in multiple simultaneous forms. To this trajectory, the Norwegian black metal from the 1990s is a recurring reference. However, affective belonging does not aspire to achieving sameness or homology. For example, even though the Korpsånd bands favor a lo-fi esthetics reminiscent of the early Norwegian bands, they employ it in new and creative ways to express black metal "inhumanity."

Musicians, fans, and the media take part in constructing the black metal scene, which implies that "scene" and "underground" refer to a variety of constellations and communities, including contested ideas of what black metal is. Keith Kahn-Harris argues for the usefulness of homology for "drawing connections between the incommensurable empirical and theoretical elements of the scene" (Kahn-Harris 2007: 22). By contrast, I find it important *not* to confuse popular and scholarly usages because scene theory does not equal scene experiences—neither the scene members' own experiences nor the ones based on fieldwork encounters. This is why I problematize metal scholars' methodological impact on the object. Scene members' own understandings (and conflicting ideas), I believe, must be included in order to understand what black metal is or means to those who play, produce, and listen—aspects that concerns black metal's ontology. The many hours I spend in company with black metal people strengthen my view of the black metal scene as fragmented, yet the same time, I understand how the various fragments share a set of so-called affective intensities. Atmospheric black metal, the Korpsånd scene, and NyreDolk's slow duka all emphasize "atmosphere," while the musical expressions of the bands are very diverse in terms of timbre, length of songs, and style of performance and production aesthetics. This is what I mean by the idea of different black metal fragments being affectively allied *without* becoming one-and-the-same.

Karl Spracklen laments that most countercultural movements have "been co-opted by capitalism and commodification in to the mainstream" (Spracklen 2018: 245) and that the existence of alternative culture is "under threat, if it survives at all" (Holland and Spracklen 2018: 2). While this may be true in some cases, my fieldwork contradicts the fatalistic idea that all music eventually will be subsumed by global capitalism. To some, black metal has become a gold mine, including "old" Norwegian bands who made anti-commercial music, or, indeed, anti-music. Nevertheless, this does not create a threat to black metal everywhere, quite the contrary. None of the bands of the Copenhagen black metal undergrounds seems to be in it "to make it" (Cohen 1999). Rather than monetary gain, they have alternative aims with their music as they invoke aggression, explore sadness, and aspire to dissolution.

Acknowledgments

Many people have generously contributed to my research. I warmly thank all of you for your time and interest in the project, and for sharing your (thoughts on) black metal. Warm thanks also go out to my peer reviewers, reviewers, and editors for your patience, support, and suggestions that helped sharpen my writing.

NOTES

1. For details concerning the interviews, see entries listed in the references section.
2. I heard this reaction before. Two musicians from the Copenhagen hardcore band Eyes were touring with Primitive Man (Denver, Colorado), who revealed that touring in Europe saved the band financially at a critical point.
3. Other festivals focusing on dark, doom, and black metal include A Colossal Weekend and Nocturnefest, both in Copenhagen.
4. The sound would not disturb the sea creatures (the glass is almost half a meter), but strobe lights and smoke were skipped, and UV-lights were angled upwards and not directly at the basin to avoid heating the water.

5. Morild prefer all quotations to appear as collective statements, which I fully respect, hence the "we."

REFERENCES

Ærekær (2019), *Avindskjold*, cassette tape, Montréal and Copenhagen: Tour de Garde and Nattetale.

Afsky (2018), *Sorg*, LP, CD, cassette tape, Berlin: Vendetta.

Afsky [Ole Luk] (2019), in-person interview, Copenhagen NV, January 8.

Ascendency (2018), *Ascending Primary*, cassette tape, Copenhagen: Self-release.

Ascendency (2020), *Birth of an Eternal Empire*, EP, Wachtendonk: Iron Bonehead Productions.

Berger, Harris M. (1999), *Metal, Rock, and Jazz: Perception and the Phenomenology of Musical Experience*, Hanover and London: Wesleyan University Press.

Berger, Harris M. (2008), "Phenomenology and the ethnography of popular music: Ethnomusicology at the juncture of cultural studies and folklore," in G. Barz, and T. J. Cooley (eds.), *Shadows in the Field: New Perspectives for Fieldwork in Ethnomusicology*, 2nd ed., New York and Oxford: Oxford University Press, pp. 62–75.

Blot & Bod (2016), *s/t*, self-release.

Blot & Bod (2017), *Ligæder*, LP, Wachtendonk: Iron Bonehead Productions.

Blot & Bod (2019), *Ormekongens argelist*, LP, Wachtendonk: Iron Bonehead Productions.

Born, Georgina (2012), "Music and the social," in M. Clayton, T. Herbert, and R. Middleton (eds.), *The Cultural Study of Music: A Critical Introduction*, 2nd ed., New York: Routledge, pp. 261–74.

Christensen, Simon (2018), "Korpsånd: Black metal-heresy should be praised!," *Passive/Aggressive*, November 22, https://passiveaggressive.dk/korpsand-black-metal-heresy-should-be-praised-interview/. Accessed April 8, 2019.

Cohen, Sara (1999), "Scenes," in B. Horner, and T. Swiss (eds.), *Key Terms in Popular Music and Culture*, Malden: Blackwell, pp. 239–50.

Cooley, Timothy J., and Barz, Gregory (2008), "Casting shadows: Fieldwork is dead! Long live fieldwork! Introduction," in G. Barz, and T. J. Cooley (eds.), *Shadows in the Field: New Perspectives for Fieldwork in Ethnomusicology*, 2nd ed., Oxford and New York: Oxford University Press, pp. 3–24.

DeLanda, Manuel (2006), *A New Philosophy of Society: Assemblage Theory and Social Complexity*, New York and London: Bloomsbury and Continuum.

Dokument #1 (2013), *Dokument #1*, various artists from Mayhem, LP, Copenhagen: Posh Isolation.

Eyes [hardcore band] (2018), conversation at a concert at the Youth House, Copenhagen, November 24.

Fanebærer (2017), *En af dem, der red med fane*, cassette tape, Copenhagen: Hævngær.

Fanebærer (2018), *Fra hånd til jord*, LP, cassette tape, Copenhagen: Nattetale.

Gabestok (2018), *DEMOS*, cassette tape, Copenhagen: Hævngær.

Gabestok (2019), *TRE*, LP, cassette tape, Aarhus: Strange Aeons Records.

Garotte (2009), *1*, cassette tape, Copenhagen: Posh Isolation.

Garotte (2010), *Count the Almonds*, 7", Copenhagen: Posh Isolation.

Graham, Steven (2016), *Sounds of the Underground: A Cultural, Political and Aesthetic Mapping of Underground and Fringe Music*, Ann Arbor: University of Michigan Press.

Grifla de la Secta (2018), *Dyrs føde*, 7", Montréal: Tour de Garde.

Hagen, Ross (2011), "Musical style, ideology, and mythology in Norwegian black metal," in J. Wallach, H. M. Berger, and P. D. Greene (eds.), *Metal Rules the Globe: Heavy Metal Music Around the World*, Durham: Duke University Press, pp. 181–99.

Hagen, Ross (2014), "'Kvlt-er than thou': Power, suspicion and nostalgia within black metal fandom," in L. Duits, K. Zwaan, and S. Reijnders (eds.), *The Ashgate Research Companion to Fan Cultures*, New York: Routledge, pp. 223–35.

Hansen, Emil (2019), "Stadionblackens lod," *Devilution*, January 26, https://devilution.dk/anmeldelser/koncertanmeldelser/behemoth-vega-25-01-2019. Accessed March 13, 2019.

Holland, Samantha, and Spracklen, Karl (2018), "Introduction," in S. Holland, and K. Spracklen (eds.), *Subcultures, Bodies and Spaces: Essays on Alternativity and Marginalization*, Emerald Studies in Alternativity and Marginalization, Bingley: Emerald, pp. 1–10.

Hviid, Jesper Bagger (2019), in-person interview (together with Emil Toft and Morten Damsgaard), Mayhem KBH, January 11, and March 27.

Jackson, Michael (2013), *Lifeworlds: Essays in Existential Anthropology*, Chicago: University of Chicago Press.

Jordslået (2018), *EP I*, cassette tape, Copenhagen: Hævngær.

Jordslået (2019), *EP II*, cassette tape, Copenhagen: Hævngær.

Kahn-Harris, Keith (2007), *Extreme Metal: Music and Culture on the Edge*, New York: Berg.

Kitchin, Rob, Perkins, Chris, and Dodge, Martin (2009), "Thinking about maps," in M. Dodge, R. Kitchin, and C. Perkins (eds.), *Rethinking Maps: New Frontiers in Cartographic Theory*, New York: Routledge, pp. 1–25.

Kolnar, Knut (2003), "Det ambisiøse selv," doctoral dissertation, Trondheim: Filosofisk institutt, NTNU (Norwegian University of Science and Technology).

Korpsånd (2018), *Korpsånd—An Introduction to the New Wave of DKBM*, digital album, https://korpsaand.bandcamp.com/. Accessed April 3, 2019.

Korpsånd/Various (2019), *Korpsånd*, a compilation 2xLP of various artists from Korpsånd/Mayhem, Copenhagen: Nattetale [Cassette, (n/a): Fallow Field (2018); CD, Montréal: Tour de Garde (2018) (see also Korpsånd 2018)].

Kripal, Jeffrey J. (2000), "Review: The enigma of the oceanic feeling: Revisioning the psychoanalytic theory of mysticism by William B. Parsons," *Journal of Religion*, 80:2, pp. 372–74.

Lind, Tore Tvarnø (2019a), "Solbrud: Stormlyd," *Danish Musicology Online*, 9, pp. 5–22, https://www.danishmusicologyonline.dk/arkiv/arkiv_dmo/dmo_09/dmo_09_artikel_01.pdf. Accessed August 11, 2021.

Lind, Tore Tvarnø (2019b), "Oceanisk black metal på Den Blå Planet," *Devilution*, January 24, https://devilution.dk/artikler/interviews/morild-interview-2018. Accessed March 13, 2019.

Mayhem (2010), "About," Facebook, https://www.facebook.com/groups/134901086539377/about/. Accessed April 3, 2019.

Michalewicz, Aleks (2007), "Gods amongst us/Gods within: The black metal aesthetic," in H. Wendy, N. Angela, and M. Chris (eds.), *Super/Heroes: From Hercules to Superman*, Washington, DC: New Academia Publishing, pp. 211–22, 385–88.

Morild (2017), *VI*, EP, self-release [re-release 2019, EP, Copenhagen: Indisciplinarian].

Morild [band] (2018–19), in-person interviews, Morild's rehearsal space in Copenhagen, September 12 and December 7, 2018; email correspondence, September–December 2018; and conversation at the release concert at Den Blå Planet, February 1, 2019.

Morild (2019), *Så kom lyset og tog mig på ordet En sort sky af minder I afgørende stunder Frosset fast i mit indre Jeg håber det forsvinder med lyset At dø eller blive fri*, LP, Copenhagen: Indisciplinarian.

Mørk, Gry (2009), "'With my art I am a fist in the face of god': On old school black metal," in J. A. Petersen (ed.), *Contemporary Religious Satanism*, Burlington: Ashgate, pp. 171–98.

Nielsen, Klaus Hedegaard (2019), "Nyredolk—forsætligt eller ej," *Passive/Aggressive*, https://passiveaggressive.dk/nyredolk-forsaetligt-eller-ej/. Accessed April 3, 2019.

NyreDolk (2018), *s/t*, cassette tape, Tampa: Caligari Records.

NyreDolk (2019a), conversation with the drummer at Loppen, Copenhagen, April 5.

NyreDolk (2019b), *s/t*, EP, Aarhus: Strange Aeons Records.

Olson, Benjamin H. (2011), "Voice of our blood: National socialist discourses in black metal," *Popular Music History*, 6:1&2, pp. 135–49.

Olson, Mark J. V. (1998), "'Everybody loves our town': Scenes, spatiality, migrancy," in T. Swiss, J. Sloop, and A. Herman (eds.), *Mapping the Beat: Popular Music and Contemporary Theory*, Malden and Oxford: Blackwell, pp. 269–90.

Orm (2017), *s/t*, LP, CD, Copenhagen: Indisciplinarian.

Orm (2019), *Ir*, LP, Copenhagen: Indisciplinarian.

Overell, Rosemary (2014), *Affective Intensities in Extreme Music Scenes: Cases from Australia and Japan*, New York: Palgrave Macmillan.

Parsons, William B. (1998), "The oceanic feeling revisited," *Journal of Religion,* 78:4, pp. 501–23.

Peterson, Richard A., and Bennett, Andy (2004), "Introducing music scenes," in A. Bennett, and R. A. Peterson (eds.), *Music Scenes: Local, Translocal and Virtual*, Nashville: Vanderbilt University Press, pp. 1–15.

Ratcliffe, Matthew (2008), *Feelings of Being: Phenomenology, Psychiatry and the Sense of Reality*, Oxford: Oxford University Press.

Reveron, Sean (2018), "Black metal demo of the month: Nyredolk," *Cult Nation*, October 16, https://www.cvltnation.com/black-metal-demo-month-nyredolk/. Accessed February 13, 2020.

Reyes, Ian (2013), "Blacker than death: Recollecting the "black turn" in metal aesthetics," *Journal of Popular Music Studies*, 25:2, pp. 240–57.

Reynolds, Simon (2011), *Retromania: Popculture's Addiction to Its Own Past*, London: Faber and Faber.

Roos, Cecilie [heavymetal.dk/Night of the Black Attack] (2018), in-person interview, Ballerup, December 28.

Saarinen, Jussi A. (2014a), "The oceanic feeling: A case study in existential feeling," *Journal of Consciousness Studies* 21:5&6, pp. 196–217.

Saarinen, Jussi A. (2014b), "The oceanic feeling in painterly creativity," *Contemporary Aesthetics*, 12, https://contempaesthetics.org/newvolume/pages/article.php?articleID=704. Accessed February 13, 2020.

Saarinen, Jussi A. (2015), *A Conceptual Analysis of the Oceanic Feeling: With a Special Note on Painterly Aesthetics*, Jyväskylä Studies in Education, Psychology and Social Research 518, Jyväskylä: University of Jyväskylä.

Seiðr (2017), *Frostbreed*, cassette tape, Montréal: Tour de Garde.

Seiðr (2018), *Withering*, cassette tape, Copenhagen: Hævngær.

Seiðr (2019), *Intethedens Afsky*, LP, Copenhagen: Nattetale.

Sejr (2013), *Demo*, cassette tape, Copenhagen: Posh Isolation.

Sejr (2014), untitled, EP, USA/unknown: Morte Creations.

Sexdrome (2009), *Sexdrome*, 7", Copenhagen: Posh Isolation.

Shelemay, Kay Kaufman (1996), "The ethnomusicologist and the transmission of tradition," *The Journal of Musicology*, 14:1, pp. 35–51.

Skoggangr [J/Genfærd] (2019), in-person interview, Farum Sø, January 12.

Slægt (2013), *DEMO*, 7", Montréal: Tour de Garde.

Slægt (2015), *Beautiful and Damned*, EP, CD, Wachtendonk: Iron Bonehead Productions.

Slægt (2017), *Domus Mysterium*, LP, CD, cassette tape, Herzogenrath: Ván Records.

Slægt (2018), *The Wheel*, LP, CD, Herzogenrath: Ván Records.

Solbrud (2012), *s/t*, LP, CD, Copenhagen, København, Oslo and Berlin: Self-Release, Euphonious Records, VME and Vendetta.

Solbrud (2014), *Jærtegn*, LP, CD, Copenhagen: Mighty Music and Target Group.

Solbrud (2017), *Vemod*, LP, CD, Copenhagen: Indisciplinarian; Berlin: Vendetta.

Solbrud [band] (2015–18), in-person, University of Copenhagen, September 26, 2018; hang out after a concert at Tagensbo Kirke, Copenhagen NV, October 12, 2018; and several earlier in-person interviews and conversations, 2015–18.

Spracklen, Karl (2010), "True Aryan black metal: The meaning of leisure, belonging and the construction of whiteness in black metal music," in S. Niall, and H. von Imke (eds.), *The Metal Void: The First Gatherings*, Oxford: Inter-Disciplinary Press, pp. 81–93.

Spracklen, Karl (2018), "Making sense of alternativity in leisure and culture: Back to subculture?," in S. Holland, and K. Spracklen (eds.), *Subcultures, Bodies and Spaces: Essays on Alternativity and Marginalization,* Emerald Studies in Alternativity and Marginalization, Bingley: Emerald, pp. 239–53.

Strange Aeons Records (2019), in-person interviews with Quentin Nicollet and Andreas Trillingsgaard, Aarhus, May 30–31.

Straw, Will (1991), "System of articulation, logics of change: Communities and scenes in popular music," *Cultural Studies*, 5:3, pp. 368–88.

Straw, Will (2004), "Cultural scenes," *Loisir et Societé (Society and Leisure)*, 27:2, pp. 411–22.

Sunken (2017), *Departure*, LP, [n/a]: Epicycle; CD, Ovar: Nordavind; cassette tape, Salem: Eternal Warfare.

Sunken (2018), *The Crackling of Embers*, EP, Berlin: Vendetta [earlier self-release under the name Arescet, 2013].

Sunken [band] (2018), in-person interviews, Radar, Aarhus, November 10, and Forbrændingen, Albertslund [Night of the Black Attack 3.0 festival], November 17.

Toft, Emil [Fanebærer/Mayhem] (2018), in-person interview, Copenhagen NV, January 18.

Torben Sloth [black metal fan] (2019), in-person interview, Copenhagen, February 13.

Vaabnet (2017), *Den Ed Du Har Svoret*, cassette tape, [n/a]: Fallow Field.

Wickström, David (2009), "*Окна открой!* Open the windows! Scenes, transcultural flows, and identity politics in popular music from post-Soviet St. Petersburg," PhD thesis, Copenhagen: University of Copenhagen.

Yellow Eyes [band] (2018), conversation at the Youth House, Copenhagen NV, November 16.

8

"Dit Is Berlin":[1] Local Metal Scene Building and Transformation in Berlin, Germany

Wolf-Georg Zaddach

In 1986, East German heavy metal band Formel 1 recorded the song "Dit Is Berlin" (also known just as "Berlin"), which is sung in the characteristic old-Berliner dialect, typical for all their songs and the Berlin metropolitan area. The title means literally "This Is Berlin." During the pre-chorus, Norbert Schmidt sings:

> Und die Leute, die hier wohnen / Ja, ich lieb auch diese Stadt / Große Fresse und dämlich quatschen / Aber sind ganz groß im Herzen—Berlin.
>
> (And the folks who live here / Yes, even I love the city / big mouth and silly talking / But gifted with a big heart—Berlin.)[2]
>
> (Translation by the author)

Within the song, Formel 1 construct an image of Berlin that distinguishes the city from other areas. Talking about Berlin though is a rather complicated undertaking due to the city's rich, diverse, and conflicting history: as seat of the government for centuries, a main center of industrialization in the nineteenth and early twentieth century, one of Europe's most vital cities between the world wars, center and last bastion of the national-socialist Third Reich, and, in the following periods, divided during the Cold War era. Berlin also has been the home of active youth and subcultures for several decades. Despite the political circumstances, heavy metal is one of those present youth cultures in Berlin since the early 1980s, and the city is an important spot for metal within Germany and Europe (for the case of Germany, see Zaddach 2017). In the following chapter, I will discuss the diverse background of heavy metal in Berlin by contrasting the 1980s and 2010s to explore the scene developments due to the political circumstances and analyze aspects concerning the local scene formation. First, I will provide a theoretical perspective about local scene formation and analysis mainly driven from German sociology.

Scene as socio-geographical concept

A theoretical concept that covers the aspects of a geographically differently spread youth cultures is scene. Scenes can generally be characterized by a thematic focus, the personal involvement of protagonists, as well as a certain infrastructure and availability of important objects. Scenes can be constituted both regionally and virtually (Bennett and Peterson 2004; Cohen 1999) and are organized to a certain extent by themselves (Bennett and Peterson 2004: 5). The protagonists often take over functions as voluntary workers (Hitzler and Niederbacher 2010: 22–25, 184–85).

The term was occasionally used in journalistic publications as early as the 1940s (Bennett and Peterson 2004: 2) and the historian Eric Hobsbawm used it for *the jazz scene* around 1960. However, still in the 1970s it was a rather negatively connoted term in scientific discourse and understood as subversive or countercultural (Müller-Bachmann 2007: 142). In the context of popular music, Will Straw picked up the term in 1991 referring to a lecture by Barry Shanks in 1988 (Straw 1991). Straw understands scenes as a cultural space in which musical practices coexist and overlap. He further emphasizes:

> The point is not that of designating particular cultural spaces as one or the other, but of examining the ways in which particular musical practices "work" to produce a sense of community within the conditions of metropolitan music scenes.
>
> (Straw 1991: 373)

The cultural spaces by no means only refer to specific locations or points on the map, as ethnomusicologist Kay Kaufman Shelemey points out (Kaufman Shelemey 2011: 363). Straw later criticized his own restriction to metropolitan scenes. In an interview in 2012, he points out that there is still a prevalent "urban bias" in the cultural sciences, and that one actually knows too little about the rural, nonurban side (Janotti 2012: 4). A major criticism of the concept of the scene is the lack of methodical precision. Straw argues that this is precisely the advantage of the concept, which allows it to adopt to different historical and geographical topics (Janotti 2012: 3). A too static method could run the risk of misjudging these spheres.

However, the term scene has been discussed in the German-speaking area as well without direct reference to Shank or Straw. For example, the youth researcher Dieter Baacke spoke of youth scenes and the meaning of the "spatial question" already in

1987 (Baacke 1987: 107, 115). The East German sociologist Manfred Stock applied the concept in his dissertation written in the GDR and emphasized the character of experience, for which bands are particularly important (Stock 1989: 93). In addition, he already recognized the peculiarity of communitization: Scenes have an "aura of the personal, the intimate and the private" (Stock 1989: 95) and are "perhaps [...] first hints for organizational forms of social life that refer to something in future which is beyond their own framework" (Stock 1989: list of notes, 13, footnote 65). In 1992, the sociologist Gerhard Schulze used the scene-concept in his social theory of the *Erlebnisgesellschaft* ["Society of experience"] (1992). Schulze understands this "specifically modern social form" as a network of publics who are characterized by experience orientation, "consumption of a particular experience-product," as well as a commitment to concrete contents and places (Schulze 1992: 375, 460). One of the more recent and the profound approaches regarding youth cultures is the conceptualization of sociologists Ronald Hitzler and Arne Niederbacher. The concept, which deals with the post-traditional neo-tribalism concept of the Frenchman Michel Maffesoli and Ulrich Beck's individualization thesis among others, defines scene as a

> form of loose network; a network in which indefinitely many people and groups of people get involved [...] A scene typically has local colors and peculiarities, but is not locally limited.
>
> (Hitzler and Niederbacher 2010: 15–16)

Hitzler and Niederbacher intend to describe social and aesthetic values in scenes. Such would be the self-chosen social localization and the experience value, in particular the meaning of the scene as prestructured experience space (Hitzler and Niederbacher 2010: 16–26). Aiming to develop a methodologically sufficient concept, Hitzler and Niederbacher have developed the approach of a "scene cartography." That means that the often ethnographic observation and documentation of the specific thematic focus, the attitudes of the protagonists, the lifestyles, the symbols and rituals, the media, the social structures and overlaps with other scenes, as well as concrete meeting places and events are taken into account. This relatively static perspective on youth cultures can be criticized (Chaker 2014: 182–86.). However, some aspects—the question of spaces, structure, aesthetic and social practices—provide insightful suggestions for quantitative as well as qualitative research. The methodical elaboration then makes it possible to compare different local scenes.

I will use Hitzler and Niederbacher's definition of scenes to identify locations and places, media, and protagonists, but will not follow their schematic approach to a full extent to avoid any bias especially for the historic perspective.

Berlin: The 1980s

Between 1949 and 1989, a border between two different states divided the city. The border and the so-called Berlin Wall, built in 1961, divided the socialist part in the East from West Berlin as part of Western Germany, which understood itself as democratic and free. The division of the city was the result of the Yalta Conference in 1945, at which the Allies decided how to split up Germany. They built Berlin Wall in 1961, and the border between West Germany and the GDR (German Democratic Republic), in general, symbolized the demarcation and isolation of GDR socialism from the West and understood as a protective wall (*schutzwall*) (Fulbrook 2005; Gienow-Hecht 2010).

However, heavy metal was popular in both parts of the city. Yet, the music was rated very differently, with different consequences. For the East German governing party SED, heavy metal was a "weapon of the enemy" in order to undermine and ideologically win over the youth—a critical position by the government against almost all youth cultures since the 1960s (see Stock 1994). The political circumstances of a politicization meant a lot of disadvantages besides the lack of LPs, merchandise goods, and concerts of western bands; due to the controlled flow of commodities, the metal scene had to face and to partly accept the rules of the system, such as the control of culture in general and censorship. In addition, during the first half of the 1980s, the SED and the Stasi observed, interrogated, and partly destroyed the scene. One example would be the official state-run youth club Ernst Knaack in Berlin-Prenzlauer Berg. This club was visited by youth in general, and among them were metal fans. With the rising popularity of heavy metal in the mid 1980s, they started to organize metal parties frequently ("Heavy-Feten"). The Stasi started officially interrogating after a civilian indicated that youth with fascist attitudes would hang out there—a trigger word in general that was met with suspicion by the Stasi, which suspected metal fans of being fascist due to their coats and the usage of skulls and SS-like runes in band logos (AC/DC, Slayer). As standard procedure, the Stasi interrogated the manager of the youth club and started to work with three so-called *informelle mitarbeiter* (IM) who were secret informants bought off with consumer goods or were forced by the Stasi.

However, those investigations did not lead to any seditious evidence. The Stasi documented that the club manager refused "any support of the security organs to identify the negative-decant youth [=metal-fans]" and that he would underestimate the danger and threat of metal fans (BStU n.d.: 448). Consequently, the Stasi planned the suppression of the venue, which was visited by up to 200 metal fans at bigger events. After closing for several months due to renovation, as was said officially, the youth club got a new manager and new orders for the cultural program, which excluded heavy metal.

Within East Germany, the metal scene in East Berlin was the most active with a high density of bands and well-known clubs far beyond the borders of the city for their concerts and metal parties. When a West Berlin journalist in 1987 got the chance to officially visit East Berlin and explore the nightlife, he compared the district Prenzlauer Berg with West Berlin's Kreuzberg, obviously amazed:

> I think I'm in Kreuzberg [West Berlin, known as party area for many decades]. Old buildings and street cafes form a milieu-idyll [...] Hippies, flippies and punkies grin or look evil, depending on the style traction that you immediately get feelings of home. A lush subculture grows and flourishes here in the barely hidden.
>
> (Starke 1987: 76, translation by the author)

Material goods are important for a music scene such as heavy metal. To deal with the lack of goods such as western metal LPs, magazines or fanzines, and merchandise the fans had to be creative. One other aspect of the lack of goods was a certain appreciation of all kinds of accesses to the scene. Those circumstances established a high esteem for insider knowledge, a high demand to get hold of copies of records or radio recordings, and the creative production of self-made merchandise such as copies of band shirts from the west. The partly well-organized black market enabled fans to get used original LPs from the west from time to time. Those "holy artifacts" were important objects to establish a sense of connection with the international metal scene regardless of the political consequences if one got caught smuggling LPs (Anonymous fan 2014: n.pag.). They were important sources of sound and information with their notes about the lyrics, studios, and producers.

To experience metal live or at least together with others, fans often gathered at official youth clubs. Since private sector clubs virtually did not exist, those clubs were one of the few opportunities to experience metal in public events. Several of those clubs were at times pilgrimage sites: The so-called Abi in Berlin-Weißensee, the FDJ youth clubhouse "Maxim Gorki" in the Charlottenburger Straße; one of the oldest FDJ club houses in Berlin, the youth club in the Langhansstraße 23; or the "Renner" FDJ youth club in Berlin-Marzahn. The "Maxim" FDJ youth club in the Charlottenburger Straße was a popular meeting place among the professional scene members: musicians, roadies, organizers, who often negotiated concert deals or initiated new projects or staff changes. For fans in the GDR, the youth center "Abi" (short for "Kulturhaus der Arbeiter-und-Bauern-Inspektion") in the north of the city became a nationwide pilgrim destination. Here, fans and musicians met, at times after traveling for several hours to get there:

> Until now I only knew what was going on here from *Metal Hammer* reports only. Here the latest and hardest metal music was played from the canning and the venue

> was crowded with metal heads. When I told my pals in Hoyerswerda, one thing was clear: The next trip goes to Berlin-Weissensee! But the crowd at the Abi was so big that it was not easy to get in there.
>
> (Vocke 2009: 25)

One of the former security members of the club remembers the frequently overcrowded events:

> Halle, Rostock, Jena, Erfurt, Wittenberg, from all parts of the country [...] fans did come to this club, without even knowing that they would get in.
>
> (Parlow 2015: n.pag.)

While members of the club got access into the club quite easily, some of the teenagers spent "three, four, five hours outside" the club, even though they partly traveled for several hours to get there:

> Well, once we arrived, let's say at half past six, there were already about one hundred men. And they were not Berliners. And they did not know when they would get into the venue. Sometimes they were unlucky and did not even get in at all.
>
> (Parlow 2015: n.pag.)

East Berlin was simply the center of the metal scene in the GDR. A certain scene infrastructure with meeting places, the contact with western, like-minded people who did "expeditions" behind the Iron Curtain, a rich black market, and large group of event operators and organizers as well as musicians were characteristic of the scene here. Nevertheless, only some parts of the city were particularly active areas: the districts of Weißensee, Prenzlauer Berg, and Marzahn. Friedrichshain for instance—and in contrast to today—was not yet an established nightlife area.

Formel 1's "Dit Is Berlin" was not the only praise about the capital. In 1987, Berlin celebrated its 750th anniversary. The East Berlin band Merlin produced a metal version of the hymn of praise "Berlin is still Berlin," based on numerous versions of the same name chanson, dating back to the Berlin operetta tradition and Walter Kollos' "Three Old Box" (1917). In particular, this song was frequently broadcast on air in 1987 and played live by the band itself.

Left of the wall

The situation in West Berlin was also surprisingly problematic. Separated from the actual territory of the Federal Republic and thus affected by restrictions on the transfer of goods and culture, West Berliners considered themselves as periphery, separated from the actual metal centers in West Germany. Here, heavy metal spread rapidly during the first half of the 1980s, with a tremendous acceleration starting in 1983 (Elflein 2016; Mader et al. 2012). With the establishment of probably the first German heavy metal fan club in Veltern in 1981, larger scene spots grew especially in North Rhine-Westphalia and the Ruhr area, Hanover, and Hamburg. Fans got involved in new heavy metal networks, which is especially evident in the founding of new journals. Götz Kühnemund, cofounder of the *Rock Hard* fanzine, which in a short span of time grew to be full-time professional enterprise, remembers the 1980s scene in the Ruhr area:

> Everyone wanted to be there, everyone had to be actively involved in this super exciting new scene. It did not matter if you started a band, ran a fanclub or a self-made booklet brought out. Main thing was, you were part of this awesome spectacle.
>
> (Quoted in Schmenk and Krumm 2010: 7)

Already in 1983, the ZDF (Second Public Television) presented the *Rock Pop—The Heavy Metal Show.* This concert series booked international metal bands or several West German bands, and this was probably the first opportunity for many fans to watch bands such as Iron Maiden, Judas Priest, or Ozzy Osbourne live. When the ZDF broadcast the recording *Heavy Metal Night* from the Westphalenhalle in Dortmund on February 4, 1984, adolescents got infected with the music.

The heavy metal scene of 1980s West Berlin experienced a fast-growing infrastructure of clubs and record shops. The booklet *Berlin Intern: Hard Rock, Punk, Heavy Metal*, which was distributed free of charge as an information brochure by fans for fans, contains numerous advertisements by West Berlin pubs and clubs. For instance, the club Surprise, located in Berlin-Steglitz, advertises itself as a regular metal bar when it says "Disco + Café. Hard & Heavy Party Wednesday, Thursday, Friday, Saturday, Sunday" (Anon. 1984: no. 2, 9). In addition, the booklet announces parties and concerts in locations such as the Amnesia, Odyssey, or Heavy Metal, which happened all over the districts of West Berlin.

Of particular importance was the founding of Noise Records in 1983 as well as Harris Johns's Music Lab Studio. Noise Records and the Music Lab Studio became important for the production of the West German thrash metal sound by bands such as Kreator and Tankard (Gehlke 2017). West Berlin thus indirectly became an important driver and pioneer of thrash metal in Germany despite the remote location. Karl-Ulrich Walterbach, the founder of Noise, experienced the special situation of West Berlin when it comes to music industry networks. The large majority of the German music industry was not present in Berlin, and "it was next to impossible for Walterbach to find music professionals in Berlin" (Gehlke 2017: 75). Harris Johns, son of an American GI and a German woman, worked at the famous Hansa Studios during the 1970s and founded the studio Music Lab Berlin during the early 1980s. Since the studio's inception, he produced bands such as Sepultura, Slipknot, also various German punk bands as well as the experimental Einstürzende Neubauten. Most prominently, he worked as the *Haus- und Hoftonmeister*, the main producer, for Karl Walterbachs labels Noise Records and Aggressive Rockproduktion (Zephyr's Odem 2017). He produced German bands such as Grave Digger, Helloween, Kreator, Tankard, Sodom—thus had a special and early role in the formation of the so-called teutonic metal—the specific sound of German power and thrash metal (in line with Karl Rudolf "Charlie" Bauerfeind). Hence, with an experienced producer such as Harris Johns, the highly motivated Walterbach was able to establish one of Germany's most important and influential independent metal labels of the 1980s in West Berlin.

1989–90: Reunification and hybridization of once separated local scenes

The 1990s and the reunification brought together the once separated scenes in Berlin. Although, folks from West Berlin usually have been able to cross the border to East Berlin, now it was possible the other way round as well. When West German thrash band Kreator played a sold-out concert with Tankard, Coroner, and Sabbath on March 4, 1990, at the Werner-Seelenbinder-Halle in East Berlin, it was the first larger unification moment of the once separated scenes.

The fans from the Eastern parts were especially amazed by the scene infrastructure of West Berlin with its several venues for live music, such as the legendary SO36 in Berlin-Kreuzberg, the Huxleys in Berlin-Neukölln, or the Kulturbrauerei in Berlin-Prenzlauer Berg. New networks of musicians had been established, which led to the rise of bands such as Depressive Age, who had been successful during the 1990s, touring with Nuclear Assault through Europe, among others. Most prominently, Rammstein, who formerly played in punk bands in East Berlin (Feeling B) and Leipzig (Till Lindemann) during 1980s, formed during the first half of the 1990s in Berlin and created a new style (Neue Deutsche Härte) of commercially successful industrial metal.

Berlin: The 2010s

The scene in Berlin's 2010s is multigenerational, stylistically diverse, equipped with a wide range of established and newer live venues, labels, booking agencies

FIGURE 8.1: Ticket for the concert of Kreator, Tankard, Coroner, and Sabbath in East Berlin, in March 1990. Source: Uwe Breitenborn, Berlin.

and promoters, and metal bars. While larger business enterprises were rare during the 1980s, there was a growing metal music industry especially since the 2010s. This is due to the history of the city as well as its changing character. When Sony

Music announced in early 2019 that the German headquarters will move from Munich to Berlin in 2020, stating that Berlin would be the creative hotspot of Europe and therefore "the place to be" (Musikwoche 2019), they reacted to an ongoing process of more than twenty years of Berlin becoming a central "creative city" in Europe.[3] According to a city's report, Berlin's general music industry spans more than 1,500 businesses.

Besides the major label Universal Music, which resides close to the former Berlin Wall in Berlin-Friedrichshain since 2010, several metal businesses are established nowadays. For instance, the main editorial team of the German-language *Metal Hammer* operates in Berlin-Kreuzberg since 2010. Many metal journalists, who are working for the three major magazines, *Rock Hard*, *Metal Hammer*, and *Deaf Forever*, are based in Berlin. Several underground and semiprofessional magazines and blogs like Metal Guardian or Zephyr's Odem operate from the capital or nearby. Besides the Austrian label Napalm Records, which opened its German headquarters in Berlin in 2016, several smaller and independent labels, such as Pelagic Records and Vendetta Records, were founded in the city. Pelagic Records was founded by Robin Staps in 2009 and is the house-label of the internationally acclaimed post-metal band The Ocean. The label features several other international post-metal bands such as Mono from Japan or LLNN from Denmark. Vendetta Records is a leftist underground label founded by Stefan Klose in 2001. Vendetta became an important international hub for contemporary underground (post-)black metal and sludge and features bands such as Sun Worship from Berlin, Ultha, Woe, or Solbrud and Sunken from Denmark.

Development and (self-)perception as local scenes during the 1980s and the 2010s

The feeling of being detached from the active metal centers in West Germany was widespread in West Berlin. The editors of the *Iron Pages* magazine, which was the third most successful magazine in West Germany after *Metal Hammer* and *Rock Hard* for some time during the 1980s, regret the "peripheral location of Berlin on the HM [heavy metal] map" in a "Berlin special" in 1986 (Mader 1986: 7). In part, this was understood as a result of lower attention and interest in bands from West Berlin which motivated the editors to emphasize that "the average [West] Berlin metal group is by no means worse than the average West German band" (Mader 1986: 7). Yet, from the point of view of the GDR scene, West Berlin was a strong western metal center, and within reach. Smuggling and traveling between the two parts of Berlin provided one of the most intense private exchanges of goods.

However, both perspectives demonstrate the influence of political circumstances on local scene formation and self-perception.

(Self-)Perception of the metal scene in East Berlin during the 1980s

The social interaction between society and the heavy metal scene was very different in both parts of the city. In East Berlin, the state politicized heavy metal. In addition, a changing public discourse appeared about the music and the scene. Journalists in particular got interested from 1984–85 onwards (Böhm 1985; Martin 1985). Since 1985, the major and controlled popular music journal *melodie & rhythmus* ("melody & rhythm"), based in East Berlin, has become an essential vehicle for this development. With the March issue of 1985, the magazine launched a two-part feature entitled "Heavy, Hard and Wild: Heavy Metal" by journalist Anja Böhm. The article seemed to pick up widespread prejudices with subheadings such as "hair-raising," "in war with Satan," or "ghost trains and nonsense" (Böhm 1985: 14–15). On a closer reading, however, it becomes clear that the informed author creates a certain distance from these prejudices. Böhm classifies heavy metal as rather harmless and provocative in a traditional sense (Böhm 1985: 15). By doing so, she benevolently weakens the threat scenarios and offers a different and affirmative perspective. Many subsequent articles were inclined to weaken widespread stereotypes about the youth culture. For example, the youth magazine *neues leben* ("new life") published by the federal youth organization FDJ in August 1985. This development culminated in an interview with the director of the ZAG Tanzmusik in 1987 (Central Working Group at the Center for Cultural Work, Leipzig). Here, the cultural politician describes heavy metal as the "current magic formula in popular music," and stated that metal is a "legitimate part of the socialist music culture" (Profil 1987: 15).

Part of this somewhat ironic turn is the raising academic interest, in contrast to West Berlin and West Germany in general. In 1983, the Research Center for Popular Music, one of the first such centers of its kind worldwide, was founded at the Humboldt-University. The musicologist Peter Wicke, who has been involved in the formation of the International Association for the Study of Popular Music (IASPM) and published several internationally acknowledged studies about rock music as well as theory and musical analysis of popular music, became the first director of the center. Though his personal interest and acknowledgment of heavy metal has been, at least during the 1980s, rather limited, he supported members of the center to work on youth cultures such as heavy metal.[4] Besides, the National Academy of Pedagogical Science (Akademie der Pädagogischen Wissenschaften) conducted a research project on youth cultures in the GDR for several years. Here, through several qualitative interviews, heavy metal was acknowledged as an important youth culture with fans (Stock 1989; Stock and Mühlberg 1990; Steiner et al. 1999). Though we have to understand that the state had a huge interest in gaining information about heavy metal and therefore may have tried to influence the researchers, the outcome was remarkably unbiased, aiming to separate empirical research from political interpretation. Thus, the state-financed research in the 1980s GDR ironically provided one of the first sociological and ethnographic studies on heavy metal worldwide.

Despite the fact that the public was interested in the local heavy metal scene, or even sought the collaboration, for instance for the production of Friedrich Schiller's *Die Räuber* with a heavy metal band in 1987 (Zaddach 2018: 305–08.), most fans felt distant from the hot spots of the international metal scene. The lack of important fan objects and the limitations of traveling made few opportunities to see idols such as Iron Maiden live in Hungary or Poland even more difficult. Formel 1, who sung about Berlin, were not able to play abroad and split up over these limitations in 1986–87. Bands after that got luckier and could play selected shows in other socialist countries after 1987.

Some fans and musicians realized that these circumstances could also work for their own purposes. In several letters to the national radio, for instance, fans demanded more heavy metal on the radio, or more concerts. In fact, the cultural politics responded to those demands and the pressuring public discourse and allowed more metal bands to play officially live and recorded music. The support also included prices and funding for young metal bands. Nevertheless, most fans realized the suppressing circumstances as late as 1989–90. The death metal band Darkland from East Berlin expressed this anger on the EP *40 Years*, recorded in autumn 1989. Every verse of the lyrics of the title track "40 Years for Nothing" starts with "40 years" respectively "28 years" referring to the Berlin Wall, criticizing the GDR. For instance: "28 years interned / 40 years Stasi power / 40 years we obeyed" (see Zaddach 2018).

Diversification and fragmentation; professionalization and DIY: Underground in the 2010s

Compared to the 1980s, Berlin's scene in the 2010s appears completely different. Due to the international and diverse character of the city, discourses and self-perception changed heavily. Important factors of influence are the diversification of the scene due to stylistic differentiation of the metal world, the aging of scene so that heavy metal in the broader sense spans several generations, and the ongoing

FIGURE 8.2: Feature about heavy metal in East-German magazine *melodie & rhythmus*, March 1985.

professionalization of metal as a characteristic since the 1970s, but with heavy impact on the local scene development.

Now, the scene in Berlin seems to offer more opportunities of engagement for fans with different interests and backgrounds. For instance, it enables queer and LGBTQ+ metal fans and artists to establish a scene within the scene, with their own parties, concerts, and such. According to Schug (2017), who conducted interviews with such scene members, this opportunity of individual flourishing while still feeling connected to the larger frame of the scene becomes an important feature. Long-term scene members describe this as a rather recent development. When I asked different scene members in the interviews I conducted, I found that hardly anyone even knew about a queer metal scene within "their" scene. Apparently, the general metal scene is more fragmented, split into sub-scenes. This partly happened due to an ongoing stylistic diversification, as a result of which a long-term death metal DIY-promoter barely knows about the activities of another long-term black metal promoter and label manager, for instance (interview with the author). In addition, aspects such as aging, political orientation, and gender play an important role. Aesthetic differences in taste and style can provoke complete differences between fans as well as general

FIGURE 8.3: Cover of East Berlin-based magazine *melodie & rhythmus* featuring the East German band MCB, a Motörhead-style trio, April 1988.

changing social discourses, such as marriage for homosexual couples (legislatively supported in Germany since October 1, 2017) which was not welcomed by all metal fans in Berlin.

Another aspect is the changing character of underground activities. This can partly be understood in connection to the ongoing professionalization of former DIY scenes such as the death metal scene as well as broader cultural developments of a "network society" and aspects of digitalization. Access, connectivity, and velocity, both physical and digital, allow local scene members to expand,

FIGURE 8.4: Fans at a live concert in East Berlin, summer 1989. Source: Jörg Ebert, Berlin.

transcend, and partly replace their local scene experiences and personal involvement in it.

During my interview with Leif Timm, a long-time death metal promoter, he noted that the DIY activities of the underground are sort of an indicator of the health of a local scene (Timm 2018). Even if there are several different sub-scenes, which know only a little about each other, as described earlier, it expresses a certain vitality and creates cohesion at least within the sub-scene. A certain oversupply of concerts and events that may result from that fragmentation and activities are rather "a paradise" for Timm. However, he acknowledges a tendency toward eventicization in the form of festivals instead of single shows. In fact, even in the 2010s, with new generations of fans, several DIY organizations with specific special interests started to work. For instance, the "Berlin Death Metal e.V.," which began in 2013 to support the local death metal sub-scene, organizes a death metal festival once a year since then. Another example would be the Swamp Conspiracy, a cohort of volunteers for the benefit of the local scene which arose from the perception of a problem:

FIGURE 8.5: Concert of the East Berlin death metal band Darkland in Berlin, summer 1989. Source: Jörg Ebert, Berlin.

> The Swamp Conspiracy has sprung from the problem that the metal scene in Berlin is very different. Everyone is trying to do their own thing. What we've seen in recent years has been that people are increasingly focused on which band they like, how much money they can make. There was a lack of support in their own underground scene. You count yourself to this scene, without supporting it yourself.
>
> (*Gritty Mag* 2015: n.pag., translation by the author)

The organization aims to set a counterpoint to that by giving local acts the chance to open for larger bands who are on a tour stop in Berlin. The team consists of a diverse pool of fans, such as photographers, students, and sometimes the unemployed:

> We have bartenders, concert promoters, electrical engineers, party organizers and graphic designers. So people who have already developed something themselves, and would like to do more for the scene.
>
> (*Gritty Mag* 2015: n.pag., translation by the author)

They consider themselves as an open group, and anyone who is interested are welcome to join them. Since 2014–15, they have organized several shows as well as the annual Swamp Fest. For Timm, one success factor of the Swamp Fest is the diversity of styles that attract fans from diverse Berlin sub-scenes. The Swamp Conspiracy have benefited from the fair and proactive conditions at the Tiefgrund, a recreational area close to the Ostkreuz station.

However, several scene members acknowledge a certain critical intensity, a scene-densification. The DIY webpage berlinmetal.lima-city.de lists an average of about 30 metal concerts monthly, with fewer concerts during the summer months due to the festival season in Europe. However, in April 2019 the page listed about 60 metal concerts. Other lists such as "Hanschi's concert newsletter" provide regular information on about 100 shows a month covering metal, punk, rock, and hardcore. There are more than a dozen metal festivals in Berlin with less than 1,000 attendees. As a DIY show organizer critically explains:

> A special feature of Berlin is the complete "hyperacidity." There is an oversupply, so your own event has to offer something special. This scene is not infinitely big. When I go to a stoner concert, I sometimes see the same people I see at a sludge concert, and when I go to a sludge concert, I see the same people going to a death metal concert. People do not have endless money to support the scene adequate.
>
> (*Gritty Mag* 2015: n.pag, translation by the author)

In addition, Berlin metal fans also travel to festivals throughout Europe, which increases the financial pressure and the oversaturation. Another fact is that in Berlin numerous metal musicians are active. In 2011, a master's thesis analyzed the Berlin scene quantitatively and determined that there are almost 300 active bands, of which about 21 percent had a record deal. Several of these bands are active for many years and playing only occasionally or little in Berlin. This is accompanied by the problem of finding adequate rehearsal rooms as well as opportunities to perform live. Voluntary collectives, the so-called *eingetragene Vereine* ("registered associations") in Germany, run creative complexes such as the "ORWO-Haus" in Berlin-Marzahn, one of the biggest independent nonprofit music complexes in Europe. Here, more than 200 bands from a wide range of genres, studios, musical instrument builders, and live venues find a home. Nevertheless, the situation regarding the price development of real estate in the city is tense.[5]

Few scene members see a change in the underground compared to five years and more ago and note that there are fewer underground activities. One reason

FIGURE 8.6: Berlin-based death/black metal-band Norkh at the club Tief in 2018. Source: Lemmor Photography, Berlin.

for this is that the ongoing professionalization makes it more and more difficult to organize concerts without larger financial risk or financial backup. Due to the decline of self-organized tours and the increasing involvement of booking agencies even in extreme metal, rising costs for venues, and the oversupply of shows in Berlin, local DIY-promoters seem to be rather hesitant now. In addition, there is a trend toward buy-ons into tour packages, which makes it problematic to include local support bands, while local bands from Berlin, for instance, have to invest a lot of money if they would like to play live. Another aspect may be the commercialization and the presence of metal in the German mainstream media (Timm refers to the regular reports and live streams in mainstream media of Wacken Open Air among others). A result of this is that a lot of international guests and tourists travel to Berlin to experience the subcultural lifestyle in Friedrichshain, Kreuzberg, and Neukölln. However, in a fragmented and oversupplied local scene, the risk for DIY promoters seems to have gotten too high to take chances on a poorly attended show.

Political differentiation

A significant change when compared to the Berlin scene(s) of the 1980s is the political differentiation. In addition to a neo-fascist mindset since the 1980s, especially in NSBM, a left-wing metal sub-scene established itself in Berlin, stimulated by and in loose connection to the leftist, anarcho, and Antifa (anti-fascist) scenes. The leftist metal scene consists mainly of younger generations, often born after 1980. The development of this part of the scene was by no means without conflict. Especially fans and musicians, who became active in the scene since the 2000s, embraced younger styles and style-fusions such as metalcore, deathcore, D-beat, and electrocore. The conflicts arose especially at the borders and transgressions of scenes, even though mindset and ideals have been similar, as the singer of Post-War Perdition, which has been a successful underground band for some time, remembers:

> It was actually going pretty well, but we never got anywhere. For the normal metalheads we were the "Zecken" [literally "tick," pejorative for punks and leftist orientations], for the alternative "leftists" we were the normal metal heads. It was always a dread to reconcile everything. The punks have always eyed us critically. They were probably worried that Manowar would now come into the room and flirt with sexist slogans or what do I know.
>
> (*Gritty Mag* 2018: n.pag., translation by the author)

Following the analysis of Fischer (2011: 78–82), the popularity of this subgenre of metal is reflected in a relatively large number of corresponding underground bands and concerts. Some bands, such as War from a Harlot's Mouth, were quite successful internationally, but also faced similar disintegrations from the major metal scene, mainly explained with generational difference (Seidel 2015). Parts of the scene describe themselves as a-political, especially older generations of fans. At the same time, they may organize or attend shows of suspicious black metal bands or even exhibit obvious behavior that favors neo-fascist ideology. From my point of view, the political differences seem to split the scene even further. The political differences are often unspoken to avoid conflicts. More often, those differences lead to a tendency to avoid the political other, which could also mean that they do not see (and like) the same metal bands—a tendency which started in the 1980s with the differentiation into heavy and early extreme metal. Apparently, Berlin's metal scene seems to mirror the general social constitution in Germany, with a potential tendency toward multicultural and leftist orientations—perhaps contrary to rural areas.

Conclusion

Metal in Berlin has a rich and diverse history and scene structure since the early 1980s. Due to the political circumstances of Germany's post-war history, Berlin's scene development reflects on the resultant political complexity. During the 1980s, two rather independent scenes developed under opposed political systems with different consequences. While the socialist state was afraid of the western youth culture and in general prevented a flow of goods from the west, West Berliner politicians did not care much about metal. In East Germany, the society was rather curious about heavy metal, so that even academics started to research about the youth culture including interviews since the mid 1980s. However, there were already early attempts to unite these as one scene. Fans from the East and West wrote each other, and West Berliners could visit East Berlin.

Since the fall of the Wall and the German reunification in 1989–90, there is one scene in Berlin with a growing diversity due to styles and subgenres, aging and generational differences, differing political orientations, and stratification in terms of music industry and DIY underground structures. In the 2010s, Berlin's metal scene appears rather fragmented and characterized by an oversupply, especially of live concerts and events. While an active underground with bands and DIY promoters can be understood as a sign of vitality, not only the aging of scene members but also digitalization may have important influences on the further development and cohesion of the local scene.

Future challenges for the local scene lie especially in the issue of gentrification. Frequently, local clubs and venues report issues with the property owners, raising rents, or suing neighbors. These pose challenges for finding not only important scene places but also spaces for musicians and bands. While rehearsal spaces are in general rare, issues with property can be problematic for metal bands as well. In 2019, the case of the Rockhaus Berlin in Lichtenberg, home of several metal bands, exemplified that issue. Berlin's senator for culture had to jump in and cofound the interest of the owner in order to save the creative space. Several bars and venues had to close in the recent past, and even though a highly debated new law that permits the raising of rents for living space for the next five years was established in early 2020 (and turned down by a higher court in April 2021), business estates such as clubs and bars will most probably face tightening circumstances during the upcoming years.

Although there are growing attempts at supporting the music scene in general in the city, mainly through public funding, the 2020s will most probably have an intensified debate about the role of the creative industry in general. The metal scene partakes only partially in such public debates; yet the outcomes may offer the potential to grow, institutionalize, and open-up further perspectives for a sustainable local scene.

NOTES

1. Song title from the East Berlin band Formel 1 from 1982. The title means literally "This Is Berlin" and is a dialect typically for Berlin metropolitan area.
2. Originally recorded in 1986 (unpublished), re-issue: AMIGA 88697498072, 2009.
3. This became part of the city's official marketing since the 2000s, especially with the campaign "be Berlin" and its slogan "be crazy, be curious, be berlin" or "You are mad, my dear, you have to go to Berlin" (all translations by the author), referring to the Austrian composer Franz von Suppé. That also included new strategies of funding and support for the start-up and entrepreneurship-scenes of the city. For the music industry, several funding institutions are based in Berlin, such as Initiative Musik, Berlin Music Commission, Musiboard Berlin, or Music Pool Berlin.
4. I'm leaving out the Central Institute for Youth Studies (Zentralinstitut für Jugendforschung), since it was located in Leipzig. Nevertheless, it contributed remarkable facts about heavy metal in the GDR as well.
5. For example, in spring of 2019 politicians discussed the expropriations of private real estate companies publicly.

REFERENCES

Anon. (1984), *Berlin Intern: Hard Rock, Punk, Heavy Metal,* no. 2–9, Berlin: n.p.

Anonymous fan (2014), interview with author, Berlin.

Baacke, Dietrich (1987), *Jugend und Jugendkulturen: Darstellung und Deutung* ("Youth and youth cultures: Portraits and interpretation"), Weinheim: Juventa.

Bennett, Andy, and Peterson, Richard A. (2004), "Introducing music scenes," in A. Bennett, and R. A. Peterson (eds.), *Music Scenes: Local, Translocal and Virtual*, Nashville: Vanderbilt University Press, pp. 1–16.

Böhm, Antje (1985), "Schwer, hart und wild: Heavy metal (Teil I+2)" ("Heavy, hard and wild: Heavy metal [part 1+2]"), *melodie & rhythmus*, 3&4, pp. 14–15.

BStU [Federal Archives, Stasi Records Archive] (n.d.), MfS, HA XX/AKG, Nr. 5653, vol. 2, p. 448.

Chaker, Sara (2014), *Schwarzmetall und Todesblei: Über den Umgang mit Musik in den Black- und Death-Metal-Szenen Deutschlands* ("Schwarzmetall and Todesblei: About dealing with music in Germany's black and death metal scenes"), Berlin: Archiv der Jugendkulturen.

Cohen, Sara (1999), "Scenes," in B. Horner (ed.), *Key Terms in Popular Music and Culture*, Malden: Blackwell, pp. 239–50.

Densky, Wolfgang, and Schmidt, Norbert [Formel 1] (2014), interview with author, Berlin, December 4.

Ebert, Jörg [Darkland] (2015), interview with author, Berlin, September 12.

Elflein, Dietmar (2016), "Restless and wild: Early West German heavy metal," in M. Ahlers, and C. Jacke (eds.), *Perspectives on German Popular Music*, New York: Routledge, pp. 116–22.

Fischer, Jens (2011), "Metal in Berlin: Chancen und Herausforderungen urbaner Strukturen" ("Metal in Berlin: Opportunities and challenges of urban infrastructures"), master's thesis, Berlin: Humboldt-University Berlin.

Fulbrook, Mary (2005), *The People's State: East German Society from Hitler to Honecker*, New Haven: Yale University Press.

Gehlke, David (2017), *Damn the Machine: The Story of Noise Records*, Berlin: Iron Pages.

Gienow-Hecht, Jessica (2010), "Cold War culture," in M. P. Leffler, and Odd Arne Westad (eds.), *The Cambridge History of the Cold War*, vol. 1, Cambridge: University Press, pp. 398–418.

Gritty Mag (2015), "Swamp conspiracy: Support the underground," https://gritty-mag.com/2015/04/05/swamp-conspiracy-support-the-underground/. Accessed February 29, 2020.

Gritty Mag (2018), "Daniel: One thousand lives," https://gritty-mag.com/2018/04/15/daniel-one-thousand-lives/2/. Accessed February 29, 2020.

Habermann, Peter [Brutus] (2018), interview with author, Berlin, May 15.

Hitzler, Ronald, and Niederbacher, Arne (2010), *Leben in Szenen: Formen jugendlicher Vergemeinschaftung heute* ("Living within scenes: Ways of youth community formation today"), 3rd ed., Opladen: Jeske + Budrich.

Janotti, Jeder Jr. (2012), "Interview—Will Straw and the importance of music scenes in music and communication studies," *E-compós, Brasília*, 2, pp. 1–9, www.e-compos.org.br/e-compos/article/download/812/599/0. Accessed February 29, 2020.

Kaufman Shelemay, Kay (2011), "Musical communities: Rethinking the collective in music," *Journal of the American Musicological Society*, 2, pp. 349–90.

Mader, Matthias (1986), "Berlin-special: Calderon," *Iron Pages*, 1, p. 7.

Mader, Matthias, Jeske, Otger, and Hofmann, Arno (2012), *Heavy Metal Made in Germany*, 2nd ed., Berlin: Iron Pages.

Martin, Wolfgang (1985), "Musik special: Heavy metal," *Neues Leben*, 8, pp. 8–9.

Molle, Jens (2015), interview with author, Berlin, August 19

Müller-Bachmann, Eckart (2007), "Strukturelle Aspekte jugendkultureller Vergemeinschaftungsformen im Zeitalter der Globalisierung" ("Structural aspects of youth cultures in times of globalization"), in D. Villányi, M. D. Witte, and U. Sander (eds.), *Globale Jugend und Jugendkulturen: Aufwachsen im Zeitalter der Gobalisierung*, Weinheim: Juventus, pp. 137–46.

Musikwoche (2019), "Sony Music verlegt Deutschlandzentrale nach Berlin" ("Sony Germany moves to Berlin"), *Musikwoche*, March 12, http://www.mediabiz.de/musik/news/x/438397?NL=lid&uid=m58115&ausg=20190312&lpos=Main_1. Accessed February 29, 2020.

Neumann, Marcel (2015), interview with author, Berlin, July 9.

Parlow, Michael (2015), interview with author, Berlin, July 15.

Profil (1987), "Heavy metal national," *Profil—Methodik zur Tanzmusik*, 9, pp. 13–15.

Schmenk, Holger, and Krumm, Christian (2010), *Kumpels in Kutten: Heavy Metal im Ruhrgebiet* ("Buddies in battle vests: Heavy metal in the Ruhr area"), Bottrop: Henselowsky Boschmann.

Schug, Lisa (2017), "'Not eager to fit in': The collective work of creating an alternative cosmology of heavy metal," master's thesis, Linköping: Linköping University.

Schulze, Gerhard (1992), *Erlebnisgesellschaft: Kultursoziologie der Gegenwart* ("Society of experience: A cultural sociology of the present"), Frankfurt and Main: Campus.

Seidel, Paul (2015), interview with author, Berlin, June 2.

Starke, Jürgen (1987), "Mit Silly in Ost-Berlin: Zum Cognac bei Honey" ("With Silly in East Berlin: To a cognac with Honecker"), *Musikexpress Sounds*, 10, pp. 74–78.

Steiner, Irmgard, Wenzke, Gerhard, and Merkens, Hans (1999), *Informelle Gruppen Jugendlicher in der zweiten Hälfte der 80er Jahre in der DDR. Forschungsberichte, Interviews* ("Unofficial youth groups in the GDR during the second half of the 1980s"), Berlin: FU Berlin.

Stock, Manfred (1989), "Zur Soziologie gegenwärtiger Jugendkulturen in der DDR—ein theoretisch-konzeptioneller Ansatz und empirische Befunde" ("About a sociology of contemporary youth cultures in the GDR—A theoretical conceptualization and empirical findings"), PhD dissertation, Berlin: Humboldt-University Berlin.

Stock, Manfred (1994), "Youth culture in East Germany: From symbolic dropout to politicization," *Communist and Post-Communist Studies*, 27:2, pp. 135–43.

Stock, Manfred, and Mühlberg, Philipp (1990), *Die Szene von Innen: Skinheads, Grufties, Heavy Metals, Punks* ("The scene from the inside: Skinheads, gothics, heavy metals, and punks"), Berlin: Links.

Straw, Will (1991), "System of articulation, logic of change: Communities and scenes in popular music," *Cultural Studies*, 3, pp. 368–88.

Timm, Leif (2018), interview with author, Berlin, May 20.

Vocke, Frank (2009), "Der schwarze Kanal—Ostmetal-Fans berichten von der Front" ("Black channel—East German metal fans report from the frontline"), *Eisenblatt*, 3, pp. 24–26.

Zaddach, Wolf-Georg (2017), "Metal in Germany," in Paolo Prato, and David Horn (eds.), *Encyclopedia of Popular Music of the World*, vol. XI, New York: Bloomsbury, pp. 357–61.

Zaddach, Wolf-Georg (2018), *Heavy Metal in der DDR: Szene, Akteure, Praktiken* ("Heavy metal in the GDR: Scene, protagonists, practices"), Bielefeld: transcript.

Zephyr's Odem (2017), "Harris Johns: Ich hätte schon gern mal mit Metallica gearbeitet, die haben mir von Anfang an gefallen," http://www.zephyrs-odem.de/backstage/backstage/harris-johns-ich-haette-schon-gern-mal-mit-metallica-gearbeitet/#.XKiv43duKIU. Accessed February 28, 2020.

9

Perspectives Old and New: Cross-Generational Community in the Dayton Metal Scene

Bryan A. Bardine and Jacob Hale

Introduction

Metal music has been around for more than 50 years, and in that time its fans have had to deal with criticism from the press, conservative governments and religions, and the ignorance of people who choose to believe anything and everything that is said about metal music and culture. Despite that, metal has, for the most part, survived and quite often thrived. Why? Because of the fans. Regardless of where metal scenes exist, there are always loyal fans who, at least in part because of the criticism they have endured, are arguably the most dedicated and supportive of any genre of music. But how do scenes maintain over long periods of time? How do members support one another? Support the bands? Support the venues so that there will be a scene in another 50 years?

This chapter is a continuation of a study begun in 2016 which examined Dayton's metal scene in a more general way. In that study, we encountered two distinct groups in the scene: the early founders, who were there at the beginning in the 1980s, and the more recent scene members, who have been in the scene a much shorter time. Our goal for the current study is to determine what has kept this scene alive for nearly 40 years by asking what both groups see as the strengths and weaknesses of the scene during their time therein. We want to understand what they believe has kept the scene going in difficult times—times when the city was in financial difficulty, when the unemployment rate was high, when there were too few places to play, when metal just was not as popular as it once was. Through interviewing early founders and current scene members, distributing a survey online and in person at shows, and through participant observation, our goal is to better understand how these two groups found metal music, supported the scene, and tried to maintain it as a community over the years.

Dayton has had a metal scene for 40 years, but there have been times when the scene was stagnant, when there were few places to play, when some members had lost interest in the scene, and even when metal itself became less popular. Through all of these issues, the scene would have died out without a supportive community. Why is it important to study this community? Because it has survived, and it often thrives, and without a strong community, it would not be able to have shows every weekend at multiple venues; it would not be able to help the greater Dayton community with fundraising concerts and benefits; and it would not be able to bring people together with cookouts, parties, and picnics, even when times are tough. By studying the Dayton metal scene, we are learning how a group of people in a medium-sized Midwestern city has been able to connect not only with its members but also with the greater Dayton population.

Background and methods

Dayton, Ohio, is the sixth largest city in the state of Ohio (United States) with a rich cultural history as well as close ties to the business world and the military. Dayton is the birthplace of Orville Wright, one of the Wright brothers—who were the first to successfully fly an airplane. Dayton is also the home of Paul Laurence Dunbar, a renowned late-nineteenth-/early-twentieth-century African American poet and novelist. It is the home of the National Funk Music Hall of Fame. Several of the inductees, including The Ohio Players, Zapp, and Roger Troutman, either hail from Dayton or have lived most of their lives there. The city is also the home of the National Museum of the United States Air Force, which is located at Wright-Patterson Air Force Base, the largest employer in the region, with more than 30,000 employees. For a city its size, Dayton has a strong arts community. It boasts of two beautiful theaters—The Victoria Theatre and the Benjamin and Marian Schuster Performing Arts Center. The city is also the home of the Dayton Ballet and the Dayton Contemporary Dance Company as well as the Dayton Art Institute, which houses works of art from all over the world.

Dayton is located in the Midwestern United States, a region of the country generally known for being a little more conservative than the East and West Coasts, but it also consistently has some of the best metal in the United States. The Midwestern United States is known to be a friendly part of the country, one where people wave to each other when they see one another. People from the Midwest respect hard work, even physical labor, and they value living the simple life and making an honest living. That same work ethic is reflected in many of the metal bands from the Midwest. Some of those bands are Slipknot (numetal), Disturbed (numetal), Ministry (industrial), Skeletonwitch (black), Chimaira (metalcore), Pelican (post-metal), Born of Osiris (progressive), and Mushroomhead (alternative), to name a few. In interviewing the participants in our study, many of these Midwestern characteristics came out, as well as in the musical intensity that the local bands showed during the concerts we attended.

In terms of demographics, the city has a population of approximately 140,407 people, of which 48.8 percent are male and 51.2 percent are female (United States Census Bureau 2019: n.pag.). About 22 percent of the population is under 18 years old, 65.7 percent is between the ages of 18 and 64, and 12.4 percent is 65 and older (United States Census Bureau 2019: n.pag.). Approximately 39 percent of the population is Black or African American, 3.9 percent are Hispanic or Latino, and 0.9 percent are Asian (United States Census Bureau 2019: n.pag.). The majority of the population is white at 55.3 percent (United States Census Bureau 2019: n.pag.). The median household income (in 2018 dollars) is $31,395, and 32.1 percent of the population is in poverty (United States Census Bureau 2019: n.pag.).

In keeping with Varas-Díaz et al. (2016), we used a mixed methods approach for our data collection, consisting of surveys, interviews, and participant observation, which produced "more detailed and nuanced results" than had we used qualitative or quantitative methods alone (Varas-Díaz et al. 2016: 285). Dr. Bardine is a member of the Dayton metal scene, which opened a number of doors for us to conduct our research. He has numerous connections to key creators and mediators within the scene, including the previous owner of Oddbody's Music Room, where we were allowed to conduct a substantial part of our interviews and surveys.

The interviews lasted between 13 and 45 minutes. Surveys and interviews were conducted in different locations in Dayton, including Oddbody's Music Room, The Courtyard Lounge, South Park Tavern, and Starbucks. Also, several interviews were conducted during a variety of events, including local metal shows and a food-drive festival. We received verbal consent from each participant after explaining the focus of our study. In total, we collected surveys from 131 individuals and conducted 24 interviews from scene members. Our participants came from more than 30 different areas in and around Dayton.

Literature review

Metal music and culture have received much critical attention and have a history of being characterized as violent, obscene, and deviant. We hypothesize that metal's stigmatization may result in especially cohesive and supportive musical collectives. Because they have been alienated from and criticized by the dominant culture, the members of the scene may feel compelled to be especially supportive of other group members, creating feelings of community and an "us versus them" mentality. Weinstein proposes that boundaries imposed on groups by external powers, in this case alienation from the dominant culture, can create a sense of solidarity among group members (Weinstein 2016: 11). Because of the potential for metal scenes to have especially supportive and cohesive relationships due to their alienation from mainstream society, we seek to determine if the members of the Dayton metal scene view themselves as a community, in addition to better understanding the history and trajectory of the scene.

Before addressing our findings, we must first address our usage of the term "scene." For metal researchers (Kahn-Harris 2000; Varas-Diaz et al. 2016; Wallach and Levine 2011), the term "scene" seems to be the primary term used to describe metal music collectives. Although there are many, sometimes conflicting, definitions of scene, we will make use of the definition provided by Wallach and Levine (2011). They consider scenes to be "*loosely bounded functional units* containing a finite number of participants at any one time" (Wallach and Levine 2011: 119, original emphasis). As opposed to the concept of subcultures (see Shildrick and MacDonald 2006), in which members' identities are defined by their membership, scenes are less rigid. A person may consider themselves a part of a local metal scene but can still be free to move in and among the parent culture. Although scenic membership is perhaps less strict, there are limits to who is considered to be legitimately within the scenes' boundaries, as, by their nature, scenes do have borders that are in some way patrolled.

Wallach and Levine's (2011) discussion of scene also provides us a way for understanding the function of local music scenes. They present four essential functions of metal scenes (Wallach and Levine 2011: 119). First, scenes help circulate the music and style of their genre. Second, scenes provide sites for the display of genre-related expertise and fashion, as well as the "collective consumption" of genre-specific "artifacts." Third, scenes offer local sites for performance and the production of artifacts. And fourth, scenes help connect local bands and artists to larger interconnected scenes. In our research, we found that the Dayton metal music collective meets all four of Wallach and Levine's criteria; therefore, we will make use of the term "scene" in our discussion of Dayton metal.

Now that our use of the term "scene" has been addressed, we should clarify our usage of the term "community." In our interviews with members of both groups being studied, numerous participants used words such as "brotherhood," "camaraderie," "family," and "community" in describing their experiences with Dayton metal. The use of such terms led us to question the nature of the community experienced by Dayton metalheads.

Among scholars in metal studies, there is ample precedent for the use of the term "community" (Weinstein 2016; Hill 2014; Varas-Díaz et al. 2016; Guibert and Guibert 2016; Donze 2010). Weinstein (2016), in particular—describing the 2013 Noctis Festival in Calgary, Canada—notes how the participants formed a type of metal community, in which members performed interconnected functions within the collective. Many of the relationships and interactions we observed among the Dayton metal scene members also seemed to transcend a scenic categorization. Many members of the Dayton metal scene serve various and interconnected functions within the scene and express a sense of unity and support that can only be described as a type of community.

Weinstein (2016) provides five characteristics of communities that are useful for examining the Dayton metal collective. Fundamentally, communities must have a set of values that the members hold in common (Weinstein 2016: 10). These shared values, which create the "culture of the community," facilitate community members' mutual identification; if we share values with another person, we are more likely to feel as if we relate to them (Weinstein 2016: 10). The third characteristic of communities is interaction among members, which Weinstein describes as the "enactment" of both shared values and mutual identification (Weinstein 2016: 10).

The first three characteristics work together to create a sense of solidarity in the community. Solidarity is not only resultant from the shared values, identification, and interaction, it works to strengthen them as well, creating a "self-reinforcing virtuous cycle" (Weinstein 2016: 11). For example, in the Dayton metal scene, members regularly hold benefits or charity functions for other members who need them, such as the benefit shows that have been held for members who needed funds to cover funeral expenses. Another example is Oddbody's Music Room, the main venue in Dayton for metal music, which has hosted multiple Restock concerts. To get into the show, attendees must bring in nonperishable food items or clothes. All of the donations are given to local foodbanks and other charities. These examples demonstrate the members' sense of solidarity, which stems from their mutual identification and interaction, as well as the shared value of helping others, whether it be other scene members or the Dayton community at large.

The fifth characteristic of communities is that they must have boundaries in some form (Weinstein 2016: 11). Without boundaries, communities would have nothing separating them from other social entities, thus negating features such as shared values and solidarity. Although many of our interviewees from the Dayton metal scene firmly believed in the scene's open and accepting nature, many of the same participants indicated that the primary criterion for being a member of the scene is coming to shows, a parameter that potentially excludes people who prefer to follow bands online or who face increased social or bodily risk in attending concerts held primarily in bars. Despite their earnest belief that the community is open and welcoming to anyone, there are inherently people who are left out. From our research, this exclusion was not intentional but more often resulted from innocuous group preferences. For instance, a person who does not like metal music would naturally feel excluded from the metal scene, simply on the basis that they do not value the same type of music. This being said, there are some potential issues that accompany the term "community" as well as communities themselves.

Because the Dayton metal scene has all five of the features outlined above, it can be, by Weinstein's (2016) metric, considered an "ideal" metal community. However, the community members' belief that they are highly inclusive—despite being predominantly white and male and favoring public participation in the scene—suggests a problematic nature of both the term "community" as well as communities themselves. Essentially, as Weinstein herself notes, communities are necessarily exclusive (otherwise they would lack social boundaries, and therefore definition), and they often rely on traditions which can be normative and oppressive. Friedman asserts that traditional communities "have harbored social roles and structures which have been highly oppressive for women" (Friedman 1999: 579) and that "many communities practice the exclusion and suppression of non-group members, especially outsiders defined by ethnicity and sexual orientation" (Friedman 1999: 581). Expounding on Friedman's work, Hill states that "the nostalgic vision of the community does not take into account the exclusionary practices and the normalizing traditions that make certain power relations appear natural and that normalize the exploitation of some community members" (Hill 2014: 180). Hill further describes how differences are often not tolerated, both because communities need a "sense of togetherness" in order to function and because they are "ill-equipped to deal with dissimilarity" (Hill 2014: 181). Day (2006) suggests that the very idea of community may be fictitious as it is based on idealized, romanticized perceptions of the past. So, although the Dayton metal scene views itself as a community of equals, this idealized community may, to some extent, exist more in their imaginations than in reality. Although it may be an example of an imagined community (see Andersen 1983; Hill 2014), this does not mean that the members are intentionally separating themselves or keeping others out of the scene. Based on our interviews, they want a community that is inclusive and open to all, but based on the results of our surveys, the demographic makeup of the scene does not suggest a highly inclusive group. What is clear is that some respondents are not aware of their lack of diversity but are aware that they feel included and welcomed.

Results from surveys and interviews

Based on the data from 131 surveys, we learned that the Dayton metal scene is composed of 70.2 percent males and 29.8 percent females. In terms of the racial makeup of the scene, it is 92.2 percent white. The next largest racial group was Native American at 6.3 percent. There were no African Americans who completed surveys. The Dayton metal scene, in general, is quite old. More than 52 percent of the respondents are over 40 years old, with the highest number of respondents in the 41–50 age range, which would put their involvement in the scene beginning, most likely, in the 1980s or early 1990s. The youngest group of scene members, 19 to 30 years of age, was just 18.5 percent of the survey respondents. In terms of the type of jobs that scene members held, 68.4 percent of the respondents have blue collar jobs, while 20.4 percent hold white collar jobs. We were unsure if the means of employment from the remaining 11 percent was blue or white collar.

Early founders' perspectives on the scene

During the course of approximately two years, we were able to interview seventeen scene members who we referred to as "early founders." To us, early founders are scene members who started in the scene more than twenty years ago—in many cases more than 30 years ago. This does not mean that they are necessarily as active today as they once were, since jobs and families tend to take up more time, but most are likely to go to a few shows or are still playing in bands. As we interviewed individuals, we would always ask them to give us names of others they had heard about or knew who were important in the early days of the scene. This approach was beneficial in helping to get interviews with some members who had not been active for quite a while. In this section of the chapter, we are going to get early founders' perspectives on a variety of topics, including what the scene was like when they first got involved, what they saw as the strengths and weaknesses of the scene, as well as if they consider their scene a community.

The founding scene members had a wide variety of perspectives[1] on the scene in its early days. One impetus for members to want to play music was that there was "no home entertainment then [...] to have fun you had to leave the house," referencing the lack of internet, cable television, or even cell phones. Several members mentioned the "do it yourself" (DIY) nature of the scene. Members talked about having to rent their own halls, lights, sound techs, and so on just to put on a show. Since most of them were teenagers at this time, they were too young to get into clubs, so renting VFWs or church halls were the only ways they could actually perform in front of people. One scene member noted, "[W]e had to rent halls on our own, rent sound and light guys and charge admission." Comments like this came up frequently in the interviews, and for the most part, they were not complaining about it; they did it because they wanted a place to play; they loved the music, and they knew people would come to the shows. One scene member even said this DIY attitude jump started the scene. Another aspect of putting on their own shows was the importance of Kinko's Copies. Marc Godsey, currently the lead guitarist for the band Forces of Nature and one of the longest serving members in the scene, remarked thus: "[P]eople would work for t-shirts, [for] bands, [...] posting fliers on telephone poles. It was very grass roots." One drawback of the DIY approach, though, was that shows did not always get the best bands. One musician noted, "[I]t was not uncommon to stomach through the opening bands" to get to the more accomplished ones.

Punk musicians also played an important role for some of the early founders. One of the early metal musicians said, "Punk was very influential to the metal scene. A lot of punk musicians were very fast, so it influenced the metal guys [to play faster]." He also noted that many of the local metal bands were playing covers because bands that could play in bars were only allowed to play rock covers. Metal was too loud and aggressive for the bars. It was the punks, however, who convinced some of the metal musicians to write and perform their own material. Possibly another influence from the punk scene was the aggressive nature of the mosh pits. One scene member commented that "all were welcome, but you might get your ass kicked [...] [M]osh pits were more uniform then, but they were also more vicious." The viciousness might be a response to the feeling of freedom among the members because there were so few adults at the shows.

Several members talked about the atmosphere of the scene then, how it had "a lot freer feeling." Another noted how important the music was for him and how it made him feel close to the local scene. He said, "Metal was more than just music to listen to—it gave me a sense of belonging that I didn't have anywhere else." At that time "everyone knew each other, a lot of things [were] going on. There was respect for each other and there was no real competition." Furthermore, unlike many shows today where all the bands on the bill are the same genre, during the early days of the Dayton metal scene, this was not the case. Steve Lukjanous, an influential member who led several important early bands in the scene, commented that "genres were together, mixed together—everyone was together hanging out." This idea of togetherness and camaraderie was crucial for the scene in the early days.

Throughout the interviews, many early founders identified similar strengths of the Dayton scene. Several mentioned how passionate and supportive the fans were then. One commented that the "fans turned out in force [...] there was a collective energy." Another noted, "[P]eople came to shows—they were huge [...] more came to shows then than now." An important issue during the early days was that there just were not that many shows to go to, whereas today there are multiple venues or clubs hosting shows each weekend. When there were not that many shows, people would be sure to attend because it was their only chance to see their favorite local band for several months. Mike Nye, an influential early scene member, remarked, "[W]hen you don't have a lot of [opportunities] to see a show, people would be there; they were religious about it." He also mentioned that there was not much metal being played in general, so when there was a show, people wanted to see it.

Although there were many strengths of the scene, the early founders identified some weaknesses in the scene as well. One issue that came up often was that there were not that many places to play. One scene member talked about how the bars were reticent to let a metal band even perform in their club. The club owners were close-minded: "[T]hey were scared of metal." This close-minded attitude may have been enhanced by the clubs' desire for only wanting cover bands. One member said, "[B]ars didn't want you; they [only] wanted cover bands," which they felt would bring in more fans.

During this time in the 1980s and early 1990s, one of the most difficult aspects of putting on a show was getting the word out. Usually bands would make fliers and staple them on telephone poles around town or just try to let people know by word of mouth. With the advent of the internet, it became much easier to let people know when and where shows were being held. Currently the Dayton scene has several ways to let people know about upcoming shows. The "Dayton metal family" Facebook page as well as the Dayton Local Music Fans and Dayton Music Scene websites, to name a few, are some popular sites where people can go to get information about upcoming concerts. Finally, the last weakness that the early founders brought up most often were the issues with DIY shows. One scene member said that there is a "lot of risk involved in DIY." As we continued to talk, he discussed that not only can the price to put on a show be high, but also because of the nature of the scene, sometimes people could get hurt, whether in mosh pits or fights. Granted, there were rarely problems, but the chance of something happening was always there.

Despite all of the positive aspects of the scene, members did not always call it a community. The main negative response focused on rivalries between scene members. One scene member said that there was "not much of a community [...] more rivalries, division [and] geographic rivalries then." This early founder stressed that problems could arise among members from different local areas outside of Dayton. He was the only interviewee to make this comment, but it is based on his own experience, and it is important because it does show a possible issue with the community within the scene.

On the other hand, more scene members felt that there definitely was a community in the Dayton scene. For instance, one early founder said that "people hung out more […] [they] went to shows even if [they] didn't care for the bands, to see friends." He stressed that back then the shows were places to just hang out and socialize. He also indicated, in contrast to what he sees in the scene today, that "more bands helped each other out […] bands traded shows," which according to him does not happen anymore. He is currently in a band and does not see the same level of commitment today as when he and the scene were younger. Another early founder believed that it was a community, and he thinks that one of the reasons it is not a community today is, in part, because the younger generation "doesn't understand our sound." He is intimating here that one reason younger members may not be coming to shows is because they do not like the kind of music that many of the older bands are playing. The genres that are most prevalent in the Dayton scene now are the more extreme genres (death, black, thrash and doom), whereas many younger people either are not interested in metal, or they are not as interested in the more extreme genres.

While there is an argument to be made that there was not a clear community in the early days, by looking at both the interviews and the surveys, it seems that while there may have been some aspects of the scene that were not perfect, most people felt that it was a community. Sixty percent of those who completed the surveys felt that community was the most important aspect of the scene. Unfortunately, that question was not broken down by early founder or new member, but we believe with such a high number as 60 percent, a significant part of both groups felt that community was the most important aspect of the scene.

While it seems that most members view the early scene as a community and acknowledge that the scene currently has many positive aspects, there was one scene member who felt that the scene today needs to make a significant change in order to progress. Before addressing the scene's potential shortcomings, we will review its positive aspects. Several early founders commented that the crowds today are more interested in the music than they were when the scene began. One noted that the fans "are more in tune with the music," while another commented that "now more [are] there to watch the music […] then it was more of a party atmosphere." The reasoning behind this could be that the music today is more complex or even more aggressive than it was 30–40 years ago. It could also be that the scene members were much younger then and were more interested in partying than focusing only on the music. Another group of early founders said that there are more places to play and more shows today than there used to be, which is both good and bad. Mike Nye, an influential early founder posited, "[P]eople can say I don't know if I can get out this week, I'll see them next week," which on the surface is good only if they actually make it to the show the next week. In the past there were fewer shows, so fans would do whatever they could to attend. Now, because there are more options, attendance tends to be lower. Another positive aspect of the scene today is that there is a social media presence that allows bands to get their music and information to the public more quickly and easily through Spotify, Twitter, Facebook, and so on, which of course did not exist when the scene first began.

While the fans today are perhaps more engaged with the music, and it is easier to disseminate information about shows, the early founders had two primary issues with the current scene. More than one of the interviewees commented that attendance at shows is lower than it used to be. There could be several reasons for this. First, because there are more shows, people have more options, so they may not want to see the same band several weeks in a row. Whereas in the past, as was previously mentioned, there were fewer shows, so attendees were more inclined to go because they knew they would not be seeing the bands again for a few months. Second, it may be that the predominant genres of metal being played today may not attract as many people. When the scene began, there was no death metal, and thrash and black were just in their nascence, so bands really were not playing them yet.

Newer members' perspectives on the scene

Over the course of our investigation, we interviewed more early members than newer members, but we were able to interview seven people who we have classified as newer to the scene, people who have joined the scene within the past 20 years. In this section of the chapter, we look at newer members' perspectives on a variety of topics, including how the members first became involved in the metal scene, what they saw as the strengths and weaknesses of the scene, and whether they view the scene as a community.

One common way that newer members found out about the Dayton metal scene was through friends and family. One participant remarked that his friend, who is also "[his] tattoo guy," got him to start coming to shows. Another participant indicated that her connection to the scene was through her father, "I got [...] introduced to it [the Dayton metal scene] when my dad started playing shows. He's the lead singer for the Hellhounds." Once she started going to her father's shows, "[she] just got interested in the other bands that were playing."

Besides connections through friends and family, the main way that newer scene members got plugged-in to the Dayton metal scene was through their connections to metal music establishments, such as music schools and venues. Two participants cited the role Trojan City Music, a music store in Troy, Ohio, played in their exposure to the Dayton metal scene. One of the participants learned about the scene while taking lessons at the store: "[T]hey [Trojan City] showed me Zuel. I bought that [CD] and liked it a lot, and they showed me Engraved

Darkness and Reefer Hut (all three are local Dayton bands)." He went on to add, "I also found out about this show [at which the interview was conducted] through them." Similarly, another participant learned about the scene because Trojan City "[sells] a bunch of local band stuff [...] That got me into the local metal bands." An additional participant suggested that he started to be a part of the Dayton metal scene because of the bars and venues. He had gone to a couple shows in the past and realized they "always have good shows." The Dayton metal scene's proximity to his hometown was also a factor in his participation in the scene. He said, "[T]his [Oddbody's] is the closest place to me that has good shows, that book all the bands that I like, so I just started coming here and finding out about bands that are from here." From these participants' responses, a strength of the scene is that its venues do a good job of bringing in their share of newer members. In our interviews, the participants also identified two other primary strengths of the scene.

The first of these strengths we have categorized as "community and/or camaraderie." Although they used different ways to communicate the idea, there was a clear feeling of unity among the participants. One participant replied, "[D]efinitely the camaraderie and working together [...] [E]verybody's all about playing a show, a good show, or just jamming out together on the same stage." Another participant indicated "family," "community," and "acceptance" as the scene's strengths. She went on to cite a food drive going on that evening as an example of the scene's sense of togetherness, "[L]ike the drives we're doing tonight, where we give back to the community. I see a lot of those." To expand on acceptance as a strength, she noted that the scene is

> a nice place just for exploration [...] You can come out one night dressed to the nines or drunk as you want to, [and] people will still accept you, even if you come back to the next show and you're not as crazy.

Related to the idea of acceptance from the scene members, one interviewee suggested that he gleaned self-confidence from being involved in the scene. He responded that the scene "helps you really not be scared of looking different [...] or expressing your music or opinions because you just adopt the 'I don't care' attitude." He continued, "[I]t makes you feel good because you care about yourself, and you don't care what others think about your looks and such." In addition to feeling confident in his choices in appearance, music, and self-expression, he elaborated that you "[build] confidence because you get that sweet anger release that you're too afraid to do in public." Even though they had been in the scene a relatively short amount of time, the newer scene members felt a sense of acceptance and support from the scene.

FIGURE 9.1: Local Dayton band Engraved Darkness' guitarist/vocalist Johnnie Wallace performing at *The Summer Slaughter Tour* at Oddbody's Music Room. Courtesy of Tom Wilson.

The second major strength that the newer members identified was "the music" itself. Many scene members were pleased with the overall quality and diversity of the metal music they encountered. One participant blended both "community and/or camaraderie" and "the music" in his answer. He responded,

> [T]he music, the people [are the strengths of the scene.] [I]t's awesome. It's basically a group of people [who] come together, listening to real good music, enjoying theirselves [*sic*], meeting new people, and understanding what kind of music they're listening to.

Another interviewee indicated that the "power" and "the mixture" of the music is the scene's strength. He expounded, "There's different kinds of metal here, all different kinds." Similarly, one participant said that "the strengths are so many different people making so much good shit [music]. We're making so much good stuff nowadays." Although it may be expected that members of a music scene enjoy the music being produced there, it is worth noting that several newer members were drawn to the scene specifically for the quality of its music, its genre diversity, and the dedication of its musicians.

In our interviews with the newer scene members, we also asked participants to identify any weaknesses they saw in the scene. Overall, there were not many criticisms, which is perhaps to be expected due to the newer members' relatively lower familiarity with the scene owing to their limited time as members. Two of the newer members of the scene that we interviewed explicitly told us that they had not been in the scene long enough to be aware of its weaknesses. An additional two participants suggested that the scene had no weaknesses. One stated,

> [The scene is] pretty much how I want it to be, like, I [...] haven't seen all the bands that are here yet, so I can only imagine what else they have in store. Everything I've seen so far is perfect.

The other participant responded in a similar manner, "I don't think that there's anything that could make it better. The only thing I think could make it better is just to let it keep going, let it evolve, and that is going to make [it] better." In other words, not only is the scene fine as it is, in this interviewee's opinion, but if it is left alone, it will continue to become better and better.

The interviewees that did cite weaknesses in the scene primarily indicated concerns about the scene's infrastructure—namely, promoters, advertising, and venues. One participant responded that the scene "definitely could use more [...] promoters, more choices." When asked to elaborate on what he meant by "choices," he clarified, "[more] options, like you're really limited when [it comes to performing] metal. You only got so many venues when you come to play [in Dayton]." Another participant, although he initially said, "[T]here's no way to make it [the scene] better," later suggested that there could be better ways to let people know about tickets going on sale. He remarked, "I think they need to clarify a way of getting more tickets out." Once the participant had thought of this idea, he suggested that there could be more video advertising and "pictures of the different bands [...] on [a] webpage."

Finally, although many of the newer members of the scene mentioned the scene's inclusivity and welcoming nature, one participant did acknowledge that it could be difficult to feel comfortable in the scene at first. She stated, "I can see it from an outsider's point of view that it could be kind of intimidating because there are obviously a lot of people who take it very seriously." It is understandable that someone from outside of the scene might initially feel uncomfortable with some of the fans' intense expressions of passion. However, this same participant did insist that the members of the scene are "honestly really accepting."

This idea of the scene being very accepting was common among interviewees. In fact, several of the newer members were quick to bring up the scene's welcoming nature or to refer to the scene as a community. Before addressing the participants' responses in this section, we should note that the newer members of the scene were not directly asked if the Dayton metal scene is a community. It was not until analyzing the interviews at a later date that we noticed the community trend in the participants' responses. Future work on this topic would certainly involve a more direct line of inquiry into all of the participant's thoughts on the scene's community status.

Nevertheless, community was a distinct theme that arose throughout the interviews with the newer members. Four of the seven newer members mentioned community or otherwise used a term or expression that suggested a communal experience. When one participant was asked what the strengths of the scene were, she mentioned community as well as family, "Well, first off, family's one [strength], and community [is another]." The same interviewee also remarked that the Dayton metal scene "almost feels like a big family." In fact, this is a common expression among metalheads in Dayton. One of the newer members we interviewed referred to the scene members as "the Dayton Metal Family." There is even a Facebook page dedicated to the group: https://www.facebook.com/groups/462039053827799/ (accessed July 2, 2021).

Another of our participants mentioned two things in his interview that, while they do not directly indicate community, suggest a sense of unity among the scene members. When asked what the strengths of the scene were, he replied thus: "[D]efinitely the camaraderie and working together." Both camaraderie and working together suggest cohesion and interconnectedness among the scene members. He also indicated that he had a strong desire to give back to members of the scene. He said, "I've always wanted to inspire others. Or give people the feeling that music has given to me [...] That's just one thing I've always wanted to accomplish, and the Dayton metal scene really gives that." He continued, "I love playing music, I love the people that come out, I love the good times that we share [...] It's just, it's a connection. It's a very strong connection." Not only did this newer member of the scene feel an intense connection with the other scene members, but he also cares passionately about giving back to the community that had given him so much. Throughout the interviews with the newer members, there were enough instances of people discussing community, family, camaraderie, and connections that we have concluded there is a general feeling of community among the newer members.

Connections/findings

The Dayton metal scene has survived for 40 years because of the resilience of its community and its love of metal music. But even with this resilience, no scene is perfect. This section of the chapter will discuss our primary findings and make suggestions about the future of the scene. First, we learned that the Dayton metal scene is aging, and it is aging quite fast. More than 50 percent of the scene members are 40 years old or older, and less than 20 percent are between the ages of 19 and 30. What this means is that the scene needs more young people to become active. Ideally, the number of older scene members and younger scene members would be about the same, but that is not the case in Dayton. There is too much of a discrepancy between the ages of the groups. So what can be done? One way to bring in more younger members would be to encourage bands playing the types of metal that the younger generation appreciates to play at the primary venues in town. Doing so could bring more young people to shows who may then choose to come more often. We did not see the scene knowingly keeping bands from playing, but it does seem like most bands play the more extreme genres, which younger fans tend not to prefer.

Marc Godsey, an early founder in the scene, noted that the conservative nature of some of the older bands needs to change. In multiple interviews, early founders talked about not liking "younger" metal or felt that the younger generation did not understand their sound. The younger generation should not have to understand the older generation's music; many younger people came to metal at a later time, so they were not influenced by bands like Black Sabbath or Deep Purple or Iron Maiden. The older generation will need to be more flexible and willing to share the stage with younger bands and to understand that there may be some differences in where the younger generation started their "metal education." They might learn to appreciate the sound of the younger musicians' music, which could help the younger crowd be more willing to come to shows and get involved in the scene.

In comparison to the older scene members, we learned that the younger generation sees very few problems with the scene. For the most part, they like it the way it is, while the early founders seemed very nostalgic about how the scene was when they were younger. While this is not surprising, many early founders are at that age when we look back fondly to when they were younger, it is important to look forward as well. The newer scene members look at the scene quite differently, which is appropriate. They have a different experience with the music and the scene than many of the early founders. What seems to unite scene members from across generations is a sense of community.

Previously, we established that there are both early and newer members of the Dayton metal scene who feel the scene functions as a community, or at least possesses communal elements. In addition to this trend, there were a number of interviewees who expressed that the scene is especially accepting. Although participants suggesting the Dayton metal scene is a community and them viewing the scene as accepting are not one in the same, there are specific instances from our interviews that suggest the two perceptions are interconnected. When asked about the strengths of the scene, one participant directly correlated community and acceptance: "Well, first off, family's one, [and] community, but also acceptance, which I guess goes with community." Another of our participants impassionedly linked the quality of the community with its acceptance, stating thus: "Nobody cares what you look like, nobody cares who you are, it's surprisingly accepting [...] It's a great community because nobody gives a fuck." It is understandable that those who view the scene as a community would also view the community as accepting and inclusive. Communities thrive on their sense of interconnectedness and solidarity. However, it is possible that the members' perceptions of the community's inclusivity are based on their existing in-group status and that the Dayton metal scene may not be quite as welcoming as its members think.

One of our primary findings is that there is a trend among scene members of viewing the collective as more inclusive and welcoming than it actually is, at least in terms of gender and race/ethnicity. It may well be the case that some members perceive a community that is more imagined than real. For instance, numerous scene members suggested that there is both an equal distribution of men and women in the scene as well as a high degree of racial and ethnic diversity. One participant stated, "I would say it's about equal [men and women], considering that metal isn't really designed to be toward one specific gender." Another noted, "[You see] about everybody here. Men and women, all kinds of races, like [it] seems to have a pretty good mixture of everybody enjoying it." Some statements of inclusivity even became hyperbolic, "[A]s far as ethnicity goes, it's all walks of life, you know, and it's really cool. Especially in today's time, it's cool to see everybody of all walks of life, *every* ethnicity" (emphasis added). According to our survey results, as well as our observations at local metal shows, these estimates are far from accurate. From our surveys, we estimate that roughly 70 percent of the scene's members are male. And rather than including people from every ethnicity, the scene is composed of roughly 92 percent white people. This does not mean that the scene members are actively trying to keep certain groups of people out, but it may mean that they want their scene to seem as diverse as possible. They are proud of their scene, and it has brought them a lot of happiness and support; it is understandable that they would speak about it in glowing, if not wholly accurate, terms.

What, then, is the cause of this discrepancy? Why do members of the scene view the collective as more demographically diverse than it actually is? We do not believe that they are lying, whether to us or to themselves. Instead, we would argue that it is the very nature of communities that would cause the members to have a heightened perception of themselves. Communities feel a sense of togetherness, which, in some ways, results from their exclusion of the Other. In extreme cases, communities outright ban people from other walks of life. But in milder instances, a person might not fit into a community simply because that person has different interests. Someone who does not enjoy metal likely would not feel as if they belong in a metal community. It is natural, then, that members of a community would feel that their group is welcoming and accepting because if they are already members of the community, then they have successfully penetrated the group's boundaries. It is hard for a group member, who has already been accepted, and is surrounded by others who are accepted, not to feel as if their group is accepting. This being said, it is the responsibility of groups that value acceptance and inclusivity and that seek to grow, as so many of our interviewees expressed, to work to expand their membership. As of now, we do not know the best ways to encourage scene members to examine the scene with a more critical eye toward gender and racial/ethnic diversity. It is possible that there simply are not many women or people of color who are interested in participating in the Dayton metal scene. However, with Dayton being composed of approximately 51 percent women and 39 percent African Americans, we are wary of reaching this conclusion. Furthermore, research suggests that there are many women and people of color who are avid fans of metal music in the United States and around the world (Walser 1993; Fellezs 2013, 2016; Dawes 2012; Patterson 2016). Therefore, there may well be metal fans from other walks of life in the Dayton area that the current scene is not reaching, who would make valuable members and would strengthen the scene's sense of community.

Conclusion

The goal of this chapter has been to analyze Dayton's metal scene through the lens of two groups—the early founders and the newer members. We examined both groups by looking at how they perceived the scene's strengths and weaknesses, whether it is a community and how/if there are connections between the two groups' perceptions of themselves and the scene as a whole. We found that while there are certainly differences between how the groups see themselves and the scene, both groups tend to have positive understandings of the scene as a whole, though the newer members tend to see fewer faults with the scene than the early founders do. The early founders generally saw the scene nostalgically, that it was better in their day compared to today, while the newer members often could find no faults at all with the scene. What we learned, though, is that while there are certainly many strengths to the scene, its members may need to begin looking at

FIGURE 9.2: Local Dayton band Zuel performing at Oddbody's Music Room. Courtesy of Tom Wilson.

it in a more realistic way. The scene is not as diverse—racially/ethnically or in terms of gender—as they believe. There are certainly faults—too much conservatism among the early founders' attitudes toward change and too few critiques from the newer members. By avoiding potential problems, the members do not have to work to solve them, to make the scene a stronger, better version of itself.

The biggest issue that we see with the scene are the differences cross-generationally. The two groups do not really see eye to eye on many things. Although the scene has survived over the years because of its sense of community, if the early founders and newer scene members do not begin to make connections and work together, then the community that has been so vital to the scene may begin to splinter. So, what can be done? One suggestion would be to have the early founders who are still in bands host shows with younger bands, to act as mentors to them. We learned that some of the older members like that multiple genres tend to perform at shows today; this could be the catalyst to bring the early founders' music to the younger members and vice versa. Furthermore, venues like Oddbody's or Turnbuckles and Brews (the only other venue in Dayton that currently has metal shows) could host events such as jam sessions or even events to bring both groups together just to talk, listen to metal, and get to know one another. In the past, Oddbody's has hosted charity concerts and even a couple of metal movie nights to bring scene members out to spend time together. An important part of the movie nights was that bands could bring their merch to the event and sell it. This would get members talking to each other, and for those that did not know each other, it is a great way to meet new people. These are the kinds of things that can further build community.

What brings all of the scene members together is metal. That is where it begins and ends. If both groups are willing to come together and hear each other, the scene will not falter—it will thrive. The Dayton scene sees itself as a community, a community that is resilient and one that has consistently dealt with whatever issues have come its way. Regardless of the problems inherent in keeping a scene going, it has always been able to survive. The city's economic turmoil did not bring it down, nor did the difficulties in finding places to play metal. The way to address the problems in the scene is that everyone must come together, regardless of age, regardless of the type of metal they listen to, and regardless of their beliefs about the scene. The way to keep the scene together and to encourage the feelings of community that have been so vital is for everyone to trust each other and continue focusing on what has made this scene so strong for 40 years—the community that supports it and the metal that they all love.

NOTE

1. All quoted text from this section on are taken from interviews/conversations during the research study.

REFERENCES

Anderson, Benedict (1983), *Imagined Communities: Reflections on the Origin and Spread of Nationalism*, Thetford: Thetford Press.

Dawes, Laina (2012), *What Are You Doing Here?: A Black Woman's Life and Liberation in Heavy Metal*, New York: Bazillion Points.

Day, Graham (2006), *Community and Everyday Life*, London: Routledge.

Donze, Patti Lynne (2010), "Heterosexuality is totally metal: Ritualized community and separation at a local music club," *Journal of Popular Music Studies*, 22:3, September 9, pp. 25, 9–82, https://doi.org/10.1111/j.1533-1598.2010.01241.x. Accessed November 5, 2020.

Fellezs, Kevin (2013), "Black metal soul music: Stone vengeance and the aesthetic of race in heavy metal," in T. Hjelm, K. Kahn-Harris, and M. Levine (eds.), *Heavy Metal: Controversies and Countercultures*, Sheffield: Equinox, pp. 182–200.

Fellezs, Kevin (2016), "Voracious souls: Race and place in the formation of the San Francisco Bay area thrash scene," in A. R. Brown, K. Spracklen, K. Kahn-Harris, and N. W. R. Scott (eds.), *Global Metal Music and Culture: Current Directions in Metal Studies*, New York: Routledge, pp. 89–105.

Friedman, Marilyn (1999), "Feminism and modern friendship: Dislocating the community," in J. Arthur (ed.), *Morality and Moral Controversies*, 5th ed., Upper Saddle River: Prentice-Hall, pp. 578–89.

Guibert, Christophe, and Guibert, Gérôme (2016), "The social characteristics of the contemporary metalhead: The Hellfest survey," in A. R. Brown, K. Spracklen, K. Kahn-Harris, and N. W. R. Scott (eds.), *Global Metal Music and Culture: Current Directions in Metal Studies*, New York: Routledge, pp. 167–89.

Hill, Rosemary Lucy (2014), "Reconceptualizing hard rock and metal fans as a group: Imaginary community," *International Journal of Community Music*, 7:2, June 1, pp. 173–87, https://doi.org/10.1386/ijcm.7.2.173_1. Accessed November 5, 2020.

Kahn-Harris, Keith (2000), "Roots?: The relationship between the global and the local within the extreme metal scene," *Popular Music*, 19:1, January, pp. 13–30, https://doi.org/10.1017/S0261143000000052. Accessed November 5, 2020.

Patterson, Jamie (2016), "Getting my soul back: Empowerment narrative and identities among women in extreme metal in North Carolina," in A. R. Brown, K. Spracklen, K. Kahn-Harris, and N. W. R. Scott (eds.), *Global Metal Music and Culture: Current Directions in Metal Studies*, New York: Routledge, pp. 245–60.

Shildrick, Tracy, and MacDonald, Robert (2006), "In defence of subculture: Young people, leisure and social divisions," *Journal of Youth Studies*, 9:2, August 16, pp. 125–40, https://doi.org/10.1080/13676260600635599. Accessed November 5, 2020.

United States Census Bureau (2019), "QuickFacts: Dayton city, Ohio," July 1, https://www.census.gov/quickfacts/fact/table/daytoncityohio/PST045219. Accessed November 5, 2020.

Varas-Díaz, Nelson, Mendoza, Sigrid, Rivera-Segarra, Eliut, and González-Sepúlveda, Osvaldo (2016), "Methodological strategies and challenges in research with small heavy metal scenes," *Metal Music Studies*, 2:3, September 1, pp. 273–90, https://doi.org/10.1386/mms.2.3.273_1. Accessed November 5, 2020.

Wallach, Jeremy, and Levine, Alexandra (2011), "'I want *you* to support local metal': A theory of metal scene formation," *Popular Music History*, 6:1&2, pp. 116–34, http:// 10.1558/pomh.v6i1/2.116. Accessed November 5, 2020.

Walser, Robert (1993), *Running with the Devil: Power, Gender, and Madness in Heavy Metal Music*, Hanover: Wesleyan University Press.

Weinstein, Deena (2016), "Communities of metal: Ideal, diminished, and imaginary," in N. Varas-Díaz, and N. W. R. Scott (eds.), *Heavy Metal Music and the Communal Experience*, Lanham: Lexington Books, pp. 3–22.

10

La Belle Endormie Awakened by Hellfest Open Air?: A Study of the Nantes Metal Music Scene

Gérôme Guibert and Sophie Turbé

In terms of number of events per capita, the Nantes metal scene is today more dynamic than any other in France. Statistics on concerts have shown that the Nantes metal scene was more dynamic in the early 2010s than those in eastern and northern France (Turbé 2017). Today all actors in the production chain have a presence in Nantes: artists, agents, producers of shows, labels, recording studios, and venues of various sizes, and this has turned the city and the area around it into a highly attractive metal scene, giving it pull on a European scale. The scene's regular activity is punctuated by several metal festivals with varied aesthetics (heavy traditional, black metal, stoner, hardcore), the largest being Hellfest, which is organized at the end of June and which floods the city with over 100,000 metalheads. Nevertheless, before Hellfest, there was nothing extraordinary about the Nantes metal music scene. Given its geographical isolation (in comparison to other cross-border regions), the lack of music industry professionals, the small number of metal fans, and the fact that Nantes does not have a big international airport, the scene was not, before then, on the map for international groups. With the arrival of Hellfest, the situation changed: groups came to Nantes for a festival that was on another scale altogether. How did Nantes become the French capital of metal and build one of the most recognized metal scenes in Europe? In this chapter we will show that the Nantes metal scene was built in a rather unique fashion in comparison to other typologies that researchers in popular music (Straw 1991) or metal studies (Wallach and Levine 2014) have been able to develop. Indeed, the reason for the scene's strength lies first of all in an external event, the Hellfest festival, which has taken place in Clisson, a small town of 10,000 inhabitants 30 kilometer southeast of Nantes, since 2006.

Some background on the city of Nantes

Nantes is a French city with a population of 300,000 (2015), rising to over 630,000 for greater Nantes, making it the sixth most populous urban area in France. It is the largest city in the French "Grand Ouest"[1] as well as being the historic capital of Brittany. Nantes was shaped by the economic activity of its port. Shipbuilding also developed gradually in the city, creating significant inward migration, mainly from the Atlantic coast of Brittany (north west of Nantes) and the Vendée (south of Nantes). It reached its zenith in the twentieth century, before the port's industrial activity drastically declined. The city's population even fell after 1968, and the shipyards closed in 1987. After this, Nantes became known as *La Belle endormie* ("Sleeping Beauty") (Grandet et al. 2011). The population of Nantes fell from 260,000 in the 1968 census to 240,000 in 1982. The city then experienced (from the early 1990s) a new period of development, founded in culture and the municipal strategy of presenting Nantes as a "creative city." Nantes' population thus grew to 300,000 in 2015.

In this chapter, we will describe the metal scene in Nantes, from genesis in the 1980s to explosion in the 2010s. We will show that in this respect Nantes has been somewhat out of step with the rest of France. The first wave of French heavy metal groups obtained a national following in the mid 1980s, when the French economy was growing. Conversely, there were few heavy metal groups in the city of Nantes, which was undergoing an economic downturn at that time. Twenty years later, in the mid 2000s, in what was a gloomy national economic climate, quality of life had improved in Nantes. No longer "Sleeping Beauty," as the twenty-first century progressed the city became *La Belle éveillée* ("Beauty awakened") (Grandet et al. 2011). The activities associated with heavy metal were absolutely not part of the city's tourist or creative communication strategy, but the local metal scene was able to piggyback on the promising local economic context and benefited from Hellfest festival crowds (the festival began in 2006) to become the leading national metal scene (Turbé 2014).

Heavy metal in France at the turn of the 1980s

After the early years of the French scene in the 1970s that we do not intend to detail here (see Hein 2003; Guibert 2019), the 1980s saw the maturing of the heavy metal scene in France. Between 1979 and 1981, the groups AC/DC (from Australia) and Trust (from France) became essential reference points on the French scene, charting strongly (Lesueur 1999). The two groups were frequently played on the main French radios. They gave numerous concerts and were broadcast on TV several times (Guibert 2018).[2]

At the beginning of the 1980s, around twenty French groups were making a nationwide impact, driven by the New Wave of British Heavy Metal.[3] Albums by Judas Priest, Thin Lizzy, Motorhead, Iron Maiden, and Saxon were thus very popular among French high school students at the time (Mignon et al. 1986). The early 1980s were characterized by a new media context. As in several other European countries (Pirenne 2019), press publications dedicated to metal began to appear as of 1983 (Guibert 2018). They were an important forum for French groups and helped publicize local events (tours, concerts, album releases). They also strengthened the links between fans of this music.

Technological developments also facilitated the circulation of music. The popularity of the audio cassette made the recording of music cheap and easy and office photocopiers did the same when it came to producing posters.

The most important changes however resulted from regulatory measures adopted following the arrival of the left in power with the election of François Mitterrand in May 1981, in particular in the media and culture sectors. The 1980s saw the arrival of national private terrestrial television channels, starting with Canal + (1984), then La 5 and TV6 (1986), the repatriation onto French soil of channels previously broadcasting from outside France prior to 1981 due to the state broadcasting monopoly (TMC, RTL, SkyChannel, TV5), local channels, and cable and satellite channels. From time to time, these channels broadcast heavy metal music. MTV became available in France as of 1988 via cable offers.

Furthermore, in 1981, with the end of the state broadcasting monopoly, the deregulation of the FM band led to the creation of numerous local free radios[4] stations. The "top down" effect of television programs and music magazines now met the "bottom up" impact of these emerging local radio stations. In Nantes, there were nearly fifteen "free radios" broadcasting music on FM at the beginning of the 1980s. According to the accounts we have gathered, the best-known heavy metal program was called *Rebel* and was hosted on Radio Nantes by Renaud.

The Nantes scene

Like everywhere else in France, these favorable conditions helped Nantes hard rock and heavy metal groups to rise to the surface. These groups, made up of amateur teenagers, either high school or university students or workers or the unemployed, rehearsed in private spaces, cellars, barns, and garages (Touché 1994). Among them were Squealer, who formed in 1979 and were very much influenced by AC/DC, and Dynasty, who formed in 1981. The year 1982 saw the arrival of Charter,

Sanz (a project from the main guitarist in Charter), Ardeur (who became Fools at the end of 1983), and Tétryl, who played hard rock inspired by both progressive rock and Thin Lizzy and Scorpions. A first monograph of Nantes rock (Thomas 1987) shows that there were very dense contact networks between these different projects. The social interaction began in rehearsal rooms, where fans were sometimes welcomed on Saturday afternoon or after high school lessons. Charter, for example, practiced at a breakers yard on the outskirts of Nantes. There were no noise restrictions (De Montbas 2010) and twenty to thirty people regularly turned up to their weekly rehearsals.

The Plein Watt festival and the rising reputation of Nantes groups

Outside the groups' close networks of influence, the rock scene gained visibility through concerts, and initially through rock springboards ("tremplins rock"). The most famous of these was Plein Watt organized by La Maison de Quartier de Doulon (a social center) and Radio Atlantic FM in 1983, 1984, and 1985. Through the groups that played at them, these springboards brought public attention to the emerging rock subcultures, especially heavy metal. In 1983, the eight finalists recorded one or two titles on a compilation album (33 rpm, 12-inch vinyl). Among them was the heavy metal group Tetryl, who contributed the titles "Les Bunkers" and "Les Mutants." In the album cover photo, they have long hair. Two of the musicians are wearing leopard-skin t-shirts, and one a studded leather bracelet. On this compilation, the musicians' looks differed according to the musical genres they played (blues, reggae, post punk, jazz fusion, etc.). The following year, in 1984, the five finalists were each offered the opportunity of releasing a two-title single (45 rpm EP). One of the bands, Squealer, played heavy metal. For the EP, they recorded two really heavy songs with shouted vocals, in the style of Accept. Their look included long hair, leather, jeans, and studs. Sanz also had a certain following and brought out an album on vinyl in 1986. Charter also recorded an unreleased demo in 1984, and they were one of the winners at the 1985 Plein Watt festival. The festival's record was never released however because it was in deficit. Nevertheless, Charter were the leading band on the Nantes scene at the time, in particular because they were able to make a video of "Fils des Loups" when they played it on French TV channel FR3 at the end of 1984, an exceptional achievement for a local band at the time. After the TV appearance, Charter were then featured in *Metal Attack,* one of the French specialist heavy metal magazines (Guibert 2017).

However, no group from Nantes were yet managing to make a living from music. The concerts took place either in neighborhood houses and social centers or in privately owned venues, or when they opened for national touring bands. Charter thus opened for Factory (from Lyon) in Nantes, and for Satan Jokers (from Paris) in Angers. Sanz opened for Trust and Scorpions in Bordeaux, and Squealer for Trust, Sortilège, Vulcain, Satan Jokers—all from Paris—and Stocks (from Lille) around the same time.

The local scene

Even though there weren't many groups, the metal subculture garnered a few hundred very committed fans in Nantes in the mid 1980s. They followed international groups, whose recordings they discovered, listened to, and shared (by means of home taping and exchanging cassettes). They went to Nantes record stores like Fuzz Disques or Nuggets, which sold new records, or used-record stores (Blue Records, La Bourse du Disque, Discoccaze), as well as following these major artists in written and audiovisual media. At the local level, they went to the concerts that were on offer. However, the time spent together was not limited to these rare events. From the early 1980s, fans of Nantes heavy metal used to meet in town at a bar near the Ecole des Beaux-Arts (fine arts school) called Le Ralliement. At the time, it had a huge jukebox which played well-known heavy metal music. When Le Ralliement closed in 1987, metal fans moved to another bar in the city center, Le Bastille.

In addition to this everyday meeting place, heavy metal fans also took up a nightclub, Les Naïades, in Avessac, 70 kilometers northwest of Nantes, for their Saturday night outings. Obviously you needed a car to get there, which made it difficult for the youngest metal fans. However, until the 1990s, Les Naïades was one of the only nightclubs in the region with a room dedicated to hard rock and heavy metal. What's more, the beer there was cheap. It was quite common for metal fans in France to go to clubs on Saturday nights.[5]

Finally, as already mentioned, the appropriation of space took place by means of the adoption of a particular look. A look was first of all inspired by a fan's favored musicians, as they appeared on record covers or in magazines. Fans bought t-shirts, badges, or patches (to be sewn on denim jackets) at the weekly markets in Nantes or on the Atlantic coast during the summer. But there were also more specialized places in the city—in particular, stores known as "stocks américains."[6] There was, for example, the place on Place du Commerce in Nantes where several people we interviewed bought t-shirts, cartridge belts, US army bags (used by high school and university students as satchels in the 1980s), or later parkas and khaki or camouflaged trousers. In addition, there were also clothing stores allowing you to work up more eccentric looks, especially for musicians influenced by the Californian glam rock/glam metal wave of the second half of the 1980s (Mötley Crüe, Ratt, Poison, but also Guns N' Roses). In this regard, the people of Nantes talk about a shop that sold tight pants as well as lace, another that sold second-hand clothes by the kilo, and yet another that sold fabrics for you to design your own look.

The end of the first Nantes heavy metal scene

Although most of the groups mentioned disappeared in the second half of the 1980s, those who gained a local following moved to Paris in search of success.[7] The only Nantes group that broke through was Squealer, who, after recording a self-produced album[8] *DFR* (released in 1987), went on to play concerts in Paris at the Elysée Montmartre and the Gibus, were featured in articles in *Hard Rock Magazine* and *Metal Hammer*, and got signed by Vogue (BMG) in 1989 for a second album. Their media success continued until the mid 1990s. Another notable group, Fools, initially influenced by Van Halen, were signed by Musidisc in 1991 (in coproduction with Warner) for a one-album deal. Charter's lead singer, Philippe Chastaing, tried his luck in Paris with the glam rock group Charms but without success. During the second half of the 1980s, new groups appeared in Nantes. We should mention Chears, formed in 1985 by two former members of Dynasty along with new singer-songwriter guitarist, Richard Royce. Chears contributed a title to the Nantes compilation *Rock'n'Noël* ("Hard on the Road") and were signed to Barclay. The group Lady's also come to mind. Inspired by the New York Dolls and Mötley Crüe, they didn't make any records in spite of attracting attention through their gigs. Other musicians moved into speed metal, like former Charter guitarist Eric Castro, who was influenced by Metallica and started the band Shark in 1987 (who played with Loudblast). Shark didn't survive the 1980s however.

Bottoming out

Beyond the ebbing of heavy metal as a specific genre, the town hall's heavily publicized cultural policy in Nantes in the 1990s did not give any room to disturbing and minority aesthetics like heavy metal. The 1990s thus marked a turning point because at national level, the new noise legislation forced amplified music events to be taken outside cities. When we look at what happened in Nantes in the long term, it can be observed that activities around music moved to the city's outlying areas. Thus, in the south, in La Roche-sur-Yon,[9] the association Piranha Décibels transformed this small town into a major venue for speed/thrash metal tours. To the north of Nantes, in Vitré, the local association organized the Monsters of Death festival in 1991. To the west, in Saint Nazaire, the Live in Metal association began by organizing concerts at the venue Le VIP (the first of which was Napalm Death in 1996) and then organized three editions of the Bloodwave Metal Fantasy festival. To the east, we could also mention what was happening in the Nantes wine-growing areas, including the Muscadeath festival, in Vallet, near Clisson.

The case of nightclub Le Floride, open since 1979 and originally installed in downtown Nantes, rue Michel-Columb, can also attest to this change. It developed alongside the punk rock, gothic, and new-wave movements of the 1980s, but it gradually moved closer to metal in the second half of the 1990s. At the end of the decade, the club received noise pollution complaints and the city curbed its opening hours, forcing it to close earlier. In 2002, Le Floride moved to the far east side of the Île de Nantes, to the former premises of a music bar, Le Saint-Domingue. It was now located on a brownfield site in the old shipyards, far from the old town. There was no street lighting or public transport. Le Floride's clientele nevertheless followed it to its new location with its capacity of a 100 where a program of metal concerts was organized by the city's young associations.

Apart from a few Nantes initiatives which did not intensify until the early 2000s, concert venues and associations developed more in other cities. Located a 100 kilometers north of Nantes, Rennes in particular saw the emergence of a hardcore scene (first made up of former punk rock and thrash metal lovers) out of which emerged groups (Stormcore, Underground Society, AWOL, etc.), fanzines, associations, and radio broadcasts in the early 1990s. The scene grew at the end of the decade with the label Overcome in 1997, and continued doing so until 2007. The Rennes scene, with the Superbowl of Hardcore festival; the Mass Prod association, formed around the group Mass Murderers in 1996; the Enragé Production label and the booker Rage Tour, initially set up around the group Tagada Jones, established links with Nantes, notably through the creation of local label Age of Venus (To Learn, 25 Ta Life, etc.) in 1995 and Nantes groups like Slamface or Right for Life. To promote extreme metal, which emerged at the same time, the concert promoter association Garmonbozia was set up in Rennes in 1998. At the beginning of the 2000s, the association grew and began to schedule concerts in Rennes which attracted many people from Nantes, as well as other concerts in Paris and Nantes, where it organized concerts at, among others, L'Olympic, a venue of Nantes' new cultural strategy from 1993 and dedicated to the promotion of popular music under the national SMAC label (Scène de Musiques Actuelles—contemporary music scene).[10]

In Nantes, the metal association Sound Effect was created at the end of the 1990s but counted among its members many exiles who arrived in Nantes for their studies, including Karen Le Goux, from Saint Nazaire (and part of the association Live in Metal). She set up the gig listing website (and hard-copy fanzine) *Sueur de Metal*, and was involved in the metal radio program broadcast by a new nonprofit station, Jet FM, *The Loopin' Wild Show* presented by Looping, which she took over in 2004 and renamed *Katharsis*. Sound Effect sought to help the new generation of Nantes groups such as Hysteresis, Side Effect, Anétia Insignis, Aliens Structure, Bloodshed, and Skunt.

The opening of Ifern An Naoned,[11] an independent record store specializing in metal in the Champ de Mars district in 2003, also served as a distribution point for albums by Nantes groups, as well as their merchandising and local fanzines. Due to the high rental costs in downtown Nantes, store manager Guillaume Delautre moved his shop to the southern suburbs, in Rezé. During the six years his store was open, Guillaume met Ben Barbaud, founder of Hellfest. The record store was initially an exhibitor at the festival for three years. In 2008, as the independent record store business was no longer profitable, Guillaume joined the Hellfest team as merchandising manager.

Hellfest as catalyst

The establishment of the CLS Crew association in 2000, which worked in the hardcore genre in the small town of Clisson, located half an hour southeast of Nantes, marked the birth of one of the biggest metal festivals in Europe. At first, it was linked to the hardcore scene which had developed in Rennes and then Nantes. The CLS association organized the Hardcore Fury Fest festival in 2002, programming Agnostic Front with a crowd of 400 people gathered at the sports complex in the small town of Clisson. Fury Fest took place for a second time over two days in 2003 at the Halle de la Trocadière in Rezé, in the suburbs of Nantes. With 7,000 people buying tickets and profits of €30,000, Ben Barbaud, its founder, set up a new association, MAN.IN.FEST, which he became an employee of. He recruited an intern, Yoann Le Nevé, who became his principal partner and continues to be so up until today. In 2004, Fury Fest moved to a site between Nantes and Paris, to the Parc des Expositions in Le Mans, but suffered a considerable loss. In 2005, the association decided to cede the festival rights to foreign promoters. A total of 30,000 people attended, and it was a success, but the association was swindled by the promoters, who kept the €600,000 which the festival earned. It should be noted that between 2002 and 2005, Fury Fest's programming had gradually integrated metal music (from Slayer to Motorhead, Anthrax to Slipknot). Following the problems of 2005, Ben Barbaud and Yoan Le Nevé relaunched the project in 2006 under the name Hellfest. It returned to Clisson to settle in the Clisson's vineyards. Initially inspired by hardcore, they now called it an "extreme music festival," opening the programming up to extreme metal and traditional heavy metal from the 1970s and 1980s. The first two years of Hellfest in 2006 and 2007 helped the association to return to financial health and strengthen the organization, leading to the sale of 45,000 tickets in 2008 and the hiring of two new people. Although at first the festival had been dependent on the municipal council's annual vote, from 2008 onward relations with local government organizations improved and the festival signed multiannual partnership agreements which helped give it stability. In 2009, 60,000 tickets were sold (Marilyn Manson, Mötley Crüe, Manowar, etc.), and the festival's fame was now definitively established, becoming an international fixture in the city of Nantes (Kiss, Judas Priest, Black Sabbath, Iron Maiden, and Rammstein were headliners and more than 250 groups participated each year).

Hellfest has already been the subject of social science research (Guibert and Sklower 2011; Guibert and Guibert 2015, 2016; Charbonnier 2016). These studies draw particular attention to the astonishment of the inhabitants of the region hosting the festival who were not used to metal during the initial years. Before Hellfest's commercial success kicked in as of the 2010s, metal culture did not have much of a foothold in the region and could even have been characterized as invisible, because it affected too few people for the media to take an interest in. The research also emphasizes the rapid growth of the festival, something that is very unusual in France (attendance figures increased from 12,000 paid tickets over two days in 2006 to 180,000 paid tickets over three days in 2019). Tourism has developed around the festival, with the festival site being turned into a park outside the period of the event, managed by the Clisson town hall and accessible to the public. The festival still has nonprofit status and therefore remains independent and has been able to hold out against multinationals that have tried without success to compete with it in France (AEG with Sonisphere from 2009 to 2011, or Live Nation with DownLoad from 2016 to 2018). It's because it grew so big that Hellfest quickly affected Nantes. First, during the festival itself there's work in transport and hotels, and technicians and specialists of all kinds are recruited several weeks before and after the festival and more generally throughout the year. The festival was the occasion for metal's coming out. Young people learned about its existence through Hellfest, and then started groups, associations, and media projects. Many people with metal-related business projects (labels, webzines, merchandising, communication, recording studios, concert production) came to settle in Nantes.

Nantes benefited from the impetus of Hellfest in Clisson, its audience, its groups, and its international media coverage. Yann Le Baraillec, founder of the Motocultor festival in 2007, which is located in Brittany 120 kilometers from Nantes, considers that the success and public recognition of Hellfest have considerably contributed to convincing municipal stakeholders, local businesses, and residents to support his festival. He believes that "[t]he fact that things have gone well at Hellfest, which is on a larger scale, has helped us to build trust here locally" (*Le Monde* 2017: n.pag.).

The beginnings of Hellfest were synonymous with the professional development of metal music in Nantes. A certain number of actors began earning a living thanks to this music at the beginning of the 2000s, whether this was in groups, as producers of shows, in clubs or record stores, or as technical personnel. Thanks to its progressive development, Hellfest helped place Nantes on the metal map and attract the metal "creative class" in a Richard Florida-style dynamic. While the city has been recognized as an important cultural actor since the beginning of the 1990s, the metal subculture was invisible there. In the second half of the 2000s, the Nantes region appeared as the breeding ground for Hellfest, which attracted mainstream national media as well as international artists.

Nantes, the French capital of metal

Following the establishment of Hellfest in Clisson in 2006, Nantes saw the birth and growth of a number of venues dedicated to metal music and associations specializing in the genre, contrasting dramatically with the cultural vacuum preponderant in the city in the past. The qualitative leap experienced by the Nantes scene from the second half of the noughts is very clear, with the appearance of independent privately owned clubs (existing without public funding) with capacities of more than 150 people, which made it possible to program groups from the local scene alongside international groups with professional technical setups. These venues resembled those only found in the three largest French cities at the time (Paris, Marseille, and Lyon).[12] A significant milestone in terms of structuring the metal scene in Nantes and bringing about its professional development (Turbé 2017) came with the opening of Le Ferrailleur in 2006, in the new creative district of the Île de Nantes, where the city decided to convert old shipyard buildings into entertainment venues. Along with two partners, Thomas Nedelec founded the club and concert venue Le Ferrailleur in response to a call for tenders by the city. He was previously a musician but also involved in the local scene, producing concerts at Le Floride and working as a sound engineer for local group Ultra Vomit[13] and for Hellfest in its early days. Playing at Le Ferrailleur quickly became a must for metal group tours. It provided the local scene with a means of development, and brought together metal fans from around Nantes, creating important social bonds. Between fifteen and twenty concerts a month are now put on there, with two-thirds geared toward the metal scene. A rapid rapprochement between Le Ferrailleur and Hellfest, which developed in parallel, created reciprocal reinforcement: Hellfest provided Le Ferrailleur with a successful metal image and at the same time Le Ferrailleur brought together the festival's local audience. Le Ferrailleur currently has seven full-time employees. In addition, since 2012 the venue has hosted the Nantes Metal Fest which programs not only national groups over three days (Loudlbast, Trepalium, L'Esprit du Clan, Klone, etc.) but also groups from the local scene in Nantes and surrounding towns and cities (Rennes, Brest, Saint-Nazaire, etc.).

Club La Scène Michelet also opened in 2009, with a bar and an upstairs room with a capacity of 150. Located to the north of the city, in the university district, the venue was accessible by public transport. La Scène Michelet currently programs around 170 concerts a year, about half of which are given over to metal. Forty associations have worked with La Scène Michelet on its programming, and, according to the venue manager Olivier Piard, the other major players on the local scene have had a significant and complementary role in the venue's development[14]: "Both Hellfest and Le Ferrailleur are drivers for us" (Anon. 2017). The manager of the club Le Floride holds the same virtuous circle discourse:

> La Scène Michelet and Le Ferrailleur are both venues that have grown out of Le Floride's success. Their owners previously organised metal nights at Le Floride. The arrival of those venues and the Hangar à Bananes in 2007 also boosted our business.
>
> (*Grabuge Mag* 2019: n.pag.)

The development of associations has also been facilitated by the existence of bars operating on a less stable economic basis with smaller capacities (less than 80 people), making them more suited to the programming of local groups. This, for example, is the case for Blue Wave Production (death/grind), Eviscer'Asso (extreme metal), Metal Invasion, and Dream Factory, which until 2015 partnered regularly with Rennes booker Garmonbozia to put on concerts in Nantes, Paris, and Lyon, as well as a more recent generation of associations such as Black Flag Production (2014), Soundfest Production (2016), and Black Speech Production (2016), whose programming has given impetus to the scene. Other venues, more peripheral but well-known nonetheless, are worth mentioning here: Le Canon à Pat' in Rezé (south of Nantes), which opened in 1997; the Café Death Porc; and the De Dannan Celtic Pub, located in the city's historic center. More recently, in 2018, the Black Shelter, an Irish pub with a 250-seat concert space, chose to locate itself in Carquefou in the northern suburbs of Nantes to escape noise restrictions. The Warehouse (2017), a nightclub located in the former Hangar à Bananes in the port of Nantes, near Le Ferrailleur, programs electronic music. However, as it has a capacity of 3,500, it occasionally hosts international metal tours. The combined activities of these venues has made the metal scene in Nantes the most dynamic in France after Paris. The Nantes scene has resonance on a regional and national level and even internationally.

Visibility and structuring of the scene

The group Ultra Vomit, founded in 1999, has a strong presence in Nantes, but is also known nationally. When they signed with Obliteration Records, a Japanese underground label oriented toward death/grind, they attempted an international breakthrough with their album release *M. Patate* in 2004, but remained confined to a subgenre that received little media attention. Then, the album *Objectif thunes* came out on Listenable Records and helped them establish a national reputation. For *Panzer Surprize!* in 2017, they signed with Verycords (Warner Music). Playing on the main stage at Hellfest in 2017 and 2019 and at their concert at L'Olympia (Paris) in 2018, which was released on DVD, brought them significant media coverage.

Karma Zero (metalcore), Stinky (hardcore), Enlightened (Stoner), El Royce (stoner), and VƆID (black metal) are just some of the local groups that have helped give visibility to the Nantes scene. VƆID is signed to black metal French label Les Acteurs de L'Ombre, whose founder, Gérald Milani, originally from Paris, settled in Nantes in the early 2010s,[15] regularly putting on concerts at Le Ferailleur. The dynamism of the local scene thus attracts people from the national scene who come to settle in Nantes. Musicians such as the group Arkhon Infaustus (black metal), for example, have set up a recording studio in Nantes. Gronibard and Alcest recorded their latest albums there. Kongfuzi Booking has also opened an office in Nantes.

Specialized media primarily working in metal have also been part of the development of, and swept along by, the Nantes scene. Here we're thinking of metal and hardcore webzine *Horns Up*, which became the producer of Hellfest TV and which has a national audience, as well as Eric Cambray, founder, in Montpellier in 2001, of the webzine *Metalorgie* which is an online reference in France on the hardcore, punk, and metal scene. Cambray moved to Nantes, organized his first concerts there in Le Floride, then launched the Metalorgie Fest at La Barakason (Rezé youth and cultural center) and at La Scène Michelet from 2009, before investing in Le Ferrailleur and then in Le Glazart in Paris.

Conclusion

Over the course of twenty years, the Nantes metal scene has gone from a circumscribed network of amateurs to a local market with national and international reach in cultural industries (Ferrary and Callon 2006). It has thereby freed itself from the need to work with Paris-based organizations, a groundbreaking situation in France (Guibert 2006). The case of the Nantes heavy metal scene is doubly unusual. Firstly, it has benefited from a local and regional cultural policy favorable to the creative industries since the early 1990s and which has been strategic in its consideration of land use planning. This public policy neglected metal music because of its confrontational image (Guibert and Sklower 2011), but Nantes has benefited from the nearby establishment, in Clisson, in the Nantes wine-growing region, of Hellfest, a huge European-scale festival specializing in metal music (more than 180,000 tickets sold for each day of the festival, in which more than 260 groups took part). This has made it possible for those involved in metal music to live in Nantes and build careers within the scene for themselves and those around them. The strength of the Nantes scene can be seen in the various events that celebrate the longevity of its best-known contributors. Hellfest's acquisition of a large bar-restaurant located in the heart of the city of Nantes and scheduled to open in 2020 (Grandet and Lambert 2019) further extends the prospects for the scene's development and the strength of links created between its local anchoring and dissemination further afield, out of which all the different players undoubtedly derive their capacity for innovation.

In 2007, for the second edition of Hellfest, Slayer guitarist Kerry King felt that it was important to play for regions as remote as that which hosted Hellfest.[16] It must be said that at the time France was not known or recognized as somewhere with a metal following and touring groups often settled for a concert in Paris, sometimes also taking in Lille, Strasbourg, or Lyon. The situation has changed radically, because Hellfest has made it possible to break new ground by establishing a durable metal festival for the first time in France since the 1970s. What with the festival infrastructure, its six stages, and its metal merchandising supermarket (Extreme Market), Hellfest works with many professionals in the region, whether they are from an artistic, administrative, or technical background. Whereas at the beginning of the 1980s the scene was made up of teenagers who were unfamiliar with the music economy, almost 40 years later, a diverse metal community in terms of age, gender, and social circles now populates the Nantes region.

The Nantes scene therefore generates today what can be called a "geographical charisma" effect (Appold 2005), with a strong force of attraction exerted on any new actors wishing to settle there. The scene's reputation has thus been built up in parallel to the successive relocations and economic and symbolic success of the agents who have established themselves there. The Nantes scene can also be described as a local proto-market in the process of maturing (Turbé 2017), because it now provides the resources necessary for the professional development of some of its players. Metal in Nantes is thus engaged in a process of innovation that is making it possible to bring about the emergence of actors on the scene on a translocal and then transnational scale. Concert opportunities are increasing, as

FIGURE 10.1: Hellfest programmes, Clisson (France), 2006 To 2013. © Becom Color Photograph.

are career opportunities and the number of qualified individuals working on group development. With the success of Nantes groups such as Ultra Vomit, it's reasonable to think that Nantes may well not yet have had its last say on this matter.

NOTES

1. An area comprising Brittany, Normandy, Pays de la Loire, and the old Poitou-Charentes region.
2. Moreover, the recording of Trust's live concert in Nantes on June 29, 1980 at the Parc des Expositions de la Beaujoire is a testimony to this period and was later released for *Record Store Day* (Trust, *Répression. Live sur Nantes 1980*, Sony, 2008).
3. Featured in the main French rock magazines (*Rock & Folk* and *Best*).
4. *Radios libres* or "free radios," originally a synonym for pirate radios and then a term used for nonprofit radio stations that continued broadcasting in the same spirit after deregulation in 1981.
5. As the French publication *Enfer Magazine* shows.

6. A distant relation of the army surplus stores set up by the US Army after the end of the Second World War in countries in which the United States retained a presence, including France.
7. The phenomenon of moving to the capital was almost systematic for developing artists in popular French music during the twentieth century (Guibert 2006).
8. The album was recorded at Eric Chauvière's studio, the only professional recording studio in Nantes at the time. Chauvière produced a lot of bands from Nantes.
9. Where the group Jinx broke onto the scene. Jinx brought out two albums, with Devil's Records (1986) and then Musidisc (1988).
10. As of 1998, the advent of state and city approved and funded venues accompanied a change in outlook in terms of cultural policies on popular music, even if these venues only hosted metal groups occasionally within their rehearsal rooms or as part of their programming.
11. Which means "Hell of Nantes" in Breton language.
12. However, in these cities, such clubs put on a much more general program in terms of musical genres.
13. Now one of the best-known French metal bands.
14. Ouest-France, "La Scène Michelet, dix ans de guitares hurlantes," which can be read at the following link: https://www.ouest-france.fr/pays-de-la-loire/nantes-44000/la-scene-michelet-dix-ans-de-guitares-hurlantes-5193731. Accessed July 2, 2021.
15. In 2018, he organized the festival for the tenth anniversary of the label Les Acteurs de L'Ombre at La Maison du Quartier in Doulon, where the Plein Watt festival and the first heavy metal concerts took place in Nantes 35 years ago.
16. DVD, Dans l'Enfer du Hellfest in *Metallian,* no. 49, September 2007.

REFERENCES

Anon. (2017), "La Scène Michelet, dix ans de guitares hurlantes," *Ouest-France*, August 18, https://www.ouest-france.fr/pays-de-la-loire/nantes-44000/la-scene-michelet-dix-ans-de-guitares-hurlantes-5193731. Accessed July 2, 2021.

Appold, Stephen J. (2005), "The location patterns of U.S. industrial research: Mimetic isomorphism, and the emergence of geographic charisma," *Regional Studies*, 31:1, pp. 17–39.

Charbonnier, Corentin (2016), *Hellfest: Un pèlerinage pour metalheads*, Tours: Throne of Thanatos.

De Montbas, Renaud (2010), "Interview Charter," *Charter*, *Turbo Metal*, 12" Records, Berlin: Fils du Metal 009.

Ferrary, Michel, and Callon, Michel (2006), "Les réseaux sociaux à l'aune de la théorie de l'acteur-réseau," *Sociologies Pratiques*, 13:2, pp. 37–44.

Grabuge Mag (2019), "Le Floride, 40 ans toujours passion," https://www.grabugemag.com/interview-le-floride-40-ans-toujours-passion/. Accessed June 10, 2020.

Guibert, Christophe, and Guibert, Gérôme (2015), "Metalheads characteristics: Some statistics from the main French metal event (Hellfest)," in T. M. Karjalainen, and K. Kärki (eds.), *Modern Heavy Metal Markets Practices and Culture*, Helsinki: MHM, pp. 64–69.

Guibert, Christophe, and Guibert, Gérôme (2016), "The social characteristics of the contemporary metalheads: The Hellfest survey," in A. R. Brown, K. Spracklen, K. Kahn-Harris, and N. W. R Scott, *Global Metal Music and Culture: Current Directions in Metal Studies*, New York: Routledge, pp. 167–89.

Guibert, Gérôme (2006), *La production de la culture: Le cas des musiques amplifiées en France*, Paris: Mélanie Seteun and Irma.

Guibert, Gérôme (2017), "La presse magazine musicale," in Claire Blandin (ed.), *Manuel d'analyse de la presse magazine en France*, Paris: Armand Colin, pp. 229–43.

Guibert, Gérôme (2018), "*Marche ou crève*: The band Trust and the singular case of the birth of French heavy metal," in G. Guibert, and C. Rudent (eds.), *Made in France, Studies in Popular Music*, New York: Routledge, pp. 89–103.

Guibert, Gérôme (ed.) (2019), *Trop fou pour toi: 50 ans de hard rock, heavy metal, metal français*, SACEM Online Exhibition, Sacem Museum, June, https://musee.sacem.fr/index.php/ExhibitionCMS/ExhibitionCMS/ComplexExhibitions?id=1241. Accessed June 10, 2020.

Guibert, Gérôme and Sklower, Jedediah (2011), "Hellfest: The thing that should not be? Local perceptions and Catholic discourses on metal culture in France," *Popular Music History*, 6:2, pp. 100–15.

Grandet, Magali, and Lambert, Stéphanie (2019), "Hellfest: Un bar restaurant s'installe à Nantes en 2020," *Ouest France*, December 17, https://nantes.maville.com/sortir/infos_-hellfest.-un-bar-restaurant-s-installe-a-nantes-en-2020_52716-3944325_actu.Htm. Accessed July 2, 2021.

Grandet, Magali, Pajot, Stéphane, Sagot-Duvauroux, Dominique, and Guibert, Gérôme (2011), *Nantes la belle éveillée: Le pari de la culture*, Toulouse: Editions de L'attribut.

Hein, Fabien (2003), *Hard Rock, Heavy Metal, Metal: Histoire, culture et pratiquants*, Nantes: Mélanie Seteun and Irma.

Le Monde (2017), "La route des festivals," http://www.lemonde.fr/la-route-des-festivals/article/2017/08/20/escapadeau-motocultor-festival-petit-frere-du-hellfest_5174341_5151848.html#jTuvxQWxqxlxkWfp.999. Accessed June 10, 2020.

Lesueur, Daniel (1999), *Hit-parades (1950–1998)*, Paris: Alternatives et Parallèles.

Mignon, Patrick, Boyer, Régine, and Daphy, Eliane (1986), *Les lycéens et la musique*, Paris: INRP.

Pirenne, Christophe (2011), *Une histoire musicale du rock*, Paris: Fayard.

Pirenne, Christophe (2019), "Né sous une (très) mauvaise étoile: Une étude de cas dans la réception de la new wave of British heavy metal," *Volume!*, 15:2, pp. 15–23.

Straw, Will (1991), "Systems of articulation, logics of change: Communities and scenes in popular music," *Cultural Studies*, 5:3, pp. 368–88.

Thomas, Régis (1987), "Enquête sur les musiciens rock de la région nantaise," master's thesis, Nantes: Université de Nantes, November.

Touché, Marc (1994), *Connaissance de l'environnement sonore urbain, l'exemple des lieux de répétition; faiseurs de bruits? Faiseurs de sons? Question de point de vue*, CRIV-CNRS research report, Vaucresson: CNRS.

Turbé, Sophie (2014), "Observer les déplacements dans la construction des scènes locales: Le cas de la musique metal en France," *Cahiers de Recherche Sociologique*, 57, pp. 97–113.

Turbé, Sophie (2017), "Observation de trois scènes locales de musique metal en France: Pratiques amateurs, réseaux et territoires," doctoral thesis, Lorraine: Université de Lorraine.

Wallach, Jeremy, and Levine, Alexandra (2014), "'I want *you* to support local metal': A theory of metal scene formation," *Popular Music History*, 6, pp. 116–34.

11

Heavy Metal in Estonia: Cohesions and Divisions, Past and Present

Toni-Matti Karjalainen

Introduction

Estonia, the small Baltic nation in the northeastern corner of Europe, with a population of 1.3 million, may not be known for metal music. The folk metal group Metsätöll is pretty much the only Estonian band that has broken through to a wider international consciousness within the global metal community. However, the Map of Heavy Metal Bands by Country Per Capita[1] which was based on the listings of *Encyclopaedia Metallum*[2] suggested that there exists quite an active metal scene in the country. In this review, Estonia had 151 bands, which averages 12.3 bands per 100,000 people. This number lagged behind its Nordic neighbors, the leaders of this comparison, Finland (53.2), Sweden (37.1), and Norway (27.0). However, Estonia was in the same group with countries like Germany (10.0) and Denmark (12.6), with numbers higher than the United Kingdom (5.1) and the United States (5.5). In comparing Estonia to some other Baltic countries—Latvia (3.0) and Lithuania (3.5), or Russia (1.4)—their scenes appear tiny in comparison to Estonia.

Albeit informative, this comparison, however, is outdated,[3] and is not particularly revealing details or the "true" state of the scene. Other kinds of information were needed, which was the start of my more active personal Estonian explorations in the Spring of 2016. I was invited to be part of the jury in the semifinals of the first Wacken Metal Battle Estonia, the globally spread band competition in which the local winners get to perform at the Wacken Open Air metal festival in Germany. The battle took place in a small club called Rockstar's in the city of Tallinn, the Estonian capital located 2.5 hours ferry ride south from Finland's capital Helsinki. This experience got me digging a bit deeper into the Estonian scene, to go beyond the sheer numbers on the surface. I soon realized that the Estonian metal scene not only has an interesting history with a peculiar cultural position but also has become viable in recent years. The scene is as of yet small and largely hobby-based, but also very versatile, consisting of a mix of younger and older metal fans and bands—some nurturing the more traditional streams of black and death metal, others developing new sounds and exploring genre boundaries in the form of modern metal, hardcore, punk, doom, stoner rock, to name a few. Representing the modern stream, Horror Dance Squad eventually won the local battle and ended up playing at Wacken in the summer of 2016.

There were two generic objectives for this exploration. The first one was to describe the state of the current heavy metal scene in Estonia and to construct a narrative of its historical development. The second objective, which also functions as the core thematic thesis of the chapter, was to investigate if there actually exists one cohesive scene or merely a set of divided sub-scenes, and, in the case of cohesion, what might keep the scene members connected and the scene viable. Furthermore, the chapter looks at how different cohesions and divisions have appeared in the past, and what impact they may have on the current scene.

The study

Local metal scenes around the globe have been extensively explored in academic studies (e.g., Wallach et al. 2011; Karjalainen and Kärki 2015; Varas-Díaz and Scott 2016; Brown et al. 2016; Elovaara and Bardine 2017; Karjalainen 2018). When searching for background information on the Estonian scene, however, the scarcity of documentation becomes clear. There are a few studies found on Estonian music in general or on particular genres (Smidchens 1996; Rüütel 2003; Pawlusz 2018), but the view of metal and hard rock are largely absent. Furthermore, while the Estonian metal scene is unexplored in academic circles, popular writings are relatively rare too.

Inspired by the book at hand, I decided to fill the gap by conducting an explorative study on the Estonian metal scene through three primary approaches and data, conducted in this chronological order:

1. Desktop research on the existing online articles and other materials on the scene,
2. In-depth interviews with selected key persons of the scene, and
3. An online survey for the scene members.

First, to build a rough overview of the scene, I started the exploration by browsing through older Estonian band and artist interviews online, the majority appearing in estonianmetal.com site.[4] Most of these interviews were conducted by small zines and blogs from different countries (all in English) and included a wide variety of Estonian metal bands. Benefiting the scope of this chapter, many of these interviews also included questions about the state and history of the Estonian scene that seemed to appear quite unknown for most interviewers. These interviews provided a solid body for the history review and state of the scene in different time periods, revealing many common themes and characteristics, historical facts, bands, and genres.

However, it was difficult to find interviews or reports from the last three to four years, as they were not collected anymore on the estonianmetal.com site, and general Google searches did not help. Neither were there any Estonian metal stories or interviews appearing in international music magazines or sites, with the few exceptions of Metsatöll. The existing online interviews were mostly short and anecdotal, lacking deeper exploration on the aspects constructing the scene, let alone possible descriptions of the scene cohesion.

In order to get more up-to-date views of the scene, as well as longer and more personal experiences and insights concerning the development of the Estonian scene by persons who have experienced it in the core, it was therefore important to arrange a set of interviews on the spot. In particular, I needed opinions from people having a wide view on the scene: those working in the industry, running the scene infrastructure and events. I did face-to-face interviews with seven key persons in Tallinn, including musicians and metal industry operators during two trips to Tallinn in January 2019.[5] The informants had multifaceted profiles and wide experiences in the scene, which is typical for a small scene like Estonia, including a musician, promoter, club owner, concert and festival organizer, band manager, record shop vendor, and others. The most experienced one had spent 30 years in the Tallinn scene; the newer ones, five to fifteen years. In addition, I had more casual conversations with a few people outside the metal scene as well.

After analyzing these insightful interviews, it then became obvious that some further and more general data would be beneficial, especially to map the current state of the scene. Albeit highly informative and eye-opening, the informants were also looking at the scene from different angles, having slightly contradictory opinions, also colored either by their experiences on the promotion and organization side of the scene (especially the promoters) or by the particular sub-scene of metal they were operating (especially the artists). Therefore, as the third step, an online survey was created to get a wider view of the current state of the Estonian metal scene. The survey (with twenty brief questions, see the appendix) was launched on September 6, 2019 and was open for 17 days. It was added on the estonianmetal.com Facebook site and shared actively.

In the remaining part of the chapter, first I start with the description of the current scene, mainly based on the survey. Then, based on the interviews and desktop study, in the next section, I will be reflecting on the history of Estonian metal, as it has a strong connection to the present state, and is interesting as such, as well as discussing a few emerging themes.

Overview of the current scene

The survey, in particular, provided an overview of the general activity and atmosphere within the Estonian metal scene, along with some basic figures concerning the demographics and size of the scene. In total, 212 responses were received. The first 100 answers came within three hours after putting the survey online, and most of the rest in the first three days, which strongly signals the activity in the scene. Only a few responses arrived in the last days, none in the final day, suggesting a well-saturated sample of the scene members. Furthermore, the survey was completely filled by most respondents, only a few did not answer some individual questions, and even the final "Anything else you want to say about the present status of the Estonian metal scene" received 107 answers from 212 respondents.

Overall, the survey participants presumably represent a good overview of the scene members, including people who are active online and follow estonianmetal.com (and gathering a likely overrepresentation of Estonian-speaking versus Russian-speaking fans due to the language and identity issues).

Scene dispersion

Based on the survey, the Estonian scene entails a pretty dispersed age range as well as a male majority, typical for metal (see Figure 11.1). Most respondents (200) were of Estonian nationality, but also four Russians, one Portuguese, one Latvian, one German, one North American, and four nonrespondents were included. As the mother tongue, 193 spoke Estonian, 10 Russian, and 1 Finnish, Portuguese, German, and English.

The versatility of the respondents was also highlighted by the high number of different occupational, professional, and educational backgrounds (open question); the range extended from students to professionals of various kinds, from construction workers to IT specialists, from laymen to PhDs. No particular groups were clearly dominating. What was striking, however, was that only four respondents marked themselves as musicians and six otherwise working in relation to music (i.e., teaching or industry). This reinforced the pre-assumption that the metal scene is strongly hobby-based, especially since over half of the respondents

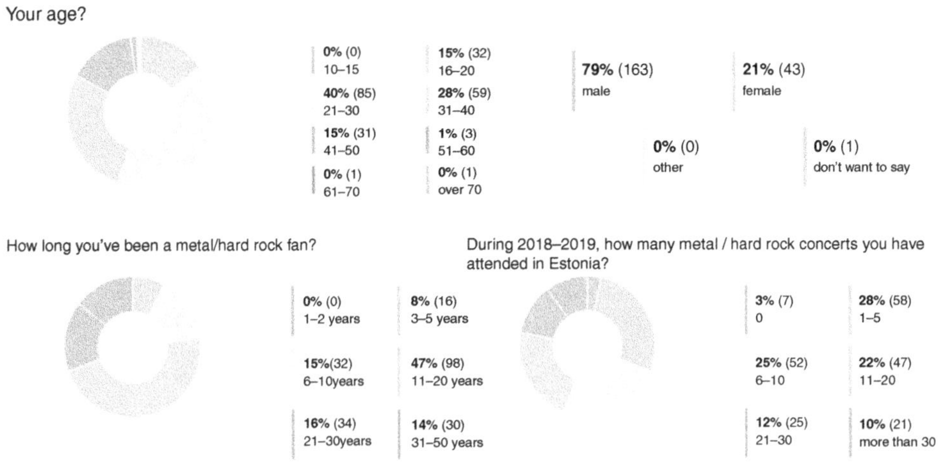

FIGURE 11.1: Survey respondents' age, sex, duration of metal fandom, and concert going activity.

(111) noted that they have been a musician in the next question. In that question, they also name 83 different bands in which they played, from newly established to long-standing ones. The instruments mentioned covered evenly the "basic" rock set of guitar, drums, bass, and vocals, with only a few others included.

Metal cohesion

Despite the dispersed representation of Estonian metal fans, overall, the metal fandom functions as a cohesive unit connecting the scene members. There apparently emerged a strong feeling of distinction: A scene around metal exists and its members recognize themselves as part of this defined community. This was not only discussed during the interviews but also particularly suggested by the survey; a question was included where the respondents were asked to estimate how many people actively listen to metal among their peers (family and friends). The numbers, shown in Figure 11.2, strongly suggest that there exists a recognizable scene, that the metal fans hang around other metal fans. Namely, as comparison, the respondents were also asked to estimate how many people actively listen to metal among the Estonian people in general. The percentages turned out to be much lower than those among their peers. Hence, 95 percent of the respondents estimated that less than 30 percent of Estonians listen to metal, the majority suggesting 5–10 percent, almost half (49 percent) saw more than 30 percent of their peers listening to metal, the majority ticking the more than 50 percent box.

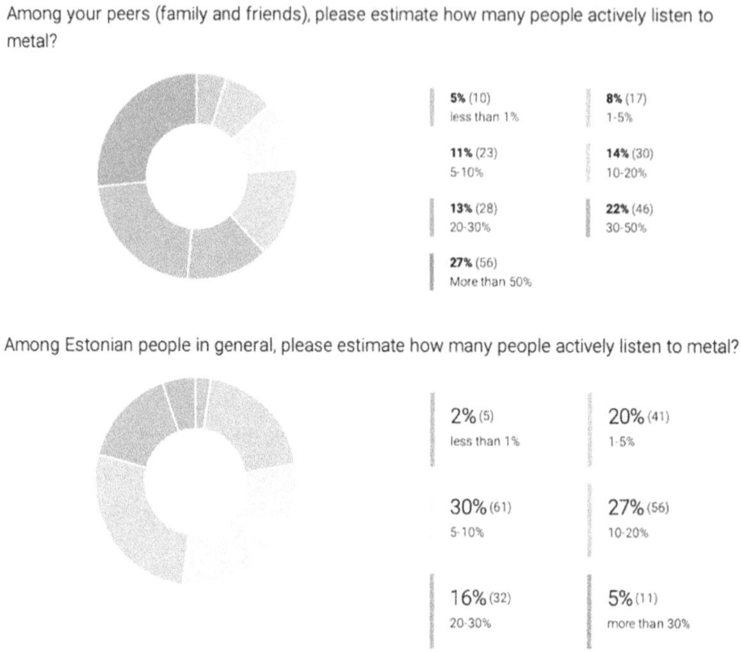

FIGURE 11.2: Estimation of the metal activity of the Estonian metal community versus the common public.

But how large was the Estonian metal community overall? In one open question, survey respondents were asked to roughly estimate the total number of Estonian metal fans (attending gigs) at the moment, and whether the number would be lower or higher than five years ago. In this category, the answers varied quite a lot. The number of fans ranged from 50 to 100,000, perhaps also suggesting the nature of the events and their audiences, from the underground gigs to the mega-concerts by Metallica and the like. However, the most typical answers saw the size of the Estonian metal community comprising a few thousand active fans. There appeared, however, quite a clear indication that the activity of the local metal scene has been increasing recently. A total of 98 respondents said the current number of metal fans is higher than five years ago, whereas 34 said it's about the same, and 38 that it is lower. Many interviewees on the second phase of the study also suggested that the Estonian metal scene is experiencing its highest peak at the moment.

Metal was considered a minor genre and predominantly underground in Estonia. Asking for the most popular music genres domestically, the respondents mostly mentioned pop, hip hop/rap, EDM, and generic rock. This is suggesting the same situation as in most other countries; all these genres also having both domestic and foreign artists. The marginal position of metal probably strengthens the sensed cohesion among the scene members. At the same time, it is however important to note that in terms of the respondents' own music listening habits, there were not many "only metal" persons. The great majority, when asking what genres other than metal they are actively following, listed a number of examples ranging from classical to different styles of rock, electronic to jazz, punk to hip hop, and so forth. In total, almost 50 different genres were named. This echoes the clearly visible dispersion of the current scene in terms of styles and subgenres, as will be discussed in the next section.

Active bands and subgenres

What were the biggest and/or most influential subgenres and local bands of the Estonian metal scene? Both in interviews and in the survey, one needs to be careful when analyzing the answers, as many may have naturally promoted their own favorite bands and genres rather than trying to look at the bigger picture. However, this is quite a large sample and is representative of the scene.

The current scene involved many bands and players from the earlier waves of Estonian metal, to be briefly summarized later in this chapter. Alongside these black, pagan, death, thrash, and other more "traditional" performers and supporters, a newer generation of Estonian metal fans and bands had emerged. In the survey, respondents were asked to give an estimation of the number of active Estonian metal bands at the moment. The answers ranged between the peaks of 5 and 5,000, but most of them stayed between 50 and 150 (86 respondents) and less than 50 (74). In the interviews, some of my informants estimated that there might be around 100 Estonian metal bands existing today, of which 50 of them are currently active.[6] These estimations were well in line with the survey answers.

The most influential bands

The survey asked the respondents to name the most influential Estonian metal bands in the current scene. This was also an open question; they could name as many as they like. In total, 85 bands were mentioned, which also suggests that there are perhaps overall some 100 active bands at the moment (also noticing that some of the mentioned bands are not actually active at the time). The top three of the listing was clear. Most of all, Metsatöll (pagan/folk[7]) was regarded by far the most influential band, getting 147 mentions, quite a few even without any other bands mentioned. Following them were Goresoerd (grindcore/death) with 57 and

Pedigree (industrial) with 40 mentions. Loits (pagan/black) and Tankist (thrash) scored 26, Tharapita (pagan/black) 24, Talbot (stoner/doom) 22, and Herald (speed/heavy) 17. The Wacken Battle winners Horror Dance Squad (modern/groove/metalcore) were mentioned eight times.

Talbot (established 2008) is also worth mentioning separately. They were the winners of the Estonian Music Awards 2019 metal category. Their first album *EOS* (2010) was nominated for the Best Metal album of the Estonian Music Awards 2010, and the second album *Scaled* (2013) won the same category in 2013. The band has been touring often in Europe and also visited Japan in 2018.

Most of the other bands, however, were rather local. The folk metal group Metsatöll (established 1999) was the only one that was more widely recognized in metal communities. The success and scale of recognition is of course difficult to assess, and all the other bands' popularity was far behind Metsatöll.[8]

Looking at the list of the most influential Estonian metal bands in its history, the responses were slightly different: 74 bands were mentioned here. Metsatöll was again on its own level (114 mentions). The rest of the top eight was populated by Loits (69), Tharapita (42), GGG (Gunnar Graps Group) (34, heavy rock), Aggressor[9] (27, death), Shower (19, thrash/speed), No-Big-Silence (14, industrial), and Manatark (11, black/extreme). The punk rock band J.M.K.E. also received ten mentions.

Active subgenres in the current scene

As the genre diversity of the influential bands suggest, there appeared some subgenre variety within the Estonian metal scene. But what were the most active subgenres of metal in the current scene? That was one of the survey questions, and the respondents were again able to list as many candidates as they wanted. Dividing subgenres is of course not as straightforward as that; bands often cross boundaries that are not clear, different evolutions appear, and so forth. There were also many Estonian bands mixing different styles like black/pagan, death/black, metalcore/death, doom/stoner, just to name a few.

One general observation from the survey, also strongly supported by the desktop study and interviews, was the amount of extreme metal throughout the whole history of Estonian metal, with the exception of its inception. The small number of melodic metal bands in the current scene was striking, for instance in comparison to the Finnish or Swedish scenes. In the survey, heavy metal got fourteen mentions, but power metal only two. The ten biggest metal subgenres listed, in turn, were black (73), death (69), thrash (36), folk/pagan (34), stoner (33), metalcore (21), doom (20), punk (15), heavy (14), and industrial (10). Altogether 24 different subgenres were listed.

In the various interviews, there appeared a division, chronologically based, between the more traditional black, death, and thrash metal especially consumed and produced by the older scene members and the more modern incarnations of metal, death, grind and hardcore, progressive, groove, stoner, industrial, and other subgenres with younger musicians and fans. This division also existed in Bardine's study in this book. The rather strong folk/pagan scene in turn was particularly influenced by Metsatöll and some bands combining those styles with black metal approaches.

Scene makers, places, and events

Concrete places and events, as well as people putting up and running those, are crucial for any scene to exist. They are also the cohesive glue keeping the community viable, despite the clear divisions between the subgenres. Such cohesive places and events were also specifically examined in the study, both in the interviews and the survey.

Clubs and festivals

There were again many varied suggestions for the most important places in the current Estonian metal scene (clubs, stores, other). However, a few stood out. First, most of the places are located in Tallinn which was generally seen as the center for the Estonian metal scene. It was also estimated in the interviews that 80–90 percent of metal bands are from Tallinn.

Even though a long list of (still running or closed) clubs and venues were mentioned, it became evident that club Tapper was considered the core place, followed by club Barbar, both purely focusing on metal and rock shows. From the key general venues hosting many metal concerts, and as one respondent summarized, they were becoming more important for "quality shows," Von Krahl and Sveta Baar received many mentions. Furthermore, other important places for many were the Rock Café, Woodstock Rock Club / Rockstar's. Outside the music venues, Nailboard Rock Shop was often mentioned as an important place as well. In Tartu, the second largest city of Estonia, club Rock & Roll Heaven and rock bar Underground were regularly mentioned as the key places outside Tallinn.

Concerning the most important events of the current Estonian metal scene, the answers were the most uniform of the whole survey. Hard Rock Laager, the annual Estonian metal festival, was mentioned by 156 respondents. Other events such as Hard Rock Camp, Howls of Winter (underground black metal festival), Barbar Fest, and concerts in the mentioned key venues were also regarded as important. Many also mentioned Tallinn Music Week and its newly established "Metal Stage" evening.

Key persons

In a small scene like Tallinn, it becomes tremendously important that there are people who commit to organize the events and run the venues. One question in the survey concerned the most important persons of the current scene (musicians, promoters, managers, producers, others). Interestingly, it was almost solely the promoters and creators/organizers of the events and venues who were mentioned. The list of names was again long but three persons clearly stood out. Kaido Haavandi (also known by his artist name "Draconic")—being active in the Estonian metal scene since the mid 1990s as musician, promoter, organizer, you name it, also behind the club Tapper and Hard Rock Laager festival—was regarded as the most influential person of the scene. He was mentioned by 78 respondents. Roman Demchenko (21 mentions) with his company Damn.Loud Agency (10) as well as Tanya Korenik (11) and her Urban Culture Entertainment (12) were the next most often mentioned key persons, both very active promoters and organizers of the current high-profile metal concerts with foreign bands. These three persons were also the key informants of my interview study. This was however the category in the survey that received the lowest number of answers overall, many also saying they don't know or don't want to say who would be the key names. And as nicely put by one respondent, "the most important persons are the active scene members who come to the shows."

In the interviews, we discussed the places, events, and the state of the scene in more detail as experienced by the industry people and musicians. Club Tapper (500 capacity) has long been, and still is, the central meeting point for the community. It hosted three to four bigger gigs per month, typically with foreign headliners.[10] Rock Cafe (1,500 capacity) was the biggest venue in terms of the size, hosting different genres and only a few metal gigs annually.[11] The local bands, in turn, and some smaller international bands typically played in different venues like Rockstar's, Sveta Baar, and Barbar.

Local-international division

A notable observation was that the local scene was quite strongly divided between the bigger shows and venues with international bands and smaller gigs and clubs hosting local bands. The rise in the activity of the scene in the preceding five years predominantly resulted from the increased number of visiting bands in Estonia, not through locally produced concerts, from the fan perspective. As was indicated by the interviewees, the smaller shows and venues, those that operate mainly with the local bands, were often struggling to get people to attend. And if seen through the bigger events with foreign bands, the scene appeared much less active. Some informants even went as far as saying it is not even a real scene in terms of the local bands, which is important to note.

The increasing number of foreign bands visiting the country was notable—as well as necessary for the local metal scene, proving some additional inspiration for the local musicians, in particular when there has been lack of big local "heroes." As explained by Anders Melts (my interview):

> Why Finland has so many big and good metal bands? I think it's because you have had these local icons for a long time. We only have Metsätöll. It has inspired lots of youngsters to establish their own bands. I think that's why we have now more those bands, because we finally have in Estonia one band that everyone is listening to, like Metallica or something.

But it was also pointed out that Metsätöll was such a specific case that it hardly functioned as any major inspiration or model for other Estonian bands' musical styles. "There's the metal scene, and there's them," commented one informant.

In providing local bands with notable support, the importance of the Hard Rock Laager festival in Vana-Vigala was hugely important. The festival, with an audience of around 2,000 people, included some semi-large international names[12] but mostly Estonian bands (e.g., 15 out of the total 22 in 2019, and 13 out of 22 in 2018). At the festival, bands had positive experiences performing to a wider crowd and finding new audiences as well. This was noted by one of the interviewed musicians. The festival has a strong following; many people are loyal and go every year, which made it one of the best places to present a band to the locals.

A remarkable, and quite recent, add-on to the local music scene was the summer mega concerts by Live Nation in the traditional *Lauluväljak* venue. With many stars like Madonna, Tina Turner, and The Rolling Stones, the recent heavier visitors included bands like Rammstein (2017); Guns N' Roses and Iron Maiden (2018); and Metallica and Bon Jovi (2019). These events had big crowds, many people also attending from the neighboring countries of Finland, Russia, Latvia, and Lithuania. For example, Guns N' Roses gathered some 60,000 people to this very same spot that experienced the legendary "Singing Revolution" events in 1987–91. Such big events for the local scene were evident, especially activating the sleeping fans as described by Kaido Haavandi (my interview):

> We call them heavy metal fans in the closet because they look like average dudes, go to their office work [...] you can be proud of yourself, saying I'm going to the Iron

> Maiden gig [...] and also of course for the younger generation to see that there's something else going on other than what they hear on the regular radio [...] maybe they start band, maybe they meet new friends and that all creates curiosity [...] and they understand that there's this parallel music, parallel society going on, people who take music much more seriously, who can name this as a lifestyle, and who are really supporting the bands as well.

The current Estonian music scene overall had been boosted by the high-profile music industry event and popular festival Tallinn Music Week (TMW) that also included a metal showcase evening. TMW, established in 2009, became an important meeting point for European music and creative communities, consisting of a weeklong music festival with local and international showcases, an industry conference, and other activities. It was recognized as a key music gathering by the likes of *The Guardian*[13] and *New York Times*.[14] Kersti Kaljulaid, the president of Estonia, inaugurated the festival in 2018, which was a big event for TMW too, as the country celebrated the 100th Anniversary of Independence.[15] All this highlights the recent emphasis on and development of the cultural and creative industries that has been visible in Tallinn.

Hence, the Estonian metal scene was, and still is, embodied through its live events. Concerning the local industry infrastructure, related to recording and publishing, activities were really small.[16] For the small local bands, the scene appeared as DIY in character, and for the local non-scene crowds, it was pretty much underground, lacking mainstream recognition. Occasional reports on the bands and events appeared in the local media, but metal was, for the most part, apparent only in the scene-related forums.[17] It is therefore no wonder that many bands were constantly looking for chances to extend their reach abroad in other Baltic States and beyond. But as the global supply of metal bands is immense, like anywhere else, they were facing tough competition. For a band coming from the small Tallinn scene, without any support, it was almost impossible to break through, as agreed by all informants. The lack of the local opportunities and subsequent difficulties to get elsewhere is like a vicious circle that seemed to frustrate many local musicians.

Cohesions and divisions in the past

The current state of the Estonian metal scene, including its overall cohesion as well as subgenre and underground versus mainstream divisions, is strongly impacted by, even directly resulting from, the different development phases of the scene in the past. The development of Estonian metal is an interesting story and would require its own much longer text, but the main stages are briefly described here as unfolding from the interviews and desktop study. The history is constructed of three main waves separated by particularly low tides.

The first wave: Moshing the winds of change, late 1980s onwards

As in many other small non-Anglo-American countries, the local metal scene started to emerge in Estonia in the 1980s and 1990s. The Estonian case is, however, peculiar due to the long period under the reign of Soviet Union—occupation started in 1939. Estonia regained independence in 1991 in the course of the dissolution of the Soviet Union. Already before that, the winds of change brought by the Glasnost and Perestroika politics started opening up the Soviet states in the late 1980s. This gradual emancipation with higher transparency and more free discussion also affected music cultures and scenes.

In fact, music played an important role in providing Estonian people a louder voice and raising the hopes of re-independence, functioning as an important catalyst for a revolutionary spirit in the form of *laulev revolutsioon* ("the singing revolution"), the events that gathered people to various singing fests with anti-Soviet concerts (Rinne 2007; Haukkala 2017). Eventually, up to 30,000 people got together at an open-air theater, *Tallinna lauluava* ("Tallinn singing stage"), to sing forbidden national songs, some of them with rock arrangements. It is the same venue that currently hosts concerts by Metallica, Rammstein, and others. Already prior to this peak period, joint singing had had a special function in forming communities, maintaining unity, and developing the national identity of Estonia for decades, even centuries (Raudsepp and Vikat 2011).

The turn of the decade also gave birth to the rock and metal scene in Estonia, as a wider phenomenon, particularly in Tallinn. In the early 1980s, a local punk scene had already emerged in Estonia, even though the Soviet authorities did not particularly like such loud and potentially rebellious music. And until these days, the punk scene had maintained its small but firm position in the country. Other genres such as heavy metal emerged, as the western influences crossed the country borders despite the censorship and the lack of open commerce. The early scene was underground, but toward the end of the decade, more activities surfaced along with the opening of society; the KGB[18] took the "observing" stance instead of the "punisher" stance, as summarized by Kaido Haavandi. Indeed, the change was clear, as Andres Volly of Bestia[19] also described (Stevenson 2011): "The Soviet regime got weaker at the end of the 1980s and it gave chance for extreme metal and punk bands to emerge."

In 1987, the first Estonian heavy festival Heavy Suvi ("heavy summer") was organized, followed by the Rock Summer festival in 1988. Another remarkable scene-founding event occurred in 1990 when Tartu Muusikapäevad ("Tartu music days") included the American thrash metal band Death Angel on the bill. As noted by Anders, "all of the same age remember that [...] Death Angel in Estonia, it was a big event." The Noorte Muusa ("young muse") festival that was mainly punk also included some metal.[20] In the beginning of the 1990s, two important clubs, 326 and Võit, were opened in Nõmme, in the southern part of Tallinn city, followed a bit later by the club La Rocco in the district of Mustamäe. The geographical closeness and cultural connection with Finland, in particular, became a strong supporting factor for the early scene. Music magazines spread south, along with the Finnish radio and television waves. People smuggled in records that were not available in Estonia. For example, Anders Melts, himself an early and still active Estonian scene member and musician,[21] remembered that even his mother, when visiting Finland, brought records back upon requests to Tallinn.

Inspired by the foreign metal influences and opening local possibilities, Estonian metal fans started to create their own bands.[22] To accompany the hard rock and punk-oriented early styles, the globally spreading extreme metal styles were also soon picked up by Estonian teenagers, and the first thrash metal bands were established.[23] The local death metal acts soon followed, becoming perhaps the biggest early band scene of Estonian metal, many blending death with thrash, doom, and other influences.[24] Many positive cycles were ignited. The independence brought along better availability of international records for the fans and gear for the musicians. The new mental and material realities encouraged people to start new bands and events. And the more events there were and clubs for the bands to perform, the more bands emerged. Also, more foreign bands started to visit the country. The scene's reputation grew, which also opened some new possibilities for the Estonian bands abroad. This development concerned not only metal; there occurred simultaneous emergence of other genres like indie rock.

This scene—events, bands and the fans—of the late 1980s and early 1990s constructed the first wave of Estonian heavy metal, characterized by the rapidly changing society and new emerging possibilities for more extreme cultural forms. The development of the first wave resonated with the common globalization and transcultural evolution in heavy metal; many local metal scenes started to visibly emerge from the 1990s onwards in different parts of the world to break the Anglo-American hegemony (see, for example, Wallach et al. 2011; Brown et al. 2016; Karjalainen 2018). In Estonia, the situation was unique due to the regained independence in 1991 and freedom that arguably also enabled and amplified formations of new subcultures and art forms.

The low tide of the mid 1990s

After the rather active start to the scene's development, the Estonian metal scene plunged in the mid-to-late 1990s. This concerned not only metal, but also the Estonian rock scene as a whole. Many of the bands of the first half of the decade discontinued around 1995, with no new major acts appearing. Anders Melts concluded that "in 95–97, nothing was left." Even though there might have been other factors, like the global low tide of the metal scene, the main explanation for the downspin was more concrete. Simply, the reality struck many bands: Many members of the first wave bands got to the "critical" age of having to make important decisions concerning their education and future profession. Musical careers were not a realistic option. And still today, it is generally not a realistic option in Estonia. Even the very established bands like Aggressor experienced this. If the positive cycle had shaped the scene, a negative spin was now suddenly gaining force, as remembered by Kaido Haavandi: "People distanced themselves from death metal because there was nothing there anymore, the audience had gone, there were no fellow bands to play with."

The second wave: The scene reestablished and blackened, late 1990s onwards

Hence much of the scene disappeared in a short time. There had not really been a long-term infrastructure built during the first wave. Kaido, who himself was a newcomer in the scene at that time, entered a very demanding reality: "We had to figure it out ourselves, the way we organized gigs, the way we rehearsed, what equipment we used and how we recorded, we didn't have much of a legacy." Besides establishing his own black metal band Manatark under his artist name Draconic, Kaido soon became a key person within the scene gradually, setting up Hard Rock Club, Hard Rock Laager, and club Tapper. The early hands-on experience played a crucial role in this development. Even today, the local scene is strongly dependent on a similar DIY mentality and personal passion.

If death and thrash metal largely constituted the first wave of Estonian metal, new styles were forming after the low-point of the mid 1990s. A distinct black metal scene started to grow in Estonia, as in many other countries, accompanied with some folk/pagan metal bands. Many of them, however, included death metal elements of the first wave.[25] From this era, Loits was the band that became perhaps the most recognized and longest lived with their self-acclaimed style of "militant flak 'n' roll" as well as their highly patriotic lyrics. Overall, a stronger national/local focus seemed to become an important component of the second wave, following the rather similar narrative traits of black and folk metal scenes in other parts of the world. When the first wave incorporated more universal themes and approaches like Anglo-Saxon influenced thrash and death metal of that era, Estonian black metal was taking influences from the original Norwegian scene, as admitted by Kaido, while it also embraced a particular DIY approach:

> Norwegian black metal [...] produced a lot of primitive bands because a lot of people had the idea that if you had the beehive sound of guitar and two riffs, minor chords on top of each other and screams, then that's already a pretty good deal.

This "Norwegian approach" was stressing a certain individualism that seemingly altered the working approaches and attitudes of the musicians, which may have boosted the whole scene but also kept it relatively closed, among a circle of like-minded people. The current small but strong black metal community in Estonia is reminiscent of this early scene.

But instead of copying the Norwegian scene, musically or narratively, Estonia had its own specific thing going on in black metal. Manatark, Loits, and others gave a much-needed boost to the future bands. The low-point gave birth to a stronger and more prevalent scene, and the scene was doing better again around the turn of the millennium. And as a new important local scene marker, Kaido and other "Hard Rock Club guys" started a new festival, Hard Rock Laager, that had its first edition in 2002. An important societal milestone was experienced in 2004 when Estonia joined the European Union, bringing more connections and financial security for the country. This also influenced the networking prospects of cultural sectors, at least indirectly.

The low tide and the modern shift of late 2000s

The Estonian metal scene was about to ride another low tide at the end of the decade and early part of the 2010s. In particular, gig attendances started to drop, and the number of gigs was reduced to the point in which practically nothing was happening. Some informants suggested this followed the global financial crisis (2007–09) which hit Estonia particularly hard, with its very practical implications like diminishing concert attendances. The financial grounds also got shakier, bringing severe times for the local industry. The struggle of the early years of the Club Tapper (established 2008) showed this in an extremely concrete manner. Kaido remembered this:

> We didn't realize it's all going to shit, and we started it with bells and whistles [...] in half a year this place was bankrupt [...] around 2010 we pulled the plug from most of the stuff we did here. It became a very do-it-yourself thing.

For the bands, again, the chances to perform were diminished. In particular, this changed the prospects of many black metal bands; instead of more serious aspirations of music as a profession, they were forced to get back to the mode of making and playing music just for fun. This is still the situation for the local bands, as noted earlier.

The crisis hit the "old" bands and subgenres in particular. But while black metal started to fade from its visible position in the scene, there were many new and different genres appearing in Estonian metal. Influenced by the emerging global metal styles in the early 2000s, nu metal and metalcore—or deathcore and different cross-overs of hardcore and metal—post metal, as well as more technically, say progressively, oriented styles started to emerge in Estonia. As pointed out by Thon from the pagan/black metal band Sõjaruun in 2009, "[a]t the time black metal is not very the issue here. Like in every country we also have *trendwavestiles* here and at the time metalcore/deathcore is at highpoint" (MLC 2009: n.pag). The new waves caused new young people to pick up heavier music, without a direct relation to earlier scenes or styles, locally or globally. Tanel Kõnd, current bass player in instrumental post-metal band Ocean Districts (established 2011), described his start with music around 2002: "We were sitting with our friends and the skateboards [...] Somebody just threw out the idea. Yeah, we should make a band [...] the band was called Stem [...] they are called the first metalcore band in Estonia."

Without Tanel onboard anymore, Stem released their only album *Marble Men* in 2007, combining ingredients from different modern scenes, like metalcore and technical metal. Such modern metal soon created its own sub-scene in Estonia, as a very different counterforce for the more traditional black, death, and folk metal approaches. These bands drew their influences from abroad, Stem members, for instance, thought highly of bands like Mnemic from Denmark and Gojira from France. Indrek Ulp from Horror Dance Squad, who got into metal around 2000 as a teenager, initially discovered the genre as a rap fan and remembered the period as an active new start: "The scene exploded and there were so many metalcore-related bands (in Estonia) around 2005 and 2006." But the overall downspin of Estonian metal also affected the new sub-scene. Even though there was an active and positive climate with quite a few bands that had promising future prospects in 2005–09, many also started to disband or discontinue their activities. One reason was, once again, other things in life requiring attention and the harsh realities of music life.

The third wave: Modern metal versatilities of 2010s

After a few pessimistic years, new things started to happen in the Estonian scene again, around 2015. And as suggested by most informants and the survey, the scene has perked up in the last five years. Further stability has been provided by Estonia's inclusion in the Euro currency in 2011, which was a notable mental shift not only soothing the effects of the financial crisis that had hit Estonia particularly hard, but also marked another, perhaps the final step away from the Soviet/Russian reign toward the "west."[26] Peoples' income and lives started to improve quite remarkably, providing new possibilities for cultural areas as a whole.

Roman "Romcha" Demchenko, who was arguably the most active promoter and manager of the scene at the time, as well as the head of the Music Festival Program and producer of the TMW, also suggested the Estonian metal scene was at its highest point at the moment:

> At some point it started to grow, I think in 2014 really actively and I'm pretty sure now it's on its peak, right now it's really many shows going on. Like basically every weekend, there are at least a few shows you can choose from [...] I'm promoting about thirty shows a year, and there are like other promoters, so I think we have, let's say, few hundred shows a year. So, it's big, especially considering the population of Tallinn.

The operational realities had also drastically changed during the previous ten years, as new kinds of networks and practices had emerged in social media. The audiences find gigs more easily, local bands have more possibilities for performances, and foreign bands realized that there were things actively happening in Estonia. The whole infrastructure was also developing quickly, and the industry appeared more networked than before. In particular, new Baltic collaborations had emerged, although Estonia and Tallinn still remain as the clear main metal hub of the Baltic countries. But more and more foreign bands were doing Baltic shows on their tours. The location between Finland and Russia made it logistically feasible for many bands to include Baltic shows in their travel schedule when visiting Finland and other Nordic countries as well as Russia.

Cohesion and divisions of the current scene

When starting my exploration, I expected to find some divisions within the Estonian metal scene, following from the versatile history, different subgenres, as well as the cultural and political positions of the country. The data however did not provide an absolute answer on the question of how unified or divided the scene might be. Both the interviews and the surveys included very different opinions; a summarized view suggests that it has at least become more unified in comparison to some instances in the past. As discussed earlier, there appeared a rather tight cohesion generally; the metal community at large was clearly identified and holding together. But then, there were also several contradictory opinions. In particular, the divisions echoed strongly between different eras, the "generations" of Estonian metal, and the respective subgenres, which was also seen in Bardine and Hale's study on the Dayton metal scene.

The activity of the scene today?

This polarization was reflected in the final open-ended question of the survey, asking if there is anything else to be said or pointed out in the current Estonian metal scene. Overall, 107 of the 212 respondents gave their opinions. Roughly, 28 of the respondents were positive (like "it's amazing"), 36 negative (like "it's slowly dying"), and the rest were neutral. This is of course quite subjective and not describing the cohesion or atmosphere in general. But some comments may be shown to highlight the controversy of the experiences and some divisions in the scene.

A few people saw the scene as lacking unity, divided, or scattered with "people stuck in their own musical bubble." One commented that people envy each other, while another noted that bands don't stick together. One respondent even saw that there are a few active people in the scene who appear as elitists who don't want more people to join the scene. Some "elitism" was also experienced toward less extreme forms of metal. These were however single comments, and, as usual, it is probable that complaints are overpresented and general contentment may not be as easily expressed in this type of context.

On the positive side, comments like "everyone is pretty friendly and open-minded," "I've only seen kind people," and "all the top bands know each other very well" were also presented. The interviews, by the promoters in particular, expressed a very positive view. This was highlighted by Roman's conclusion (my interview): "[T]he scene is small and we're all a, say, small family." Perhaps we can count on this view that undoubtedly is based on wide experience and perspective, and conclude that currently there is a rather strong overall cohesion and community spirit within the scene.

Historical divisions?

Based on the history, some divisions in terms of the concert attendances had been recognized between different generations/waves, metal subgenres, and styles. One survey respondent saw the scene divided in the groups of 15–25 years old, 25–40 years old, and older. The interviews also somewhat supported the existence of some divisions in terms of the different waves and subgenres. They are not always present though, as many current events reportedly involve both the "oldies" from the first and second waves and younger "third wave" audiences. Sometimes, however, the differences between the generations and the stylistic focuses of the three waves were visible. The older scene members populated the more "traditional" extreme metal shows, black and death in particular, whereas modern metal bands were typically followed by younger audiences. These differences were however case specific and not necessarily constant. Overall, stronger subgenre divisions were reported being strongest during the second wave, following the more coherent first wave. Kaido summarizes thus:

> Strangely enough, in the 90s we had a more united scene. Then we split apart because there were no big concerts anymore and people just dropped into different, smaller places, kept to themselves, created their own scene, like nu metal, black metal but I think nowadays the scenes are not polarized at all.

The role of the key persons like Kaido, Tanya, and Roman had been crucial in bringing more unity to the scene. They organized events in different subgenres, often combined to get bigger audiences, hence bringing different fans together in concerts. For example, Tanel acknowledged their role (my interview):

> They are so passionate about this music and the scenes [...] They don't stick to one genre, they bring together every different kind of genre, and I guess people who follow them then discover those new genres, and that makes the scene bigger.

The strengthened cultural cohesion in metal may also be partly explained by the fact that the younger metal generation just tended to have less personal friction with each other due to the lack of personal historical experiences. And perhaps, the scene was not very politically charged in the first place, as vividly illustrated by Kaido's comment (my interview):

> You can easily have a right-winger guy, a left-winger guy sitting together, drinking beer. They're wearing different outfits, you can see that they shouldn't be getting along, but on the other hand they are—we know each other from 20 years back, should we start fighting now?

Nonetheless, specific subgenre gigs were constantly organized. And as a general observation from the study, the people from different subgenres were not necessarily fully aware of the bands, events, or states of other subgenres. For example, there existed a small community called "Black Magic Estonia" organizing its own private invite-only clubs for an audience of 50–100 black metal fans. Some

Russian metal fans also at times gather at specific events. Estonia still accommodates a large Russian population, and the cultural division between the Estonian and Russian populations was rather strong in many areas of the society, due to their obvious historical and political history. In general, it was noted by many that in metal such frictions are not clearly visible, but this study did not provide any data on that matter, also because of the lack of Russian respondents in the survey. It was said to be a small number of people in any regard.

Estonian metal identity?

Some of the subgenres, black metal and partly folk metal in particular, had typically also involved strong ideological and narrative tensions between the claimed "original" and "other" cultures of countries and nations, making those members of the scene predominantly Estonian. For historical reasons, these sub-scenes had provided avenues for expressing national pride, even nationalist aspirations, to boost the Estonian agenda and strive for stronger independence. In the current scene, it seems that the national characteristics or historical aspects were treated merely as a coloring narrative by bands like Metsätöll. Estonian cultural history and folklore offers a rich source for stories. Metsätöll, Goresoerd (interestingly, the "biggest" Estonian bands), and some other bands also use the Estonian language as a particular feature to mark their cultural roots. Andres from Bestia commented on this in an older interview:

> Singing in native tongue is very special thing for us. Lyrics deal mostly about ancient times and battles, nature and there is also some inspiration taken from Nordic and Estonian mythology [...] I feel great respect for this kind of music (folk), as it has direct connection to our roots.
>
> (Mordant 2009: n.pag.)

As a contrast to national echoes in folk and black metal, the modern metal subgenres and the third wave offspring were not bearing any clear traces of a joint Estonian (or Tallinn) identity, nor did the musicians feel any particular pride about being from Tallinn/Estonia, or admitted nurturing any clear national character in their music, or in the narratives of the bands. One could argue that the vast modernization of Estonia and Tallinn is reflected in the approach—or "sound" in that sense—of some of the modern metal bands of the scene. The comment of Karl Mesipuu of Horror Dance Squad is interesting:

> We all have our day jobs, we all work in big companies. For example, our guitarist Mikk works at Skype, and Indrek works at the mobile phone company Ericsson.

> I work at the British financial sector. Yeah, we all have these office jobs, and I guess that maybe influences how we write. Maybe it inspires us differently [...] we're trying to keep this electronic vibe as the main part in our songs, so that people will recognize our sound [...] And the gear we use is also very digital, so it all blends together very well, I guess.

Well, Skype was established in Tallinn and got hugely famous by 2011 when it was acquired by Microsoft, the same year when Horror Dance Squad was established. And overall, the band's approach is an interesting representation of Estonia's strong identity shift from a post-Soviet nation toward a digitally advanced information society during the last twenty plus years (Runnel et al. 2009; Tammpuu and Masso 2018). Perhaps this is a topic deserving more attention in future research.

Conclusion

The current Estonian metal scene appeared relatively active, involving lots of energy and a new force that might strengthen the base for new bands and people. The division between the events with international bands and those of the local scene was strong. The scene was also quite heterogeneous and, despite improved overall cohesion, it involves many subdivisions based on different development streams during the three historical waves, as well as on the overall difficult realities of a small scene.

To write this overview within the limits of a book chapter was somewhat challenging. Lots of insights and stories from the long interviews, materials from the secondary data, details of the survey, and other data could not be included. They would provide a base for a much longer text that hopefully will be realized in the future. Needless to say, the goal of this chapter was certainly not to provide the reader with a comprehensive summary of the scene, nor a precise history report, but to construct a selective view into the scene as experienced both by some of its core figures (interviews) and a larger number of scene members (survey)—to reflect the nature of *living metal scenes*, in accordance with the approach of this book. Of course, the story may have taken slightly different routes with other informants, but, eventually, I believe I managed to gather a pretty representative picture of the scene and to summarize part of it in this chapter.

Epilogue

Characteristic of a viable scene, lots of new activities and changes have occurred in Estonia since completion of this study, and more will definitely surface before the eventual publication. The long cycles of academic publishing do not support timely information sharing; the state of the scene as described in this chapter is specifically that of spring and summer of 2019. Already in 2020, further scene-expanding things have surfaced including the Grom MMXX festival in Tallinn. Rock Café has also moved to a new location and is actively hosting bands throughout the year, in addition to other active venues like Tapper, Sveta Bar, and Barbar. Moreover, Metsätöll will tour America with TYR, and Loits was added as supporter for Finnish Moonsorrow in their Finland tour in spring 2020. Just to name a few examples.

However, the situation and prospects described in this chapter are dated before the COVID-19 crisis shook the world. The outbreak paralyzed the live scene in Estonia, as everywhere in the world, and it remains to be seen what the pace and extent of the post-crisis recovery will be in the forthcoming years.

Appendix: Survey questions

ESTONIAN METAL SCENE

Welcome! I'd greatly appreciate if you could answer some quick questions about the Estonian heavy metal scene (or hard rock, let's be general). I will use the answers as the background in my forthcoming book chapter that I've been working on. If successful, it'll be included in a US-based academic book on global metal scenes. All answers will be treated anonymously. The survey is open until September 22. Thanks for your time and metal on!

Toni-Matti Karjalainen, Aalto University, Espoo, Finland

1. Your age?
2. Your sex?
3. Your nationality and mother tongue?
4. Your occupation/profession and education?
5. If you are/have been a musician yourself: name your band, instrument, years active.
6. How long you've been a metal/hard rock fan?
7. What other genres you listen to actively (up to 5 genres)?
8. Among your peers (family and friends), please estimate how many people actively listen to metal?
9. Among Estonian people in general, please estimate how many people actively listen to metal?

10. What are the most popular music genres in Estonia at the moment, in your experience?
11. Your rough estimation of the total number of Estonian metal fans (attending gigs) at the moment? Is it lower or higher than 5 years ago?
12. Your estimation of the number of active Estonian metal bands at the moment?
13. What are the most influential Estonian metal bands in the current scene?
14. What have been the most influential Estonian metal bands in the history?
15. What are the most active subgenres of metal in the current scene?
16. What are the most important places in the current Estonian metal scene (clubs, stores, other)?
17. What are the most important events of the current Estonian metal scene?
18. Who are the most important persons of the current scene (musicians, promoters, managers, producers, other)?
19. During 2018–19, how many metal/hard rock concerts have you attended in Estonia?
20. Anything else you want to say about the current status of the Estonian metal scene, something I should be aware of? Please have a free word, answers will be confidential.

NOTES

1. See, for example, https://www.gislounge.com/map-of-heavy-metal-bands-by-country-per-capita/. Accessed July 2, 2021.
2. https://www.metal-archives.com/browse/country. Accessed July 2, 2021.
3. On September 30, 2019, Metal Archives had already listed 210 Estonian bands and 3,920 Finnish bands, for example.
4. Including altogether 83 interviews, with 30 different Estonian bands/artists. The ones with most interviews are Loits (24), Metsätöll (8), Bestia (6), and Manatark (6). The site was active in 2004–15 and is later mostly replaced by the Facebook group (https://www.facebook.com/estonianmetal/ [accessed July 2, 2021]) in which the most posts appear in Estonian language.
5. The seven personally interviewed key informants—to be greatly acknowledged for their interest and time—included Anders Melts, Kaido Haavandi, Indrek Ulp, Karl Mesipuu, Roman Demchenko, Tanel Kõnd, and Tanya Korenik. All the informants are particularly acknowledged for their time and insights. In the chapter, the direct quotes from these informants are made with their first names.
6. Estonianmetal.com site is listing 217 bands, representing a variety of different genres. The listing is however clearly incomplete, for example Tankist, Talbot, and Horror Dance Squad

one of the visible current bands, are not included there. Metal Archive (https://www.metal-archives.com/browse/country) in turn names 210 Estonian bands (September 30, 2019). As this is a history collection, many of these are however disbanded or inactive.

7. I hereby use the subgenre definitions of estonianmetal.com (or other sources, if not listed), even though such straight categorization may not do full justice for some of the bands.
8. For example, when looking at the Last.fm for the most listened Estonian bands, the list includes: Metsatöll (32,015 listeners), Loits (5,420), Tharaphita (2,521), Human Ground (1,021), Manatark (1,482), Must Missa (1,507), Bestia (1,756), and Ceremonial Perfection (1,998).
9. Aggressor and No-Big-Silence are practically the same band, and the two counted together would make 41 mentions.
10. When doing the interviews, the list of upcoming headliners consisted of a pretty wide international and sub-genre mixture: Sirenia, Orange Goblin, Septicflesh, The Black Dahlia Murder, Threshold, Combichrist, Napalm Death, and Moonspell.
11. The metal/rock shows in 2019 included bands like U.D.O., Riverside, Bullet for My Valentine, Alice in Chains, and Powerwolf.
12. For example, Carcass, Dark Funeral, Metsätöll, and Keep of Kalessin in 2019.
13. https://www.theguardian.com/travel/2014/oct/30/top-10-music-festivals-winter-breaks-france-australia-sweden. Accessed July 2, 2021.
14. https://artsbeat.blogs.nytimes.com/2015/03/20/whats-on-this-week-around-the-world-16/?_r=0. Accessed July 2, 2021.
15. Estonia's "original" declaration of independence in 1918, later cut-off by the Soviet Union years.
16. Indie metal labels Nailboard Records and Hexenreich Records and studios like Around Sound exist, but basically most local albums are worked on and released independently. If there is a chance, the bands may release through international labels, but that is pretty rare. The big corporations like Universal and Sony are of course present in Estonia too but, as commented by the informants, they don't really release anything metal-related here.
17. There is, for example, the weekly "Metallion" radio show of the nationwide Raadio 2, Radio Mania, "the only Estonian rock radio" and Rock FM –however hardly playing any Estonian music at all—as well as the underground metal magazine *Pläkk*. In addition to various social media and online resources like Estonianmetal.
18. Komitet gosudarstvennoi bezopasnosti, the national security committee of the Soviet Union.
19. A black/death metal band established in 2000.
20. For example, the very first Estonian black metal band Spout, who never released anything, performed during the festival.
21. Anders Melts is also the establisher of the death/doom band Forgotten Sunrise.

22. It is difficult to name the very "first" bands as reportedly many bands existed but did not record anything, and the genre borders between rock genres were rather fluid. Some of the first "official" (traditional) heavy rock/metal bands of late 1980s include Metallist (1983), Gunnar Grasp Group (GGG) (1984), and Omas Kojas (1986).
23. For example, Palat (1987), Shower (1989), Flytrap (1992), and Ascent (1992).
24. These included bands like Aggressor (1989), Nekropol (1989), Postmortem (1990), Rattler (1991), Mortified (1992), Forgotten Sunrise (1992) (Death/Doom Anders), Obscured (1992), and Decease (1992) in the late 1980s.
25. In addition to Manatark (1998), other notable black/pagan metal were, for example, Winter Night Overture (1994), Tharaphita (1995), Loits (1996), Tarbatu (1996), and Vaikus (1997).
26. See BBC's article titled "Estonia becomes 17th member of the euro zone," December 31, 2010, https://www.bbc.co.uk/news/world-europe-12098513. Accessed July 2, 2021.

REFERENCES

Brown, A. R., Spracklen, K., Kahn-Harris, K., and Scott, N. W. R. (2016), *Global Metal Music and Culture: Current Directions in Metal Studies*, New York: Routledge.

Elovaara, Mika, and Bardine, Bryan (2017), *Connecting Metal to Culture: Unity in Disparity*, Bristol: Intellect.

Haukkala, Hiski (2017), "Ripe for revolution? The role of loud popular music in revolutionary social and political processes," *Metal Music Studies*, 3:3, pp. 387–403.

Karjalainen, Toni-Mtti (2018), *Sounds of Origin in Heavy Metal Music*, Newcastle: Cambridge Scholars Publishing.

Karjalainen, Toni-Mtti, and Kärki, Kimi (2015), *Modern Heavy Metal: Markets, Practices, and Cultures*, Proceedings of the Modern Heavy Metal Conference 2015, June 8–12, Helsinki: Aalto University.

MLC (2009), "Interview with Sõjaruun", *My Last Chapter* zine, May 11, https://www.estonianmetal.com/interviews.php?id=85. Accessed April 1, 2019.

Mordant (2009), "Interview with Bestia", *Minacious Webzine*, September, https://www.estonianmetal.com/interviews.php?id=86. Accessed April 1, 2019.

Pawlusz, Emilia (2018), "Can musicians build the nation? Popular music and identity in Estonia," in A. Polese, J. Morris, E. Pawlusz, and O. Seliverstova (eds.), *Identity and Nation Building in Everyday Post-Socialist Life*, New York: Routledge.

Raudsepp, Inge, and Vikat, Maie (2011), "The role of the phenomenon of joint singing in the development of national identity in Estonia," *Procedia—Social and Behavioural Sciences*, 29, pp. 1312–19.

Rinne, Harri. (2007), *Laulava vallankumous: Viron rocksukupolven ihme*, Helsinki: Johnny Kniga.

Runnel, Pille, Vergerfeldt-Pruulmann, Pille, and Reinsalu, Kristina (2009), “The Estonian tiger leap from post-communism to the information society: From policy to practice,” *Journal of Baltic Studies*, 40:1, pp. 29–51.

Rüütel, Ingrid (2003), “Traditional music in Estonia today,” *Fontes Artis Musicae*, 51:3&4, pp. 295–303.

Smidchens, Guntis (1996), *A Baltic Music: The Folklore Movement in Lithuania, Latvia, and Estonia, 1968–1991*, https://scholarworks.iu.edu/dspace/handle/2022/20479, Bloomington: Indiana University Press.

Stevenson, Rhys (2011, “Global metal scene report #5 Estonia,” *theRabbitMusic*, March 1, https://therabbitmusic.wordpress.com/2011/10/22/global-metal-scene-report-5-estonia/. Accessed April 1, 2019.

Tammpuu, Piia, and Masso, Anu (2018), “Welcome to the virtual state: Estonian e-residency and the digitalized state as a commodity,” *European journal of Cultural Studies*, 21:5, pp. 543–60.

Varas-Díaz, Nelson, and Scott, Niall (2016), *Heavy Metal Music and the Communal Experience*, Lanham: Lexington Books.

Wallach, Jeremy, Berger, Harris M, and Greene, Paul D. (eds.) (2011), *Metal Rules the Globe: Heavy Metal Music around the World*, Durham: Duke University Press.

12

From the Sound of the Lathes to the Noise of the Amplifiers: Heavy Metal and the Music Scene of the Greater ABC Region (São Paulo/Brazil, 1980–90)

Rui Luiz Ferreira Granado and Heloísa de Araújo Duarte Valente

Introduction

This chapter is a historical survey of the metal scene of the "Greater ABC" metropolitan region of the State of São Paulo (Brazil), between the years 1980 and 1990. As a starting point, we sought to identify the main factors that contributed to the formation of its identity and profile, such as the military repression in Brazil in the 1980s, the workers' culture through union movements, and the influence of punk culture. In this context, the relationships between the local sound landscape[1] and its implications on the behavior of a group of fans of the genre, the ABC Headbangers, precursors of the metal scene in the region, stand out. To understand the relevance of these factors, we raise the following question: How does the sound landscape influence the musical conception? And vice versa: How does the music scene reinforce and compose elements of the local sound landscape? Based on studies of heavy metal (Janotti Junior 2004), the music scene (Vasconcellos 2015), and the sound landscape (Schafer 1991, 1997, an analysis of personal collections, period magazines, and documentaries was undertaken, thus allowing the identification of these determining factors for the introduction and popularity of the heavy metal genre in the region. We also examined the historical context and the political landscape of the country in the period in question as well as the opening to democratic rule after a period of military rule that lasted from 1964 to 1985.

After the successful Brazilian tour of the band KISS in 1983, heavy metal started to attract the attention of Brazilians, a fact that would be confirmed later with the success of the Rock in Rio festival in 1985. In this period the country went through political changes after the end of the dictatorship and the process of democratic rule in the country. During the 1980s, the Greater ABC region was the stage for one of the most expressive cultural movements of the Brazilian underground music scene: heavy metal. During this period, a group of young fans of heavy metal called The ABC Headbangers emerged in the region, and they gained such prominence that they influenced the national metal scene. Known across the State of São Paulo, the group was responsible for the consolidation of heavy metal in the region and served as reference and inspiration for other metal scenes in Brazil. The Greater ABC region is located in the metropolitan region of the State of São Paulo, and consists of seven cities: Santo André, São Bernardo, São Caetano do Sul, Diadema, Mauá, Ribeirão Pires, and Rio Grande da Serra.

As an important industrial hub for the national automobile industry, the Greater ABC region became known as the "Brazilian Detroit." If we compare the musical scene of Detroit in the United States with the scene of the ABC of São Paulo, we will find many similarities, especially with regard to the influence of the sound landscape from assembly lines and their relationship with both the sound and content of the compositions, as reported by the anthropologist Sam

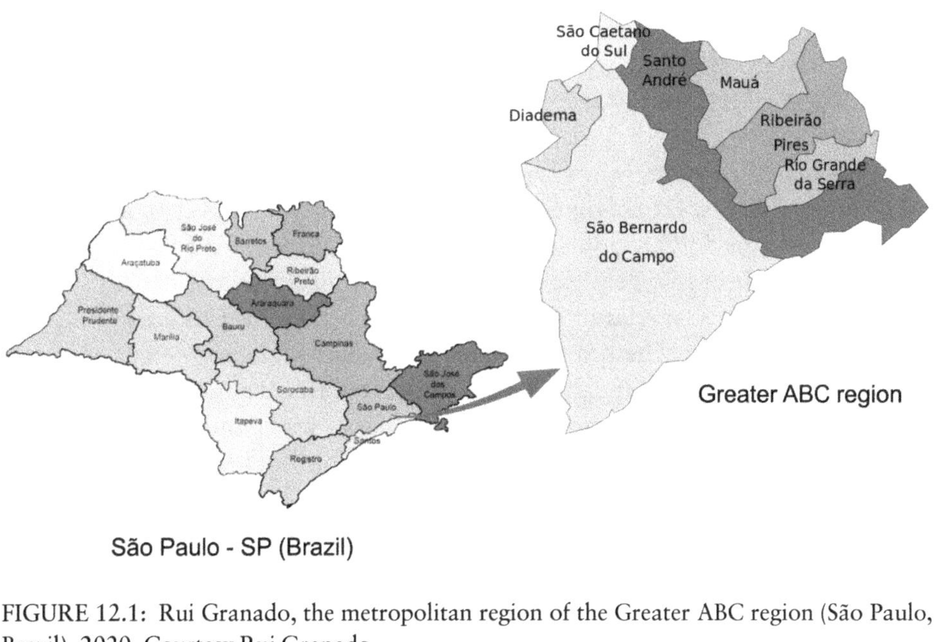

FIGURE 12.1: Rui Granado, the metropolitan region of the Greater ABC region (São Paulo, Brazil), 2020. Courtesy Rui Granado.

Dunn in his documentary *Metal Evolution* (2011).[2] This kind of relationship is evidenced in an excerpt from an interview from the site "ABC Rock You," where Paulo "Gepeto," vocalist of the band Ação Direta, talks about the influence of the environment on compositions:

> The music reflects very much the way we live. Today we see it that way, maybe in the 80s they weren't seen that way. We're in the globalized world and you realize that each place has its own pro rock sound. ABC bands also have this characteristic and it has to do with what we live here, right? The factory thing, the ash and the urban chaos, right? And this reflects directly in the music, for sure.
>
> (Gepeto 2011: n.pag.)

In almost all ABC cities, there was core activity involving members of the ABC Headbangers, especially in the cities of Santo André (A), São Bernardo do Campo (B), and São Caetano do Sul (C), considered central and strategic regions because of efficient and accessible public transport. The ABC headbangers used to use the train stations as a meeting point before the concerts, which often took place in other cities in the state of São Paulo. Since they were all using train travel, they inevitably met members of other rival groups, which ended up causing widespread conflict. With unemployment being a reality for many young people, and the lack of prospects both personally and professionally, these headbangers found working-class jobs as their only options. It was precisely these elements that served as inspiration for several bands that appeared in the Greater ABC region during the 1980s. The lyrics presented themes related to war, nuclear conflicts and social and political conflicts, a legacy of workers culture, as well as coexistence with punk rockers who shared the same space with the headbangers in the assembly lines of the factories. This more politicized characteristic was the difference between the bands of the Greater ABC and the other scenes of the State of São Paulo since it was very common that bands outside the ABC region still approached themes related to occultism and Satanism in their music. Because of this difference, little by little the ABC Headbangers gained the respect and admiration of almost all lovers of heavy metal in the State of São Paulo. These fans attended many shows, always coming as a large group, reinforcing the group spirit, union, and commitment among their members.

During the shows, the group held banners and posters high, becoming a kind of trademark, besides the traditional war cry known by all: ABC HEADBANGERS! ABC HEADBANGERS! ABC HEADBANGERS!

Among many memories marking the participation of ABC Headbangers in events, none stood out more than the famous episode of the show of the English band Venom. It was Venom's first tour through Brazil in 1986. Even after 33 years, this report is still remembered both by ABC Headbangers and by headbangers

FIGURE 12.2: Patrick Nicholas Korb, ABC Headbangers reunion before a show, 1987. Color photograph. Courtesy MX band website.

from other locations. Based on what I was able to personally witness, and reports from some of the members of the ABC Headbangers, mostly through informal conversations, we have tried to present different points of view from those who witnessed this event, an opportunity to know and feel a little of the electric atmosphere created by ABC Headbangers:

> The year is 1986. A group of young people from ABC Paulista prepares to watch a show of the English band Venom, one of the biggest bands of heavy metal in the world. There is a lot of expectation because this would be the first time that the group performed in Brazilian lands. A bus is chartered exclusively for this occasion, and little by little the people from Santo André, São Bernardo do Campo and São Caetano do Sul arrive at the galleria. The group was composed of approximately 50 members with long hair and a "different" look causing people to turn and notice

> them. It's time to get on board and the anxiety increases. Everyone checks their tickets, settles in their seats and, finally, the bus continues to the Corinthians gymnasium, in the Tatuapé neighborhood, in the eastern zone of the city of São Paulo. Upon arriving at the destination, the bus passes by the long line of headbangers waiting to enter the gym. People in line at the gym start watching the bus slowly looking for a place to park. Some even think that this bus is the Venom band itself and its team, but to the surprise of all present there, a collective voice chants their business card and reveals who had just arrived: *ABC Headbangers! ABC Headbangers! ABC Headbangers!* The crowd that waited in line starts shouting and greeting the ABC people in a sign of respect and admiration. This chant would become traditional in almost every event involving ABC Headbangers, a kind of trademark.

This is just one of the many eyewitness accounts still remembered with pride, even after 33 years, by fans who experienced this era of such strong fan devotion and organization. But how did this group reach such a celebrity status—their own ability to rouse a fan base for any musical act that came through? How did ABC Headbangers achieve this kind of solidarity? It's important to this study to understand how such strong groups form, and so we want to look carefully at the rise of ABC Headbangers to see if there are strategies we can borrow for future movements.

The beginning: Forged in dark years

The 1980s were a difficult time in Brazil, marked by issues and movements working against the government at the time. The 1964 military coup consolidated the dictatorship, instituting censorship and the end of freedom of expression throughout the nation. Until 1985, there was censorship or repression by the authorities against any expression of opinion contrary to the military regime. Many people were persecuted, imprisoned, and even tortured for taking a stand against the government. People were taken to military bases and facilities and never returned to their homes. To this day many are reported as "missing," without their relatives having any information about their whereabouts. With regard to music, censorship was ruthless, prohibiting the concentration of political groups and demonstrations during concerts and artistic events. There was a curfew, prohibiting movement at night in the streets. The military violently repressed any kind of demonstration, using horses, shields, batons, and gas bombs, seeking to intimidate and demoralize as well as disperse and repress the demonstrators. The lyrics of several songs were censored because of themes that might convey any message considered "subversive" or present any content contrary to the military ideology prevailing in the country.

The artwork on album covers was also censored. Any cover with themes considered "forbidden" was prohibited and changed, a rule that was valid for both domestic and foreign artists. According to the researcher Wlisses James de Farias Silva (2014), during this period, from an economic point of view, Brazil was experiencing a deep crisis, with uncontrolled inflation and a large social gap, aggravated by a huge external debt and a succession of economic plans which failed. It was with this background that the ABC region began to draw attention with both the strength and performance of their workers and their labor movements.

For the interest of this study, it is important to talk about the strengthening of the trade union movement of ABC. At the end of the 1970s, a movement in Brazil called New Syndicalism formed between 1978 and 1980. This movement resulted in the creation of confederations as the Unified Workers Central (CUT) and the Workers Central Union (CGT), in addition to the Workers Party (PT). This framework of struggles and demands became a hallmark of the ABC region, consolidating a profile of mostly politicized workers engaged in social and labor causes. This profile was reflected in such diverse cultural movements as theater, dance, poetry, and also in the music produced in the region. According to Silva (2014), heavy metal is a reflection of the crisis that came from the 1970s, and it burst like a bomb in the faces of 1980s youth.

The day-to-day conflicts served as inspiration for songs that expressed the opinions of thousands of working-class young people in relation to economic inequality and social problems. According to Silva (2014), these ordinary young people could not rise economically in the individualistic society of the 1980s. Usually with little formal education, they were eventually absorbed by the labor market of the service sector or even as factory workers. In the 1980s, almost 50 percent of the labor force was composed of young people between the ages of 18 and 30, and 34 percent over the age of 21 (Leonelli and Oliveira 2004). The young workers who worked on the assembly lines began their professional career in institutions such as National Service of Industrial Learning (SENAI), which provided activities related to the work routine of an assembler, enabling and offering the possibility of hiring by the companies registered in a partnership system, such as Volkswagen of Brazil, Ford, General Motors, and Scania. In addition to providing the necessary education to work there, the school environment allowed the integration of social groups that were related according to common interest and affinity with a certain subject, such as music.

Workers were underpaid, and also suffered because those low wages relegated them to a lower class in society and reduced them to a form of servitude. In the Greater ABC region, specifically in the early 1980s, there were few prospects for change, but according to Bosi (1972), wherever these workers were found, despite their seemingly hopeless situation, they brought their intensity for living and a humanity to this mechanized, inhuman factory.

Amplifier noises as a form of expression

In an assembly line, the sound of machines merges into the work routine, creating a kind of symphony. The title of the chapter "From the sound of the lathes to the noise of the amplifiers" is an attempt to emphasize the reality experienced by thousands of young people, most of them workers, during the 1980s and the influence on their music. These narrow professional options, amplified by politics and oppression, were passed from father to son, as a meager inheritance for those who had so few possibilities. As mentioned before, on an assembly line, the sound of the machines merges with the work environment and creates a kind of "musical composition." It becomes a common "sound landscape" composed of various elements, according to Schafer's concepts (1991, 1997). Heavy metal as a musical genre presents distinct elements with respect to sound, thus establishing their own "sound brand." According to Schafer (1997), this term refers to a sound of unique to that community or that has certain qualities that make it especially significant or noticed by the people of that place. Once this *sound brand* is identified, it is necessary to protect it because that sound brand reflects the unique acoustic life of the community. This sound mark of the ABC region is directly linked to its history involving the punk movement, the working class, and the culture of industrialization that served as inspiration both in the construction of the lyrics and in the sonority. In an interview to the site ABC Rock You, Marcelo D'Castro, guitarist of the band Necromancia, corroborates the influence of the environment in relation to the compositions:

> This "violence," of course, has influenced it. We wanted to have a heavier, more aggressive, dirtier sound, but we didn't know how to play properly. We wanted to make a sound with attitude and that was sincere, the messages of the songs.
>
> (D'Castro 2011: n.pag.)

Having said that, it is worth noting some particular aspects of heavy metal playing in the Greater ABC. For decades, the region was known as a true center of reference for rock bands of different styles, among them heavy metal. According to journalist and musical critic Tom Leão (1997), rock and consequently heavy metal, have always been the music of young proletarians and suburban people, who did not need much musical knowledge, besides the fury of youth, to express themselves. In this aspect, the amplifier represents that argument, that fury through music, the will to break the paradigms, that which really disturbs the order and causes discomfort to the conventional standards of society, and from the point of view of researcher Jeder Silveira Janotti Junior (2004) that which was previously considered noise, *distortion*, ends up being positively reappropriated. According to R. Murray Schafer, the increase in the intensity of sound power is the most striking characteristic of the industrialized sound landscape:

> The industry needs to grow: therefore, its sounds need to grow with it. This is the theme established in the last two hundred years. In fact, noise is so important as a means of drawing attention to the fact that if it had been possible to develop silent machinery, the success of industrialization might not have been as complete. For greater emphasis, let's put it more drastically: if cannons had been silent they would never have been used in war.
>
> (1997: 115)

In addition to the power and growth of the sound produced by the machines, high in many decibels, the sound power of the amplifier represents a way to express the seizure of power, by demonstrating with noise its position before society, as Janotti Junior says:

> The sound emitted by the amplifier is first of all a way to express the indignation, desires and frustrations of a certain group. Somehow this powerful and distorted music spoke of feelings and anguish that young people felt, but did not know how to express, a mixture of friendship, dreams and common values.
>
> (Janotti Junior 2004: 115)

Taking again the theory developed by Schafer, this attitude is explained: making noise is one of the privileged ways to hold power (Schafer 1997: 115). According to Janotti Junior (2004), this relationship between intensity and power is also evidenced by Weinstein (2000):

> The type of power that height provides is a dose of youthful vitality, a power of resistance to the violence of sound that expands one's own energy to respond to this with a physical and energetic push of one's own power. The height of heavy metal is not deaf, irritating or painful (at least for the fan), but energetic.
>
> (Weinstein 2000 quoted in Janotti Junior 2004: 23)

According to the sociologist Leonardo Carbonieri Campoy (2010), the context of Brazilian thrash metal is represented by the survival of war situations, the memory of the nuclear bomb, science without limits, and the destruction of the environment. Influenced in large part by the political ideology and the aggressive sound of punk music, the heavy metal bands of ABC began to emerge in the region's music scene. In the early 1980s, the punk movement gradually gave way to heavy metal, which in turn exponentially grew a true legion of fans—who may have started as punk fans or rock fans or heavy metal fans but who identified themselves more and more with the heavy metal genre. During this period, several bands appeared in the region, and heavy metal was beginning to consolidate.

We can't deny that in its beginnings the ABC heavy metal scene was strongly influenced by the existing scene in São Paulo's capital. Much of what was consumed by the region's headbangers came directly from the capital, such as cassette tapes, records, magazines, t-shirts, and accessories in general. Unlike the well-known musical scene in the capital and other locations in the state of São Paulo, in relation to heavy metal, the Greater ABC region stood out for presenting its own style. According to historian Silva:

> In the 1980s, heavy metal became a cultural movement present in all continents of the world, but it is clear that this presence in so many places also modifies heavy metal itself, which ends up adapting to cultural or political patterns of societies where parts of youth adopt it as a musical style.
>
> (2014: 105)

Another factor would be fundamental for the development and creation of the musical style of the bands of the region: the influence of music and punk culture. At the beginning of the 1980s, as previously mentioned, many punk fans and musicians worked in neighboring factories, and consequently, were linked in some way to the ABC trade union movement. This coexistence of punk rockers and headbangers, working side by side, was important to awaken the political and social interest that began to emerge in the compositions of ABC region heavy metal bands. According to the sociologist Aldemir Leonardo Teixeira (2007), who at the time was a member of the punk group Anjos do ABC,

> [t]he ABC punks, being in an industrialized region in a period of innumerable striking movements, followed and acted in parallel with the union movements between 1979 and 1983. The Angels of São Bernardo do Campo, in their majority, were workers in the metallurgical sector and articulated political actions, participating in strikes, demonstrations, pamphlets, pickets and marches. They were more politically active, being engaged in social issues.
>
> (Teixeira 2007: 3)

Initially, this coexistence was not possible because of the dispute between rival groups that fought for ideological divergence, or even for territory disputes in the central regions of ABC cities. Sharing the same work environment, in this case the factory, punks and headbangers shared information that enabled a cultural exchange between the groups. In this respect, the factory was of paramount importance for the socialization process, since, according to Vasconcellos:

> [i]t is possible to observe the existence of spaces that, even not presenting the complexity of a first order public space, are fundamental for the coexistence between the actors of more or less specific groups. These are places chosen for the realization of social practices linked to the values of these groups and, for this reason, we can say that they are spaces of first order for these individuals.
>
> (2015: 28)

While most of the national heavy metal bands approached subjects related to the occult (demons, monsters, black magic, and Satanism) and epic themes (dragons, battles, medieval legends, and Nordic culture), the bands of the Greater ABC, for ideological reasons, were influenced by factors related to the culture of the region, their daily lives, political and social problems that explicitly demonstrated their indignation and awareness in relation to their positions in society, the urban chaos, the threat of war, poverty, diseases, and the political situation of the country.

And it was precisely with this change of attitude and posture that the ABC region heavy metal scene took shape and emerged for the national scene. During this period, several bands appeared in the region: Karisma, Performances, Mammoth, MX, Necromancia, Blasphemer, Cova, Slaughter, Desaster, Warhate, Esfinge, Hammerhead, Deflagração Atômica, Ação Direta, Titânio, and Revenge.

This change of posture and awareness is visible in the trajectory of the band Necromancia, from São Bernardo do Campo. In the beginning, the band had themes related to Satanism and occultism as we can see in the lyrics of the song "Death Lust" ([1993] 2012):

> The seven entrance of the underground has opened
> The only sky entrance is closed again
> The Antichrist flames burn forever
> Demons devour the flesh of humanity

But over the years, they matured both from the point of view of sound and in relation to the themes addressed in their songs, as we can see in the lyrics of "Check Mate" (2002):

Raise the chase
There are reasons to fear the worst
Rack of nation
Wage war until obliteration
Old conflicts
Scars of war.

This change of attitude also occurred with the band MX, from Santo André, as we can see in the lyrics of "Dead World." This song is part of the album *Simoniacal*, released in 1988 by Fucker Records:

Between trash and shit scattered
Making noise to bleed through the mask
Causing agony and despair
No, we're not in hell
Hell that will be less cruel
Close to this
Reality that we were waiting for
So soon in the nuclear future.

Heavy metal and the ABC music scene

When we refer to the expression "musical scene," we should understand it as a cultural space in which various types of musical practices coexist, interacting with each other within a variety of differentiation processes (Straw quoted in Vasconcellos 2015: 33).

In the 1980s, the Greater ABC was the setting and meeting point of several urban tribes: punks, headbangers, skinheads, rappers, goths, rockabillys, and skaters. These groups met in specific places known as redoubts, marked territories that were frequented and defended by their members. The relationship and coexistence between the tribes were not always friendly, but were marked by rivalries and violent confrontations that resulted in some deaths. In the Greater ABC region, these conflicts also occurred frequently, especially in the central region of Santo André. The territories or meeting places were located at strategic points, mainly easily accessible near train stations and bus terminals. Also, according to musician and researcher Victor Vasconcellos,

> [a] scene can be understood as a scenario, that is, it exists through the relationship that operates between people (actions, behaviors, social practices, issuing of

> symbols) and spaces (material places invested with meaning). From this, we argue that in each scene there are spaces that are more valued and that become central depending on the "positive" attributes they offer. The greater their centralities, the more complex and periodic the social interactions (sociability) will be
> (Vasconcellos 2015: 18)

In almost all the cities of the ABC region there was some type of activity on the part of the ABC Headbangers; however, the largest number of members of the group were concentrated in the central region of the cities of Santo André, São Bernardo do Campo, and São Caetano do Sul.

Based on this finding, we took as a reference the statement by Vasconcellos (2015), according to which activities and social practices developed in these spaces which made the scene revolve around the ABC Headbangers. The scene is formed by a circuit of places where it is necessary to communicate with the other members of the group. These events took place in the central regions precisely because of the ease of access and proximity to train stations and bus terminals. These spaces have a large area of influence, serving as a reference for visitors from other locations. For Vasconcellos (2015), this centrality was observed both through the number of people who frequented such spaces and the routes that people took to reach them. In the Greater ABC region, although most of the activities took place in the central regions of cities, the local scene had specific nuclei that formed in the neighborhoods of cities in places such as bars and schools. According to Janotti Junior (2004), affirming the group traits, taking over the city, as well as showing up and demarcating its space are ways of celebrating the group experience in the face of the threats, uncertainties, and anguish experienced by these young people.

Specialized stores: More than a place to buy LPs

In the early 1980s, there was no heavy metal record store in the ABC region. Therefore, this made the region's heavy metal fans travel to downtown São Paulo to acquire heavy metal material. This conviviality between the young people of both regions was peaceful and respectful, allowing the exchange of experiences and the participation of the bands in concerts spread throughout the State of São Paulo. From the point of view of the concept of the music scene, Vasconcellos states that these stores are characterized as places that are frequented often and, depending on their importance to the group, receive people from other cities and even from other regions. This way

> [t]he specialized stores, for an underground scene, are not simply a place of commerce in which people go only to buy products. They are also meeting places where individuals who are part of the scene go to listen to music, discover new bands, promote events, talk about the scene, meet other members of the group.
>
> (Vasconcellos 2015: 42)

Over the years, the Greater ABC region began to create its own identity, something that really represented the interests of the region and, above all, an emerging music scene. In 1984, Metal Music, the first store in the region to specialize in rock and heavy metal, was opened in the center of the city of Santo André. Undoubtedly Metal Music was a place that became part of the tradition in the city, being of fundamental importance for the local culture—for adolescents in 1984, in particular. The year the store opened would become a milestone in the history of the city. Metal Music is characterized in the heavy metal scene by Vasconcellos (2015) as a "central" location both from the point of view of relevance within the movement and in relation to the ease of access through the train station and the bus terminal, both located in the center of the city of Santo André. In an interview to the website Strangers Atratores, Jean Gantinis, owner of the Metal Music store, talks about the beginning of the store's activities in the region:

> When I opened the store, the collection was my own, I put it to sell and then, with time, I started to build a heavier collection, with heavy metal and thrash metal of that time, for the store. With this, the kids started to show up. I'm aware of the importance that Metal occupies in the city. I see here, for example, a guy who is now a father and his son, today, goes to the store. There are already cases of grandchildren of this first Metal client. This is our work here.
>
> (Gantinis 2017: n.pag.)

Another central point in ABC's heavy metal scene was Fuckers Records, which started its activities as a record store and later became an independent label that produced and promoted several bands in the region. In testimony to the program *Pegadas de Andreas Kisser*, of Radio 89 FM, presented by Andreas Kisser, guitarist of the band Sepultura, Leandro dos Santos, owner and founder of the store, spoke about how the initiative to create the label and produce the bands of the region came about:

> We imagined at the time having a record store where we could work and have fun. We were 21, 22 years old and even with all the difficulties in three years, from 86 to 89, we created a record store that also ended up becoming a small record company in which we released some records, collections and compact, which at the time was

> a tradition. We started organizing concerts and then we painted the idea of making records with the people from the region who went to the store to buy records. The idea was in fact to expand everything that the store could do. We had something that was very strong, something that was pre-internet. We had a catalogue that we did the design ourselves, printed and sent by mail. So we sold cassette tapes and vinyl to all of Brazil, t-shirts, and we thought we could also do something for the local bands.
>
> (Carvalho 2017: n.pag.)

In the air: The weight of ABC heavy metal in radio waves

Another important element for the heavy metal scene at ABC was Radio 97 FM, the "Alternativa." Located in the city of Santo André, the radio station is considered the first in Brazil to have had a program dedicated to rock music, as Martins points out:

> When the radio appeared in 1983, the censorship that had been ruthless until then began to lose strength, and in this post-dictatorship scenario the radio appeared in Santo André that would be a source of pride for the residents of the region. It is worth remembering that until that moment MTV did not exist, much less 89 FM, and in this sound mosaic in which Brazilian rock began to reach maturity, 97 already stood out from other radios for presenting a profile that resisted artistic banality, becoming an example of vanguard among the stations.
>
> (2011: n.pag.)

Vasconcellos (2015) points out that radio stations are not considered as physical spaces from the point of view of the music scene, but play an important role in scene development as that they act as channels through which the information linked to these groups is circulated.

For the musician and researcher André Barbosa Filho (2003), regionalism is a key brand of radio, because it offers visibility to local information. This principle stimulates the relationship between radio and the community. Despite being located in the ABC region, Radio 97 FM also reached the capital, coast, and interior parts of the State of São Paulo. Among the heavy metal programming, the program *Sessão Rockambole* ("Rockambole session"), the first radio program in Brazil dedicated exclusively to the genre, stood out. It was broadcast weekly on Sundays and presented by the announcer and broadcaster Beto Peninha. The program brought news from the music universe, mainly through foreign material which until then was unpublished in the country. Beto Peninha promoted several events in the ABC region and in the city of São Paulo, promoting shows of national and international bands. *Sessão Rockambole* not only provided its listeners information about renowned foreign bands but also brought latest news from the heavy metal universe, such as the most recent albums released, schedule of shows, and general details related to the national and foreign bands.

From the assembly line to the stages: The heavy metal shows in the ABC region

Heavy metal shows took place in almost all cities of the Greater ABC, most of the time in places like bars, theaters, clubs, sports courts, and school auditoriums, where usually some band member studied or had some kind of contact. During the 1980s, attending a heavy metal show was a deeply satisfying experience for fans who felt greatly obligated to attend such events. More than a moment of intense emotions, the show was an event that promoted the meeting of the elements of the scene and strengthened the bond between its practitioners. According to the sociologist Leonardo Carbonieri Campoy (2010), for the practitioner, the underground as an "organic whole" is evidenced only in these events. Thinking with them, it is in the show that "the flame of the underground" is lit, and it is in the show that it will shine with the greatest intensity.

For economic reasons, the bands promoted concerts together; there was mutual collaboration to loan instruments and promote the event in question. According to Silva (2014), in addition to doing the zines, in most cases it was the fans and members of bands, without space or sponsorship, who organized the shows and promoted festivals as a way to have place for their own bands to perform. On the issue of concerts, Marcelo D'Castro, guitarist and vocalist of the band Necromancia, spoke to the site *Polvorosa Zine*:

> The first difference I see is the number of concerts there are today and at that time there were few. Today you have many friends on Facebook, but only some will hang out together. I talk about ABC that at the time we were in a crowd of more than 30 people easy and went to salons or shows that were rolling and often just by meeting. We were very united. I miss it today. In compensation the shows are better, the scene in my opinion is growing, the media also and I hope for better days in relation to Brazilian metal.
>
> (Anon. 2014: n.pag)

According to Marcelo D'Castro's report, today this practice of watching heavy metal shows in large groups has become increasingly rare. Although the metal scene has grown and consolidated in the Greater ABC region, this concept of

FIGURE 12.3: Anon., MX band performing live at a show, n.d. Color photograph. Courtesy MX band website.

group, of brotherhood, has been lost over time. There was this feeling of pleasure in being part of a group, or rather, there was pride in saying "I'm from ABC!" It was more difficult to get some kind of material from heavy metal bands of that time, which was considered very important and that gave a kind of status to those who were the first to get an LP imported from bands like Metallica, Slayer, and Venom. To walk in a group represented the union between its members, a feeling of protection, because all of them fought for the same ideal. The information was more difficult to share, so it was essential to be in a group to get information like the promotion of concerts, releases of LPs, and even possible conflicts with other groups. Walking in large groups made it possible to take advantage of fights, give more security to their members, and intimidate rival groups. Today things are more accessible. Social networks allow information to be shared almost instantly, without effort or difficulty. Concerts still take place, but in greater numbers and in more accessible places. People are connected by computers, and physical presence is not so relevant, making them more "individualistic," causing the concept of the group to get lost over time.

FIGURE 12.4: Rui Granado, cover art of the collection *Headthrashers Live*, 2018. Black and white photography. Personal archive/Rui Granado.

Remaining members of some groups from the 1980s still promote nostalgic encounters, most of which take place annually on birthdays of cities or places of importance to the scene, such as bars or record stores that remain active for more than 30 years. During these meetings, members reminisce about many stories as well as the first shows that took place in the region. Watching a heavy metal show in the 1980s was a real "saga," which started with the difficulty of finding an available place, getting sound equipment and musical instruments, and finally making the journey to the shows that almost always ended in conflicts with other rival groups. For all that, participating in a show was a sign of attitude and respect among the ABC Headbangers. Because they didn't happen as often as today, the shows were essential to gather the groups and strengthen the scene. It was precisely during one of these shows that the first live record was made involving several heavy metal bands from ABC: the collection Headthrashers Live, recorded on January 29, 1987, at the Teatro Municipal de Santo André, with the participation of the bands MX, Cova, Necromancia, and Blasphemer. The show was highlighted in the national media because of an article in the specialized magazine *Rock Brigade*, which in this period was no longer a zine, being distributed almost throughout Brazil. Thanks also to this review, headbangers from other states got to know the ABC metal scene.

The end...or, uh, a fresh start?

In the 1990s, with the advent of MTV Brasil, a channel with daily programming aimed at teenagers, most of the rock and heavy metal bands fell into ostracism. The music video culture not only brought new musical trends, but also dictated rules and standards to be followed and copied by young people. At the Greater ABC, a climate of mistrust hovered in the air because of the uncertainty about the future of the heavy metal music scene in the region, since the ideals and purposes were no longer the same as in the previous decade. On the one hand, the big media conglomerates stopped investing in heavy metal; on the other hand, the bands found in technology their greatest ally. In this period, new technology revolutionized the music industry: the CD or compact disc fundamentally change the face of the music industry. The bands of ABC region that initially recorded their first compositions through cassette tapes, and later on vinyl records, were now facing not only a new trend or technology, but a possibility.

With the popularization of the CD, many bands that until then were not able to produce albums in the 1980s, due to lack of resources and financial conditions, sought in this new technology the possibility not only of producing an album, but also of improving and evolving technically while deepening the process of musical production; in addition, bands were able to reduce the costs as the price of recording and producing an album on CD was lower. That was the case with some ABC region bands such as Necromancia, MX, Hammerhead, and Ação Direta. The MX band was the only ABC band to produce their own albums in the 1980s; the other bands mentioned were able, during the 1990s, not only to produce albums on CDs, but also to disseminate them outside the country, since the national market was not so favorable and in a way accessible to heavy metal, which generated a new media phenomenon and further strengthened the underground heavy metal scene.

After the period of dissemination and consolidation of heavy metal in the ABC music scene, the region was positively impacted as a result of the popularization of culture focused on this genre. On another level, heavy metal established a kind of sound brand, from the sounds of the factories. Taking into consideration that the increase in the intensity of sound power is the most striking characteristic of the industrialized sound landscape and that the ABC region is precisely an area of concentration of machinery, the relationship between noisy sound landscape and heavy metal seems pertinent. In a way, heavy metal followed the development of the region and vice versa, through a relationship of reciprocity, which was born around the local proletarian culture and which later served as a reference for other regional scenes, almost throughout the country. Rock and heavy metal are so present in the culture of the region that, in 2016, the city council of the city of São Bernardo do Campo, through the bill of Law 60/16, instituted in the official calendar of the city the "Day of Rock." In the project, the band Necromancia is revered for completing 30 years of activity and for its contribution to the music scene of the ABC region. In that same year, the city hall of Santo André paid tribute to the Metal Music store, also for its 30 years of existence and cultural contribution to the regional music scene. Little by little, the ABC bands left their garages and broadened their space inside and outside the country. The young man who until recently was marginalized and discriminated due to his appearance and his musical aesthetic became a reference not only of a musical subgenre or of his "urban tribe," but also constituted a relevant element in the formation of a cultural scene that presented the ABC region to the whole of Brazil. Heavy metal is part of the Greater ABC's culture, something that is rooted and ends up being confused with the region's own history when it comes to rock 'n' roll.

Epilogue

The purpose of this research was to promote and preserve part of the musical and cultural memory of the Greater ABC through heavy metal and its influence on the region's music scene. Because it is research in the field of culture and media, this study allowed the organization of photographic, literary, and audiovisual materials for future researchers and professionals in the field and will serve as a basis for a possible video documentary or literary record. During the development of this project, I confess that I tried my best to separate the fan from the researcher, which was not easy, since I experienced the growth of the genre in the region and was a member of the ABC Headbangers of São Caetano do Sul. In this period, I also ventured as a musician, having my first and only band, the Devastação Nuclear, created.

In Figure 12.5, we can see the band Devastação Nuclear and its members: from left to right, me, Rui Granado (bass and vocals), Sérgio Teixeira (guitar and vocals), and Alexandre Godoy (drums). After a few years, the hair is no longer long and the black t-shirts gave way to social shirts and collar polo. Friends... Yes, I still have contact with almost everyone, others unfortunately no more, but other opportunities for meeting will come. With all this, I close my participation in a nostalgic way and with one certainty: While you may not be able to dress and act like a headbanger all the time anymore, heavy metal and its essence will never leave you...

FIGURE 12.5: Anon., Devastação Nuclear band, 1987. Color photograph. Personal archive/ Rui Granado.

NOTES

1. The expression, created by the composer R. Murray Schafer (1991), refers to every acoustic environment, regardless of its nature.
2. In this documentary, the anthropologist Sam Dunn travels through several countries in search of the roots of heavy metal.

REFERENCES

Anon. (2014), " Necromancia: 30 years of trash metal in the vein", *Zine gunpowder,* http://polvorazine.com/?p=4497. Accessed November 27, 2016.

Barbosa Filho, André (2003), *Radio Genres: Audio Formats and Programs*, São Paulo: Paulinas.

Bosi, Ecléa (1972), *Mass Culture and Popular Culture*, Rio de Janeiro: Voices.

Campoy, Leonardo Carbonieri (2010), *Darkness over Light: The Underground of Extreme Heavy Metal in Brazil*, São Paulo: Alameda.

Carvalho, André (2017), "Andreas Kisser's footprints with people from Fucker Records," YouTube, March 19, https://www.youtube.com/watch?v=94kv_5Urub0/. Accessed September 25, 2017.

D'Castro, Marcelo (2011), "Necromancia: Meet the band," YouTube, http://www.youtube.com/watch?v=09-ZRVRRplc. Accessed March 11, 2017.

Dunn, Sam (2011), *Metal Evolution*, DVD, Canada: VH1 Television Series.

Gantinis, Jean (2007), "Metal music: The story of ABCD's most beloved store," *ABCD Maior*, http://www.abcdmaior.com.br/materias/cidades/santo-andre-464-anos-metal-music-a-historia-da-loja-mais-querida-do-abcd. Accessed April 7, 2017.

Gepeto, Paulo (2011), "Ação Direta: Meet the band," YouTube, https://www.youtube.com/watch?v=eUMyDoABWew. Accessed April 21, 2017.

Janotti Junior, Jeder (2004), *Heavy Metal with Dendê: Heavy Rock and Media in Times of Globalization*, Rio de Janeiro: E-papers.

Leão, Tom (1997), *Heavy Metal: Guitarras em Fúria*, São Paulo: 34.

Leonelli, Domingos, and Oliveira, Dantas (2004), *Diretas Já! 15 Days That Shook Brazil*, São Paulo: Record.

Martins, Ricardo (2011), "ABC and the pioneer in rock radio," memoriarockabc, https://memoriarockabc.wordpress.com/2011/11/26/abc-e-o-pioneirismo-nas-radio-rock/. Accessed April 15, 2017.

MX (1988), "Dead World," *Simoniacal*, CD, Brazil: Fucker Records.

Necromanica (2002), "Check Mate," *Check Mate*, CD, Brazil: Hellion Records.

Necromanica ([1993] 2012), "Death Lust," *Back From The Dead*, CD, Brazil: Voice Music.

Schafer, R. Murray (1991), *O Ouvido Pensante*, São Paulo: UNESP Publishing House.

Schafer, R. Murray (1997), *A Afinação do Mundo*, São Paulo: UNESP Publishing House.

Silva, Wlisses James de Farias (2014), *Os Incômodos Perdedores: Heavy Metal in Brazil in the 1980s*, São Paulo: USP.

Teixeira, Aldemir Leonardo (2007), *The Punk Movement in ABC Paulista—Os Incômodos Perdedores*, São Paulo: PUC.

Vasconcellos, Victor (2015), *The Geography of the Underground: A Study on the Spatiality of Heavy Metal Scenes in Brazil*, Berlin: New Academic Editions.

Weinstein, Deena (2000), *Heavy Metal: The Music and Its Culture,* Nova York: Da Capo Press.

13

"This Is the City of Hate": Surveying the Hull Metal/Hardcore Scene

Lewis F. Kennedy

The ongoing expansion of metal studies into a global research field continues to produce innovative work on metal/hardcore scenes around the world (e.g., Wallach et al. 2011; Brown et al. 2016). Within the United Kingdom, Birmingham has often taken precedence as the supposed birthplace of metal (Cope 2010; Weinstein 2014), but contemporary metal/hardcore scenes in Leeds (Riches et al. 2014), across northern England (Yavuz 2018), and throughout the United Kingdom (Emms and Crossley 2018) have received scholarly attention more recently. Alongside metal/hardcore's more well-known or exotic locales, one can identify countless scenes that generally receive less attention because of their apparent ordinariness; this chapter is devoted to just such a scene.

With around 260,000 inhabitants (CPPI 2018), Kingston upon Hull—more commonly known simply as Hull—might be considered a typical small-to-mid-sized city in the northeast of England. Like many other British cities born of heavy industry, Hull experienced a sharp decline during the post–Second World War, post-industrialization years of the twentieth century. Despite these ostensible similarities with other comparably sized British cities, there is a perception among its members that Hull's metal/hardcore scene is broadly inferior to its counterparts elsewhere. Based upon a mixed methods ethnography of the Hull metal/hardcore scene, this chapter identifies and explores themes arising from online survey data and face-to-face interviews. Following a brief overview of the city's history and contemporary state, I introduce some of the key findings of the scene ethnography. Hull's physical location and symbolic position within the wider British metal/hardcore scene network emerge as focal points for local scene members and the rest of the chapter considers both positive (independent, identifiable) and negative (isolated, insular) characterizations of the local scene. Rather than cast Hull as a unique case, I seek to further ongoing discourse(s) on metal/hardcore scenes around the world by adding another piece to the mosaic of metal/hardcore as a global cultural phenomenon.

Given myriad competing definitions of the term "scene" (and related terminology like subculture, tribe, neo-tribe, art/music world, etc.) across numerous disciplines and academic fields, it is pertinent to briefly explain usage of the term in the present chapter.[1] Following previous work on music scenes generally (e.g., Bennett and Peterson 2004) and metal/hardcore scenes specifically (e.g., Wallach and Levine 2013), "scene" here refers to a variable combination of people, institutions, and artefacts. Hence, for present purposes, "the Hull metal/hardcore scene" might be best understood as comprising all those people who are in some way involved in metal/hardcore in and around the city of Hull (musicians, concert attendees, promoters, venue operators, recording engineers), all those institutions that support metal/hardcore (gig venues, pubs/clubs, rehearsal spaces, music studios), and those artefacts that emanate from people and institutions that are part of the scene.

Setting the scene

Founded in the late thirteenth century (Miles 2011: 3; Starkey et al. 2017: 9), Kingston upon Hull is a city in the East Riding of Yorkshire in northeast England. Located some 20 miles inland of the North Sea at the confluence of the River Hull and the Humber Estuary, the city's fortunes have long been linked to maritime trades including wool and the importation of timber (Miles 2011: 3), and later, whaling and distant-water fishing (Starkey et al. 2017: 2). During the twentieth century, Hull experienced a significant decline thanks to a combination of increasing automation and containerization (CPPI 2018: 23), disruption and destruction of industry during the Second World War (Atkinson 2017: 239), and the so-called Cod Wars (Avery 2008: 53).[2] By the new millennium, Hull had "for decades [...] been among the most economically deprived areas in the country" (Richardson 2017: n.pag.), and "Hull's schools were at the bottom of the national league tables and the city council itself was designated the UK's worse performing authority in 2004 and 2005" (Avery 2008: 57). This apparently downward trend of the city continued into the second decade of the twenty-first century, with higher-than-average rates of people seeking unemployment benefit and cuts in core government funding contributing to an austere present and uninspiring future: "More than one in three children living in Hull lives in poverty" (Rickett 2018: n.pag.).[3] Negative perceptions of the city were challenged, however, when Hull was designated the 2017 UK City of Culture, a "title awarded by the Department for Digital, Culture, Media and Sport every four years to a city in the United

Kingdom, with the winner hosting a year-long programme of cultural events and celebrations" (British Council n.d.: n.pag.). The resultant £32.8m "cultural programme" (CPPI 2018: 7) was evidently sorely needed, with the team behind the award bid portraying the city as "coming out of the shadows" (Flinn 2014: n.pag.), and even the British Council acknowledging that "Hull is a city that has often been overlooked" (n.d.: n.pag.).

Despite recent efforts to the contrary, many of the city's inhabitants (including members of the metal/hardcore scene) grew up in a broadly negative milieu. As will become apparent throughout this chapter, my ethnographic data suggest negative views of the city sit alongside more positive, prideful perspectives on the local metal/hardcore scene. Indeed, this dual narrative of Hull as negative and positive may be observed in the scene's musical output. Black Tongue, a so-called sludgewave band (Handmaker 2015) from Hull, begin their debut EP, *Falsifier* (2013), with a song dedicated to the city of their founding: "H.C.H.C." Vocalist Alex Teyen paints a bleak picture of Hull as "the city of hate [...] a dead city of forgotten people," but introduces the song's climactic breakdown by declaring "We are Hull City Hate Crew, fuck you!" A similar conceit underlies claims from fellow Hull bands Mastiff, who refer to themselves as a "[m]iserable band from a miserable town" (Mastiff 2020: n.pag.), and Battalions, who describe their music as "[d]irt ridden sludge from the wastelands of Hull" (Battalions 2020: n.pag.). While depictions of Hull as somewhat austere are not entirely without cause, these sardonic, self-deprecating perspectives on the city appear in popular discourse as well as in metal/hardcore. Moreover, such views surface elsewhere in Hull's metal/hardcore scene, articulated by various members in survey data and during interviews.

Studying the scene

Following the methodology utilized by Bryan Bardine in an earlier study of the metal scene in Dayton, Ohio (see Bardine, this volume),[4] my ethnography of the Hull metal/hardcore scene employs a mixed-methods approach, combining data gathered from both a quantitative survey of and qualitative interviews with scene members. Hosted on Google Drive and disseminated through various social media channels (Facebook, Twitter, Instagram), the online survey received 60 responses during the period September 15 to October 2, 2017. To produce the broadest range of responses, the survey was advertised as open to anyone who considered themselves to be or have been part of the Hull metal/hardcore scene. Adapted from Bardine's earlier study, respondents were invited to answer fifteen questions covering demographic information (gender, age, ethnicity, occupation, location), their thoughts on metal/hardcore music (favorite genres, favorite artists, why they like the music), on the Hull scene (length of scene membership, where they attend concerts, favorite local artists), and on their habits of travelling to other scenes. Select questions were altered from Bardine's questionnaire to account for local differences (e.g., the addition of lower age categories reflecting a greater volume of all-ages concerts and a lower legal age for alcohol consumption), or to provide the opportunity for more expansive answers (e.g., changing a multiple-choice question on what respondents like about metal/hardcore to allow open-ended responses).[5]

Perhaps unsurprisingly, the Hull metal/hardcore scene largely mirrors the extreme metal scene in nearby Leeds, which is "characterised as predominantly masculine, white, working class and heterosexual" (Riches et al. 2014: 92). Among Hull survey respondents, 85 percent identified as male (13 percent female, 2 percent nonbinary), 73 percent were 30 years old or younger,[6] and 93 percent identified as white British or some variation thereof. Slightly more than 80 percent of survey respondents (49 of 60) lived in or near Hull city center, within walking or bus distance of the main metal/hardcore venues, while the remaining respondents were scattered among areas surrounding the city, including satellite towns and villages. Possibly reflecting the generally young age of respondents, the primary occupations of surveyed scene members were retail, student, and the service industry (e.g., bar staff), but the range of professions included software analyst, nurse, civil servant, and forklift truck driver. The Hull scene appears to enjoy a relatively healthy balance of new and old members, with most having been part of the scene for five years or fewer (28 of 60) only slightly outweighing those who have been members for ten years or more (23 of 60). While the majority of respondents (46 of 60) attended at least one metal/hardcore gig per month in Hull, including five scene members who claim to go to such gigs five times or more every month, the rest of the surveyed scene members were less-frequent gig attendees.

The predominance of white male respondents is likely a result of utilizing a scene framework that relies heavily upon public, visible engagements with music (e.g., performing at or attending gigs). Given that "historically such frameworks have omitted women from the picture" (Hill 2016: 29), alongside Hull's higher-than-average white British population (CPPI 2018: 76), it is worth noting the caveat that my survey data may not include those scene members whose participation is largely private, a group who could incorporate higher percentages of women and people of color. Hosting an online survey promoted through social media was an attempt, however unsuccessful, to reach those less visible members of the Hull metal/hardcore scene.

To add qualitative perspective to the largely quantitative data accumulated through the scene survey, I conducted face-to-face interviews with six Hull metal/

hardcore scene members (drawn from the pool of survey respondents) during the period January 23 to February 13, 2018. Comprising eighteen questions designed to provide in-depth personal reflections to complement survey data, interviewees were asked open-ended questions regarding their views on the local metal/hardcore scene. Three interviewees were in their early twenties, originally from other parts of the United Kingdom having moved to Hull to attend university, and had been part of the local metal/hardcore scene for around three and a half years. The other three interviewees were all from Hull, with two in their late twenties having been scene members for twelve to thirteen years, and one in his late forties having been a member of the scene for 32 years. All six originally became fans of metal at a young age (either preteen or teenaged) and performed in various bands during their teens and early twenties. At the time of interview, five were members of metal/hardcore bands in Hull (with one of those also a record producer), while the other interviewee was a promoter, live sound engineer, and venue operator. Highlighting methodological issues similar to those encountered with the survey, all six of my interviewees were heterosexual white males. As such, the breadth of experiences captured during the interview portion of the ethnography was severely limited; however, responses provided by my interviewees are nevertheless valuable as part of the ongoing patchwork of metal/hardcore research.

Reflecting the prominence of Hull's geographical location in much discourse surrounding the city in both popular press and academic literature, my ethnography of the scene included an additional focus of Hull's location and its potential effects upon the scene. Supplementing questions drawn from Bardine's earlier study, the Hull metal/hardcore scene survey included questions pertaining specifically to Hull scene members' habits of travelling elsewhere to attend metal/hardcore gigs—where they travel outside the city for such gigs, how often, and their primary reason for doing so. In a similar vein, scene-member interviews included questions related to perspectives on the potential effects of Hull's location on its metal/hardcore scene, and on its proximity to other metal/hardcore scenes in nearby cities. The remainder of this chapter is devoted to exploring the significance of location in discussions of Hull and its metal/hardcore scene, mixing extant literature with the thoughts of scene members drawn from my ethnography.

Locating the scene

For most of its history, the city's position on an estuary near the North Sea provided sustenance, wealth, and purpose, but beginning in the latter half of the twentieth century, "[t]he loss, contraction and reconfiguration of Hull's industrial and maritime functions led to socio-economic decline, and this was compounded by the city's relative geographical isolation, resulting in high levels of unemployment and deprivation" (CPPI 2018: 23). No longer seen as advantageous, Hull's location now denotes "geographical isolation," fostering notions of the city as "provincial" (Atkinson 2018: 97) and "peripheral" (Starkey et al. 2017: 10). While the ferry port and nearby Humberside airport provide ready access to continental Europe, perceptions of Hull as isolated persist due "more to relatively poor road and rail links than to objective geographical remoteness" (CPPI 2018: 25). Despite connecting Hull to much of the rest of the United Kingdom, the M62 motorway has become enmeshed within negative perceptions of the city and its inhabitants: "There is something about being at the end of the M62—geographically it is the end of the road. There's a kind of cultural disconnect with the rest of the world because of that" (Hull-born filmmaker Sean McAllister quoted in Curtis 2017: n.pag.).

While the environment of postwar Birmingham may have been conducive to the foundation of heavy metal (Cope 2010: 26–35; Weinstein 2014), the city's location, especially in relation to transport networks, appears essential to the musical development of bands like Black Sabbath and Judas Priest. Situated toward the west of central England's Midlands region, "the geographical positioning of Birmingham was crucial to the emergence of specific musical innovations during the 1960s and early 1970s" (Cope 2010: 9). Birmingham's "central location, excellent transport links, large population, and numerous music enthusiasts" allowed the city to become a pivotal hub for artistic activity wherein "musicians from other areas came to Birmingham to play gigs, and local bands could travel elsewhere" (Weinstein 2014: 44). Consequently, the city enjoyed an "ebb and flow of musical concept and style" that "directly influenced the musical and aesthetic direction of influential bands such as Black Sabbath and Led Zeppelin" (Cope 2010: 9).

Birmingham's centrality juxtaposes sharply with Hull's position near the east coast: "Seen from the rest of England, Hull appears to be peripheral: a port tight against the east coast, detached from the heartland of Yorkshire and England more generally" (Starkey et al. 2017: 10). Members of the Hull metal/hardcore scene articulated a sense of the city being "peripheral" when characterizing the scene as "quite small, quite isolated" (Interviewee 4). When compared to nearby cities in Yorkshire, Hull's apparent isolation is highlighted further: "When you think of where Leeds is placed, you've got Manchester less than an hour away, you've got Sheffield less than an hour away, you've got Nottingham just over an hour away" (Interviewee 6). By contrast, in Hull "you are an hour from anywhere, whichever direction you want to travel in" (Interviewee 6), effecting the flow of artists and audiences both to and from the city.

For members of the metal/hardcore scene in, say, Leeds, there seems little reason to travel to attend or play gigs in Hull when other locations are in closer proximity, not to mention a higher volume of such gigs happening in Leeds (see below).

Hull scene members travelling elsewhere face similar issues, but while additional travel time "doesn't really bother bands," the extra cost of such travel can be prohibitive: "if you've got three vehicles to Newcastle, it's going to be £20–30 to get there, each, so you're going to be asking for £90, which is not gonna happen" (Interviewee 5). Likewise, scene members attending gigs outside Hull identified financial constraints as a factor in their interaction with other scenes, with one survey respondent noting that they travel "not very often as money is tight," while another suggested that when going to gigs outside Hull they travel "wherever is closest [...] depending on the bands coming. Not cheap nowadays." While these additional travel times and expenses may seem relatively insignificant (especially to those encountered in countries larger than the United Kingdom), they can result in perceptions of Hull and its metal/hardcore scene as inaccessible compared to other cities in Yorkshire or along the east coast of England.

Characterizing the scene

Perceptions of Hull's isolation are further exacerbated because the city is "a dead-end, you don't pass through it to get anywhere. So touring bands [...] pass through Leeds or they'll hit Lincoln and turn inwards" (Interviewee 6). A dearth of outside influence provided by a relatively low volume of touring bands performing in the city results in Hull lacking the "ebb and flow" so crucial to Birmingham's scene in the late 1960s. As part of their analysis of what they call the United Kingdom's underground metal world, Rachel Emms and Nick Crossley conducted research at venues in Birmingham, Bristol, Leeds, Liverpool, London, and Manchester. These cities were selected "on the basis of information gleaned from interviews with tour managers and promoters" who "identified our six localities as the main stops on the underground metal touring circuit" (Emms and Crossley 2018: 119). Surveyed Hull scene members compiled a similar list when asked about their habits of travelling to attend metal/hardcore gigs in other cities, naming sixteen different locations, mostly in the north of England but also as far away as Cardiff and Brighton. Leeds (27 mentions), Sheffield (16), and Manchester (15) were the most commonly cited cities to which scene members travel for gigs, with Nottingham and London receiving five mentions apiece. Thus, while scene members will travel relatively large distances to attend metal/hardcore gigs, the most common destinations are large cities in the north of England.

While some Hull scene members reported travelling outside the city to visit particular venues, see specific bands, or attend major festivals like Download, most suggested they left Hull due to the scale of artists on offer elsewhere. A common refrain among survey respondents suggested that they travel to cities like Leeds,

Sheffield, and Manchester to see "bigger bands" than those performing in Hull. The majority of surveyed scene members identified well-established, international touring bands as among their favorites—Slipknot, Metallica, Mastodon—the kinds of "big" bands very unlikely to perform in Hull. Thirteen bands received three or more mentions as "favorite" among survey respondents, but with only four British artists (six from the United States, and three Australian) and the newest band forming nearly a decade before the survey (Northlane, formed in 2009), the chances are slim for a Hull scene member hoping to see their favorite band perform locally. As such, Hull metal/hardcore fans travel elsewhere "because bands I like never play Hull" (survey response). Some scene members recognize that "[n]ot all events and localities are equal in a translocal world" (Emms and Crossley 2018: 131), with one noting that "most of the bands I want to see play a limited number of dates in the country. Not usually in Hull" (survey response).

Within the "core-periphery structure" of interconnected local metal/hardcore scenes in which "[s]ome events and localities are more important than others" (Emms and Crossley 2018: 131), Hull remains steadfastly on the periphery: "Although Hull has seen it's [*sic*] fair share of quality over the past few years it is still been [*sic*] overshadowed by other Northern cities" (survey response). In effect, the Hull metal/hardcore scene is doubly handicapped by its proximity to larger scenes in nearby cities. As its scene members attest, Hull is not a common destination for the kinds of international touring artists they describe as favorite, but, as identified by Emms and Crossley, the city also falls outside the core of the United Kingdom's underground metal/hardcore tour circuit. In both instances, Hull and its metal/hardcore scene are understood as peripheral—outside and isolated from the country's main metal/hardcore network.

Peter Atkinson points toward the relative geographical isolation of Hull as a significant aspect of the city's "soundscape," positing that David Bowie's *The Rise and Fall of Ziggy Stardust and the Spiders from Mars* (1972) "was shaped by an interaction between two *distinct* soundscapes: metropolitan London and provincial Hull" (Atkinson 2018: 97, original emphasis). In comparing Hull to London, Atkinson describes the former as "provincial" (2018: 97), a "small northern town" (2018: 103), and an "unexceptional town" (2018: 109). More than simply acknowledging London's hegemony among British cities, Atkinson implies broader connotations of provincial—peripheral, small, insignificant—to characterize Hull as the cultural opposite of London. In Atkinson's reading, David Bowie's use of backing musicians from Hull (the Spiders from Mars) shaped "[t]he essence of the *Ziggy Stardust* project and its meaning is a double coding of 'alterity' (embodied in the metropolitan suburbanite Bowie's performance) and authenticity (embodied in that of the northern, provincial band)" (Atkinson 2018: 106). Notably, it is not merely the case that the musical worlds of London and Hull were different, but that one was subordinate to the other: "London had the elaborated soundscape; Hull had a soundscape that was secondary to this, one subject to the former's influence" (Atkinson 2018: 100). Hull-based band The Housemartins displayed a stubborn riposte to the city's inferiority complex when they titled their debut album *London 0 Hull 4* (1986), but a sense of inadequacy remains on the part of some local metal/hardcore scene members.

Unlike larger, better-connected cities elsewhere in the United Kingdom, for Hull there are "geographical limitations of it being a dead-end, of it being somewhere you don't pass through—there's not that same sense of vibrancy" (Interviewee 6). For many in Hull, the local metal/hardcore scene seems adversely effected by its proximity to scenes in cities like Leeds, Sheffield, and Manchester, since "those cities are a more viable option for bands, or bigger bands especially, because there's more people localized in that area compared to here" (Interviewee 3). Hull may not seem such a "viable option" for metal/hardcore bands as "there's few places to play metal, very few places" (Interviewee 1). Asked where they usually attend gigs in Hull, 52 of 60 surveyed scene members identified one of two venues: O'Rileys or Gorilla Studios. With relatively few touring bands passing through the city and the scene centered so heavily around just two venues, it may be unsurprising for one of the longest-serving scene members to observe that Hull metal/hardcore "can be a little conservative" (Interviewee 2). A paucity of venues and tendency toward tradition combine to form a scene that is "very focused within itself and doesn't draw from elsewhere [in terms of] influence" (Interviewee 3). This sense of a scene "focused within itself" is compounded when observing the apparently unidirectional travel between Hull and other scenes: "I'm aware of bands from Hull playing in Leeds, in Sheffield, in Manchester being well-received, but that isn't reciprocated in terms of people coming back to see them" (Interviewee 6).

When asked to identify what they like about the Hull metal/hardcore scene, some survey respondents expressed decidedly negative views. One member suggested that "the scene has become more fractured and sometimes seems cliquey to outsiders," with another characterizing the scene as "an impenetrable clique if you're not one of the 'cool' bands." More damning, a few respondents contended that they like very little about the Hull scene—"Not much, weak bands, weak crowds, weak shows"—with two members even asserting they like "nothing" about the scene. For another respondent, the question drew a simple, derisive response of "what scene?." Despite the best efforts of some Hull bands and scene members, it seems the city's relative geographical isolation, comparatively poor transport links, and proximity to larger "core" scenes have resulted in a local metal/hardcore scene that might be characterized as insular. Hull falls outside the touring circuits of many metal/hardcore bands, both national and international, while bands from nearby cities likely see little reason to incur additional time and monetary costs to perform to smaller audiences. While local scene members travel outside the city to attend or perform gigs when able, Hull's scene nevertheless seems largely disconnected from the wider UK metal/hardcore scene network, fostering perceptions of the scene as isolated and insular.

Reinterpreting the scene

Recalling the dual narrative of the city and its location as both positive and negative, perceptions of the Hull metal/hardcore scene as insular only form part of the story. While the local scene may be smaller than those elsewhere, its size is beneficial when forming and maintaining a community: "[I]t is a small scene and, because people know each other, people develop an actual compassion and actual empathy for each other; we know what each other goes through" (Interviewee 6). Indeed, several survey respondents identified a sense of community as important in metal/hardcore generally and the Hull scene specifically, echoing research on small metal scenes elsewhere (e.g., Varas-Díaz et al. 2015). Many of those surveyed described the scene as friendly and welcoming to new members as well as bands from elsewhere, characterizing the scene as "small, supportive, welcoming, active in hosting/engaging bands from other regions" (survey response). One advantage of a small, community-driven scene is that "when the scene gets behind a band, [...] they can be really supportive and they'll stand up for that band, they'll go to the gigs wherever they're playing" (Interviewee 2). Numerous survey respondents commented on the generic diversity and quality of local metal/hardcore bands, with one suggesting that despite the scene's size "[t]here's something for everyone and I think if you're into metal hardcore we're pretty fortunate to have the scene that we do" (survey response). Hence, while Hull may not enjoy the "core" status of larger scenes, its limited size allows members to foster personal relationships and be visible in their support of local artists.

Where the small, close-knit nature of the Hull scene may provide its members with a strong sense of community, the city's literal and metaphorical isolation can also be interpreted positively. While many British and North American bands seem to bypass Hull on their regular touring routes, the city's location relative to continental Europe has its benefits. As explained by one interviewee, "being a port, we've had a few bands come straight in off the ferry and done a Hull gig on the first night of the tour [...] we're in the perfect position to connect with Europe" (Interviewee 2). Though the interviewee conceded that such gigs are infrequent, they nevertheless represent a potential future in which the Hull metal/hardcore scene becomes a significant part of regular touring networks, with scene members utilizing the city's location to their advantage.

Rather than consider Hull as disconnected from the rest of the United Kingdom and/or other British metal/hardcore scenes, we might recognize that the local scene has "got its own thing. Hull, as a place, is very independent [...] It does sound its own way" (Interviewee 1). Indeed, "Hull enjoys an often-stated reputation as an independent, free-thinking place" (Starkey et al. 2017: 10), a trait that appears to permeate its metal/hardcore scene. The apparent remoteness of the city has led its artistic community to develop a particular character: "[P]eople in Hull do their own thing; because we're at the end of the M62 and the other side of the town is the North Sea, people have evolved their own music, their own styles" (Interviewee 2). Reflexively feeding into narratives about the city from bands like Black Tongue and Mastiff, one interviewee observed that "there seems to be a different level of anger from the people of Hull. I don't know what they're angry about, but they seem pretty angry to me" (Interviewee 1). Mastiff guitarist James Lee recognizes the influence of Hull on his band's music, observing "[t]hat sense of isolation being stuck in this crumbling post-industrial city certainly helps feed the miserable sound that we go for" (quoted in Davies 2019: 33).

By reinterpreting the limitations of their location to form a creative impetus, some members of the Hull metal/hardcore scene have shaped notions of independence into a distinct identity: "The town [*sic*] is slowly building a hefty reputation for birthing some truly unholy tunes and while we may not know what is causing it, we should be thankful" (MacLennan 2019: n.pag.). These scene members have recast ostensible isolation and insularity into an identifiable, independent local approach to metal/hardcore often imbued with a sense of anger and injustice born of the city's location and the scene's position within the national metal/hardcore scene network.

Conclusions

Hull's location near the coast in the northeast of England and its relative socioeconomic deprivation contribute to disparaging perspectives on the city from within and without. A city once central to trade and industry was repositioned as peripheral in the wake of deindustrialization, and a population that once had a clear identity moved toward anonymity. For many members of the local metal/hardcore scene, Hull has always seemed isolated and inauspicious. Larger Yorkshire cities like Leeds and Sheffield occupy comparatively central locations within the United Kingdom and, thanks to well-developed transport links, enjoy a privileged position within the touring circuits of most metal/hardcore bands. The unidirectional travel of bands and audiences from Hull to other scenes does little to ameliorate the issue of potential stagnation within the Hull scene, "because it's not a place where bands pass through, there isn't that kind of melting-pot dynamic that you might have [elsewhere]" (Interviewee 6). But rather than allow apparent isolation and insularity to overwhelm them, members of the Hull metal/hardcore scene repurpose the negative elements of the city's location and environment to positive ends. The limited size of the scene affords a more personal sense of community and visible support structure. Hull bands have found recent success in part by adapting notions of isolation and bleak prospects into an identifiable local sound.

Compared to larger world-renowned metal/hardcore scenes, not to mention those in supposedly unusual places, Hull may seem strikingly ordinary. This chapter has sought to investigate the apparent mundanity of the Hull metal/hardcore scene by employing an ethnographic approach. Through responses to surveys and interview questions, local scene members expressed a variety of perspectives on the Hull metal/hardcore scene, both positive and negative. The city's location emerged as a frequent point of contention, affording a supportive, independent scene for some, creating a stagnant, isolated scene for others. Hull's geographical location and metaphorical position within national scene networks provides the space for a small, community-driven scene that has developed an independent identity; however, those same factors restrict the wider impact, interconnectedness, and perceived importance of the local scene. While the group of survey respondents and, especially, interviewees was limited in size and perspective, the resultant data portray a scene adapting to its literal location in the world and metaphorical position within metal/hardcore culture.

The nature of the Hull metal/hardcore scene is at once accommodating and restrictive: "[W]hile it brings to us on a personal level a lot of benefits, a lot of warmth and happiness, as a scene it prevents the kind of growth that would see people shooting off in other directions" (Interviewee 6). The location of the city and the mentality of its people mirror the duality of the local metal/hardcore scene—at turns isolated and independent, insular and identifiable. The city and its scene are analogous, both attempting to forge an identity and redress a perceived inequity: "[E]verything about it geographically limits what the scene can become and breeds the peculiarities of what the scene is" (Interviewee 6).

NOTES

1. For a thorough explication of "scene" and related terms in the context of twenty-first century popular music, see Kennedy (2018: 152–85).
2. "The so called 'cod wars' with Iceland ended in 1976 with Iceland setting up a 200 mile exclusion zone which cut off the rich fishing grounds to English trawlers. With other grounds already over-fished, the number of Hull trawlers able to make a living declined and the once crowded and lively fish dock became virtually empty" (Avery 2008: 53).

3. In 2011, "7.9% of Hull's population was claiming Jobseekers' Allowance. This had dipped slightly to 7.2%—still more than double the UK average—by 2013" (Mistry 2016: n.pag.); "Since 2011, Hull City Council has seen £121 million of core funding removed, with another £10 million due to be taken away this year" (Rickett 2018: n.pag.).
4. My thanks to Bryan Bardine for the impetus to conduct this research. I was fortunate enough to present early findings of my ethnography alongside Bryan and Ed Banchs (see Banchs, this volume) at the 2018 annual meeting of the International Association for the Study of Popular Music (US Branch) at Vanderbilt University (Nashville, TN).
5. This change highlights a significant difference in how the two studies were executed: while Bardine's questionnaire was completed by scene members in physical concert spaces (during and post-concerts), my digital questionnaire allowed more time and space for respondents to consider and provide longer, more detailed answers if they so chose.
6. Age ranges of respondents as presented in the survey: 15 or under (0 percent), 16–24 (48 percent), 25–30 (25 percent), 31–40 (13 percent), 41–50 (10 percent), 51–60 (2 percent), 61 or over (2 percent).

REFERENCES

Atkinson, David (2017), "Trauma, resilience and utopianism in Second World War Hull," in D. J. Starkey, D. Atkinson, B. McDonagh, S. McKeon, and E. Salter (eds.), *Hull: Culture, History, Place*, Liverpool: Liverpool University Press, pp. 239–69.

Atkinson, Peter (2018), "The contrasting soundscapes of Hull and London in David Bowie's *Ziggy Stardust and the Spiders from Mars*," in E. Mazierska (ed.), *Sounds Northern: Popular Music, Culture and Place in England's North*, Sheffield: Equinox, pp. 96–111.

Avery, Alan (2008), *The Story of Hull*, Pickering: Blackthorn Press.

Battalions (2020), Battalions' Bandcamp site, https://battalionsdirt.bandcamp.com/. Accessed February 19, 2020.

Bennett, Andy, and Peterson, Richard A. (eds.) (2004), *Music Scenes: Local, Translocal, and Virtual*, Nashville: Vanderbilt University Press.

Black Tongue (2013), *Falsifier*, CD, Boston: We Are Triumphant.

Bowie, David (1972), *The Rise and Fall of Ziggy Stardust and the Spiders from Mars*, Vinyl, London: RCA Victor.

British Council (n.d.), "Hull: City of culture," https://www.britishcouncil.org/arts/hull-city-culture-tour/city-of-culture. Accessed February 19, 2020.

Brown, Andy R., Spracklen, Karl, Kahn-Harris, Keith, and Scott, Niall W. R. (eds.) (2016), *Global Metal Music and Culture: Current Directions in Metal Studies*, New York: Routledge.

Cope, Andrew L. (2010), *Black Sabbath and the Rise of Heavy Metal Music*, Farnham: Ashgate.

Culture, Place and Policy Institute (CPPI) (2018), *Cultural Transformations: The Impacts of Hull UK City of Culture 2017, Preliminary Outcomes Evaluation*, Hull: University of Hull.

Curtis, Nick (2017), "Sean McAllister, curator of Made in Hull: 'We're showcasing 75 years of a proud working city,'" https://www.theguardian.com/uk-news/2017/jan/01/sean-mcallister-made-in-hull-city-of-culture. Accessed February 19, 2020.

Davies, Hywel (2019), "Mastiff: Thick, disgusting and indigestible hardcore: What's not to love?," *Metal Hammer*, June, p. 33.

Emms, Rachel, and Crossley, Nick (2018), "Translocality, network structure, and music worlds: Underground metal in the United Kingdom," *Canadian Review of Sociology*, 55:1, pp. 111–35.

Flinn, Jon (2014), "Stepping out of the shadows," Arts Professional, January 6, https://www.artsprofessional.co.uk/magazine/270/article/stepping-out-shadows. Accessed February 19, 2020.

Handmaker, Simon (2015), "Starter kit: Sludgewave" July 2, http://www.heavyblogisheavy.com/2015/07/02/starter-kit-sludgewave/. Accessed February 19, 2020.

Hill, Rosemary Lucy (2016), *Gender, Metal and the Media: Women Fans and the Gendered Experience of Music*, London: Palgrave Macmillan.

The Housemartins (1986), *London 0 Hull 4*, CD, London: Go! Discs.

Kennedy, Lewis F. (2018), "Functions of genre in metal and hardcore music," PhD thesis, Hull: University of Hull.

MacLennan, Matt (2019), "Mastiff: The hard behind the core," Heavy Blog is Heavy, February 7, http://www.heavyblogisheavy.com/2019/02/07/mastiff-the-hard-behind-the-core/. Accessed February 19, 2020.

Mastiff (2020), "Miserable band from a miserable town," https://twitter.com/mastiffhchc. Accessed February 19, 2020.

Miles, Philip C. (2011), *Hull through Time*, Stroud: Amberley Publishing.

Mistry, Pritti (2016), "City of optimism: Hull relishes Siemens investment boost," *BBC News*, December 1, https://www.bbc.co.uk/news/uk-england-humber-38130988. Accessed February 19, 2020.

Richardson, Nigel (2017), "Why it's time you gave Hull a second chance," *The Telegraph*, January 1, https://www.telegraph.co.uk/travel/destinations/europe/united-kingdom/england/yorkshire/kingston-upon-hull/articles/uk-capital-of-culture-hull-what-to-see-and-do/. Accessed February 19, 2020.

Riches, Gabrielle, Lashua, Brett, and Spracklen, Karl (2014), "Female, mosher, transgressor: A 'moshography' of transgressive practices within the Leeds extreme metal scene," *Journal of the International Association for the Study of Popular Music*, 4:1, pp. 87–100.

Rickett, Oscar (2018), "This film shows the reality of life in austerity Britain," Vice, https://www.vice.com/en_uk/article/mb4wp3/this-film-shows-the-reality-of-life-in-austerity-britain. Accessed February 19, 2020.

Starkey, David J., Atkinson, David, McDonagh, Briony, McKeon, Sarah, and Salter, Elisabeth (eds.) (2017), *Hull: Culture, History, Place*, Liverpool: Liverpool University Press.

Varas-Díaz, Nelson, Riverra-Segarra, Eliut, Rivera Medina, Carmen, L., Mendoza, Sigrid, and González-Sepúlveda, Osvaldo (2015), "Predictors of communal formation in a small heavy metal scene: Puerto Rico as a case study," *Metal Music Studies*, 1:1, pp. 87–103.

Wallach, Jeremy, and Levine, Alexandra (2013), " 'I want *you* to support local metal': A theory of metal scene formation," in T. Hjelm, K. Kahn-Harris, and M. LeVine (eds.), *Heavy Metal: Controversies and Countercultures*, Sheffield: Equinox, pp. 117–35.

Wallach, Jeremy, Berger, Harris M., and Greene, Paul D. (eds.) (2011), *Metal Rules the Globe: Heavy Metal Music Around the World*, Durham: Duke University Press.

Weinstein, Deena (2014), "Birmingham's postindustrial metal," in B. Lashua, K. Spracklen, and S. Wagg (eds.), *Sounds and the City: Popular Music, Place and Globalization*, Basingstoke: Palgrave Macmillan, pp. 38–54.

Yavuz, Mehmet Selim (2018), "'The Barghest O' Whitby': (A genealogical study of) Death/doom music(al) network in northern England," PhD thesis, Leeds: Leeds Beckett University.

Contributors

Dr. Heloísa de Araújo Duarte Valente holds a PhD in communication and semiotics (Catholic University, São Paulo, Brazil). She is associated researcher in the post-graduation program at Sao Paulo University Music Department (Brazil). Her main research interests are related to musical semiotics, especially the connections between musical performance and the media; also, the musical role in cultural processes: music as a kind of memory in the media and of the media. She has organized several books and published many articles concerning musical media culture and musical semiotics in specialized magazines.

Edward Banchs, MA, is a freelance writer and independent researcher based in Pittsburgh, Pennsylvania whose writing has appeared in various publications including *The Guardian*, *Metal Hammer*, *Decibel*, *Afropop*, and *Metal Music Studies*. He holds a BA in political science from Florida Atlantic University and an MA in African studies from the University of London's School of Oriental and African Studies. He is the author of *Heavy Metal Africa: Life, Passion, and Heavy Metal in the Forgotten Continent* (Word Association Publishers, 2016), listens to a lot of heavy metal, and owns entirely too many metal band t-shirts.

Dr. Bryan Bardine is a professor in the English department at the University of Dayton, USA. He has co-edited two previous collections on *Metal Music and Culture: Heavy Metal Studies and Popular Culture* (Palgrave Macmillan, 2016) and *Connecting Metal to Culture: Unity in Disparity* (Intellect Books, 2017). He has also organized two professional conferences: *Metal and Cultural Impact* (2014) and the *Metal in Strange Places Conference* (2016, both at the University of Dayton). His recent scholarly work has examined connections between gothic literature and metal lyrics, teaching metal studies, and analyzing metal scenes and culture. He is the chair of the International Society for Metal Music Studies organization as well as the outgoing president of the College English Association of Ohio. He teaches graduate and undergraduate courses in metal studies, composition, American and gothic literature, film, and pedagogy. He earned his PhD in literacy and curriculum and instruction from Kent State University in 2004.

Rui Luiz Ferreira Granado, MA, holds a master's in communication and media culture by UNIP - Paulista University. He has been working in higher education since 2007 as a teacher for the majoring courses of radio broadcasting and television, audiovisual production and advertising, and publicity. Currently part of the faculty crew in RTVI (Radio, TV and Internet) at USCS - Municipal University of São Caetano do Sol. He has 20 years' experience acting as an audiovisual producer.

Dr. Gérome Guibert is a sociologist and is associate professor at the Université Sorbonne Nouvelle, Paris. He has published many books including *Made in France: Studies in Popular Music* (Routledge, 2018). His research areas are live music and local music scenes, and he studies heavy metal culture since the beginning of the century. Gérome has especially directed two issues of *Volume!*, the French popular music studies journal, in 2006 ("Metal Scenes" with Fabien Hein) and in 2018 ("Paradoxal Metal"). He has also published many papers in English––one in the *Popular Music History*'s "Heavy Metal Controversies and Counter Culture" Special Issue (2011) and another in *Global Metal Music and Culture* (Routledge, 2016). He is a member of the *Metal Music Studies* journal's editorial advisory board since 2015. He was the convener of the French *Heavy metal et sciences sociales* conference (2014) and also the convener of the 4th ISMMS international conference in Nantes, 2019.

Jacob S. Hale, MA, received his bachelor's in integrated language arts from Mount Vernon Nazarene University and his master's in English from the University of Dayton. His presentations include: "Searching for connections: Community in the metal, rap, and hip-hop scenes in Dayton, Ohio," with Bryan Bardine, *Popular Culture Association National Conference*, March 2018; "On intersections and dead ends: Reading street lit with incarcerated juveniles," *Literature and Social Justice Conference*, Lehigh University, March 2018; and "Unnatural selection: Anthropomorphic and supernatural animals in Alice illustrations," with Alexis Ancona, Manchester Metropolitan University, April 2017. Jacob is currently teaching composition at Hondros College of Nursing and Columbus State Community College.

Pierre Hecker, MA, is a researcher and lecturer at the Centre for Near and Middle Eastern Studies at Philipps-University Marburg, Germany. He is the author of the book *Turkish Metal: Music, Meaning, and Morality in a Muslim Society* (Ashgate, 2012; Routledge, 2016). His recent publications include "Islam: The meaning of style" (Sociology of Islam, 2018) and "The 'Arab Spring' and the end of Turkish democracy" (*Palgrave*, 2019). He is the head of the research group " 'Ne mutlu ateistim diyene:' Atheism and the Politics of Culture in Contemporary Turkey" funded by Stiftung Mercator and co-editor of the forthcoming volume *The Politics of Culture in Contemporary Turkey* (University of Edinburgh Press, 2021).

Dr. Catherine Hoad is a lecturer in the School of Music and Creative Media Production at Massey University, Wellington, and chair of the International Association of the Study of Popular Music Australia-Aotearoa/New Zealand branch. Catherine's research critiques and theorizes constructions of ethnonational and gendered belongings in heavy metal scenes, with a particular focus on geolocalized discourses of metal and whiteness. Her edited collection on Australian heavy metal scenes, cultures and practices was published in 2019, and her first monograph is forthcoming.

Dr. Toni-Matti Karjalainen is the recently appointed professor of arts management in Sibelius Academy at the University of the Arts Helsinki, Finland. He is also adjunct professor (docent) of music management and culture export at Aalto University in Espoo, Finland, where he also previously worked as academy research fellow and research manager. Karjalainen holds a Doctor of Arts degree in art and design and Master of Science in economics. He has been a visiting lecturer and researcher in various countries and produced over 100 academic publications in different outlets, ranging from design and brand management to heavy metal music. Karjalainen created and organized the *Modern Heavy Metal Conference*, an international research event, in Finland 2015–2020, acted as secretary of *International Society for Metal Music Studies* in 2015–2019 and is actively involved in the music industry. Homepage: www.tonimattikarjalainen.info.

Dr. Lewis F. Kennedy is a curriculum manager (popular music) at Leeds Conservatoire and musicologist based in Hull (UK). In 2018, he completed a PhD in music at the University of Hull writing a thesis on functions of genre in metal and hardcore music, conceptualizing genre as an active, emerging, and determining force in the production and consumption of contemporary popular music. Having been involved in metal studies for several years, he is the current treasurer and membership officer of the International Society for Metal Music Studies, and co-edited the 'Metal & Musicology' Special Issue of *Metal Music Studies* (2019). Recent publications include book chapters on NWOAHM and notions of heritage(-making) in metal/hardcore historiography, and a study of the interplay between *aidoru* and metal themes in the lyrics of Babymetal.

Dr. Tore Tvarnø Lind is associate professor, PhD, holding a position in the anthropology of music at the University of Copenhagen. He is currently doing fieldwork in—and publishing on—the metal scene in Denmark, music festivals and black metal in particular. Tore plans to include the Greek metal scene in his future research. Tore has done extensive research on monastic Greek Orthodox chant, and he is the author of *The Past Is Always Present: The Revival of the Byzantine Musical Tradition at Mount Athos* (The Scarecrow Press, 2012), and his interests include music censorship and conflict, music torture, music and medicine, and a variety of issues from the field of ethnomusicology. Tore has studied at the University of Copenhagen, the University at Athens, and the University of Chicago.

Dr. Douglas Mattsson is a PhD student at the department of religious studies at Södertörn University in Stockholm, Sweden. He has held senior scholarships from the Swedish Research Institute in Istanbul and the Orient Institute in Istanbul, for his research on the Turkish black metal scene. His most recent publications include "Spreading VX-Gas over Kaaba: Islamic semiotics in Turkish black metal" in the forthcoming anthology *The Politics of Culture in Contemporary Turkey* (Edinburgh University Press, 2021) and he co-authored "I am Satan! Black metal, Islam, and blasphemy in Turkey and Saudi Arabia" (*Contemporary Islam*, 2018). He is currently working on his dissertation which is an ethnographic study of the Turkish black metal scene.

Dr. Méi-Ra St. Laurent holds a PhD in musicology from l'Université Laval (Québec, Canada). Her doctoral thesis ("Métal noir québécois: L'analyse du récit identitaire d'une communauté black metal marginale") focuses on a community of black metal groups from Québec, where she draws links between music, texts, and discourses emanating from them. Her previous studies also included the analysis of extreme metal songs using narratology and musicology, and encompassed the influence of Wagnerian musical elements in the music of symphonic metal bands. She is currently pursuing a postdoctoral fellowship at Concordia University (Montréal, Canada), where she focuses on the increasing concern about the use of inclusive discourse (so-called "political correctness") in the North American context of popular music.

Dr. Peter Pichler is a postdoc researcher at the University of Graz. He leads the project " 'Breaking the law!?' Norm-related sonic knowledge in heavy metal culture: A case study of the heavy metal scene in Graz and Styria, *c.*1980 to the present." He studied history, media studies, and philosophy in Graz and Mainz. His fields of expertise are European cultural history, metal music studies, and historical theory. He has published four books in this regard: *Acht Geschichten über* *die Integrationsgeschichte. Zur Grundlegung der Geschichte der europäischen Integration als ein episodisches historiographisches Erzählen* (Innsbruck, 2011); *Leben und Tod in der Europäischen Union* (Innsbruck, 2014); *Europa. Was die Europäische Union ist, was sie nicht ist und was sie einmal werden könnte* (Graz, 2016); and *Zeitgeschichte als Lebensgeschichte. Überlegungen zu einer aktuellen und emanzipativen Zeithistoriographie* (Frankfurt/M., 2017).

Dr. Kei Saito is currently a senior lecturer at the Research Institute for Japanese Traditional Music, Kyoto City University of Arts, Japan. His research focuses are on folksong and folklore movements in modern Japan, historiography of Japanese music, and localization of heavy metal music. His recent publications are *Ura Nihon Ongakushi: Igyo No Kindai* (*Darkside of Japanese Music History: Malformed Modernity*, Shunjusha, 2015, in Japanese) and *1933 Nen Wo Kiku: Senzen Nihon No Oto-fukei* (*Listening to 1933: Soundscape of Pre-war Japan*, NTT Publications, 2017, in Japanese). He obtained a doctorate in literature from Osaka University in 2009.

Henkka" Seppälä, MA, was the bass player and one of the original members of Children Of Bodom. The Finnish melodic death metal band has sold close to two million albums worldwide and played shows in more than 50 countries. He was born in the city of Espoo in 1980. The dream of becoming a professional soccer player faded away once he joined a local death metal band in a suburban garage in 1994. While constantly playing music, Seppälä graduated with a master's degree in political history from the Faculty of Social Sciences, University of Helsinki in 2012.

Jerome Stueart, PhD, earned his PhD in English from Texas Tech University (2005), and has edited four anthologies of science fiction stories, including *Wrestling with Gods: Tesseracts 18* (EDGE Science Fiction and Fantasy Publishing, 2015) and *Imaginarium 4: The Best Canadian Speculative Writing* (ChiZine Publications, 2015). His academic work is published in *Mosaic, The Walt Whitman Review*, and his fiction and essays are published in *The Magazine of Fantasy and Science Fiction*, *Lightspeed's Queers Destroy Science Fiction*, *Fantasy, Strange Horizons*, and other magazines and journals. His first collection of stories, *The Angels of Our Better Beasts* (ChiZine Publications, 2016), was longlisted for the Sunburst Award. Both Canadian and American, Stueart is a fulbright fellow, a lambda literary fellow, and a graduate of Clarion Science Fiction/Fantasy Workshop. Currently he's in the middle of an MFA in illustration/painting at the Columbus College of Art and Design. He lives in Columbus, Ohio, and edited this bio 15 times over the course of an hour.

DR. SOPHIE TURBÉ IS a sociologist and associate professor at the Université de Lorraine in France (Metz) within the Department of Art, where she directs a professional dilploma in popular music management. Her PhD is entitled "A multisited ethnography of three local metal scenes in France: Amateurs practices, networks and territory" (2017—an ethnographic study based on three areas in France (East, North and West scenes), and enlights how the forms of anchoring and of the mobilities, both of objects and humans, contribute to the production of local scenes, which is always caught in an entanglement of scales and networks' actors.

WOLF-GEORG ZADDACH, PhD, studied musicology, music management and history in Weimar and Jena/Germany and jazz guitar in Prague/Czech Republic. Since 2011, he has been teaching and researching in the fields of popular music, jazz, artistic research, and music business. He is currently a research assistant at the University of Music Weimar and a lecturer at the British and Irish Modern Music Institute Berlin and the Popakademie Baden-Württemberg.In 2018, he received his PhD for a thesis on heavy metal in the 1980s GDR/East Germany (Bielefeld: transcript, 2018). His most recent publications also include a book about contemporary jazz research with Martin Pfleiderer (Berlin: EMVAS, 2019) and entries on heavy metal in Germany (*Encyclopedia of Popular Music of the World*) and on Black Sabbath, Iron Maiden, and Doro Pesch in the German musicological encyclopedia *Musik* in Geschichte und Gegenwart (MGG).

www.ingramcontent.com/pod-product-compliance
Lightning Source LLC
LaVergne TN
LVHW060728310826
846742LV00016B/50
9781789387582